1/00

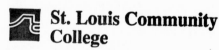

The WORLD ENCYCLOPEDIA OF CONTEMPORARY THEATRE

VOLUME 4

THE ARAB WORLD .

The WORLD ENCYCLOPEDIA OF CONTEMPORARY THEATRE

VOLUME 4

THE ARAB WORLD

DON RUBIN

LONDON AND NEW YORK

First published in 1999
by Routledge
11 New Fetter Lane, London EC4P 4EE
29 West 35th Street, New York, NY10001

Typeset in 9/10½ pt Sabon and Optima by MCS Ltd, Wiltshire
Printed in Great Britain by Biddles Ltd, Guildford and King's Lynn
Printed on acid-free paper

This encyclopedia is a project implemented with the support of UNESCO and at the request
of four non-governmental organizations. The opinions expressed in the various articles are
those of the authors themselves and do not necessarily reflect the point of view of the
sponsoring organizations.

British Library Cataloguing in Publication Data
A catalogue record for this book is available from the British Library.

Library of Congress Cataloging-in-Publication Data
A catalog record for this book is available on request.

ISBN 0–415–05932–1

INTERNATIONAL EDITORIAL BOARD

The World Encyclopedia of Contemporary Theatre would like to acknowledge with sincere thanks the financial contributions of the following:

REGIONAL SPONSORS

Canadian Department of Communications
Ford Foundation
Japan Foundation (Asia Centre)
Ontario Ministry of Citizenship and Culture
Rockefeller Foundation
Routledge
Social Sciences and Humanities Research
    Council of Canada
UNESCO
York University

NATIONAL SPONSORS

Autonomous National University of México
Cameroon National UNESCO Commission
Canadian National UNESCO Commission
Cultural Ministry of France
Department of Foreign Affairs and
    International Trade of Canada
German Centre of the ITI
Higher Institute of Dramatic Arts, Damascus
Mexican National UNESCO Commission
Joseph S. Stauffer Foundation
University of Bordeaux
Cheik Anta Diop University, Dakar
Herman Voaden
Woodlawn Arts Foundation

STATE SPONSORS

Apotex Foundation
Austrian Ministry of Education and the Arts
Samuel and Saidye Bronfman Family
    Foundation
Floyd S. Chalmers
Faculty of Fine Arts, York University
Finnish Ministry of Education
FIRT
Georgian Ministry of Culture
Greek Ministry of Culture
Calouste Gulbenkian Foundation
International Theatre Institute (Paris) and
    National Centres in Bangladesh, Belgium,
    Bulgaria, Canada, Czech Republic,
    Finland, Hungary, India, Netherlands,
Poland, Romania, Slovak Republic,
    Switzerland, United States and
    Venezuela
Israeli Ministry of Foreign Affairs, Division of
    Cultural and Scientific Relations
Japan Foundation Cultural Centre, Bangkok
Japan Foundation, Toronto
Henry White Kinnear Foundation
Ministry of the Flemish Community
    (Cultural Affairs)
Moldovan Theatre Union
Organization of American States
Polish Ministry of Culture
Republic of Macedonia Ministry of Culture
K.M. Sarkissian and the Zoryan Institute
Conn Smythe Foundation
Turkish Embassy in Canada

LOCAL SPONSORS

Marion Andre
Arts Development and Promotions
Australian Council
Mariellen Black
Lyle B. Blair
Canadian Theatre Review
Centre de Recherches et de Formation
    Théâtrales en Wallonie
Max Clarkson Foundation
Joy Cohnstaedt
Freda's Originals
H. Ian Macdonald
John H. Moore, FCA
Erminio G. Neglia
Farouk Ohan
Ontario Ministry of Skills Development
Peter Perina
E. Marshall Pollock
Rodolfo A. Ramos
Calvin G. Rand
Lynton Reed Printing
Don Rubin and Patricia Keeney
St Lawrence Centre for the Arts
Storewal International Inc.
Anton Wagner

Special thanks to:

Margrethe Aaby (Norway), Eric Alexander (Netherlands), Ebrahim Alkhazi (India), Ina Andre (Canada), Gaida Barisone (Latvia), Curtis Barlow (Canada), Isabelle Barth (France), Alexei Bartoshevitch (Russia), Shaul Baskind (Israel), Jean Benedetti (United Kingdom), Eric Bentley (United States), Don Berkowitz (Canada), Mariellen Black (Canada), Lyle B. Blair (Canada), Gaston Blais (Canada), Monica Brizzi (Italy), Robert Brustein (United States), John Bury (United Kingdom), Judith Cameron (Canada), Richard Cave (United Kingdom), Katarina Ćirić-Petrović (Serbia), Martin Cloutier (United States), Joy Cohnstaedt (Canada), Martha Coigney (United States), Communications Committee (International Theatre Institute), Leonard W. Conolly (Canada), Robert Crew (Canada), Renée L. Czukar (Canada), Esther A. Dagan (Canada), Gautam Dasgupta (United States), Donna Dawson (Canada), Susan Frances Dobie (Canada), Jason Dunda (Canada), Francis Ebejer (Malta), Krista Ellis (Canada), John Elsom (United Kingdom), Claes Englund (Sweden), Debebe Eshetu (Ethiopia), Martin Esslin (United Kingdom), Alan Filewod (Canada), Stephen Florian (Malta), Joyce Flynn (United States), Mira Friedlander (Canada), Julia Gabor (Hungary), Bibi Gessner (Switzerland), Madeleine Gobeil (UNESCO), Mayte Gómez (Canada), Sevelina Gyorova (Bulgaria), René Hainaux (Belgium), Bartold Halle (Norway), Peter Hay (United States), Ian Herbert (United Kingdom), Nick Herne (United Kingdom), Frank Hoff (Canada), Eleanor Hubbard (Canada), Huang Huilin (China), Djuner Ismail (Macedonia), Jasmine Jaywant (Canada), Stephen Johnson (Canada), Sylvia Karsh (Canada), Naïm Kattan (Canada), Ferenc Kerenyi (Hungary), Myles Kesten (Canada), Valery Khasanov (Russia), William Kilbourn (Canada), Pierre Laville (France), George Lengyel (Hungary), Henri Lopes (UNESCO), Meredith Lorden (Canada), Paul Lovejoy (Canada), Margaret Majewska (Poland), Lars af Malmborg (Sweden), Georges Manal (France), Suzanne Marko (Sweden), Bonnie Marranca (New York), Vivian Martínez Tabares (Cuba), Ruth R. Mayleas (United States), Giles R. Meikle (Canada), Paul-Louis Mignon (France), Ian Montagnes (Canada), Mavor Moore (Canada), Richard Mortimer (Canada), Judi Most (United States), Julia Moulden (Canada), Irmeli Niemi (Finland), Farouk Ohan (United Arab Emirates), Louis Patenaude (Canada), Oskar Pausch (Austria), André-Louis Perinetti (International Theatre Institute), Natasha Rapoport (Canada), Donald S. Rickerd (Canada), Roehampton Hotel (Canada), Charles-Antoine Rouyer (Canada), Mr and Mrs Irving Rubin (United States), Marti Russell (Canada), Raimonda Sadauskienė (Lithuania), Suzanne Sato (United States), Willmar Sauter (Sweden), Richard Schechner (United States), Petar Selem (Croatia), Małgorzata Semil (Poland), Mary Ann Shaw (Canada), Neville Shulman (United Kingdom), Mikhail Shvidkoi (Russia), David Silcox (Canada), Phillip Silver (Canada), Singer Travel (United States), Ron Singer (Canada), Mike Smith (Canada), Prince Subhadradis Diskul (Thailand), Anneli Suur-Kujala (Finland), Péter Szaffkó (Hungary), Carlos Tindemans (Belgium), Graham Usher (Canada), Indrassen Vencatchellum (UNESCO), Janusz Warminski (Poland), Klaus Wever (Germany), Don B. Wilmeth (American Society for Theatre Research), Claudia Woolgar (United Kingdom), Yoh Suk-Kee (South Korea), Piet Zeeman (Netherlands), Paul Zeleza (Canada).

DEDICATION

This series is dedicated to the memory of Roman Szydłowski of Poland (1918–83), a former President of the International Association of Theatre Critics. His vision for all international theatre organizations was truly world-wide and his tenacity in the service of that vision was genuinely legendary. It was Dr Szydłowski who first proposed the idea for a *World Encyclopedia of Contemporary Theatre*.

THE ARAB
WORLD

CONTENTS

VOLUME FOUR · THE ARAB WORLD

Contents • **The Nations and Their Theatres**

VOLUME FOUR

THE ARAB WORLD

AN INTRODUCTION

OF NATIONS AND THEIR THEATRES

The encyclopedia has been with humankind since the ancient Greeks. Aristotle's works are certainly encyclopedic in nature; that is to say, they encircle particular aspects of knowledge, some extremely specialized, some more general. Pliny the Elder (AD 23–79) compiled a thirty-seven-volume encyclopedia of natural science. The largest encyclopedia seems to have been edited by the Emperor of China, Yung Lo, in the fifteenth century. Called the *Yung Lo Ta Tien*, it required 2,169 scholars to write it and ran to 917,480 pages in 11,100 volumes.

The *World Encyclopedia of Contemporary Theatre* (*WECT*) is a somewhat less exhaustive encyclopedia than Yung Lo's. When complete, we expect it to run to only 3,000 or so pages in a mere six volumes. However, Yung Lo sought to cover a much wider range of subjects than *WECT*. His goal was to examine nothing less than all of Chinese literature from the beginning of time.

WECT makes no such claims about its comprehensiveness. *WECT* is specifically an encyclopedia of nations and their theatres. The starting point is 1945, the end of World War II, a time of change politically, socially and culturally for much of the world. Sketching out a social and political context for each of the countries being studied, *WECT* seeks to explore in a comparative fashion each country's theatrical history since that time. The assumption from the beginning has been that theatre is an art form which grows from its society and which feeds back into it through reflection, analysis and challenge.

No other international theatre encyclopedia has attempted such a comparative, broad-based, cross-cultural study. The fact that every one of our writers is from the country being written about adds still another level of authority and uniqueness to this work, which is attempting to present each nation's view of itself, a view not of politicians or propagandists but of each country's theatrical scholars and theatre artists.

It should also be made clear here that *WECT* is not intended as a guide to individuals, companies, festivals or forms. One will not find here analyses of Stanislavski, Brecht, Craig, Brook, Grotowski or Artaud. Nor will one find biographies of Soyinka, Fugard or Havel. *WECT* is also not the place to look for a history of the Comédie-Française or the Stratford Festival, Venezuela's Rajatabla or Japan's Tenjo Sajiki. Nor will readers find extensive documentation on the Carthage Festival or Edinburgh, on BITEF or Adelaide, on the Cervantes Festival or even Avignon.

The world of theatre is far too large and has become far too specialized for that. Information on the lives of everyone from playwrights to puppeteers, choreographers to composers, directors to designers can be readily found in a wide range of reference works available in every major language. There are book-length analyses and histories – some critical, some just documentation – of all the major companies and festivals that one could ever want to know about. There are also dictionaries available that focus on virtually every specialized theatrical subject from semiotics to cultural anthropology. Many fine theatre journals around the world maintain a valuable and continuing dialogue and documentation of current issues.

What has not existed before – and what *WECT* has attempted to create – has been a theatrical reference work looking at a wide range of *national* theatrical activity on a country-by-country basis from a specifically *national* standpoint. As we near the end of the twentieth century, as nations in many parts of the world finally shed their colonial pasts, and as new nations emerge in the aftermath of the collapse of the Soviet Union and Yugoslavia, such a gap in our cultural knowledge may seem curious. What, for example, does Romanian theatre look like to a Romanian in this post-modern world? Canadian theatre to a Canadian? What is of import to an Australian about his or her own theatre? To a Sénégalese? A Brazilian? A Vietnamese? An Egyptian? And what of all the individual republics that once made up the Soviet Union, Yugoslavia and Czechoslovakia? What is the self-perception of theatre professionals in the new Germany, where two totally different systems were uncomfortably reunited as the 1990s began?

To allow the reader to draw conclusions and to allow comparability, each of *WECT*'s writers was given the challenge of bringing together just such a national impression in a very specifically structured essay which would include not lists of names and dates but rather a context – in some cases, contexts – for international comprehension. That is, each of *WECT*'s extensive national articles – ranging from 3,000 to 30,000 words per country (small books in some instances) – has been written so as to provide theatrical professionals and those concerned with research on the profession with not only the basic material they would need if they were going to work in or visit a particular country for the first time, but also the basic material necessary to identify international trends and movements in the decades since the end of World War II.

Those who already know their own or some other country's theatre very well, no doubt, will find the information contained on those countries useful but probably too basic. Even at 30,000 words, these articles cannot possibly replace the library that would be needed to completely cover the theatre of any one country. In any event, encyclopedias historically have been intended only as introductions. Indeed, it is difficult to imagine them being anything more than that on any given subject. The philosopher and encyclopedist Denis Diderot (1713–84) argued that encyclopedias should be seen as basic libraries in every field but the reader's own. In this case, it is a theatre library for every country but the reader's own. To this end, we have asked writers to think of their ideal reader as a sophisticated professional from abroad.

In this light, we believe that *WECT* will be most important to readers for the breadth of its coverage; in this case, for the distance from home that each reader can travel through these articles. This is not in any way to suggest a lack of depth but rather to honestly recognize given limitations. *WECT* is therefore providing extended and extensive articles on every theatre culture in the world, more than 160 countries by the time the project is concluded. Looked at as a whole, they will be more than able to help theatre professionals in every part of the world put plays, companies, policies and productions into a national context, and in our complicated world this seems an important and unique contribution.

WECT material can be accessed in one of two ways: by either reading vertically (from beginning to end in any particular country) or horizontally (focusing on only a single subject such as Puppet Theatre or Dramaturgy across several countries). Having suggested earlier that this is not an encyclopedia of individuals, companies, festivals or forms, the fact is that one *can* identify individuals, companies, festivals and forms by referring to the index at the back of each volume or to the comprehensive multi-volume index planned for the final volume. By going to specific pages, the reader will then be able to follow the influence and development of particular figures or groups both within their own countries, within regions and ultimately in the world.

Whichever approach one is using, whether professionally focused or casual, it is probably useful at this point to understand the many section headings in each of the national articles and what each section is intended to include.

How To Use This Volume

Each national article in this volume is divided into twelve sections: History, Structure of the National Theatre Community, Artistic Profile, Music Theatre, Dance Theatre, Theatre for Young Audiences, Puppet Theatre, Design, Theatre Space and Architecture, Training, Criticism-Scholarship-Publishing, and Further Reading. These sections are intended to provide the following information.

History: Each national article opens with basic geographical, historical and/or socio-political material. In the cases of countries whose histories may not be well known outside the immediate region, we have encouraged writers to provide a more extensive background than might be normally found. Included is a history of the country's major theatrical movements and events since 1945, treated on a decade-by-decade basis or treated thematically. In each case the intent has been to give the national writer flexibility in interpreting the material being discussed.

Structure of the National Theatre Community: This is essentially a demographic section intended to offer information on the types of theatres (commercial, state-supported, regional or municipal) and the numbers of theatres operating in a particular country, their geographical distribution and relative sizes (both in terms of employees and budgets). One will find in this section information on the various infrastructures that have developed (national associations, national and international linkages), unions, as well as information on the major festivals in the country and national awards.

Artistic Profile: Divided into sub-sections, this examination of the major artistic trends in each national theatre since 1945 begins with **Companies**, goes on to **Dramaturgy** and concludes, where writers did not already deal with these areas in previous sections, with a discussion of **Directors, Directing and Production Styles**. Because our intent has been to look at the relationship between theatre and society, readers of this section are urged to look as well at the first two sections. Once again, the intent has been to provide the *foreign* theatre professional with an understanding of which groups, writers and directors are the most significant in the country and to put them into a national perspective. The sub-section designated as 'Dramaturgy' was initially called 'Playwriting' but was changed to 'Dramaturgy' to allow *WECT* to recognize the many companies that have worked collectively during the period being examined and to acknowledge the significant role of the director in script development. In no way is this intended to demean the importance of the playwright, whose work, we believe, still remains central to the process of theatrical creation.

Music Theatre and *Dance Theatre*: We start in both these sections with the assumption that there has long been a relationship between music and theatre, and dance and theatre; we have asked our writers to examine those relationships from a theatrical rather than from a musical or dance standpoint. In suggesting such

differentiations we have proposed that the writer take into account the kind of training needed to perform the work (music/dance or theatrical) and how the work is professionally assessed (by music/dance or theatre critics). In cases where the answers come down firmly on the side of music or dance, we have proposed not including the material in *WECT* since it might more appropriately be included in a music or dance encyclopedia. In some cases writers have focused exclusively on the line where the forms connect – often in multimedia experiments; in other cases they have written about more traditional opera and important dance or music groups. Those specifically interested in mime will find it discussed – where it has some national artistic significance – in the **Dance Theatre** section.

Theatre for Young Audiences: In many countries – especially in the period since 1945 – theatre for young audiences has developed significantly. By including a separate section in these articles, *WECT* intends to acknowledge the importance of this very special area of contemporary theatre life. The light thrown on such work seems of significance in the long-term development of theatrical art generally since 1945.

Puppet Theatre: Sometimes linked with the **Theatre for Young Audiences** section but most often recognized on its own, puppet theatre is at once one of the oldest of the popular theatrical arts and, where it has been rediscovered by contemporary theatrical practitioners, one of the most avant-garde. Within this section we have asked writers to trace developments in the form from its theatrical mimetic roots (imitation of actors) to what has come to be known as Object Theatre in which things take on a dramatic life of their own thanks, very often, to black light techniques that emerged during this period in eastern Europe. We have asked our writers to look at experiments involving the interrelationship between live actors and puppets or live actors and objects. This is a fascinating and important area which theatre professionals ignore at their own imaginative risk.

Design: This section examines the work of each theatre community's visual artists. In some cases this has been done thematically; in other cases, on a decade-by-decade basis since 1945. Again, we have asked our writers to avoid lists. Instead of just naming names, we have asked them to choose a small number of representative designers and discuss their individual work.

Theatre Space and Architecture: When we

began, this section was simply titled 'Theatre Architecture'. The words 'Theatre Space' were added as the articles began to arrive. Many of our writers originally interpreted this section as being only about buildings created specifically as theatrical venues. Clearly this would have eliminated many of the experiments relating to theatrical space which began in the 1960s and are still with us in the late 1990s, experiments which seem to have begun in North America out of sheer desperation and which evolved in many parts of the world to the total breakdown of proscenium theatre with its visual accoutrements as an *a priori* requirement for theatrical events.

Training: This section discusses the most important theatre schools and other professional training programmes in each country, their types of curriculum and the traditions they follow.

Criticism, Scholarship and Publishing: The most important theatre research and documentation centres in each country, major performing arts museums and the types of critical approaches being taken by leading critics and theatre scholars are identified in this section. The discussions here range from journalistic reviewing to more analytical philological, anthropological, semiological, and/or other types of structural approaches. In some cases historical context is provided; in others, contemporary developments are emphasized. As well, writers have been asked to identify the most important theatre journals and magazines along with the major theatre publishing houses in their countries.

Further Reading: Each national article concludes with a brief bibliography identifying the major works available within the national language as well as the most important works about the country's theatre that the authors are aware of in other languages. We have tried to follow the bibliographical form recommended by the University of Chicago but in some instances writers followed their own scholarly form leaving us with certain Chicago-style omissions. Though we attempted to fill these gaps it was not always possible. In general, however, enough information has been provided to allow the diligent reader to find the works mentioned.

To some, this structure may seem overly complicated and perhaps even contradictory in terms of allowing each writer or team of writers to identify and define their national theatres. But in every instance, the key was to maintain comparability country-to-country and ultimately region-to-region. It is our belief that as interesting and informative as each national article may be, the real value of *WECT* will ultimately lie in its ability to provide comparability of theatres world-wide, in its ability to allow directors, playwrights, dramaturges, designers, critics, scholars and even those in government to look across a wide range of theatre communities.

Certainly this structure was not arrived at quickly or casually and it continued to be refined almost until publication. When this project was first conceived by the Polish theatre critic Roman Szydłowski (1918–83) in the late 1970s, it was seen simply as an opportunity to provide accurate and up-to-date documentation for theatre critics who were being confronted more regularly than ever before with theatre from all over the world as part of their daily reviewing duties. Visiting groups were no longer rare and exotic events on a critic's schedule. They were appearing with amazing regularity and the best critics simply wanted to do their homework.

But where could a working critic go to find quickly information on Turkish *karagöz*, on Thai *khon* or South Africa's Market Theatre? Critics just seemed expected to know everything and everyone. Even when some information did exist, the sources were too often out-of-date or existed only in a language not widely spoken.

Most scholars would probably point to the nine-volume *Enciclopedia dello spettacolo* as the standard reference in the field. Available, however, only in Italian, the vast majority of the documentation included there was gathered before World War II and was, to say the least, Eurocentric. Published after the war, this encyclopedia of world theatre history was certainly strong the further one went back in time. But despite the fact that non-European theatre generally and the twentieth century specifically were not especially well served, the *Enciclopedia dello spettacolo* did become a standard. Most libraries found it essential for their reference sections. By the 1970s, however, it was clearly out-of-date even in its approaches to some of its early material.

Through the years, less ambitious attempts were made. Along with specialized individual volumes, these were very useful but, because of their specificity or, in some cases, their purely academic approach, they were not always useful to theatre professionals. It was at this point in time that Roman Szydłowski proposed a new type of world theatre reference work to the International Association of Theatre Critics, one of many international theatre communications organizations that had sprung up in the wake of two world wars.

At this organization's Congress in Vienna in 1979, Szydłowski, its president, received wide support for the proposal but no clear directions on how to proceed. Within eighteen months, however, he had convinced the International Theatre Institute's (ITI) Permanent Committee on Theatre Publications – a loose association of editors of theatre magazines and journals – to take up the challenge. The ITI, it was felt, being affiliated with the United Nations Educational, Scientific and Cultural Organization (UNESCO) at a higher level than the other international theatre associations, seemed to be the right agency to bring the idea to fruition on the world stage. At its 1981 Congress, this committee (subsequently to be called the Communications Committee) endorsed the idea and recommended it to the organization as a whole. It was the ITI's new secretary-general, Lars af Malmborg from Sweden, who decided that the project would be a concrete contribution to world theatre communication.

Malmborg, with the support of the ITI Executive Committee, brought the idea forward and in early 1982 called a meeting of interested international theatre organizations and individuals who might be able to help realize the project. It was from this meeting, held under the aegis of the Fine Arts Museum in Copenhagen, that specific plans began to be made. Four organizations – the ITI, the International Association of Theatre Critics (IATC), the International Federation for Theatre Research (FIRT) and the International Society of Libraries and Museums for the Performing Arts (SIBMAS) – agreed to combine efforts towards the realization of what was now being called the *World Encyclopedia of Contemporary Theatre*.

By 1983, with the support of the Faculty of Fine Arts at York University in Toronto and with the initial interest of a major Toronto publishing house, *WECT* was incorporated as an independent not-for-profit project under Canadian law. Initial grants came from York University, UNESCO and, the largest grant to that time, from the American-based Ford Foundation (thanks to a willingness to risk on a project that did not fit neatly into any previously established programme by its Theatre Officer, Ruth Mayleas). During 1984, representatives of the four sponsoring organizations met in Toronto (courtesy of Canadian philanthropist Floyd S. Chalmers) to set up parameters. Without this initial support and all the faith it implied in an unprecedented vision, *WECT* would never have got off the ground.

The year 1945 was established as a starting point though it was agreed that nothing ever really starts or ends neatly in the world of theatre. It was agreed that television and radio would not be dealt with but that music theatre and dance theatre would be included. It was agreed that a socio-cultural approach would be taken and that the relationship between theatres and the nations from which they grew would be explored. It was agreed that comparability would be emphasized and that writers should be chosen from within each country.

During 1984 an outstanding international team of editors was selected to coordinate the work and to advise in such specialty areas as theatre for young audiences (Wolfgang Wöhlert), music theatre (Horst Seeger), dance theatre (Selma Jeanne Cohen) and puppet theatre (Henryk Jurkowski) among others. Over the years the International Editorial Board would expand and contract as needs appeared or as particular individuals found themselves unable to continue the work. But throughout, the notion of self-identification for each national article was maintained and continued to be the primary reason why *WECT* searched for leading writers, critics, scholars and theatre professionals within each country.

The first full International Editorial Board meeting was held in Toronto in 1985 during the twenty-first World Congress of the ITI. There were five people present from North America, another five from Europe (including *WECT*'s two associate editors, Péter Nagy of Budapest and Philippe Rouyer of Bordeaux) and another six from Latin America, Africa, the Arab countries, and Asia and the Pacific. It was one of our Asian editors who put the first question to the gathering. 'What exactly do we think *we* mean when we use the word theatre?' he asked. 'I'm really not sure there's a definition we can all agree on. And if we can't come to an agreement on this basic question, how can we possibly agree on anything else?'

The apparently simple question led to an enormously involved discussion about the various types of spoken drama that had evolved in Europe and North America. Objections were quickly raised that we were ignoring musical theatre forms and forms involving movement. Others objected that we were locked into text while our puppet theatre editor was concerned that we were leaving out everything from *wayang kulit* to Punch and Judy. Our African colleagues suggested that our preliminary definition seemed to be ignoring the social relationships in much African theatre, from wedding ceremonies to circumcision rituals. And what of traditional forms in Asia such as *kathakali*, *noh*, *kabuki*, Chinese opera, or even the Vietnamese *hat boi*? What of folk forms in so many parts of the world? What of contemporary experiments?

What had appeared to be a rather innocent question in the beginning quickly turned into a life-or-death debate on the whole future – not to even discuss the international credibility – of the project. During the next few days, we turned to various standard texts on theatre in search of a suitable, internationally acceptable definition. It was a fascinating, though ultimately frustrating, exercise. To our amazement, we couldn't really find such a definition. Examinations of standard dictionaries – including the *Oxford English Dictionary* – were of even less help. Most simply defined 'theatre' as a building.

So we created our own international, intercultural working definition of the word. It is offered here not as a conclusion but rather as a starting point for a continuing consideration of what those of us working in the field mean when 'theatre' is spoken of in a contemporary global context.

> *Theatre*: A created event, usually based on text, executed by live performers and taking place before an audience in a specially defined setting. Theatre uses techniques of voice and/or movement to achieve cognition and/or emotional release through the senses. This event is generally rehearsed and is usually intended for repetition over a period of time.

By the time *WECT's* International Editorial Board next met, it had become clear from discussions with the various international organizations that *WECT* would have to respect various national differences in approaching this work and would have to take, as the American poet Robert Frost once said, 'the road less travelled by' in seeking its writers; that is, it would go to source for its information and interpretation in every instance. Indeed, *WECT* has through the years taken pride in this unique approach, slow and costly though it has been. But it has also been an approach which has led the project to develop close working relationships with theatre people *in* each of the more than 160 countries now involved in what has become the largest international cooperative venture in the history of world theatre, and certainly the largest international publishing venture in world theatre today.

In focusing the work this way, it was obvious that the *WECT* project was taking many risks. The approach was obviously going to make this a much longer project than anyone had ever dreamed of. By the time this work is concluded, it will have taken almost fifteen years. The approach would also force us to find significant international funding at a time when economies were just beginning to go into recession in many parts of the world.

But we believed when we started – and still believe – that our approach was one which would afford the best opportunity to ensure both the long-term goals and the highest standards of international scholarly excellence and accuracy. This approach was also one of the key reasons why UNESCO decided to support the project and why UNESCO ultimately named *WECT* as an official project of its World Decade for Cultural Development (1988–97). Such recognition is unusual for a scholarly work and we feel with some pride that it is an important model for future intercultural, interdisciplinary arts research.

A few words are needed here about world politics and its effect upon our work. For most people, political change is simply interesting newspaper fodder or the stuff to support opinions – pro or con – on particular subjects. The closer that politics gets to home, however, the more directly it impacts on one's reality and the more it affects how one goes about one's daily business. Political change has constantly impacted on *WECT's* reality and profoundly affected its already complicated work.

To give but one key example, when work began on our European volume, there were only two dozen or so countries to deal with, and those in eastern Europe were guaranteeing they would cover all our writing and translation fees for the region. That was 1985. By 1990, the two Germanys had become one (requiring a significant restructuring of our German material) while the USSR, Yugoslavia and Czechoslovakia went from three separate national entities to twenty-three separate countries (fifteen individual republics from the Soviet Union, six from Yugoslavia and two from Czechoslovakia). Not only did the already completed major articles on the USSR, Yugoslavia and Czechoslovakia have to be completely revised and turned into what we decided to call 'historical overviews' but also new writers needed to be found and new articles had to be commissioned on each of the republics, republics that were, in many instances, in the midst of social, political or armed revolution.

With such changes swirling around us, we read the newspapers each day with genuine trepidation. By the time of publication, the volume had expanded to some forty-seven articles. Suffice it to say here that trying to keep up with this ever-changing political landscape continues to be *WECT*'s greatest challenge, a challenge we are trying to meet through computerization and, we hope, the establishment of *WECT* as an international theatre database.

It was precisely these political changes which Martha Coigney, president of the ITI, was referring to when she said, perhaps optimistically, at the opening of the ITI's 1993 World Congress in Munich that in the future it would no longer be wars between superpowers that people of peace would have to be concerned about, but rather confrontations between cultures. If this is so then we believe that *WECT* may well be able to make a real contribution in at least introducing those cultures to one another. *WECT*'s goal from the beginning has been nothing less than that.

In helping the project to achieve this end, many organizations, many theatre and government agencies, many foundations and individuals have played important roles. A list of the financial sponsors and those who have worked with us appears elsewhere but we would like to specifically acknowledge the ongoing help of UNESCO, the Ford and Rockefeller Foundations (Rockefeller came to *WECT*'s aid at precisely the moment that recession and the enormous political changes in Europe threatened to kill the project), the Faculty of Fine Arts and the Office of Research Administration at York University, the Canadian and Ontario governments, the German Centre of the International Theatre Institute and particularly Rolf Rohmer, who has long served as president of the project's International Executive Board. This project would not have survived without the help of the Canadian Centre of the ITI (especially Curtis Barlow in the early years of the project) and the various members of the Canadian-based Board of Directors who worked to find funds to realize this work. The support of our two recent Board presidents has been particularly appreciated – Calvin G. Rand (founding president of Canada's Shaw Festival) and Professor Leonard W. Conolly, former president of Trent University in Ontario.

This project could also not have survived without the ongoing support of the Faculty of Fine Arts and the department of theatre at York University, its deans and its chairs (including Lionel Lawrence, Joyce Zemans, Joy Cohnstaedt, Seth Feldman, Ron Singer, Phillip

Silver and Robert Fothergill) and especially the sponsors of the Walter A. Gordon Fellowship, York University's highest research award, which allowed me the time to bring the first volume to fruition. The fourth and fifth volumes were completed during a sabbatical year in France.

This project would not have succeeded had *WECT* not had the active support and understanding of all the members of its International Editorial Board, particularly the wisdom and advice of Péter Nagy, whose diplomacy in the face of *WECT*'s own political struggles was never less than brilliant. Nor would it have succeeded without the stubborn belief in this project of its Managing Editor and Director of Research, Anton Wagner, whose work was long funded by the Canadian Social Science and Humanities Research Council, and the project's indefatigable administrators Donna Dawson and Catherine Matzig. Our editors at Routledge – Alison Barr, Michelle Darraugh, Robert Potts, Mark Barragry, Samantha Parkinson and Fiona Cairns – along with our brilliant copy-editor Christine Firth – have been most understanding in working with us on what must have appeared to them as a mad dream at times. Without their personal commitment – and a special thanks here to Routledge's theatre editor Talia Rodgers – and the corporate support behind them, *WECT* would still be in the planning stages.

If I have personally been seen through the many years of this project as its architect, I can only say that the building would never have stood without the strength, determination and belief of my wife and too rarely recognized co-visionary, Patricia Keeney. Against all her writerly instincts and sometimes against all logic, she bravely sat through meeting after meeting of every one of this project's boards, a duty she took on because she believed in the work. Without her faith and goodwill, *WECT* might well have foundered.

There are far too many people to thank here by name. It would be remiss to try, for too many would be left out. But to all of them, particularly to all our editors, writers, national editorial committees, ITI Centres and translators, to all the sponsoring and other organizations which supported this work and then left us the space in later years to actually realize it, thank you for believing with us and in us. We trust that your patience and support will have proven to be worth all the time, the pain and the effort.

Don Rubin
June 1998

THE ARAB WORLD

CROSSING UNSEEN BORDERS

It happened the first time in Sénégal. That was when I became aware of it. It happened again in Canada. And then again in France. All our editors and/or board members would arrive for an international meeting and everyone would get through immigration and customs without incident. Except one of our Arab editors or one of our Arab colleagues or one of our Arab consultants. Never the same person. But always an Arab. And always the same uncomfortable, good-humoured jokes afterward.

'I guess I look like a terrorist,' said one. 'They must have thought I was carrying a bomb,' said another. 'It doesn't bother me anymore,' said a third when it happened. 'I'm travelling on an Iraqi passport. What can I expect?'

As the person most often responsible for inviting these people to our meetings I felt exceedingly uncomfortable. I had seen systemic racism in North America from my youth, particularly to Blacks, but what was it about Arabs that seemed to bring out the worst in customs officials? These were scholars and artists and they always looked far more respectable than I ever did. Yet they were consistently stopped and asked to provide more explanations about why they were there in West Africa, in North America, in Europe. Did these people really need to be treated this way? Did they need to be 'more perfect' than everyone else? Why couldn't they just be themselves?

As the years of this work went on and the *WECT* project moved away from what was essentially Euro-American literary tradition and began to focus as well on 'performative' traditions, particularly in Latin America, Africa, Asia and the Pacific, I saw increasing enthusiasm among our editors in those regions. Our working principle was to be inclusive rather than exclusive, 'both-and' rather than 'either-or' and much valuable and relatively untouched material seemed to be coming forward.

But the same positive responses were not evident among our Arab colleagues. Indeed, there seemed to be little enthusiasm for the indigenous and almost a determination by many Arab scholars to simply ignore not only the performative in the society but even well-acknowledged genres such as shadow theatre. I wound up on numerous occasions debating with colleagues from the region the necessity of including material on its rich oral traditions, traditions that began with the emergence of the public poet, the wandering storyteller, the singer of epic tales and the bringer of news. It was this figure – *al-hakawati* (the storyteller) or *rawi* (narrator) – who seemed to hold so many connections to early elements of populist theatrical art. Certainly it was in these figures that one could look for the roots of what we now call acting, characterization, public entertainment and what was later to be recognized as music and/or dance theatre in this part of the world.

Perhaps part of the reason for their response could be found in the notion that in much of the present-day Arab world there is a crisis of identity, a crisis brought on by the fact that change is occurring with enormous rapidity here and social adjustments are having to be made almost daily at every level of society. Such changes are real and have led to distrust and confusion both in the region and out. The most basic questions can still be debated. For example, what is an Arab? Someone specifically from the Arabian peninsula or anyone who speaks Arabic? Is an

Arab of necessity a Muslim? Indeed, not all Muslims are Arabs.

This confusion of identity is palpable whether one is dealing with local governments or foreign customs agents; newly created societies based on recent oil wealth or ancient civilizations which have tried to link to new worlds while maintaining elements of earlier religious, social and cultural traditions; whether one is dealing with generally closed and conservative societies as one tends to find in the Gulf or with rapidly westernizing societies as one finds in the Arab states of North Africa. The world is coming to this region rapidly and the region, in response, wishes to show the world a modern and, of course, a 'proper' face. When the region is told to just be itself, when theatre people are asked to just show their own traditions, the problems of identity begin to emerge.

What then is the Arab world? Is there one?

Years ago I had a friendly debate over dinner with the eminent American scholar and cultural provocateur Richard Schechner, who wanted to know how we justified having an Arab World volume if all the others in the series were to be based purely on geographical distinctions – Europe, the Americas, Asia and the Pacific, Africa. Schechner was cautioning us against putting together a volume which was really from several geographical regions and which seemed to be based on religion more than anything else. Richard, as always, was right to some extent, but by the end of the evening he grudgingly accepted that an Arab world did exist both geographically and culturally.

My basic argument then and now was that the Arab world was as culturally distinct as sub-Saharan Africa, Asia or Europe. Diverse in the same ways that any region is, there is nevertheless a cultural unity to be found within that diversity. It is this unity that the present volume has sought to acknowledge, document and understand. Certainly it has been this region which has historically linked Africa, Asia and Europe. And certainly there are cultural links to be found in this huge area that extends from Morocco and Somalia in northwestern Africa to Iraq and the eastern borders of Asia, from Egypt south and west across the Sahara to the eastern limits of the Persian Gulf, from the Arabian peninsula dominated by Saudi Arabia to the many smaller nations and emirates which share the peninsula with the Saudis, including the descendants of the ancient Arab-Bedouin peoples who make up the population of modern Yemen.

The connecting tissue of this world is dual – the Arabic language and Islam, a religion which reaches out to include not only the Middle East and Africa (where it is dominant) but also many parts of Asia where it emerged through Iran, the Americas where Muslim immigrants brought its teachings and practices especially strongly in the last half of the twentieth century, and even to Europe where it emerged through medieval Spain.

Islam grew as a dominant religion in the Arabian peninsula and from the seventh century was brought with evangelical zeal and even conquest to other lands that now make up the Arab world. With classical Arabic as part of its arsenal, Islam – Earth-centred more than heaven-centred – marched across this part of the world. The religion's deceptively clear tenets are to be found in the religion's Holy Book – the Quran – still apparently an almost impossible work to translate according to scholars and linguists. It is said by Islamicists that the Quran truly opens only to those who can read it in Arabic and over the past thirteen or so centuries the learning of classical Arabic has therefore been as much a tool of religious education as it has been of culture and community in this region.

In fact, so committed have traditionalists here been in their determination to ensure that the Quran's linguistic secrets are understood and shared in 'proper' Arabic that many have looked down on Arabic in the vernacular to the point that for centuries colloquial Arabic was actually denied a written form. Perhaps this too reveals something of the hesitation of many Arab scholars to pay attention to more populist forms, forms not rooted in the proper and poetic Arabic. One can imagine the social and cultural problems posed by this for the *al-hakawati*, who sought to link the glories of the past and the soaring poetry of classical Arabic with the need to communicate to larger and less educated audiences in ways and in words that they would understand. The problem of writing it all down in some non-offensive form would come later.

Complicating all this further was the position taken by many conservative religious scholars in the region that Islam did not allow imitation of the human form. In the visual arts this led to abstraction very often built around Quranic written structures while in theatre it led to shadow theatre and single person narratives. As the more mimetic western forms of theatre began to be seen in the country, especially forms involving public appearances by women, new challenges to such traditional beliefs began to be

11

seen. The struggle to create a literary theatre in this part of the world was clearly a long and a real one and in many countries in the region it is ongoing. To give serious recognition to older forms may therefore be seen as being both culturally old-fashioned and politically reckless.

Literary theatre for its part seems to have been first brought to the region by European tourists, from Napoleon (who visited in 1798) to colonial powers including Britain, France and Italy. In many countries, it has now come to dominate, particularly when mixed with politics, satire, music and dance. When early drafts of our national articles started with some form of the sentence 'the theatre here began in the nineteenth century' or 'the theatre here began in 1950' or some such culturally revealing statement, we asked writers to rethink the concept and to explore their cultures for earlier performance traditions and not simply those European-style literary traditions that emerged. In some cases, the writers succeeded; in other cases, national editorial committees debated our requests and informed us that they were not willing to revise their contributions in this way.

Yet even with some inconsistencies, it seems to me that this volume is immensely important – the first Arab study of pan-Arab theatre and theatre forms. The fact that it is being done as part of a series of international volumes in cooperation with theatre professionals from other parts of the world and that it is being published in a major western language adds further to its usefulness. Much still needs to be documented in this area and we recognize that like any early overview it will doubtlessly be revised by scholars in the decades to come. But it is a starting point for serious intercultural examination of Arab world theatre and it is, I believe, a milestone of considerable proportions.

Why has it taken so long for such cultural recognition to be given here by other parts of the world? Perhaps there are some still agitated over the Christian Crusades (1098–1291), 200 years of violence in the name of God pitting Arab believers against European believers. Or perhaps, more realistically, it is because Islam is not particularly open to those who do not practise it; indeed, Islam's holiest city – Mecca – is still not open to non-believers. The Arabic language too is not so very easy to learn being, I am told, like a piece of poetry in which root sounds are clustered, often carrying several simultaneous or even contradictory meanings.

That said, the region does have its own literary masters – some, like Egypt's great dramatist Tawfīq al-Hakīm and Syria's Sa'dallah Wanous, recognized widely through productions in many parts of the region. A dozen or more major dramatists – Egypt's Ahmad Shawqi for one – can be found with a careful look through this volume.

For most Arab countries, the general pattern of the emergence of this Europe-inspired literary theatre was similar. First introduced during colonial periods for expatriates at private clubs, its base later expanded as touring groups from Europe began to play in Arab capitals such as Cairo, Damascus and Beirut. Eventually Arab business people and government officials viewed theatre on travels to Europe or other parts of the world and, as Arab students started to travel, they too began to be interested in such literary forms. In universities, adaptations of Shakespeare and Molière were particularly popular. Inevitably local writers tried their own skills at bringing local – often political – subject matter into the theatre. Eventually major actors, actor-singers, actor-dancers, actor-writers, actor-directors and even actor-dramatists and actor-administrators emerged who became quite expert at such things as 'Arabizing' plays from other parts of the world or heavily adapting plays from other Arab countries for local production.

In some countries of the region, private, usually commercial, theatres came into being. In others, the state got heavily involved (partly to control its access) through Ministries of Culture, Education or Youth and now these ministries often control theatres, funding and even casting. In dealing with theatre and its relationship to society as these volumes are, one cannot underestimate the influence of such government involvement in the Arab world. It was the Egyptian commercial groups that were the first in the region to tour and to bring in women. Names such as the Egyptian actor-manager George Abyad and the great actress-singer Fatimah Rushdie are only now beginning to be heard and their contributions appreciated in the rest of the world.

As the extraordinary range of articles in this volume illustrates (twenty-two Arab nations stretching from Algeria to Yemen) it is possible to divide the Arab world into three theatrical segments – that of the conservative Gulf states where religion and government are aligned most closely to 'protect' their citizens against intrusions from the outside world; that of the Maghreb – the westernmost Arab states of north Africa – which tend to be most closely connected to French cultural traditions; and those countries of what is generally called the Middle East which have not only been the earliest and most enthusiastic practitioners of their indigenous arts but also the most enthusiastic countries in this region to embrace the more literary-style European theatre.

Some countries connected to this region – Iraq, for example – have links to more than one of these distinctive cultural areas, an exception which perhaps best proves the general accuracy of this division. Palestine, it should be noted, which has a major article in this volume and whose problems of identity are discussed as well in several national articles, is probably most closely linked to what is called here the Middle East traditions.

The volume also includes a number of equally revealing introductory sections which put the region into both a regional and a world context. More specifically, they explain something about the important issue of language for the Arab world theatre, the relationship between women's rights and Islam and the revealing arts of dance and puppetry as practised in this region.

This volume would not have come into being without the support of many international agencies, without several travel grants to visit the region from York University in Toronto or without the help of the noted Egyptian actor, director, teacher, government deputy minister and good friend Ahmed Zaki (and his wife Geraldine, who on more than one occasion helped to bridge linguistic and cultural divides). The project was aided as well by playwright Samir Sarhan, head of the Egyptian Book Organization, whose advice was always appreciated. Early on in this project, important groundwork was laid by Ghassan Maleh of the Higher

Institute of Theatre in Damascus. I should also like to acknowledge the encouragement of my colleague Farouk Ohan of the United Arab Emirates, who has done much field research for *WECT* over the years.

Most of the editing of this volume was done during 1997 and 1998 while I was on sabbatical leave from York University and living in Provence. Many French colleagues and friends helped me keep the proper focus through the year, among them Marie-Claire and Philippe Rouyer of the University of Bordeaux and Marie-Claude Hubert of the University of Aix-Marseille.

My administrator and managing editor Catherine Matzig maintained the operations of our international editorial office in Toronto nobly and with continuous good humour, being forced to deal with me almost exclusively through the miracle of electronic mail. My life partner in this work – Patricia Keeney – continued to drive me onward when I felt most frustrated and irritable.

To all these people and to the many editors, scholars, writers, translators (particularly our translators Maha and Tony Chehade) and theatre professionals I consulted along the way, my sincere thanks.

The goal of this entire series has been to open doors into other cultures for those interested in the theatre. Many doors in this volume are being opened for the first time. The trust shown to this outsider in opening those doors by so many in the region has been deeply appreciated and has been, as always, a most extraordinary privilege.

Don Rubin
Vaugines, France
June 1998

ARABS AND AFRICA

SHAPING A CONTINENT

Each day of my childhood in the late 1930s and early 1940s, through the half-light of daybreak in the northern part of the coastal town of Winneba, Ghana, the cool morning air would vibrate to a call in a very strong voice from a tower close by. A *muezzin*, in long and melodious verses, was inviting Muslims in the neighbourhood to pray. Over the next little while, the *muezzin*'s voice would dissolve and groups of rising voices could be heard reciting from the scriptures as the congregation formed in the town's little mosque for morning prayers. Eventually the heterophony would grow thinner as the *muezzin*'s voice would rise again in an animated closing paean to Allah while the congregation filtered back out to return to its daily chores. The first prayer session of the day had ended. The next three would be observed, more quietly but no less piously, in smaller groups or in privacy before the group evening worship just before dusk.

Years later, I realized that the prevailing language of this worship was a mix of Hausa and Arabic. As a child, the profound meaning of this and other similar experiences remained beyond my ken. But Islam was then and still is very much a part of west Africa to where it had come many centuries ago. Indeed, many Africans converted to it over the millennia, practising a great Arab religion. In my small village, the Arab himself was present only by proxy, represented not in person but by the Holy Quran and its hierarchy of representative ministers. I came to understand that such influences were only one of many formed from a mighty force that had originated on the Arabian peninsula more than a thousand years earlier.

Eventually the Muslim community in my home town outgrew its old prayer site and built a splendid, modern and permanent mosque in the Zongo area, a kilometre away. Their original building, covered with corrugated iron sheets, was abandoned. Over the coming years it would become an outdoor cinema and much later a place of worship for the local Assemblies of God.

Much later, as a teacher at the University of Zambia, I found myself once again in contact with Islam. In order to observe a dance form I had not encountered before – the *zikili* dance – I joined many others in Chiwala village in the Copperbelt Province for a worship service at a mosque. The intonations of the Quran passages, I realized as the prayers were chanted, featured phraseology and cadences that showed close associations with Fante Church lyrics in Ghana. This surprised me and I wondered how this could come to be. Had some Fante Muslims (Fante Nkramo) passed on such melodic practices which, through the generations, later church people had borrowed when urged by the missionaries to contribute to the Sunday liturgy in their own language and music? I had earlier written about this music (*International Review Missions*, 1960: 183–8) and thought I knew it quite well. But I had not found any such connections. Until then.

My earlier study had indicated only that the ancestors of the Swahili speakers of this area were traders and warriors from Tanzania. But I eventually came to understand that their trading and frequent fighting expeditions led them from Malawi through Mozambique and into Zambia, where they sojourned within or around Chiwala, Petauke and Luapula (through Katanga, in Zaïre); finally they settled at

Chiwala, near Ndola, capital of Zambia's Copperbelt from where some migrated to Kalonge village and elsewhere. Wherever these warring traders passed, some of their number remained behind, intermarrying and hiring servants and other staff. It was apparently through such contact that the *zikili* was first sung and later danced to Arabic renderings.

Three Swahilicized Arabic religious song texts, in fact, came from the *zikili – Lailaha ilala Abdulikadili Shalila* (There is no other God among us, except Allah!), *Lailaha ilala Adam wo mawaliya* (La [God] says there is no one in the world like God; Adam is his first creation) and *Mohammed wolihi; Wasihabihi Waralama* (Muhammad is with his disciples; He went with them to paradise). These then – done as a mosque dance suite – connected the few Swahili communities in Zambia with the wider Muslim world, a world usually found only in urban Zambian centres.

When my career as an educator later took me to the University of Ilorin in Nigeria to help found a department of performing arts, I noticed that the Arab influence was even more obvious. Here, on a campus that blended with the city's downtown, every Friday without fail, from just before noon onwards, a huge congregation of worshippers would begin to spread out around our buildings. If I did not wind up my teaching and administrative chores quickly at that point, I would literally have to leap between a sea of outstretched legs blocking all the entrances while listening on worship mats to the *muezzin*'s invitation to prepare for prayer. Later, the Imam's voice could be heard delivering the message of the Quran, always following this with a homily.

Even larger numbers in the city could be found streaming to the official Prayer Ground for worship. But even both these crowded venues paled into insignificance compared with the scene at Ilorin's Central Mosque, probably the greatest and most magnificent in west Africa, with its shining white domes and minarets. The traffic after worship time on Fridays in Ilorin was staggering, but obviously adequately compensated for by the satisfaction of having called upon Allah on Allah's own day.

What is clear in such examples is the extent of Africa's conversion to Islam over the centuries, the zeal of its worshippers and the extent of the Arab sphere of influence even in non-Arab cities. How did this happen? Ilorin for centuries was one of the great entrepôts lying on the north–south trading routes that linked North Africa, the Sahara and the Sahelian belt of Africa, linking up with myriad smaller routes to the rich gold, kola and ivory centres of the forest zone further south. Through trading Islam had spread but it was not the only way.

Across the northern half of the continent, Islam was established by conquerors bearing the banner of the *jihad* (Holy War) while in the forest areas south of the Sahelian belt from Ethiopia, through Chad, to Liberia, the bulk of Islam's gains was made through more peaceful evangelizing. The strong winds of Islam had obviously borne Arabs around the world – across North Africa to Spain, northeastwards to Iran, Afghanistan, India, China, Japan, Indonesia, the Philippines as well as to east, west and central Africa.

The comparative ease with which the East Horn was Islamicized contrasts sharply with the fierce resistance of the Berbers of the Maghreb (the northwestern belt of Africa) and the obstinate nonchalance of Black communities of the Guinea and central African forests. Militant Islam halted at the fringes of the African forests leaving traders and proselytizers to take up the task of carrying forth the message of Muhammad by more peaceful approaches.

In the wake of the conquest of North Africa, new Arab dynasties arose. The most relevant of these were the Almoravids of the eleventh century. While ruling over Morocco and much of Spain, these dynasties extended their presence (one after another) across the Mauritanian desert to Sénégal. Fired by glowing reports of an unlimited gold supply from ancient Ghana (a land made legendary by Muslim writers from the eighth century), the Almoravids, a Muslim-Berber people (also known as al-Murabitun or garrison people and noted for their ascetic withdrawal and holy warfare) rose upon this part of Africa and overthrew the kingdom of Ghana in AD 1076. In the twelfth century, the Almohad (al-Murabbidun or followers of the Oneness of God) also invaded what was left of ancient Ghana and founded the ancient kingdom of Mali. This was followed by the establishment of the Songhai Empire. Meanwhile nascent groups had long been forming the Bornu States, the Hausa States and several others.

Arab influence was clear even then. And lest anyone suggest that Arab influence was a late bloom, it should be noted that the open maritime borders between Africa and the Arabian peninsula have long served as a tempting invitation to visiting adventurers, peaceful nomads, fugitives seeking refuge from embattled settlements at home and even common outlaws. Many of these simply wandered across uncontrolled maritime borders and through the years blended beyond recognition into local populations on African soil. The search for significant beginnings for Arab presence in Africa therefore must take into account such more or less casual influences as well as very extensive time frames.

One might even go back as far as the time of the first state navigation of Africa's east coast on the orders of Queen Hatshepsut of ancient Egypt in about the year 1493 BC. These voyages included surveys of the east coast as far south as Punt, a region interpreted by some to extend as far as present-day Mozambique. Her sailors are said to have returned with their ships laden with merchandise, perhaps the earliest record of trade relations between Africans and Arabs.

About 900 years later – in 596 BC – Phoenician adventurers (a land connected to modern-day Lebanon) sailed under orders from Pharaoh Necho of Egypt starting from the Suez Gulf southwards through the Red Sea and around the Cape of present-day South Africa returning to the mouth of the River Nile through the Pillars of Hercules (in the Straits of Gibraltar), accomplishing the first known circumnavigation of the African continent. 'Each year,' according to the famous Greek historian Herodotus, 'they landed for three months and grew and harvested a crop' (Horrabin 1960: 33). We do not hear of Arabs in this account specifically, but we may take them for granted as being represented in the populations of the east African coast. Nearly a century later, Hannibal, the Carthaginian admiral, sailed westward from Carthage (present-day Tunisia) with a fleet of sixty ships carrying thirty-thousand men and women. The fleet stopped at various points and dropped off groups of men and women in an attempt to establish colonies as far south as Cerne in present-day Sénégal (Horrabin 1960: 33).

Arab colonies had also been established on the east coast where traders from Arabia had settled some two thousand years earlier, according to Davidson (1964: 17) 'intermarrying with local people and producing, as time went by, a civilization that was distinctive to the seaboard' peopled by an essentially African population called Swahili, which over time accepted Islam and Arab culture. One can add into this an even earlier reference by an Egyptian Greek in the *Periplus of the Erythean Sea* (c.AD 800) in which the author says that 'Arabs had been trading and establishing coastal settlements' in east Africa

under the rule of Arabs from Oman since the first century AD. Exports included rhinoceros horn and (domestic) slaves (Horrabin 1960: 49).

Graham Connah (1987: 177) refers to a visit by an Arab, al-Masudi, to the east coast of Africa during the tenth century in which he notes that 'Every man worships what he pleases, be it plant, animal or mineral' (quoted by Freeman-Grenville 1975: 31–2). Clearly at the time of al-Masudi's visit, the Arabs had not yet established a significant presence nor had Islam yet penetrated this part of the continent. By the fourteenth century, however, when Ibn Battuta visited Kilwa (a principal trading centre on the east coast), Islam had already been accepted by the people.

Assiduously continuing through notes on 'pre-mosque periods' Connah (1987: 177) works his way towards the earliest knowable starting point to reckon the beginnings of Islam in east Africa. Quite a plausible position is given in his statement: 'At Kilwa, its excavator thought that Islam began to arrive in the eleventh to the twelfth centuries.' Through the maze of broad and reasonable estimations available, it is quite possible to affirm that by the fourteenth century 'a mercantile civilization, heavily influenced by Arabian culture, flourished along the east African coast' (*Third World Guide 1993/94*). During this same period, Islam, the acme of Arab culture, facilitated by the bond of the KiSwahili language, had taken a firm hold on the populations along the east coast and was making occasional thrusts inland.

The arrival of the Portuguese on the east African coast during the fifteenth century affected the region yet again, brutally plundering even where there was no resistance. Basil Davidson offers a description of a scene in 1505 at Kilwa:

> The Vicar-General and some of his Franciscan fathers came ashore, carrying two crosses in procession and singing the *Te Deum* (*We Praise Thee O God*). They arrived at the palace, one cross is put down. The Captain prays – and the plundering of the town follows.

The Portuguese held the east coast during the sixteenth and seventeenth centuries. Eventually, however, Arabs from Musqat and Oman who had held titular supremacy from the eighth to the fifteen centuries recaptured both Zanzibar and Mombasa, driving the Portuguese south to Mozambique and thus re-establishing Arab control of the east coast from (present-day)

Tanzania to Kenya. In a much later development a Sultan of Oman leased the Tanzanian coast to a German trading company. The rest of the story of the east African coast here merges into European colonial history in Africa.

Moving away from history, it should be said that there is a general tendency these days to link the ethnic-Arab with everyone who practises Islam. In fact, these are not one and the same as the example of Africa clearly attests. Even scholars make this error. Lewis (1958: 9–10), for example, is on record as defining Arab-ism this way: 'All those are Arabs for whom the central fact of history is the mission of Muhammad, the memory of the Arab Empire and who, in addition, cherish the Arabic tongue and its cultural heritage as their common possession.' This definition, of course, rules out non-Arabic-speaking Muslims. Even Arab leaders have defined the Arab as 'whoever lives in our country, speaks our language, is brought up in our culture and takes pride in our glory.' This version too rules out individuals born, bred and living in non-Arab territories, however Arabicized they may be (many Sénégalese for instance). The fact is that there are many Muslims who are not Arab at all. But the widespread presence of Arab populations in Africa and the fact they are all Muslims and follow Arab styles of living certainly leads many to the assumption that all Muslims live as Arabs and use their language and lifestyles.

There are commonalities to be sure. Certainly all who follow Islam recognize Allah as the One and Only Supreme God; accept the Prophet Muhammad as His Messenger; study the Quran (for which knowledge of the Arabic language is highly desirable); pray five times a day facing Mecca, the Prophet's birthplace; are required to give alms to the poor; participate in a month's fasting before the feast of Ramadan; and go on pilgrimages to Mecca, circumstances permitting. But once again it is important to recognize that all who follow Islam are not ethnic Arabs.

On the other hand, it is true that in many parts of Africa, the Arabic language is now spoken by millions. From Sudan to Morocco, Arabic, in fact, predominates and has become the lingua franca in countless market centres. There are also large populations who speak Arab-influenced African languages, the best example being KiSwahili, the national language of Tanzania and Zanzibar.

In west Africa, the African peoples of northern Nigeria and several neighbouring areas speak Hausa (a Hamitic language) and an Arab-Berber blend with African dialects in the northwest. Across the Sahara Desert, Berber languages remain resilient, in spite of the adoption of Islam by the people. In Morocco, for instance, about one-third of the country's inhabitants still speak Berber dialects, mostly in the mountain areas. There are also Arab communities who, thanks to the continuing existence of ancient desert trade routes, still share desert oases with Tuareg and other nomadic Berber peoples. Around these oases, Arab-Hamitic bilingualism still prevails.

Arab philosophy is also a mix of traditions – ancient and medieval Greek and Christian Hellenism for example – and it was in such blends that many of these ideas first made their way to the continent. A few examples of careers will illustrate this point. The teachers of the Arab scholar al-Kindi (c.813–70) included Nestorian Christians while he himself mainly followed a neo-Platonist line of thinking. Avicenna (c.980–1057) sought to reconcile Greek philosophy with the demands of Quranic religion. Averroes (1126–98) studied the stoics rather than Aristotle which were rejected by Muslims as well as by Christians. He was banished by the Caliph of Cordoba (Spain) for following philosophy instead of Islam.

The record of the Arab world and Islam in the realms of learning and science are uncontestable and these also were contributions which were eagerly taken up and adapted to African needs and realities. Clearly, the Arabs who came to Africa so many centuries ago drew this great continent not only into their own empire but through it into an ever-expanding Islamic civilization that is now playing an even greater part in contemporary reality. As such, one can say simply and accurately that the Arab world was a significant influence in the shaping of contemporary African reality and by its many contributions added much to the continent's cultural richness.

Atta Annan Mensah

Further Reading

Ayiku, Emmanuel. *African Business Promotional Yearbook of Appointments 1996*. Toronto: Toronto Networking News, 1996.

Boyd, Andrew and Patrick van Rensburg. *An Atlas of African Affairs*. New York: Frederick A. Praeger, 1962.

Connah, Graham. *African Civilizations*. Cambridge: Cambridge University Press, 1987.

Davidson, Basil. *The African Past*. London: Longmans, Green, 1964.

Fernandez-Armesto, Filipe. *Millennium: History of the Last Thousand Years*. New York: Scribner, 1995.

Flew, Anthony. 'Islamic Philosophy'. *A Dictionary of Philosophy*. London: Pan with Macmillan Press, 1979.

Freeman-Grenville, G.S.P. *The East African Coast*. London: Collings, 1975.

Grun, Bernard. *The Timetables of History*. New York: Simon & Schuster, 1975.

Horrabin, J.F. *An Atlas of Africa*. London: Gollancz, 1960.

Lewis, Bernard. *The Arabs in History*. London: Arrow, 1958.

Osborne, Richard. *Philosophy for Beginners*. New York: Writers & Readers, 1992.

Third World Guide 1993/94. Montevideo, Uraguay: Instituto del Tercer Mundo and Oxford: OXFAM, 1994.

Vesey, G. and P. Foulkes. 'Islamic Philosophy'. *Collins Dictionary of Philosophy*. London: Collins, 1990.

ARAB THEATRE AND LANGUAGE

THE CONTINUING DEBATE

Theatre historians credit the introduction of European-style theatre in the Arab world to three pioneers – Marun al-Naqqash (1817–55), Ahmad Abu Khalil al-Qabbani (1851–?) and Ya'qub Sannu (1839–1912). Their plays and productions introduced the concepts of dramatic literature and spoken theatre to Egypt, Syria and Lebanon and through these countries to the rest of the region. Until their pioneering work, this type of verbal/literary art was all but unknown.

Indeed, the awe with which these men looked up to the European theatre would explain why, in their efforts to establish a similar art in the Arab world, they virtually ignored the importance in this region of the indigenous shadow plays, puppet theatre or even performances of the 'Muhabbatheen' Samir troupes. Clearly they sided with Edward Lane, who will be best remembered for his Arabic dictionary and book on manners and customs of modern Egypt, who saw the latter in the 1820s, and dismissed them as 'low and ridiculous farces [performed] prior to weddings and circumcisions . . . scarcely worthy of description: it is chiefly by vulgar jests and indecent actions, that they amuse, and obtain applause'.[1]

But because the European-style play was so new to audiences, it was decided that explanations and introductions were needed to make them comprehensible. Early companies added independent prologues and even encouraged actors to engage in direct discussions with the audience. This led to often chaotic and even rude behaviour in the theatres and eventually a list of regulations governing such behaviour was drawn up by directors. By agreement, police officers were stationed in every theatre to enforce proper conduct. In many cases, though, the often illiterate police themselves had no idea what was part of the production and what was not and wound up interfering with the production and causing even more hilarity and disturbance. But it was not just the police who had trouble understanding the rules of European theatre. For audiences the very language of the plays being staged was at least half the problem. Even now, the question of language – or, more specifically, the type of language used in the theatre – remains a significant one throughout the Arab world.

In early attempts to write, translate and adapt European drama for the Arab world, dramatists were faced with a very basic problem: the existence in Arab society of two mutually antagonistic language entities. The first is Fusha (also known as classical, written, literary, formal, prestigious and, to most, correct Arabic). The second is colloquial Arabic (the vernacular or spoken form of the language which is different in many essential ways from Fusha and from its own many variants the further one gets from the Arabian peninsula). Such a linguistic dichotomy has been described by Charles A. Ferguson as 'diglossic' and he has used the terms 'High' and 'Low' to separate them.[2]

The prestige of Fusha derives mainly from its being the language of the Quran and the language of Islamic teaching throughout the centuries. It is also a symbol of Arab identity. The survival of Islam depends, many Muslims believe, on keeping Fusha, in its purest form, alive and intelligible. Language teaching has therefore been, through the centuries, directed not merely towards the propagation of Fusha but also towards the 'eradication' of the colloquial in

19

formal instruction. Indeed, it has been considered by some as blasphemous to develop a writing system for colloquial Arabic or to print books in colloquial Arabic for fear that it may undermine Fusha or challenge its position.

But the many varieties of colloquial Arabic are mother tongues for people in this region and obviously they cannot be banished by the will of any state. Indeed, Fusha is learned only in school. Given this situation, these two forms of Arabic over the centuries have had to learn to coexist, sharing tasks of communication on a more-or-less complementary basis: written communication in Fusha but oral communication in colloquial, with a slight (and codified) overlapping. Notwithstanding, colloquial Arabic has never attained respectability in the eyes of many Arabs despite the fact that it is the only language medium in which they normally express themselves. As a result 'respectable' and prestigious societal functions, regardless of their nature, always take place in Fusha.

Add into this the Arab world's growing official contacts with European culture some two centuries ago – a growth spearheaded by Napoleon's Egyptian Expedition from 2 July 1798 to 18 October 1801 – and it is possible to have some idea of the serious linguistic problems at that time. Such new types of state contacts uncovered language questions relating to social status and proper usage that had never before been dealt with. The French Expedition also introduced into Egypt the printing press and with it the profession of journalism which, in its Arabic manifestation, injected new life into the Fusha, being as it were a written genre. What a problem then when Napoleon himself decided to send to Egypt the Comédie-Française in order to entertain his armies and to 'change the customs of this country by arousing people emotionally', as he wrote in a letter sent from France to General Kleber in Egypt.[3] But how would this new art be translated and explained? Because it was based in literature, because it was official, imported and therefore prestigious, it was first decided to deal with it in Fusha. But because it dealt with personal issues, linguistic questions arose immediately. Perhaps colloquial Arabic was more appropriate for such an art. And there the question remained.

It was in Beirut in 1847 that Marun al-Naqqash staged at his home an original play called *al-Bakhil (The Miser)* written in the European style and based only loosely on Molière's play *L'Avare*. This first Arab-written, European-style play, was mainly in Fusha with some colloquial utterances scattered here and there in order to give local taste to the dialogue. We must assume that the public accepted this mixed-language choice. But it was not until twenty years later and after his death that the play was published. In an introduction by his brother Niqula, apologies are offered for some of the substandard speech 'because the author was concerned only with comic content'. He cautiously added that his brother's use of 'incorrect language was not due to any linguistic incompetence . . . but to the fact that he purposefully selected incorrect words in order to encourage others in this genre.' He added 'those who doubt what I say here should consult [al-Naqqash's second play] *al-Hasud (The Envious One)* in order to acquaint themselves with the author's clear knowledge of Arabic language and grammar.'[4]

But through the years, other linguistic choices were made as well. Ya'qub Sannu, a Syrian Jew born in Egypt in 1839 and one of the first there to write in the European style, used colloquial Arabic throughout his plays including different forms of spoken Arabic to reflect divergent cultural and educational levels (including pidgin for resident foreigners). Such a daring mix became characteristic in all his comedies. Not surprisingly, his choice of language was severely criticized as being incorrect and without dignity.

Sannu (nicknamed the 'Molière of Egypt' by no less a personage than the Khedive of Egypt) defended his position in a French-style impromptu he wrote under the title *The Molière of Egypt and What He Suffers*. In this text, written after an attack by a famous Alexandria newspaper against an Arabic theatre group that had produced one of his plays, a character points out that the person writing the most violent article was actually of Italian extraction. This man, says the character in Sannu's play, would no doubt have them use made-up words in place of Fusha (here he gives some words moulded into quasi-Fusha forms: for example – '*nahnu yadkhuluun wa yalbas il bantaluuny*'. After more laughs at the expense of the Italian journalist, Sannu says that 'comedies should contain only what actually is said by real people'.

By the end of the nineteenth century, hundreds of translated, adapted or original plays – some in Fusha, some in colloquial Arabic and some in a mixture of both – were staged. Many were adaptations from French and English classics, with Molière, Racine and Shakespeare particularly favoured. Of the original plays, many were based on Arab history or on the history of ancient Egypt. It is probably fair to say that over the next century a pattern would emerge whereby historic, epic and translated plays, particularly dramas and tragedies, would be in Fusha while the colloquial would be used for all comedies and plays with local themes. The justification for this division was the claim that colloquial Arabic with its meagre repertoire of vocabulary, particularly in the area of abstract ideas, was, unlike the rich Fusha, incapable of accommodating grand or culturally complex ideas.

The founding of the National Opera in Cairo in 1869 was of particular help to the supporters of Fusha, for plays only in Fusha – apart from those in foreign languages – were staged there. Nevertheless, dramatists who used colloquial Arabic, even in comedies, continued to be accused of being unable, because of 'lack of proper education', to use Fusha. The great Egyptian man of letters, Taha Husayn, as late as the 1950s, argued that the dramatist Osman Galal (1838–98) had little classical ability because of his adaptation, in 1901, of Molière's *Tartuffe* into colloquial prose, rather than Fusha.

Unforeseen events, however, were to upset this relationship between the two language forms in theatre. First, the Cairo Opera House was closed down as part of a state economy drive, thus denying plays written in Fusha the continuing prestige and glamour of production. Second, a campaign for the use of colloquial Arabic in education and science began to be waged at the close of the nineteenth century by a very influential lobby which included senior officials of the British occupation authority in Egypt. One of the British activists, in fact, set out to disprove the notion that colloquial Arabic was incapable of dealing with serious topics. As proof and as a model for others he translated into colloquial Arabic parts of Shakespeare's *Henry IV* and *Hamlet* and excerpts from the Old and New Testaments, writings that had until then been written only in Fusha. The translations were published in 1893 in *al Azhar*, a magazine that had as its main goal the propagation of the cause of colloquial Arabic.

The language issue soon took on nationalistic dimensions. 'Trying to curry favour with the British' became a common accusation levelled against dramatists who decided to write in colloquial Arabic at this point. Galal, one of the most successful playwrights of his time because of his expressive and lively language, was himself accused of yielding to British moral pressure. Many writing in colloquial Arabic decided to simply try and avoid the attacks by writing under pseudonyms or by not signing their names to a work at all.

The end of World War I and the severance of the ties between Egypt and the Ottoman Caliphate in Turkey brought with it an awareness, among the Egyptian intelligentsia, of a specific Egyptian identity marked, among other things, by an interest and support for an Egyptian brand of Arabic completely distinct from Turko-Islamic or Arab-Islamic Arabic. The emergence of such an Egyptian identity brought with it a call, particularly by the 'Egyptianist' Ahmed Lutfi al-Sayyed (the first president of the first Egyptian university) for the recognition of what was vaguely described as Egyptian traits in the Arabic language as it is used by all Egyptians including ordinary individuals. To mark this new spirit of Egyptianism, state prizes for best plays began to be offered in 1926 in two categories: colloquial Arabic and Fusha.

In keeping with this new spirit, the Opera House reopened its doors and produced Galal's colloquial plays for the first time. Fusha, however, found a haven in the rapidly developing school and amateur theatre, particularly in the 1920s. Egypt was soon to back away from its support for colloquial plays, however, and, from 1932, the state prizes were awarded only to plays written in Fusha. There was apparently no shortage of such scripts with more than 140 plays entered in the competition that year.

Outside of Egypt, language also continued to flare as an issue. In Morocco, the 1920s coincided with the national struggle against French occupation. Writing in Fusha and invoking epics from the grand history of the Arabs were seen as ways for the newly born Moroccan theatre to break colonial ties with French culture.

The Lebanese playwright Farah Antun (1874–1922) challenged the longstanding dichotomy between colloquial Arabic and Fusha in the introduction to his play *Misr algadida wa misr alqadima* (*Modern and Traditional Egypt*). He suggested that the two language styles were living together in Arab societies with no 'gaping void' between them. His argument was for a third type of language which he described as being mid-way between Fusha and colloquial. He suggested the new language could be called 'diluted Fusha' or 'bright colloquial'. He also suggested the use of a blend for theatre – the mid-language for private discussions on stage, Fusha for the speech of the educated, colloquial Arabic for the rest. Not surprisingly, when

Antun tried to apply his principles, the lines of demarcation between each of the language varieties seemed extremely muddy. Antun the artist was obviously at odds with Antun the theorist.

Perhaps it was because of this unsuccessful attempt that the issue of a middle variety of Arabic was not taken up again by other dramatists until 1956. Meanwhile, Mahmud Taymur (1894–1973), who is usually remembered more for his way of treating the language issue than for the artistic merits of his dramas, brought back the Fusha–colloquial Arabic debate. He argued that Fusha is a medium suited only for our eyes in our own capacity as readers whereas the colloquial is for our own tongues and ears in our capacity as locutors. Therefore, playwrights who wish to have their plays staged must write in the colloquial, the medium most suited for the theatre.[5] On the other hand he felt that if a text was to be studied, it should be written in Fusha. In an attempt to prove this, he wrote six of his thirteen plays in two versions: one in Fusha and the other in colloquial Arabic.

Taymur's solution, while appeasing those conservatives who insisted that colloquial Arabic should not be accorded the status of a written language, also suggested in effect that theatrical performance fell outside the domain of Fusha altogether. His views in a way returned the argument to where it was decades earlier. Perhaps even more revealing is the fact that late in his career, Taymur, in a speech following his election to the Arabic Language Academy, called for the use of Fusha alone in playwriting.

The issue was taken up yet again up in the work of the Egyptian playwright Tawfiq al-Hakīm (1899–1987), still the most prominent playwright in the Arab theatre. Al-Hakīm, for his part, expressed dissatisfaction with all the linguistic choices that playwrights had made to that point. His own early work had blended Fusha with the colloquial having 'each of his characters, in plays set in our time, speak in their own specific way' and although he was 'not the first to fit speech to character among Arab playwrights, al-Hakīm was greatly responsible for diffusing this conception and popularizing it'.[6] Some of his scripts written primarily in colloquial Arabic ultimately found their way into the cinema – the most famous of these was his 1944 classic Rasasa fi l-Qalb (A Bullet in the Heart) – and he wound up influencing other writers through this medium. Indeed, not a single week passes nowadays without one or more television channels in the Arab world showing this film. Despite his great success, however, he was troubled because so many of his plays never actually made it to the legitimate stage.

In 1956, in the introduction to his play Al-Safqah (The Deal), al-Hakīm acknowledged that Fusha was the language of the ages and that it let dramatists transcend the geographic boundaries separating one Arab region from another. He said, though, that it was really right only for historical plays. As for contemporary plays, he felt that something else was necessary because Fusha simply did not appeal to contemporary audiences in the theatre specifically because it was resistant to change. To write in colloquial Arabic, on the other hand, was also not totally satisfactory because its expressions dated quickly, tended to be used for cheap laughs and was by definition not as widely understood.

Al-Hakīm looked at the example of journalism, a profession that had developed a new type of written Arabic which seemed to satisfy more than one need. He therefore sought 'a third language' for the theatre which when written would look like Fusha but when acted on the stage would lend itself, thanks to the syllabic, non-vowel system of written Arabic, to variations in existing colloquial norms.[7] His play Al-Safqah was written with this in mind and he followed it (albeit ten years later) with Al-Warta (The Dilemma, 1966), another language experiment which sought to bring together Fusha and colloquial Arabic. Unlike Antun, al-Hakīm was not calling for a language already in existence in Arab society but was rather calling upon playwrights to develop a new language capable of satisfying both artistic and nationalistic-religious requirements.

It turned out to be an impossible task and critics ultimately said so. One well-known literary journalist, Muhamad Mandur Awad, described the language used in Al-Warta as 'Arabic Esperanto, doomed to failure like its international sister.'[8] Another linked al-Hakīm's 'third language' to a non-existent 'third sex' in biology and called it an 'hermaphroditic language'.[9] On the stage, Al-Warta was a complete failure; only 600 people (mostly invited guests, critics and journalists) saw the play during its week of performance before it was prematurely closed.

Twenty years later, in an unprecedented move, al-Hakīm, who always prided himself on being called the 'Father of Modern Arabic Theatre', allowed a young playwright, Fathi Salama, to rewrite Al-Wartha in a language that seemed rather close to that 'base colloquial which would induce cheap laughter in an audience'. On the stage, however, the new play – *Mugrim Taht al-ikhtibar* (*A Criminal Subjected to Experimentation*) – did meet with moderate success 'thanks to its language'.[10] The new version was never published, however. Perhaps in this way, the issue of a third language in the theatre for al-Hakīm was finally put aside. The very controversy which surrounded al-Hakīm's theatrical experimentation with language and the essays and debates that it generated were the core of the development in what came to be known and recognized by the 1960s on the stage as 'educated spoken Arabic'. Of all spoken varieties it is the most dynamic, versatile and the one, notwithstanding certain regional peculiarities, most readily understood right across the region even in the 1990s.

It was also during the 1960s that life in the Arab world changed greatly because of the Nasser regime in Egypt and its stated goal of emancipation of the 'common people'. Many at this time argued for a new pan-Arab socialism, a pan-Arab communism in some quarters. A propaganda campaign eventually emerged which quite blatantly idealized the common people including their language. Many who were earlier considered political radicals wound up in control at this point of the arts and media. Suddenly colloquial Arabic was being hailed not by 'bad-intentioned' foreigners, but by officials of the state. In fact, with new-found linguistic freedom, the theatre, like the rest of the arts, enjoyed a golden period in the 1960s.

Perhaps the most remarkable new play of this period, linguistically speaking, was the 1964 drama *al-Shab'aniin* (*The Sated*) written by the Cairo-based Ahmed Said. Said, until the Arab–Israeli war of 1967, was director of Cairo Radio's 'Voice of the Arabs', a station aimed at the propagation of socialism and Arab nationalism. In his play, Fusha and colloquial Arabic were very pointedly and crudely used as elements for characterization. Those who represented the sated (who by definition were always corrupt) spoke Fusha. The others spoke colloquial Arabic. It became quickly apparent in the play that the higher and more abstract the Fusha, the greater the character's corruption. In one scene, showing how remote and insensitive to the sufferings of the people around them the Fusha speakers were, the speech of the corrupt begins to take on an ever more ethereal Fusha until by the end they are speaking a type of nonsense. Fusha was thus shown as an instrument of subjugation while colloquial Arabic was openly hailed in the play as the tongue of the decent – the workers, peasants, soldiers and other of society's so-called have-nots.

Only three years before that play, Fathi Radwan (for several years the Egyptian Minister for National Guidance) had written *Shuqqa li'l- Ijar* (*An Apartment for Rent*, 1961), the first half of which was in colloquial Arabic and the rest in Fusha. In his introduction to the play, he expressed the wish that Fusha alone be the medium of Arab society. When the National Theatre of Egypt came to stage the play, however, he was prevailed upon to rewrite the Fusha parts in colloquial Arabic because, in the words of one critic, 'this new experiment denies the dialogue a unity and turns serious situations into what could be construed as comical ones'.[11]

In the late 1970s, Tunisia became the first Arab state to officially accord colloquial Arabic equal status with Fusha. In a 1979 directive issued to everyone connected with the theatre in the country, the Minister of Culture, stating conditions governing eligibility of plays for staging, declared under Article 3 – Style – that the 'text of a play should be written in a correct language; Fusha or colloquial; urban or Bedouin'. The directive went on to say that for the colloquial to be correct it must only be 'genuine'.[12] The mere association of correctness with colloquial in an Arab ministerial document was indeed unusual. It was not surprising therefore that of some 3,000 plays submitted to the ministry for production/approval over the next decade, almost 60 per cent were in colloquial Arabic. Syria later came to accept this as well although there long remained a clear and official bias towards Fusha in that country. As in Egypt, Fusha plays found their greatest support in Syrian schools and amateur theatres. Christian clubs there, however, tended to produce mostly in colloquial Arabic.

The same pattern could be found in the Gulf States, a situation seen clearly during the first Gulf States Theatre Festival held in Kuwait in 1988. In the play *Al-Suuq* (*The Market-Place*), presented by the Bahrain State Theatre, narration of historical events was in Fusha while the dialogue was in colloquial Bahraini. Arthur Miller's *Al-Thaman* (*The Price*), translated by Abdul Aziz al-Surayyie, on the other hand, was completely in colloquial Kuwaiti. Calls were heard again here for finding a common-to-all artistic language with communicative powers suitable for use right across the Arab theatre.[13]

In the 1990s the language issue has taken still another twist as Arab-written drama seems to have become more of a literary genre than ever with productions of such plays becoming relatively rare. At the same time, a populist theatre using only colloquial Arabic has begun to emerge in which plotted plays and literary texts are giving way to scripts with loosely drawn plots, a great deal of dancing, singing and heavy doses of sexually loaded jokes. It is a situation that is ironically reminiscent of earlier performance periods in the Arab world.

Where this issue will go in the future, no one, of course, can know. What is clear is only that in the Arab theatre, perhaps more than any other theatre in the world, the problem of language still looms large for both dramatists and those who care about this language-based art.

Elsaid Badawi
American University in Cairo
Cairo, Egypt

Notes

1 Jacob Landau, *Studies in the Arab Theatre and Cinema*. Philadelphia: University of Pennsylvania Press, 1958, p. 51.
2 Charles A. Ferguson, 'Diglossia'. *Word* 15 (1959): 325–40.
3 Mohamed Yousuf Najm, *al-Masrahiyyah Fi l-Adab al-Hadiith* [The play in modern literature]. Beirut, 1956, p. 27.
4 Marun al-Naqqash, '*Arzatu Libnan* [The cedar of Lebanon]. Beirut, 1869, pp. 26–7.
5 Mahmud Taymur, *al-Makhba' Raqm* 13 [Air-raid shelter no. 13]. Cairo, 1949, pp. 7–9.
6 Pierre Cachia, 'The Use of the Colloquial in Modern Arab Literature'. *Journal of the American Oriental Society*. 87 no. 1 (1967): 12–22.
7 Tawfiq al-Hakīm, *Al-Warta* [The Dilemma], postscript. Cairo, 1966, pp. 198–9.
8 Muhammad Mandur, *Masrah Tewfik al-Hakīm* [Tawfik al-Hakīm's theatre]. Cairo, n.d., p. 133.
9 Abbas Khidr, 'al-lughatu al-khuntha' [The hermaphrodite language]. Cairo, n.d.
10 From a lecture delivered by Mr Fathi Salama in the Arabic Language Institute, American University in Cairo, Egypt.
11 Fouad Dawwarah, *Fil-Naqd al-Masrahi* [On theatre criticism], Cairo, 1963, p. 80.
12 Omar Binsalim, *al-Rasiid al-Masrahi Biwazaarat al-Thaqaafah* [The drama-stock on the records of the Ministry of Culture]. Tunis: Centre for Sociological and Economic Studies, 1993, p. 259.
13 Adnan Binthurayl, *Ruwwad al-Masrah al-Suurii* [Pioneers of the Syrian theatre]. Damascus: Ministry of Culture, 1993, p. 35.

WOMEN IN ARAB THEATRE

FINDING A VOICE

Contrary to common knowledge, Islam gave women numerous rights and privileges: it prohibited female infanticide, allowed women full management of their own money, gave them the right of inheritance, the right to be educated, and the right to be consulted before being given away, by their male guardians, in marriage (to name just a few). Unfortunately, many of these Islamic rights have been denied to Muslim women over the centuries by conservative patriarchal systems within certain Islamic communities.

In the nineteenth century, many upper-class Muslim women were forced (later many actually chose it as a status symbol) to live in the female world of the harem while being denied social mobility and the right to work. Such seclusion was, however, impossible for the Muslim poor, who could not afford such things as keeping their women idle. By the second half of the nineteenth century, more and more women began to demand social and educational emancipation, particularly in Egypt where major socio-economic transformations were taking place. As a new middle class was created, and as extensive immigration from rural areas to the capital increased, national capitals such as Cairo expanded in population and new entertainment and cultural venues were developed to suit the tastes of the new middle class, which was more educated than ever before, more westernized and, in many ways, more elitist.

Despite this major social change in Egypt and other Arab countries, women remained marginal and in seclusion, with those of the upper and middle classes benefiting only slightly from this upheaval by being tutored at home. The Egyptian feminist movement – one of the first in the Arab world – came from those women who had the privilege of education. The leader of the movement was Huda Sha'rawi (1879–1947) who founded (with other feminists such as Nabawiyyah Musa and Malak Hifni) the Egyptian Feminist Union in 1923 and the feminist journal, La Égyptienne, in 1925. This movement advocated a gradual approach to the processes of the unveiling and confinement of Arab women and it steadfastly refused to advocate rapid change. The movement maintained that women's liberation was recognized in Islam and that a woman's education as well as her emancipation would contribute to the development of the emerging spirit of nationalism in the Arab states.

The first Arab women's magazine, Al-Fath, had been established as early as 1892 by Hind Nawfal. Between then and 1913 no fewer than fifteen other such magazines had come into existence across the Arab world, defending women's rights and calling for equality between men and women in all spheres of life. In 1919 Huda Sha'rawi led her countrywomen – marching alongside men – in independence rallies against the British occupation of Egypt. She attended and organized fourteen international conferences and visited Syria, Lebanon and Palestine to meet with other leaders of the feminist movements in these Arab states. More than any other, it was the Egyptian feminist movement which was emulated by women in other Arab countries. It was Sha'rawi who managed to convince King Su'ud of Saudia Arabia to open the first school for girls in that kingdom. It was Sha'rawi who headed the First Conference for Arab Women's Organizations in Cairo in 1937, primarily to discuss women and the growing Palestinian crisis.

The idea of women's education spread quickly and widely. In 1926 the first Egyptian woman, Khadijah Hifni, graduated from London University's Faculty of Medicine. In 1933 the first five Egyptian college-educated women graduated from Cairo University, an event that was celebrated by both that institution and the Egyptian Feminist Union. By the 1950s thousands of university-educated women were taking their places across the Arab world, women who were at last participating fully in the social and economic life of their countries.

In the area of theatre, the pattern was similar. Pre-nineteenth-century Arab performing groups took an essentially non-mimetic approach to art and as a result did not need to include women in their shows. In the spirit of fantasy and social convenience, men wore women's costumes and played women's roles. However, with the arrival of more mimetic dramas (mostly borrowed from western theatre) women's participation in the theatrical event became more essential. So during the second half of the nineteenth century the need for women who were willing to appear on a public stage increased. Unfortunately, no concomitant need for women playwrights or directors was felt. The first actresses in the new literary theatre in the Arab world actually came from among the non-Arab, non-Muslim communities.

Ya'qub Sannu, the father of Egyptian theatre, could find only two poor, illiterate (but virtuous, he insisted) girls willing to go on the stage, therefore his scripts had to be limited to no more than two female roles. In fact, he had to teach them to read and write and then he had to train them to act. According to Nihad Selaiha in *The Voices of Silence*, these first two Arab actresses were, in fact, Jewish – Milia Dayan and her sister.

As for reactions to women in the theatre, Sannu recounted in an interview (related by Ali al-Ra'i in his excellent book *Theatre of the People*, 1993), that audiences were generally dissatisfied by all European conventions. One night's audience, he said, actually refused to applaud at the end of a performance and demanded that Sannu come out and talk to them about what was going on. When he came out, they chastised him – not for having women on the stage, but for not finding the heroine a suitable husband. They warned that if he didn't change the ending, they wouldn't attend any of his plays in future. In 'Drama and Audience: The Case of Arabic Theater' (*Theater Three*, 1989), Roger Allen recounts other anecdotes that

depict such a reception by Arab audiences. Such episodes not only highlight early Arab resistance to the authority of text but also in their way reveal that women were already accepted at this period as a part of the theatre as long as they were neither Arab nor Muslim and were treated properly. Their participation in plays was accepted as a necessity, neither a reprehensible act threatening public morality nor a gratuitous one designed to evoke the sexual or the promiscuous. By the end of the nineteenth century, audiences had obviously completely accepted women on stage as a necessary part of the new trend toward realism.

Yet in the areas of playwriting and directing, as Nihad Selaiha has stated, 'the written text remained the property of men though it was often inscribed on women's bodies and voices.' On the other hand, the contribution of women in theatre continued to be enormous in the areas of performance, management, patronage and audience support. During the first two decades of the twentieth century three major Egyptian theatre companies led the way in giving women leading roles: George Abyad's company (founded 1912) which produced stage adaptations of world literature and translated western dramatic classics; the company of al-Rihani (founded 1916) which was the most commercially successful, producing comedies for the most part and what were called Franco-Arab pieces (Arabicized comedies that included long dance segments); and the Ramsis Troupe (founded 1923), established by two pioneers, Yusuf Wahbi and Aziz Eid (1881–1942), and which produced both original Egyptian melodramas as well as western classics in translation. Many other small companies existed during this period including a number of musical theatre groups such as those of Sayyid Darwish and Salama Hijazi, which were also hugely successful.

Munira al-Mahdiyyah was actually the first Muslim woman to appear on a stage. Known to the Egyptian public as a singer, she made her first appearance in 1915 as an actress-singer with the Arabic Comedy Troupe run by Aziz Eid. Al-Mahdiyyah's first appearance was the biggest entertainment event of that year: not only was a Muslim woman now appearing as an actress, but also for the public it was an opportunity to see its favourite singer in a dramatic-musical role. A huge success in Salama Hijazi's musicals, she ultimately quit working with his Arabic Comedy Troupe and went on to form her own company, thus becoming the first owner-producer-artistic director and star of the first female-owned musical theatre company. From about 1917 to 1929, her troupe reproduced earlier successes as well as adapting internationally known operas and operettas which were being seen on the Arab stage for the first time. Although al-Mahdiyyah in her heyday was certainly able to compete on a stage with such pioneers as Sayyid Darwish, Zakariyyah Ahmad and Da'ud Husni, she ultimately was unable to compete with the rising medium of the cinema, and she had disbanded her troupe by 1930.

In 1916 the first Arab dramatic actresses to reach stardom were Fatimah al-Yusuf and Dawlat Abyad. Both made their premières through Aziz Eid who had no company of his own at that time but was working with al-Rihani's troupe. Al-Yusuf was a teenager when she met Aziz Eid. He took the risk of casting her as a 70-year-old grandmother because none of his leading actresses (six Christian Syrians) would take the role. Appearing on stage under the name Rose al-Yusuf, she apparently played the role exceptionally well and from that day became the star of the troupe. She later moved with Eid to the Ramsis Troupe, starring in virtually all its productions from 1923 on.

In 1925 Rose al-Yusuf decided to quit acting altogether and started her own cultural magazine which she edited until her death. Calling it simply *Rose al-Yusuf*, it still survives as one of the most influential cultural and political magazines in the Arab world. In her autobiography *Dhikrayati* (*My Memories*, 1953) she recalled starting the magazine:

> twenty eight years ago, women weren't given the right to participate in most aspects of life. Society knew them only as slaves with veils covering their faces. Breaking into the field of magazine writing was certainly difficult for men then, so you can imagine how it was for women. I found myself heading an organization in which all the employees were men. I had to meet with men who were well-known to the public as ministers and important personalities, but who in fact just considered women as existing only for male amusement and satisfaction.

Dawlat Abyad (1894–1978), on the other hand, continued to act until her death. Also introduced to the public by Aziz Eid in 1917, she was a member of several important companies for short periods of time but eventually settled in as the star of George Abyad's theatre troupe, a company that toured widely in the Arab world.

Considered the queen of both tragedy and melodrama, she later married Abyad. In 1925, 'Aziza Amir (1901–52) joined the two-year-old Ramsis Troupe, when its owner/director Yusuf Wahbi (then only an aspiring young actor-director) placed an ad in the newspaper calling for new talent. She sent him her photograph and a letter explaining her background. A few days later, Wahbi himself showed up at her door and invited her to join his company, an invitation which she at once accepted. Amir played numerous roles with the Ramsis Troupe and later joined others, including al-Rihani's troupe. 'Aziza Amir's success was huge. Her last stage role was in 1935, after which she turned her attention and energy to film (she had earlier produced the first Egyptian silent film, *Layla*, 1927). In film she had to endure both domestic opposition from her husband's family and ridicule from the media. However, when *Layla* became a smash hit, she again became a darling of the media. Amir ultimately produced and starred in twenty-five films. Her favourite subject matter was the formidable difference between rich and poor, and in her films it was the poor who invariably won. Among her best films were *The Labourer, My Daughter, My Countryman* and, in reaction to the Palestinian crisis, *A Girl from Palestine* and *Nadia*.

Fatimah Rushdie (1908–97) was often called 'the Sarah Bernhardt of the east'. She rose to stardom very young coming from a poor but musical family. She arrived in Cairo at the age of 12, but it wasn't until she was 15 that she got her first chance to appear on stage in a small role. She joined the Ramsis Troupe where her first few roles were those of boys (inverting the tradition of boys playing women's roles). Her ambition to become a great actress was unfortunately impeded by her illiteracy for which even her natural talent could not compensate. Aziz Eid personally took it upon himself to educate her and improve her acting skills. While she proved to be a persistent and diligent student, Eid's relationship with her ultimately changed from mentor to husband, and he eventually converted to Islam in order to marry her.

An early power-couple in the world of Arab theatre, Aziz Eid and Fatimah Rushdie left the Ramsis Troupe and formed their own company, the Fatimah Rushdie Troupe, which operated from 1927 to 1935. Their first play was *Love* by Sarah Bernhardt, directed by Eid and starring Rushdie. The troupe earned itself an excellent name and built up a wide repertoire; it also established new trends in theatre marketing by selling discounted tickets to school and university students. The company found large audiences and earned acclaim, something that eventually made it the major rival to the Ramsis Troupe. For years the two companies competed. To ensure her company's leadership in the field, however, Fatimah Rushdie began playing the roles of men, taking on Yusuf Wahbi on his own turf. She played Hamlet, Mark Antony and Qays, the melancholic lover, in an adaptation by Ahmad Shawqi (the poet laureate of Egypt) of the famous pre-Islamic Arab literary tradition *Majnun Layla*. Also for her troupe, Shawqi wrote the verse play, *The Death of Cleopatra*.

Rushdie explored the field of directing, which she did most ably at one point, staging an adaptation of *Anna Karenina* and at another *The Resurrection* by Tolstoi, thus becoming the first woman director in the Arab world. In 1927 she starred in her first silent movie, *Catastrophe Atop the Pyramid*. In 1933 she starred in, directed and wrote the script for her second film, *The Husband*. Sadly, Fatimah Rushdie, perhaps the most distinguished Egyptian actress of the century and an icon of stardom and success, died in 1997 poor and alone.

In *The Voices of Silence*, Nihad Selaiha notes the name of the first woman playwright in the Arab world, Sophie 'Abdallah, who wrote a play called *Sweepstakes* which was performed in 1951–2. Unfortunately, no manuscript of the play exists. Those who witnessed the performance do not feel that anything major was missed, however. They remember it as being an essentially unimpressive piece, reminiscent of Gorki's *Lower Depths*. But the idea of a woman writing a play had been established and during the 1960s a number of plays by women began to be published. It took until the late 1960s and early 1970s before women's writing was again seen on an Arab stage.

One of the earliest of the women dramatists is Fathiyyah al-'Assal who ultimately made a career writing for the theatre. Born into a strict family that was against education for women, al-'Assal never had formal schooling as a child. She later married a journalist who helped and encouraged her to get an education and got her interested as well in Marxism and left-wing ideology. In her work, al-'Assal advocated the emancipation of women from the confines of home and from roles ascribed to them by society as only mothers, daughters and wives. She also argued that women could become good playwrights only if they watched more plays, since writing for the theatre imposes participatory

terms not required for novel and poetry-writing.

Al-'Assal's first play, *al-Murjihah* (*The Swing*, 1967) was staged at the Alexandria National Theatre in 1969 and her second, *al-Basbore* (*The Passport*) at the Gomhuriyyah Theatre in 1972. She also wrote *Bila Aqni'a* (*Without Masks*, 1982), which was mounted at al-Salam theatre, and *al-Bayn Bayn* (*Betwixt and Between*, 1985), which was never performed. Her last play, *Sijn al-Nisa'* (*Women's Prison*) was published in 1993. Al-'Assal also wrote more than twenty television dramas and scripts for twenty-two television series.

Through the 1960s and the availability of education for both genders, a new generation of educated Egyptian and Arab women came to participate in virtually every facet of professional theatre life. Actresses suddenly were university graduates who partook fully in the administrative as well as artistic side of theatre. The first woman to head the National Theatre of Egypt was Samihah Ayyub, a well-trained, highly respected actress who has played, since the 1950s, a wide and impressive repertoire of classic stage and screen roles. Married to the late Egyptian playwright Sa'd-Allah Wahbah, she began her stage career as a member of the National Theatre company. Her most famous roles were Phaedra, Cleopatra and Shen Te/Shui-Ta in Bertolt Brecht's *The Good Person of Setzuan*. Artistic director of the Modern Theatre (1973–5) and director of the National Theatre (1975–8 and 1984–9), Ayyub has proved herself as competent in administration as she is in acting.

Tahiyyah Karyioka, the famous Egyptian belly-dancer turned actress, formed another important woman-run theatre troupe in 1962 with her husband at the time, Fayiz Halawah. The importance of this company did not emerge until the 1970s when Egypt's theatre generally was muffled by censorship. Amidst this silence, Karyioka's theatre was the only politically subversive venue that remained. When the censorship tried to stop her play *Yahya al-Wafd!* (*Long Live the Wafd!*) by court order, she took the case to court, won the lawsuit and mounted the play. Halawah was the director, dramaturge and star of most of the theatre's performances, but the audience most often came to see its favourite dancer turned actress perform, responding to her political satire, her comments on current affairs and her candour. The Karyioka/Halawah company closed its doors for good in the early 1980s with the demise of the couple's marriage and professional association.

Since the 1980s and particularly with the growth of the Free Theatre movement in Egypt (in the 1990s), women's contributions have continued to be strong, with many of these smaller groups having women as performers, directors, artistic directors, stage-managers and playwrights. This younger generation of women all across the Arab world is both growing in number and becoming more assertive in the ideas they wish to convey through their work.

One such notable figure was Nihad Jad (d. 1989). A graduate of the Faculty of English Literature at Cairo University, she did her Master's in the United States. Upon her return she took up writing for the stage. Her first play, a one-woman show, 'Adila, was written, acted, directed and designed by women. The play was produced at al-Tali'a Theatre in Cairo in 1981. A realistic portrait, her female characters caused controversy partly because they were real but also because they were not full of virtue and goodness. Her second play, 'Azizah and Firdaws, went unproduced but her next play, 'Ala ar-Rasif (On the Pavement, 1986) was a huge success. Here again, Jad did not occupy herself with the ideal but with the real. Her play made headlines and earned her a great deal of money. Before her untimely death from cancer, Jad wrote three other screenplays and two television scripts. She remains one of the few women writers in the Arab world to have achieved both artistic and commercial success through the stage.

In 1981, Egypt's foremost feminist, Nawal al-Sa'dawi, published her only play, Isis, and a controversial play it has been. Interesting as a text, the play is difficult to stage as it is filled with scenes involving rape, circumcision and castration. Nihad Selaiha has said, 'It is perhaps unperformable – not on account of its structural faults (worse texts have been performed), but on account of its iconoclastic message and radical views. Its unflinching questioning and intellectual audacity remain unparalleled in writing by Egyptian women.' In this play, Isis is a powerful goddess equal to male-gods in stature and power.

With two plays to her credit Nadia al-Banhawi is another Egyptian woman dramatist of genuine promise. Her first play, al-Wahj (The Glow, 1996) is both a philosophical and psychological drama which transcends gender and delves into feelings of loss and alienation. The Death and Love Sonata (1997) is an almost expressionistic drama that projects the various components of its female protagonist's mind.

Other women of note now occupy powerful academic, artistic and executive positions. Foremost among those is Huda Wasfi (b. 1942), artistic director of both the National Theatre of Egypt since 1995, and al-Hanajir Theatre since 1992. Wasfi earned a doctorate in literary criticism from the Faculty of French Literature at 'Ayn Shams University and later worked as a professor of comparative drama and literary criticism there as well as at the Academy of Fine Arts, the Institute of Arts Criticism and the Higher Institute of Theatre Arts. During that time she translated a large number of plays from and to Arabic, and conducted research in a number of topics related to Arabic and French dramatic studies. She produced a large number of critical essays on Arab women's literature, short stories and French poetry which were all published in major literary magazines. Wasfi was director of the Annual Experimental Theatre Festival in Egypt and the first to popularize the notion of workshops in state theatres. She also created many opportunities for artistic exchange with foreign artists.

Two of the leading female theatre critics in the present-day Arab world are Nihad Selaiha (who has already been quoted widely here) and Minha al-Batrawi. Sehaila is the main drama critic of al-Ahram Weekly and is an accomplished literary critic, with many books and translations to her credit. Her support for young and aspiring artists shows in her constructive criticism of their activities as well as her positive reinforcement of their achievements. Al-Batrawi assisted in establishing Hebdo (the French al-Ahram) and continues to write for it theatre reviews in both French and Arabic. Minha al-Batrawi's educated criticism and objectivity have earned her the respect of both the theatre milieu in Egypt and a trusting readership who count on her evaluation and perception in assessing dramatic works. As for women's dramatic writing in French in the Arab world, the works of several established novelists should be noted. One of the most important is Assia Djebar, an Algerian. Born as Fatima-Zohra Imalayen in 1936, she published her first novel, La Soif (Thirst) in 1957. In 1969 she wrote her only play, Rouge l'aube (Red Dawn), in collaboration with her husband. Performed at the third Pan-African Cultural Festival in Algiers, the play reveals her strong anti-colonial sentiments and raises issues of post-colonialism.

Fatima Gallaire-Bourega, another Algerian writer now living in self-imposed exile in France, has written a very daring one-act play entitled

Témoignage contre un homme stérile (*Testimony Against a Sterile Man*, 1987). In it, we meet an old woman who reminisces about her husband's sexual violence towards her and admits that she enjoyed some of it. Starting the play by revealing a love–hate relationship with the husband, she ends by declaring a deep affection for him precisely because of his sexual acts. Gallaire later wrote *Princess You Have Come Back* (1988), where she draws a grim picture of a woman's homecoming to her native village from France. Caught between western values and a patriarchal east where male domination assumes absolute power, she returns, married to a Frenchman, and is condemned by the whole village as a blasphemer who has deserted Islam.

Representing another part of the Arab world is Hanan al-Shaykh, who left Lebanon for London in the 1970s as a refugee of the civil war. Another novelist experimenting with playwriting, her candour, unique characters, and visions of war-ravaged Lebanon have earned her renown. She has written two plays to date of which the second, *Paper Husband*, was staged in London at the Hampstead Theatre. It is about a Moroccan woman who escapes the poverty of her country and seeks new dreams abroad.

Dina Amin
University of Pennsylvania

Further Reading

Abou-Saif, L. 'Creating a Theatre of the Poor at Wekalat al-Ghouri in Cairo'. *Arab Cultural Scene* (1982): 100–4.

——. 'Najib al-Rihani: From Buffoonery to Social Comedy'. *Journal of Arabic Literature* 4 (1973): 1–17.

Al-Khozai, Mohamed A. *The Development of Early Arabic Drama 1847–1900*. London: Longman, 1984.

Allen, Roger. 'Arabic Drama in Theory and Practice: The Writings of Sa'dallah Wanous'. *Journal of Arabic Literature* 15 (1984): 94–113.

——. 'Drama and Audience: The Case of Arabic Theater'. *Theater Three* 6 (1989): 25–54.

——. 'Egyptian Drama after the Revolution'. *Edebiyat* 4 no. 1 (1979): 97–134.

Al-Ra'i, Ali. *Masrah al-Sha'b* [Theatre of the People]. Cairo: Dar al-Sharqiyyat, 1993.

Awad, Louis. 'Problems of the Egyptian Theatre'. In *Studies in Modern Arabic Literature*. Edited by R.C. Ostle. Warminster, England: Aris & Phillips, 1975.

Awad, Samir. 'The Father of the Modern Egyptian Theatre: Ya'qub Sannu'. *Journal of Arabic Literature* 16 (1985): 132–45.

——. 'Medieval Arabic Drama: Ibn Daniyal'. *Journal of Arabic Literature* 13 (1982): 82–107.

——. *Modern Arabic Drama in Egypt*. Cambridge: Cambridge University Press, 1987.

——. 'Modern Arabic Drama Outside Egypt'. *Theater Three* 6 (1989): 53–64.

——. 'Women in the Egyptian Theatre'. *Journal of Experimental Theatre Festival in Cairo*. Cairo: Ministry of Culture, 1997.

Badran, Margot. 'The Feminist Vision in the Writings of Three Turn-of-the-Century Egyptian Women'. *British Society for Middle Eastern Studies Bulletin* 15, nos. 1–2 (1988): 11–20.

—— and Miriam Cooke, eds. *Opening the Gates: A Century of Arab Feminist Writing*. Bloomington: Virago/Indiana University Press, 1990.

Cooke, Miriam. 'Mothers, Rebels, and Textual Exchanges: Women Writing in French and Arabic'. In *Postcolonial Subjects: Francophone Women Writers*. Minneapolis: University of Minnesota Press, 1996.

Gellner, E. 'The Struggle for Morocco's Past'. *Middle East Journal* 15 (1961): 79–90.

Kourilsky, Françoise and Catherine Temerson, eds. *Plays by Women: An International Anthology*. New York: Ubu Repertory Theater Publications, 1988.

Lancaster, Pat. *Hanan al-Shaykh's Paper Husband*. London: IC Publications, 1997.

Landau, Jacob. 'The Arab Theatre'. *Middle Eastern Affairs* 4 no. 3 (March 1953).

——. 'Egyptian Stage Actresses'. *The Bulletin* 22 (March 1948): 15–17.

——. 'Popular Arabic Plays 1909'. *Journal of Arabic Literature* 17 (1986): 120–5.

El-Lozy, Mahmoud. 'Brecht and the Egyptian Political Theatre'. *Alif: Journal of Comparative Poetics* 10 (1990): 56–73.

Makward, Christiane P. and Judith G. Miller, eds. *Plays by French and Francophone Women: A Critical Anthology*. Ann Arbor: University of Michigan Press, 1994.

Malti-Douglas, Fedwa. *Men, Women, and God(s)*. Berkeley: University of California Press, 1995.

Selaiha, Nihad. 'Voices of Silence: Women Playwrights in Egypt'. *Egyptian Theatre, A Diary: 1990–1992*. Cairo: Dar al-Kutub, 1993.

DANCE

MEADOWS OF GOLD AND MINES OF GEMS[1]

Geographically and culturally, the Arab world is large and diverse, a fact that can be seen in the wide array of traditional dance and patterned movement styles found in this area, which stretches from the Atlantic Ocean to the Persian Gulf. Because Arab Islamic tradition requires a strict segregation of men and women, except within permitted degrees of family relationships, how, where and by whom dance is performed is an important issue. Distinctions must also be made between what may be legitimately considered dance and what is simply patterned movement.

Such distinctions often separate dance as a form of entertainment and leisure from movement found in spiritual ceremonies such as *dhikr* (a recitation and invocation of God's name) and non-sacred ritual activities (such as the performance of certain weapons dances and the performance of healing ceremonies such as *zar*, *buri*, *isawiyya* and *guedra*). Such distinctions can vary among Arabs themselves, some calling the exorcism *zar* ritual a 'dance', while others consider it something very different because of its uncontrolled and frenzied unpatterned movements which often evoke a trance or altered state.

Social context and location also determine the propriety of a specific dance performance and those individuals who perform outside of those conditions call forth negative reactions well known to scholars of dance in Islamic societies.[2] Of course, it is mostly with the extremely conservative that these negative reactions find expression in dance although, in and of itself, there is no specific prohibition against this art in the Quran. Again, the key is that like all social activities in an Islamic context, dance perfor-

mances must occur only within proper, permitted social environments. Female professional performers who perform before audiences of non-related males, for example, are viewed as being outside of permitted social parameters and call forth the negative reactions masterfully described in Karin Van Nieuwkerk's (1995) study of Egyptian attitudes toward professional dancers, a view reinforced by numerous Egyptian films, dating from the 1930s, which depicted belly-dancers as fallen women. Except for a small minority of individuals who have adopted western viewpoints and lifestyles, such as may be found among certain classes in large cosmopolitan cities such as Cairo, Casablanca or Beirut, the vast majority in the Arab world follow these traditions in maintaining the separation between men and women in their social interactions, including dance performances.

Adding to the variety of response is the fact that the types of dance and movement in the Arab world are so vast that many occur only within specific regions (such as the city of Alexandria in Egypt or in the High Atlas in Morocco) and are not found elsewhere. In contrast, other dance types such as the *dabka* and belly-dancing are performed over large areas. In the twentieth century, new venues for stage adaptations of traditional dance and, more rarely, performances of western theatrical dance traditions such as classical ballet and modern dance, may now be encountered in large cities such as Cairo and Beirut.

While at first such a variety of dance forms may seem difficult to grasp, it is possible to conceptually identify two major types of traditional dance in the Arab world: solo improvised dancing and regional folk dances performed in groups. The former, often associated with city life, may also be found in the countryside. The most famous manifestation of solo improvised dance is, of course, belly-dancing, especially the type of professional dancing seen in cafés, hotels and films emanating not only from the Middle East (especially Egypt and North Africa), but also in highly orientalist – using Edward Said's (1978) well-known concept – productions from the west.

The focus on professional performances of Egyptian cabaret belly-dancing as the representative dance form of the Arab world, almost to the total exclusion of other solo improvised dance and regional folk dance traditions of the twentieth century, has resulted in a spate of articles found in popular sources attempting to connect this style with dances that occurred in Pharaonic Egypt. Some of these make specious and often exaggerated claims for ancient origins and religious connections that simply cannot be substantiated through historical documentation. Movement practices generally – even those of the Baroque and Renaissance periods of Europe from which we have copious written and choreographic notations – leave lacunae regarding how people actually moved. Such documents are totally absent for the Middle East and North Africa.[3] The principal sources left by natives of these areas are iconographic and, as dance historians Lillian Lawler (1964) and Sharon Fermor (1987) have demonstrated for Ancient Greece and the Renaissance, such pictorial sources are highly unsatisfactory for the reconstruction of historical movement practices. This does not mean, of course, that the movements of this dance tradition are not old, but rather that we cannot, with any certainty, establish historically verifiable evidence.

Belly-dance, versions of which were seen during the various world fairs of the late nineteenth and early twentieth centuries in Europe and the United States, titillated audiences of that period who were in search of the exotic. As Edward Said and others pointed out, images of the unbridled sexual east have long been publicized in the writings of well-known literati such as Flaubert, whose intimate encounters with a professional public dancer Kuchek Khanom (which he described in some detail) helped establish western views of the Orient as a place of passion (Wood and Shay 1976). Further images were projected in Hollywood films with performances of the naughty 'hootchie-kootchie' being one of the predominant images of the Middle East. Many Arabs express frustra-

tion and occasionally outrage that such a form has come to dominate the images that symbolize and represent Arab life in the rest of the world. One must acknowledge the fact though that belly-dance performances are easily accessible to tourists in Cairo and other large Middle Eastern cities.

By contrast, scholarly research on other regional dance traditions in the Arab world has lagged because many Arab countries are still politically or geographically difficult to visit. The financial expense and physical difficulties of travel to remote areas, the lack of specific linguistic skills and the sexual segregation of society have, until recently, retarded Arab dance research. Further complicating research in an Islamic context is the fact that domestic versions of solo improvised dance occur in more private circumstances. In such contexts investigators have limited access to these milieux which are exclusively attended by participants of the opposite sex.

Probably the first important documented research of dance in the Arab world was the meticulous survey of Egyptian dances conducted by Magda Saleh in her groundbreaking study that she filmed and recorded in the 1970s (Saleh 1979).[4] Among her conclusions was that belly-dance was only one form of choreographic expression in a wide range of dance genres.

As for regional folk dance, the most popular and well known is the *dabka*, a dance found throughout the Levant (Lebanon, Syria, Palestine, Jordan, Israel) and Iraq. In this dance the participants dance in lines or semicircles and generally hold hands in a variety of ways, or hold one another by the shoulders. A leader often carries a kerchief or other object in his or her hand and directs the changes of step and movements. The leader may also leave the line and execute special figures. *Dabka* steps, figures and movements have many local variants in patterns and hand holds, some of which are highly complex. A wide variety of folk music is played on traditional instruments to accompany the *dabka*, whose unmistakable rhythms are utilized in many popular songs by stars like Sabah, Samira Tawfik and Fairuz. These singers often feature several highly theatrical *dabka* routines (created by individuals such as Abdul Halim Caracalla) in their club or concert performances.

Many dances from the Arabian peninsula, Sudan, Egypt and North Africa are performed using opposing lines of dancers, usually, but not always, of the same sex. The lines move toward and away from one another with the dancers often performing complex cross-rhythm patterns by clapping. Dancers sometimes sing in response to the vocal soloist who might be sitting between the two lines of performers. In these dances, the dancers do not hold one another, but move in unison. These dances vary widely in the difficulty of movement, some being very simple, others displaying great choreographic complexity in foot patterns, squats and rapid turns, particularly some of the dances from the Arabian peninsula.

Among North African Berber tribes, where mores regarding the segregation of men and women are not as strictly observed as in other parts of the Arab world, men and women, generally in segregated lines or semicircles, but sometimes alternating, perform in the same space. In such dances as the *ahwash* and *ahidou*, which combine dancing, singing and rhythm, the men play musical instruments while the women dance or, conversely, lines of men and women also face one another and further subdivide, creating intricate spatial formations as the lines move about the performing area. In some of the dances, the performers also carry and play percussion instruments during the dance.

Dances in which weapons are used are also widespread through the Arab world. Some of these do not come under the native category of dance (*raqs* in Arabic), such as the *bar'a* of Yemen described and analysed in two important studies by anthropologist Najwa Adra (1985 and 1993), because they form part of rituals. In many parts of the Arab world such rhythmic patterned movement practices, although dance-like in appearance, constitute other categories. When a king, an emir or other important political figure dances, often carrying a sword, his performance would be diminished in the eyes of viewers if he were regarded as 'dancing'. Underscoring the need to understand native categories – which movement activities are regarded as dance and which are not – is Najwa Adra's observation: 'When *li'ba* (a type of social dance) and the playing of musical instruments were banned on religious grounds by the Hamid al-Din Imams (who ruled Yemen in the first half of the twentieth century) *bar'a* was not included in the ban' (1985: 282).

Dances, or rhythmic patterned movement activities in which weapons are carried exclusively by males, form two types. In the first, such as the *bar'a* of Yemen or the many sword dances and dance rituals found in Saudi Arabia, and the *taskioin* of Morocco, the daggers, swords and rifles are manipulated and brandished by the

performers, but they are not used in actual combat during the dance. These are occasions of displaying nobility and they honour a specific social, ethnic or political group.

By contrast the *seif wa tirs* (sword and shield) performance, found in some of the mountain villages of Lebanon, which has parallels to the performances of the more well-known sword and shield dance of Bursa (Turkey) is a form of true combat, and the dancers can receive wounds in the heat of performance. For this reason the dancers generally have only one partner for life, often a brother or close cousin. When one dancer dies or quits, the partner also stops dancing.[5] This dance, generally performed by a single pair, is often accompanied by a brass band.

Many weapon dances, because of their ritual quality and importance in tribal life, are considered an honour for the performers and for this reason require exceptional skill and practice. The *bar'a*, as described by Adra (1985), is highly complicated and participation in it is expected of all men who qualify; it is performed in all significant village and regional events. The *bar'a* and Saudi sword dances are generally performed in circles, with the dance leader in the centre directing changes of movement, or in a line with the leader at one end or facing the other performers to ensure synchronization of movements.

Another all-male dance requiring extraordinary athletic skill, enormous stamina and strength is the *gnawa* (named for the Berber tribe who first did it) which can be seen in the main square of Rabat and other areas of Morocco. This dance, which the men perform both solo and in groups, also has the dancers playing *qerqbat* (large wrought-iron clackers). They typically wear hats decorated with cowrie shells with balls attached by long strings which are then manipulated in whirling patterns as they gyrate their heads. The popular version is done by agile acrobats who often perform in the public squares of Moroccan cities. They wear bright silk costumes rather than tribal clothing and form human pyramids, balance trays on their heads and execute a range of entertaining and difficult feats, employing both gymnastic and dance figures in their well-rehearsed routines designed to attract coins from the public.

Such movement activity, in a wide variety of forms is also used in spiritual contexts such as Sufi or dervish gatherings called *dhikr* (recitation, invocation). These activities, because of their spiritual connotations, however much they may resemble dancing, cannot be considered as dance because dance *per se* never forms part of religious rites in Islamic contexts. Rather, these performances fall into a category that can be termed simply rhythmic, patterned, movement activity. The different orders of Sufis or dervishes use different types ranging from a simple rocking back and forth of the whole body or head to complex movement patterns. Such movements are said to help the participants achieve altered states. As well, many individuals who participate in spiritual gatherings resent the 'deceitful, exhibitionist dervishes who would dance in the market-place, undress in public, sit on hot coals, swallow glass, engage in acts of self-mutilation and, in general, misuse the ceremony of *sama*' (Shiloah 1995: 141). These spiritual events or aspects of them, particularly the *zar*, also serve as a subject for new market-places: nightclubs and theatres. In sum, using the term 'dance' to characterize the movements found in spiritual contexts needs to be questioned and native categories must be closely scrutinized and acknowledged.

Anthropologist Susan Rasmussen (1995) has analysed the *zarraf*, a wedding dance performed in groups by Tuareg women in North Africa, which contributes to the discourse of sexuality in Tuareg society that is not permitted verbal expression. Her important study, like those of Najwa Adra, among others, demonstrates the recent, and promising, direction of scholarly dance research in the Arab world.

Another genre is that of solo improvised dance, the most widespread dance type in the Arab world. This form comes in a wide variety of performance styles and contexts offering individual performers great latitude within their stylistic parameters. In the Arab world this dance genre, to a large degree, celebrates a joyful sensuality, which dictates that its social contexts be within permissible limits. It is performed by both men and women, young and old, and by all social classes. In its domestic context, its performance is usually strictly segregated by sex, although occasionally men of permitted relationship might be present (see Deaver 1978). Sexual segregation varies by family and region, class and education. This dance genre is not, as some have stated, a specifically female dance form; such misconceptions largely emerge from the highly visible public appearances of professional performances by female dancers, but until recently both male and female dancers performed professionally.[6] The form – popularly called belly-dance in the west because of its isolations of the torso in which the performer creates rapid, sometimes minute, highly controlled muscular movements and shimmies with the shoulders, chest, stomach and hips – is performed both domestically (that is at private parties and other semi-private celebratory and social settings) as well as in public settings such as hotels, cafés and large wedding celebrations in which its professional practitioners may be seen. In different parts of the Arab world, such as Morocco and Tunisia, the stylistic parameters differ from those of Egypt and the Levant, Iraq and the Arabian peninsula, but everywhere the dance is marked by individual improvised choices of movements and performance style. Each performance is considered fresh, unique and individual.

Some rare belly-dances do exist for pairs, such as the Yemeni *li'ba* or *lu'ba* (from the verb to play), in which the two dancers, who can be either two males, two females, or a male and female within a proper kin relationship, stand in front of one another and mirror each other's movements. According to ethnomusicologist Amnon Shiloah, 'this intricate, highly refined dance that enhances family celebrations and social gatherings calls for skillful, agile dancers with extraordinary bodily control [it can also] involve highly skilled acrobatic performances' (1995: 152).[7]

Even domestic belly-dance performances can be as virtuosic and athletic as those found in professional contexts. Because of this, and because professional competition is strong, professional performers have always attempted to add in unique aspects either through extraordinary athleticism or unusual skill in manipulating objects such as finger cymbals, balancing objects on the head or hands in order to attract patronage away from competitors. Since the 1960s, some professional dancers perform using set choreography to specific music, a major departure from the improvised tradition that has long prevailed. It is also the professional performers who have mostly borne society's negative attitudes.

Historically, public entertainers throughout the Middle East were often born into the trade and operated in family groups. Most were not eligible for marriage outside the group where they received their training. Often, they also danced, sang, played musical instruments, and/or performed gymnastics and magic tricks. Generally, professional dancers, both male and female, were and still are widely considered to be available sexually on a commercial basis and various governments in the region have sporadically attempted to control aspects of professional performances, including what dancers are allowed to wear. As well, professional dancers could not testify in court (Schimmel 1994) while Islamic historian C.E. Bosworth enumerated public entertainers among the denizens of the medieval Islamic underworld (1976: 1). In various parts of the Arab world different names are applied to the professional dancer, most carrying negative connotations – *almeh*, *ghawazi* and *shikhat* being just a few.

Any discussion of solo improvised dance, or, if preferred, movement practices, must finally include the many rituals in which healing and exorcism constitute the main goals of the ceremonies. *Zar*, *isawiyya* and *guedra*, among many others, are accompanied by clapped and percussion instrument rhythms and sometimes musical instruments. These latter are important since there are several well-known spirits, some highly malevolent, that must be summoned to the gathering and the musicians know which specific melodies and rhythmic patterns will call each of them. These rituals vary according to geography. The *guedra* is primarily performed in the Goulemine region of Morocco (although it is widely seen in festival contexts), while the *zar* ritual is performed in a wide band from Baluchistan and the southern coastal regions of Iran, the Arabian peninsula, most of east Africa and Egypt. During these rituals the afflicted individuals are led into trances by the lead healer, often a woman, and by the musicians present in order to effect a cure (which is to say a deal is struck with the particular spirit to release the victim for a specific time). Because a permanent exorcism is never achieved, the afflicted must continuously return to the *zar* gatherings, which for many participants constitute a supportive and pleasurable social activity (see Bourguignon 1968; Eisler 1985; Saleh 1979).

Some words may be useful here about where and when dance works are seen in the Arab world. Venues such as proscenium arch stages and western-style nightclubs, and, of course, the presence of films and television have not so much replaced the conditions and context of dance performances as added new layers to them. Nevertheless, the addition of tourist venues in which one can see choreographed spectacles featuring the biggest names among belly-dance performers along with variety shows which include some version of local folklore has affected only the richest of Arab patrons. What has had impact, though, has been the Egyptian

film industry, which since the 1930s has produced hundreds of films, almost all featuring belly-dancing. Few successful films can be found which do not prominently feature music and dance. Through such films, exceptionally talented dancers such as Tahia Carioca and Samia Gamal have become famous throughout the Arab world. On the other hand, the image of belly-dancers as fallen women again abounds in these films (see Franken 1996).[8]

The role and growing influence of western dance – especially ballet – needs to be examined, particularly the 'ballet diplomacy' practised by the former USSR through which many young Arab dancers received scholarships to study with the Bolshoi Ballet in Moscow. As well, a ballet company was founded, financially underwritten and even staffed by officials from the former USSR in Cairo in the 1960s, which was soon touring world-wide. The subsequent influence of ballet, and the importance accorded it as a cultural icon by various Middle Eastern governments, ultimately led to the founding of state companies in several other Arab countries using western theatrical dance techniques and sometimes telling stories through dance. Although mime is not entirely absent from dances of the Arab world, there is no real narrative tradition. As Islamic scholar Lois Ibsen Al Faruqi pointed out: 'It is an "abstract" rather than a descriptive or delineative art. . . . there is little or no evidence of attempts to coordinate steps, formations, movements or gestures with a story or with the description of events or things' (1987: 7). Magda Saleh has detailed how Russian elements and influences began to be used in new stagings of folk dance found in the repertoires of groups such as the Reda company of Egypt. In Lebanon, choreographers such as Abdul Halim Caracalla have created highly theatrical *dabka* extravaganzas based on storylines from Shakespeare (Trendle 1992: 50). Saleh (1978) has actually decried the intrusion of these new western elements, urging Egyptian choreographers to go back to their roots and to steep themselves in their own traditions.

Knowledgeable observers of the Reda company in Egypt concur with the assessment that these companies do not represent authentic tradition, but rather are trying to cover what they consider to be embarrassing aspects of the native dance tradition. The scholar Lois al Faruqi has also commented: 'In the Middle East, recent attempts at programmatic dance by companies like Firqah Reda of Egypt are obvious attempts to imitate an alien tradition (European dance) rather than one native to Egypt' (1987: 7). The connection of this new tradition to belly dance has been looked at by Monroe Berger, a former director of the programme in Near Eastern studies at Princeton University, who has observed:

> As the fame of belly dance spread to the western world, it became something of an embarrassment to the cultural and political custodians of the East, who began to consider themselves above their own popular arts. . . . This is because the government encourages instead the performance of a sort of folkloric dance that only vaguely resembles the belly dance.
>
> (Berger 1966: 43)

Although companies like those of Caracalla and Reda rely heavily on western elements, creating orientalist, highly sanitized and spectacular images of their respective dance traditions, successful attempts at presenting authentic folk and professional dances to represent national traditions have also been made. In 1979, the 'Musicians of the Nile', a group of musicians and dancers representing a variety of Egyptian traditions, curated and narrated by Magda Saleh, toured several cities of the United States under the sponsorship of the Smithsonian Institution. The Egyptian government, pleased by the positive responses to this tour, began to give additional government support to local traditional artists. A similar group, under the same title but with different artists, toured to rave reviews in 1995. The Moroccan government sponsors annual festivals in Marrakesh where tribal and urban groups display the wide range of folkloric traditions found in that country.

Other governments, including those of Saudi Arabia and Yemen, have now created state-sponsored companies though, following Islamic tradition, with relatively few theatrical trappings. It should be noted that these are also all-male companies.[9]

Change, as in many parts of the world, is a constant factor in all Arab countries. The very strategic geography of the Arab world itself ensures constant contacts with other peoples, each of these leaving cultural, economic, political and linguistic evidence of that contact, just as the Arabs have imprinted their presence on the traditions of others. These traditions will, no doubt, continue as long as they are relevant to audiences. Scholars (both in and out of the region) rather than attempting to harken back to a 'golden era' when everything seemed 'purer' and more 'authentic', need to put such 'changes' into a living context when dealing with the ever-metamorphosing art of dance in this part of the globe.

Anthony Shay
Pomona College
Claremont, California

Notes

1 The title refers to the title of an important historical treatise in which dance is mentioned (Shiloah 1995: 137).
2 In his insightful work *The Formation of Islamic Art*, Oleg Grabar (1987) makes the point that for several centuries following the appearance of Islam there was no specific artistic form which one could call Islamic. In fact, the art form now known as 'Islamic' reworked materials, designs and other elements from former, largely Sasanian and Byzantine civilizations that were used throughout the area. I suggest, based on Grabar's concept, that pre-Islamic attitudes toward professional dancers in the Arab world were also negative (one need only remember the Byzantine Empress Theodora's shady past as a public entertainer which the entire propaganda machinery of the Byzantine Empire was unable to hide). By contrast, in Islamic areas such as Java, dance is a courtly art and its practitioners are highly honoured artists. Thus, negative attitudes toward dancing are not pan-Islamic, but specifically a cultural (rather than religious) attitude in large parts of central Asia, the Middle East and urban areas of North Africa.
3 In one self-revealing passage, Ibn 'Arabi, the famous medieval Sufi, described his abandoned life prior to his commitment to a spiritual path: 'As the night drew to an end my wicked companions and I went off to get some sleep because we were exhausted after all the dancing' (*'wa qad ta'ibna min kathrati ma raqasna'*) (Addas 1993: 31). Frustratingly, and typically, Ibn 'Arabi does not detail what kind of dance he and his friends performed. This is a rare passage, for the mention of dance and dancers was beneath the dignity of most Arab scholars until the late 1970s.
4 The film that accompanies Saleh's dissertation is available for viewing at the Dance Collection of the New York Public Library at Lincoln Center. For the interested, the film merits a visit to New York City. It may not be copied and it is not available elsewhere to my knowledge.
5 This information was given to me by performers of this dance/ritual in the village of Mtein (Lebanon) during a field trip in December 1975.

6 There is a good deal of confusion and some-times embarrassment over this issue. Scholars have contributed to this misunderstanding through the misuse of articles and books written by belly-dance enthusiasts pushing a feminist agenda (see Sellers-Young 1992.) There is also an unwarranted assumption seen in several recent studies that when men perform the solo improvised dance they are 'parodying' women rather than simply dancing. 'These men undu-late their shoulders and hips in what looks like a self-mocking parody of traditional gender roles, combined with a sheer delight in rhythmic physical movement' (Jonas 1992: 116). Jonas, in a book which accompanies an eight-part US Public Broadcasting series 'Dancing', assumes, without proof, a parody. He states in a caption for a photograph that 'perhaps because dancing in Arab countries tends to be segregated by gender, there is an undercurrent of male dancing that parodies the social dancing of women' (1992: 113). These observations require some attention because they appear in other writings as well. Indeed, the young man shown in the photograph is not impersonating a woman; he is wearing men's clothing and sport-ing a moustache. Second, this is the dance form common to all – men and women – in urban (and some rural) settings. The assumption that these movements are feminine in a Middle Eastern context is a patent display of western orientalist notions being projected on the move-ment vocabulary of other cultures because the movements in a western context might be inap-propriate to a male dancer. The disreputability that Jonas posits attaches not to the dancing itself, but to dancing professionally which is, in the minds of many, accompanied by a strong negative symbol of being sexually available. That is not to say that the dance is not consid-ered by some post-colonial individuals to be a feminine activity; in fact, it is considered by many to be so. For example, Mohammed Chtatou, a Moroccan sociologist, states in the same television series that dancing is 'womanly, not manly'. This position is often taken by post-colonial scholars, politicians and others for they regard the open and frank sensuality which often characterizes this dance form as an embar-rassment. Yet Chtatou's argument, in my opinion, is belied by a large group of men depicted in the film (dancing in a Moroccan party) using the same movements we have just seen in the women's domestic party, during which Chtatou's voice is being heard narrating his opinions. In other words, I am positing that these dance traditions and their movement vocabularies are shared by all members of the culture. It is, in my opinion, an orientalist posi-tion that this is an exclusively female dance because of its potentially sensual movements, and that the participation of males must somehow be explained and wished away. Men, too, may exhibit sensuality.

In 1975, as a folklorist doing a project for the Smithsonian Institution, I was sent to Lebanon to investigate folk dancing and music. In the village of Mtein, a mixed Druze and Christian settlement, I saw several dances, including the domestic version of the belly-dance performed by most of the men who were present. Lebanese government officials and some Smithsonian Folklife staff were most anxious, exhibiting con-siderable squeamishness, that this dance not be shown performed by men on the Mall in Washington, DC lest the viewers 'get the wrong impression'.

7 A similar dance/game, *raqs-e ayineh*, (the mirror dance), also exists in Iran and is very popular with some children and young adults.

8 It is beyond the scope of this essay to discuss Arab dance outside of the Arab world; however, I must mention that belly-dance constitutes a hobby among hundreds of thousands of non-Arab women in the United States and Europe. The earliest professional dancers of non-Arab background who began their careers dancing in ethnic (Greek, Syrian and Lebanese) nightclubs often learned their techniques by watching films of these dancers. These films, which I attended regularly in the 1950s, were shown each week at the local Syrian Orthodox Church in Los Angeles, a venue for experiencing the dancing of the *dabka* as well.

9 These companies are utilized in what I term the 'choreographed politics' of state visits: the Saudi Arabian national dance company appeared in Los Angeles in August 1989 for a week of per-formances in conjunction with a large exhibit by the Saudi Arabian government. The Tunisian State Folk Dance company, which has both male and female dancers, appeared for two weeks on the Mall in Washington, DC in 1975. Members of the Reda company accompanied Anwar Sadat on a state visit to Los Angeles, where they danced in the rotunda of the City Hall. Unlike the world-famous and popular Moiseyev Ballet or Ballet Folklorico de México companies, these dance ensembles do not appear on commercial circuits, but rather, they represent their respec-tive governments at special events like the Olympics, world fairs and other large interna-tional functions and state visits where they fulfil the creation of a positive national image. In the same vein, they appear to entertain important guests in their home countries.

Further Reading

Addas, Claude. *Quest for the Red Sulphur: The Life of Ibn 'Arabi*. Translated by Peter Kingsley. Cambridge: Cambridge University Press, 1993.

Adra, Najwa. 'Tribal Concepts in Yemen Arab Republic'. In *Arab Society: Social Science Perspectives*. Edited by Saad Eddin Ibrahim and Nicholas S. Hopkins. Cairo: American University in Cairo Press, 1985: 275–85.

——. 'Tribal Dancing and Yemeni Nationalism: Steps to Unity'. *Revue du Monde Musulman et de la Méditerranée* 67 no. 1 (1993): 161–8.

Al Faruqi, Lois Ibsen. 'Dance as an Expression of Islamic Culture'. *Dance Resource Journal* 10 no. 2 (1987): 6–17.

Bosworth, Clifford Edmund. *Mediaeval Islamic World: The Banu Sasan in Arabic Society and Literature*. Leiden: E.J. Brill, 1976.

Bourguignon, Erika. *Trance Dance*. New York: Dance Perspectives 35, 1968.

Deaver, Sherri. 'Concealment vs. Display: The Modern Saudi Woman'. *Dance Research Journal* (summer 1978) 14–18.

Eisler, Laurie A. ' "Hurry Up and Play My Beat": the Zar Ritual in Cairo'. *UCLA Journal of Dance Ethnology* 9 (1985): 23–31.

Fermor, Sharon. 'On the Question of Pictorial "Evidence" for Fifteenth-Century Dance Technique'. *Dance Research* 5 no. 2 (1987): 18–32.

Franken, Marjorie A. 'Egyptian Cinema and Television: Dancing and the Female Image'. *Visual Anthropology* 8 (1996): 267–85.

Grabar, Oleg. *The Formation of Islamic Art*. New Haven, CT: Princeton University Press, 1987.

Haeri, Shahla. *Law of Desire: Temporary Marriage in Shi'i Iran*. New York: Syracuse University Press, 1989.

Jonas, Gerald. *Dancing: The Pleasure, Power and Art of Movement*. New York: Harry Abrams, 1992.

Lawler, Lillian. *Dance in Ancient Greece*. Middletown, CT: Wesleyan University Press, 1964: 17–21.

Mernissi, Fatimah. *Beyond the Veil: Male–Female Dynamics in a Modern Muslim Society*. New York: John Wiley and Sons, 1975.

Rasmussen, Susan. 'Zarraf, a Tuareg Women's Wedding Dance'. *Ethnology* 34 no. 1 (1995): 1–16.

Said, Edward. *Orientalism*. New York: Vintage Books, 1978.

Saleh, Magda Ahmed Abdel Ghaffar. 'Dance in Egypt – A Quest for Identity'. *Dance Research Annual* 10 (1978): 215–18.

——. 'Documentation of the Ethnic Dance Tradition of Egypt'. Unpublished PhD dissertation, New York University (University Microfilms International, Ann Arbor, MI), 1979.

Schimmel, AnneMarie. 'Raks'. *Encyclopaedia of Islam*. Leiden: E.J. Brill, 1994: 414–16.

Sefrioui, Ahmed. *Festival of Marrakesh*. National Tourist Office of Morocco, n.d.

Sellers-Young, Barbara. 'Raks El Sharki: Transculturation of a Folk Form'. *Journal of Popular Culture* 26 (fall 1992): 141–52.

Shay, Anthony. 'Choreophobia: Solo Improvised Dance in the Iranian Diaspora of Southern California'. PhD dissertation, University of California, Riverside (University Microfilms, International, Ann Arbor, MI), 1997.

Shiloah, Amnon. *Music in the World of Islam*. Detroit, MI: Wayne University Press, 1995.

Trendle, Giles. 'Lifting the Veil'. *Middle East* 213 (July 1992): 50–1.

Van Nieuwkerk, Karin. *A Trade Like Any Other: Female Singers and Dancers in Egypt*. Austin, TX: University of Texas, 1995.

Wood, Leona and Anthony Shay. 'Danse du Ventre: A Fresh Appraisal'. *Dance Research Journal* 8 no. 2 (1976): 18–30.

PUPPETRY

THE SHADOWY ROOTS

In comparison to other more ancient performance genres in the Arab world, puppetry has a relatively modest history. This is traditionally explained by the nomadic roots of parts of Arab society and/or by the Islamic interdiction of the figurative representation of God and people. Neither of these explanations, though, is completely satisfactory. Suffice it to say here that in the Arab world, it is the shadow theatre more than the formal puppet show which has traditionally ranked highest in popularity.

Shadow puppetry, in fact, is quite ancient here and Arab literature features many metaphoric references in which shadow figures are seen as reflections of the ephemeral existence of human beings animated by the hidden manipulator that is God himself. Certainly historical proof is available to show that Arab masters long knew the many visual principles which lie behind the development of the shadow art. Indeed, we also know that in many Arab countries the art was forbidden. In the seventh century in Kufa, for example, a Jewish shadow artist named Batrûnî gave a demonstration of his art in a mosque. In his show, a South Arabian king riding a horse appeared at one point. So frightened did many in the audience become that Batrûnî was denounced to authorities as a magician and decapitated.

Shadow plays were seen in Spain in the eleventh century by Ibn Hazim. 'What I saw', he wrote, 'was similar to the real world but was done in shadows fixed on a metal windmill and arranged so that while they were turned round rapidly, one image after another came into view.'

We cannot be sure whether any of these early players were Arabs or whether they were from somewhere else. Documents describe them only as *jonglers*, a popular name for wandering players. Sometimes their small companies included female dancers and puppeteers, who certainly were not Arabs since Arab girls were not permitted to dance. More likely they were purchased slaves, often Christians, who could help their masters earn money with their performances.

Starting from the thirteenth century the art of the shadow play spread across the Arabian peninsula and into North Africa. The figures were beautiful and quite elaborate, as good as any ever seen. Produced with great refinement, they were as thin as glass with strong outlines, many perforations and splendidly ornamented. Among the many figures, *Dahabiya on the Nile* is probably the most complicated and certainly the most beautiful. During this time as well, we are able to identify the first Arab shadow theatre author, Ibn Daniyal (d. 1311), who staged shows which presented the life and manners of his time with narration done by the buffoon Taif al-Chajal. Ibn Daniyal called his shows plays of ideas and high education with nothing to do with the street'. They included prayers to Allah and his prophets as well as prayers for the wellbeing of the sultan.

Shadow players are on record as having frequently performed at the Egyptian royal courts, mostly presenting a repertory of historical tales dealing with the Punic and Persian wars. It is quite possible that one of these sultans in the sixteenth century took some of the shadow players to Istanbul and this is one theory for the beginning of the famous Turkish shadow theatre, *karagöz*. On the other hand, it has been argued that it is actually the other way around with shadows groups from Egypt being the ones who first absorbed the mime and buffoon shadow tradition of the Ottomans.

Whichever version is true, it is clear that Turkish shadow masters eventually brought their *karagöz* figures to Egypt and other North African countries where *karagöz* adopted local names such as *karakouche* or *karagouz*. These shows were always performed during Ramadan and documentation exists indicating that they were sometimes presented in harems. The figure of *Karagöz* himself was at first just a comic and talkative commentator on local manners but gradually he became more negative and obscene, boasting a large visible phallus. It was in this form that he was most often presented in countries such as Algeria and Tunisia.

In Egypt *karagöz* gradually transformed, under the name of Aragouz, into a hand-puppet controlled by a one-man street puppeteer, who would use a portable stage for his shows involving Aragouz and a series of his companions. These hand-puppets had carved heads, hands and feet, boasted painted features and hand-sewn costumes. Aragouz dominated the Egyptian puppet stage for a century behaving a little like an English Punch, always fighting his adversaries. This is also apparently the only puppet theatre in the Arab world which took such a comic turn. One other form of puppetry emerging at the time was string-puppetry (*marionnettes à la planchette*), known in Europe from the sixteenth century.

We can only guess at other influences in the region, especially the influence on North African countries of animist Black African traditions which have long used puppets (particularly in rituals). European traditions in these fields must also have come to north Africa by sea. We can certainly recognize animist influence in the use of puppets in the Tunisian exorcism ritual *Stambali* as well as in the Tunisian initiation ceremony *Oumouk Tangou*. The European

tradition for its part is represented by Sicilian rod-marionettes which can also be found in a somewhat adapted form in Tunisia.

During the second half of the twentieth century, many Arab countries adopted European-style puppetry particularly in the area of children's theatre. That happened especially in the 1960s in Egypt and Sudan, which in many cultural and social areas had begun to follow Soviet models. These two countries, for example, invited from socialist Romania puppet experts who helped to found the national puppet theatre in Cairo and Khartoum respectively. Following Romanian tradition, string-marionettes were featured in these new theatres.

In other parts of the region – most notably in Algeria, Tunisia and Morocco – French cultural policy was followed with puppeteers regularly participating in courses and seminars in France and founding national puppet theatres using glove- and/or rod-puppets. All of these new theatres in the first period of their activities dramatized national tales, including indigenous dances and music which they showed on stage in what became folkloric puppet presentations.

Henryk Jurkowski
Warsaw

Further Reading

Aziza, Mohamed. *Les Formes traditionnelles du spectacle* [Traditional forms of spectacle]. Tunis: Société Tunisienne de Diffusion, 1975.

Jacob, Georg. *Geschichte des Schattentheaters im Morgen- und Abendland* [The work of the shadow theatre in East and West]. Hannover: Orient-Buch Handlung Heinz Lafaire, 1925.

Spies, Otto. *Türkisches Puppentheater* [Turkish puppet theatre]. Emsdetten/Westfallen: Verlag Lechte, 1959.

THE NATIONS AND THEIR THEATRES

ABU DHABI

(see **UNITED ARAB EMIRATES**)

ADEN-YEMEN

(see **YEMEN**)

AJMAN

(see **UNITED ARAB EMIRATES**)

ALGERIA

(Overview)

One of the wealthiest countries in Africa, Algeria's economy is based largely on the exploitation of its natural resources, especially oil and petroleum products buried in the sand and gravel of the Algerian Sahara. Also known as the Democratic and Popular Republic of Algeria, and part of the Grand Maghreb, it is bordered on the north by the Mediterranean Sea, on the south by Niger, Mali and Mauritania, on the east by Tunisia and Libya, and on the west by Morocco. Covering an area of 2,381,750 square kilometres (919,600 square miles), the Sahara Desert blankets more than 90 per cent of the country's land area.

A former French colony, Algeria's population in 1995 was estimated to be 28.5 million, 99 per cent of whom were ethnically Arab-Berber. Arabic is the official language and is spoken by about 80 per cent of the population; the remainder speak various Berber dialects. French is also widely spoken and read. The vast majority of the population are Sunni Muslim, the official state religion. The country's capital is Algiers.

The earliest known inhabitants of Algeria were hunters living in the Al Hajjar region between 8000 and 2000 BC who may have been tribal Berbers. Much later, Phoenicians settled some of the coastal areas of Algeria from their north African state of Carthage, part of modern-day Tunisia. The first Algerian kingdom was established by the Berber chieftain and Roman supporter Massinissa during the Punic wars between Rome and Carthage in the third and second centuries BC. With the decline of the Roman Empire, Roman armies were withdrawn and in the third century AD, the Donatists, a North African Christian sect that had been suppressed by the Romans, declared a short-lived independent state in the region. Algeria was invaded by the Vandals – a Germanic tribe – in the fifth century and the country was again occupied for a hundred years before being overthrown by the Emperor Justinian's Byzantine army. It was Justinian's aim to restore the Holy Roman Empire but the spread of Islam and the Arab conquest of North Africa during the seventh century thwarted the expansion of Byzantium and permanently changed the character of North Africa.

The Arab invasion was not without resistance. The Berbers, led by a tribal high priestess named Kahina who claimed conversion to Judaism, fought the invaders but eventually surrendered to the Umayyad Khalif. The Berbers quickly embraced Islam but forcefully held on to their own language thereby withstanding total Arabization. In the eighth century they formed their own Islamic government. Several tribes embraced Shiism and founded Shiah tribal kingdoms, the most powerful of which was the Rustamid kingdom at Tahert in central Algeria, which flourished during the eighth and ninth centuries. The remaining tribes adopted Islam in the form of Maliki Sunni with strong Sufi tendencies.

From the eleventh to the thirteenth centuries, under two subsequent Berber dynasties – Almoravid and Almohad – northwest Africa and southern Spain were united into one territory. The regional capital Tlemcen became known for its elaborate mosques and Islamic schools and as a crafts centre. Algerian seaports carried on a thriving trade in horses, wax, leather and fabric with European markets. The collapse of this dynasty in the thirteenth century created trade competition among both Muslim and Christian seaports and, in order to gain advantage, city governments hired pirates to seize competing merchant ships and hold cargo and crew for ransom. Algiers became a primary centre for this kind of activity.

By the sixteenth century Christian Spaniards controlled much of North Africa and Muslims asked for help from the Ottoman sultan. The Spaniards were eventually driven out but a sultan's representative – Khayr ad-Din – was installed in Algeria. Because of the vast distance between Algeria and Constantinople, the centre of the Turkish Empire, Algeria nevertheless maintained a fairly independent state during this period. Their pirates dominated the Mediterranean, bringing great riches to the nation. In the eighteenth century, however, European forces with more firepower and better ships were able to challenge the pirates; subsequent international agreements outlawing piracy

brought Algeria's sea domination to an end. As a result, in 1830 Algiers, after the destruction of its defensive forces by an Anglo-Dutch fleet, was captured by the French army.

With the French occupation, Algerian life from the late nineteenth century until the middle of the twentieth century was dominated by French tradition with the French formally annexing Algeria in 1834. This regime sparked bitter resistence from people who by this point were used to the much more unobtrusive Turkish rule. A leader emerged, Abd al-Qadir, an Islamic holy man who claimed direct descent from Muhammad. He launched a rebellion against the French which lasted for more than a decade. Abd al-Qadir remains to this day a folk hero to Algerian nationals for the nationalist feelings he inspired. In 1847, the French began to colonize Algeria in very large numbers and Algerian nationals, although benefiting from French services and economic development, remained a subjugated minority. Though they were French subjects, full French citizenship had its cost: to become citizens Algerians had to renounce their Islamic faith. Very few did so.

Among the Muslim population, there were those who sent their children to be educated at French schools and it was from this group that French cultural traditions – including the staging of a literary theatre – spread to the larger community. Yet even among this group, few were accepted as equals by the ruling class. Interestingly, it was also this group which in the 1930s led a new movement toward Algerian nationalism, a movement aimed at reviving national interest in Algerian origins. With independence, this became national policy.

The French colonial strategy in the nineteenth century was clear to all: to isolate Algeria from other Arab countries and to distance it from the political, social and cultural changes occurring in the Arab world. As a result, Algerians – denied the larger world – turned inward, adhering more than ever to inherited Arab and Islamic traditions. Positive in one way, this approach had a negative effect on Algerian cultural development since the community was also forced to cut itself off from the world around them and was late in recognizing the uses and value of such things as literary theatre.

Algerians, of course, were never devoid of their own indigenous performance forms, either in earlier centuries or during the long period of colonial occupation. Musical forms, dance forms and storytelling along with poetry recitals and recitals from the Quran were long connected to celebrations of such things as seasonal changes and community and family events long before a French-style theatre was introduced. The history of these forms can be traced back to at least the period of the Arab Islamic conquest of what is called *al-Maghrib al-'Arabi* (the Arab 'west' or Maghreb), an area that, for all intents and purposes, makes up most of North Africa. Public storytelling, for example, included improvised dramatic elements, singing and dancing and almost always took place amidst a large group of spectators who would form a *halqa* (circle) around the performers. The style is still popular. Most public entertainments began with the telling of heroic stories such as *Abu Zaid al-Hilaali*, a saga that is still capable of injecting confidence in the national soul. Such popular forms effectively expressed a deeper national reality during this period of Algerian history, so deep, in fact, that French authorities began to censor both the stories and the storytellers. But they were never completely eradicated and they continue to be performed even now as a mode of expression of the national psyche. Such presentations continue to depend on the virtuosity of a single person performing all the various roles aided by a few key props of which a cane remains one of the most useful. In the style known as *al-Maddaah* (also called *al-Qawwaal*, literally meaning 'Praise'), the *rawi* (narrator) chooses a subject, usually historical or religious, and improvises praise in verse utilizing either classical or colloquial Arabic. The *rawi* would also tell stories in prose dealing with daily life or historical events.

Also popular at that time and continuing in popularity at the present time is the puppet form known in Algeria as *al-Qaraaqoz*, a term also used to describe a scarecrow and linked theatrically to *khayal al-zhil* (shadow theatre) in the Arab east and the Turkish *karagöz* (literally meaning 'black eye'). The form's three leading characters are al-Qaraaqoz, a clever but basically good-hearted man, Laala Sunbaya, and her inseparable servant, both of whom ultimately resist all the tricks of Qaraaqoz. The form includes direct interaction with the audience and improvised words, gestures and actions. During the period of French occupation, the form was used to attack and ridicule the French and their collaborators. By 1843, it too was officially banned though it continued to be seen all across the country in various disguises over the next hundred years. This is confirmed by diaries of travellers as early as 1847 and 1862 when similar puppet forms were seen in both eastern and western parts of the country. One variation dates from the period 1910 to 1919 when an unknown Turkish performer in Algiers was noted by travellers as playing for children from beneath a table with a space cut out for his head. Appearing to the audience as if his head had been cut off, he talked and joked with the audience and played whole scenes utilizing only his head.

The earliest recorded examples of European-style theatre in Algeria date to the mid-nineteenth century when plays were done by amateur actors in French for audiences almost totally composed of French soldiers, their families, and some early European settlers. By 1853, the French government had built a large theatre for the purpose in Algiers.

The impact of such experiments on the local community was virtually nil, however, in great measure because of linguistic problems (see introductory essay on ARAB THEATRE AND LANGUAGE). One of the major problems was simply what language theatre artists should be using to perform in. Even when attempts were made to perform in classical and colloquial Arabic, audiences still had no interest. The fact that Algeria has several regional dialects and choosing one over another would obviously cause problems just added to the confusion. Other potential audience members, educated in the classical or Quranic Arabic, refused to accept art in a language that they perceived to be unrefined. Then there was the vast number of people who were functionally illiterate (some put this figure as high as 90 per cent before 1955) who stayed away from anything regarded as literary.

Even as late as the beginning of the twentieth century, the lack of general interest in a literary theatre – even among those who spoke French – was clear when a number of Algerians attempted to begin a company of their own. Again, the attempt failed for lack of audiences.

It was not until after World War I that interest in a modern literary theatre began to be seen. Intellectuals and artists were the first to feel a need for a theatre that could deal with serious issues, a theatre that would parallel the more general Algerian cultural awakening which had its beginnings in the early part of the century. Students were among the first to write and perform satiric plays, many presented as part of public celebrations where poetry, speeches and songs were well accepted. Many such events were organized by social and cultural clubs especially during the month of Ramadan.

The first and most important of these groups was the Widaadiyat at-Talaba al-Muslimeen (Society of Muslim Students) founded in 1919. In the spring of 1921, the Beirut-born dramatist George Abyad and his Egyptian Theatrical Company visited Algeria as part of a tour from Cairo. This event was a precious opportunity for students and writers to get acquainted with not just the theatre but specifically an Arab-language theatre at close range. The company staged its performances in classical Arabic which, though limited to an educated minority, had the benefit of being understood more widely than a performance in colloquial Arabic would have been. Productions included *Fat-h al-Andalus* (*The Conquest of Andalusia*), *Tharaat al-'Arab* (*The Arab Revenge*) and *Salaah ud-Deen al-Ayyoubi* (*Saladin's Story*). Abyad's company reached only small audiences at the beginning but many of those who attended would become leaders of the next decade. Attendance improved by the end of the tour as word got out that something important was happening.

The next year another Egyptian theatrical company, the 'Izz ud-Deen Troupe, visited Algeria, presenting two Shakespearian dramas in classical Arabic – *Julius Caesar* and *Romeo and Juliet*. The performances of 'Izz ud-Deen attracted larger audiences partly due to the fact that they also presented Middle Eastern songs and chants between acts of the play, a feature that was subsequently used by many Algerian groups. Yet even with these tours, attendance was still relatively low because of a continuing problem with language and a general lack of interest by the public at large in non-indigenous theatrical traditions. As Sa'd ud-Deen Bin Shanab explained in an essay in the magazine *Majallat ath-Thaqaafa al Jazaa 'iriyya* (no. 55 (1980): 31) the Algerian public was simply not yet prepared to embrace the theatre and regularly attend theatrical performances. Another important contributing factor was that the subjects dealt with on the stage were far removed from people's daily realities and worries despite the undisputed literary values of the plays.

In the years following, students began to stage their own theatrical productions in classical Arabic to audiences in the capital, expending considerable efforts to secure locations, obtain costumes, raise necessary funds and engage in rehearsals. Mostly producing melodramas dealing with issues such as drinking, some productions found audiences. Eventually, though, even these attempts were doomed to failure because of a lack of financing and the suspicion and harassment by colonial and religious authorities.

Such young theatre enthusiasts looked both to the east (where Arab-language theatre had already begun to develop in countries such as Egypt and Syria) and to the north (where they could see advances in European theatre though it was far away from them in both style and content). These theatrical pioneers continued their attempts and trials until 1926, the year, most scholars agree, that the Algerian theatrical movement was most effectively launched. It was in that year that the play *Juha*, co-authored by the actor-writer-director-designer 'Alaalu (b. 1902) and a theatre colleague, Dahmoun, premièred in Algiers at the Corsal Theatre. In this play all the elements finally came together: traditional style, content (the reality of contemporary living conditions), recognizable comedy, familiarity with the popular character of Juha and the use of a widely understood Algerian colloquial Arabic. The production also included elements from popular Algerian folklore such as music and chanting.

'Alaalu, the first genuine Algerian *homme du théâtre*, was born Salaali 'Ali in Algiers and attended French elementary school. During World War I he worked in a pharmacy where he began meeting Europeans. Through these contacts he became attracted to western music. His superb voice brought him into the theatre as a musical star. He worked first with the Maheddine Bachetarzi (1899–1986) theatre company and later formed his own group with which the play *Juha* was launched, the first of innumerable plays and productions that became part and parcel of the battle for independence. It should be noted here that the same year as *Juha* (1926) came the birth of the political party Najm Shamaal Afriqiya (Star of North Africa), the first Algerian political party to demand complete independence for the country.

Gabriel Audisio, a distinguished poet and writer whose father, Victor Audisio, was the director of the Opéra d'Alger, who had been living in Algeria during that period, wrote in his memoirs *Shurouqal-Masrah al-Jazaa'iri* (*The Dawn of the Algerian Theatre*) about the meaning of these early theatrical activities. He said,

> the important matter in my view is that Algerians have started openly expressing themselves about their existence and character in their own language and have confirmed

that existence through the development of their theatre in its individuality, destiny and capabilities. That would not and could not have happened casually for there were no companies, no stage plays, no theatres and no audiences. . . . There was a need to create or formulate these elements . . . the authorities did not find any harm in it and as they knew it was wise not to deny the people what entertained them especially when they had been denied their rights. Gradually, acting companies began to be formed though not without hardships. . . . That was the birth of their art and how it was transformed from a medieval comedy to a national theatre.

Juha was such a success with audiences that its run was extended several times. From that date, the Algerian theatre began to find its own audiences and supporters. These early actors and dramatists (all without previous theatrical training) became determined to learn about theatre, read about theatre, attend performances of visiting theatrical companies and critique one another's work.

The serious plays – both comedies and dramas – presented during this period were almost all socially critical, challenging the bitter reality of occupation in a format using colloquial Arabic. The shining star in the theatre was without doubt Rasheed Qasanteeni (1887–1944), an actor, dramatist and singer and known now as the Father of the Algerian Theatre. Born Rasheed Balkhudre in the city of Qasanteena (from which he took his stage name), he first attended Quranic schools and later was enrolled in a French school where he first encountered European-style drama and learned to play the guitar. Poor and in need of work, he found employment in the port of Algiers and through his connections there travelled to various parts of the world. Returning to Algeria in 1926, he made his début in Allalou's production of *Ziyedj Bou-Akline* (*The Marriage of Bou-Akline*), then continued his career as a director and eventually as an author. Over the next dozen years he was responsible for more than thirty productions.

It was in 1927 that another pioneer, the actor-singer Maheddine Bachetarzi, first emerged as a playwright. The possessor of a beautiful and rare voice, he had come from a wealthy family and had studied with a French music teacher who taught him western singing styles as well as those of the Arab world. The first script he wrote was *Juhalaa' Mudda'oun Fi l-'Ilm* (*The Ignorant Claiming Knowledge*) and it was also the first in a series of successes. Criticizing the commercialization of religion, the play was staged continually for several years. All these early artists – when in need of funding for a new show – were not averse to utilizing their musical skills commercially. Their concerts generated sufficient sums to allow them to stage more serious dramatic works later on.

The year 1930 – the centenary of France's occupation of Algeria – saw few artists willing to take the stage lest their appearance be misconstrued by the public. The following year, however, a relatively large number of shows was seen, several dealing with historical subjects in socially critical ways.

During this formative period, the Algerian theatre was almost completely concentrated in Algiers and women were not allowed on stage. Indeed, they were rarely seen as audience members in theatres. The conservative Algerian society of this time simply did not permit a proper Muslim girl to expose herself to public view. As a result, male actors performed all the roles. It should be noted here that 'Alaalu said that he did use women in his theatre as both performers and singers, one of the exceptions to the general rule.

For some, the value of stage plays was to provide public entertainment but more and more the theatre was urging people to think about the reality of occupation, to enlighten them about it and subtly to urge them to do something about it. Such plays were also solidly urging the idea of Arab unity. The French also understood that theatre was being used as an impetus for a national renaissance. As a result, a number of pioneers – including Bachetarzi – paid for their views by being regularly harassed by French authorities, who questioned everything they did including such 'provocative' acts as putting up theatre posters in Arabic. Many performances wound up being banned.

The plays of the 1930s also grew in quality and commitment. Audiences attended in larger numbers than ever before. A good example is Bachetarzi's play *Faaqou* (*They Awoke*) – a play which suggested that a newly awakened Algeria understood the tricks and deceptions of imperialism. This play attracted more than 8,000 spectators, a number which worried authorities who in turn increased the pressure on theatre people.

But supportive Arab artists continued to come from abroad as well. In 1932, for example, the theatre company of the Egyptian actress Fatimah Rushdie played in Algiers, an event that

Actor-singer Maheddine Bachetarzi.

deeply affected artistic circles. It seemed not a problem that the star was female and on her arrival an unprecedented welcome was organized. Her performances were filled to capacity with spectators coming from all corners of the country. Among the plays presented were *Masra' Kilyubatra* (*The Fall of Cleopatra*), *Majnun Layla* (*The Mad Lover of Layla*) and *al-'Abbasa Ukht al-Rashid* (*Abasa, the Sister of al-Rashid*). Two years after Rushdie's appearance, Algeria's best known Muslim actress first appeared on stage: Kulthoum was her stage name and she began a comedy career that continued into the 1980s. Born in Algiers, she starred in some 200 plays during her long career and late in her career played on occasion in France. However, before Kulthoum first appeared on stage, Marie Soussan, another Algerian Jewish actress, was well known.

Other Arab groups came to Algeria from Tunisia and Morocco during the 1930s. Eventually these groups played outside Algiers as well and Algerian troupes based in the capital followed their lead. The result was that amateur acting companies began to spring up in the major cities. Political support and encouragement was also given to the Algerian theatre by the National and Reform Movements generally. This led to the development of new audiences from all social strata, from workers and craftsmen to students and even leaders of the nationalist political parties.

In April 1935, the Star of North Africa party sent a theatre group of eighteen to France to perform for Algerian immigrants. The play they did – *'Ala n-Nayyif* (*Excess*) – which had previously been performed sixty-one times in Algeria, was presented in Paris and in several other French cities. The production, however, was banned in Lyon with authorities objecting to the play's urging of Algerians to continue clinging to their own beliefs and values. From this point, French authorities in Algeria began to fear the effects of such theatre and banned performances. Also banned was the circulation of Bachetarzi's political songs and the texts of Qasanteeni's sketches, many of which had been recorded and circulated by a company called Gomophone.

With the outbreak of World War II in 1939,

all theatrical activities came to a halt. By the end of the war, though, still another generation of theatre people appeared – playwrights, actors and directors who started working side by side with those who remained from the pioneering generation. The defining feature of the immediate post-war period took place on 8 May 1945, a turning point in the life of the Algerian people as a whole. On that day, 45,000 people were killed in demonstrations demanding freedom and independence. This event reinforced the belief that there was no recourse but armed struggle in the battle against French colonialism. Artists were among the first who gave expression to that new reality building an even closer relationship between theatre and the independence campaign. Many shows, in fact, were done as benefits for political prisoners and their families while others were done for the building of mosques and schools where Algerian children would be taught in their own language and about their own religion. The People's Party itself started organizing theatricalized political events with the aim of urging people towards revolution. Colonial administration policy, however, remained violent and repressive.

A new approach was attempted in 1947 when colonial authorities gave not only a small grant for the creation of a theatre group but also the right to utilize the Municipal Opera House every Friday. Maheddine Bachetarzi was elected director of the group working there (the so-called Arab Division of the theatre) with Mustafa Kaatib as his deputy. Choosing the best playwrights, actors, directors and musicians from all the then existing theatre groups, they formed a new group which they called simply and proudly the Algerian Theatre Company. In short order, the municipalities of Oran (the capital of western Algeria) and Constantine (the capital of eastern Algeria) decided to offer similar financial assistance to theatre groups in their own cities. Tickets were made available at reduced prices to encourage audience attendance even further.

A decision to stage special matinee performances for women proved quite successful in attracting even larger numbers to Bachetarzi's new theatre, an approach later utilized by other groups as well. Even a government committee was established to read and select appropriate scripts for production. Headed by Ahmed Tufeeq al-Madani (1899–1983), this committee actually improved the quality and variety of theatrical texts. Under the management of Mustafa Kaatib, the links with other arts – particularly music, dance and singing – began to be broken in favour of a genuinely Algerian literary drama.

Unfortunately, a year after financial assistance began in Algiers, it was cancelled. Theatre was clearly too political for the authorities. Future grants would appear in a budget for national promotion rather than for cultural endeavours. Yet even more theatrical production emerged, some in classical Arabic, some in the local dialect. One of the most daring plays of this period was *Fi Sabeel al-Watan* (*For the Fatherland*) which had been written in the 1920s. Though the events of the play were set in a non-Arab country (to avoid repression from authorities), audiences understood clearly what was being said and attended the play in large numbers. Also seen at this time were plays by Molière, Alfred de Musset and Shakespeare, all in Arabic adaptations. And the tours continued. One star, Egyptian Yusuf Wahbi, played in Algeria in 1947, 1950, 1951, 1952 and 1954 and also participated in round-tables with Algerian dramatists. But it was the continuing existence of Bachetarzi's Algerian Theatre Company which was most instrumental in giving the country's artists a new sense of professionalism. Amateur troupes continued to spread with new groups opening in cities such as al-Bulaida and Constantine.

One of the popular genres to evolve at this time was the historical play, drawing upon the past with its glories and heroism and embodying in it events, attitudes and distinguished personalities from Algerian history. One of the first plays of this type was *Hannibal*. Written by Ahmed Tufeeq al-Madani about this famous African personality, it was staged in Algiers in 1948. The play was still another statement about freedom, in this case a battle between the invading Romans and the people of Carthage under the leadership of Hannibal. *Hannibal* was followed by *Yughurta* by 'Abd ur-Rahmaan Madawi, a look at the ancient struggle of the Algerian people against Roman colonization. Both plays were written in classical Arabic.

Another writer of historical plays was Ahmed Rida Houhou (1911–56). Houhou began his literary career in Saudi Arabia in 1934 publishing stories, essays and playscripts in the Hijaazi magazine, *al-Manhal* (*The Fountain*). During the 1940s he returned to Algeria where he became a member of the Jam'iyat al'Ulamaa' al-Muslimeen al-Jazaa'iriyyeen (Society of Religious Leaders of Algerian Muslims). His first staged plays were *Sanee' al-Baraamika* (*The Baraamika Deeds*) and *Malakat Gharnaata*

(*The Queen of Granada*). Both dealt with social reforms and moral values, utilizing history as a reflection of contemporary reality. In 1949 he established the al-Mizhir al-Qasanteeni Artist's Company.

At the same time, a number of plays focused on religious issues, most often trying to separate belief from myths and heresies. One such was *Bilaal* by the poet Mohammed al-'Id Aal Khaleefa (1904–79). In his eloquent poetic language, he sought to bring the life of Bilaal Bin Rabaah to the stage, a man who had endured much suffering for his belief. The play dealt with the struggles of the pioneers of Islam as models for the modern Algerian struggle against colonialism. Another play of note was *al-Mawled an-Nabawi* (*The Birth of the Prophet*) written by al-Shaikh 'Abd ur-Rahmaan al-Jilaali.

Socially rooted plays became increasingly more mature in the post-war period. Mostly written in the colloquial dialect, the best of these plays were written by Budiyya Mursali, Mohammed al-Touri (1914–59) and Mohammed Waneesh. All these plays were concerned with social reality and negative manifestations that impeded its awakening and advancement. The backgrounds of these writers

were connected to their playwriting styles. For example, al-Touri was born in Baleeda and started his career as an actor/singer with the Amal Theatre Company in Algiers. An active militant in the independence struggle, he was imprisoned on several occasions. His most important play was *Qaatil Akheeh* (*Fratricide*), presented in 1936.

In the early 1950s, the years leading up to independence, the plays became more and more openly revolutionary. One such was *Shamshoum al-Jazaa'iri* (*The Algerian Samson*) whose presentation stirred a huge furore especially in Oran, where at the end of the show young people started demonstrating in the streets. Dealing with the prohibition of marriage between Algerians and foreigners, the play's symbolic meanings were clear to a colonized people. The company was harassed and warned of dire consequences if the show continued. Another in this style was Mursali's *Tahya al-Ukhuwwa* (*Long Live Brotherhood*). Attracting large audiences, it dealt with the meaning of cooperation among people as a way to strengthen the struggle.

The revolution itself started on 1 November 1954 and obviously affected the Algerian

Playwright Mohammed al-Touri.

theatrical movement. The early days were filled with chaos, and companies began to disband since many wanted to carry arms and join the National Liberation Army. Some died as martyrs to the cause on the battlefield; others were arrested and spent long periods of time in prison. Of interest here is that the prisons – contrary to what the colonial authority intended them to be – began to be transformed into schools teaching nationalism and spreading revolutionary awareness. Inside prisons, theatrical artists established small theatres in which they presented productions and sketches. Among those were Hasan al-Husni and al-Tayyib Abu al-Hasan, who became quite famous. Al-Husni (1916–88), well known as an actor and famous for his character Bou Baqara, was born in al-Madiyya and began acting in 1936. Imprisoned many times, he joined the Algerian Theatre Company in 1947 where he became a star. Within the prisons, most of the theatrical activity was satiric with an emphasis on politics and nationalism. Such shows – and many others done by fighters in the mountains – kept morale high during a very difficult period. Virtually no records exist of any of this work.

In 1958, Mustafa Kaatib established an Algerian theatre troupe in exile in Tunisia called the National Liberation Front Arts Company. From Tunisia, the company disseminated information about the revolution by presenting stage shows in various cities across the Arab world and then in friendly countries such as China, the

Mustafa Kaatib.

Soviet Union and others. That company was able to project the voice of the struggling Algeria through the art of drama, to refute French claims about colonialism and to expound Algeria's just cause to the people of the world. Kaatib, who later taught at the Burj al-Kifaan Drama Institute and in the 1970s headed the Cultural Promotion Section of the Ministry of Higher Education, said of the role of this important early company:

> When we visited friendly countries, we realized the truth about the colonialists' lies in that foreigners used to believe that the Algerian was created to fight and that he was born with a rifle in his hand and, therefore, he was against peace by nature. Contrary to that, we showed, in our activities, that the Algerian thirsts for peace, liberty and an honourable life.

The subjects that the company dealt with related to the popular struggle including the horrors of the liberation war. The company initiated its activities with Abd ul-Haleem Raayis's play *Nahu an-Nour* (*Towards the Light*) in 1958. The central image in the play connects to Picasso's *Guernica* and the destruction being heaped on the heads of innocent citizens in Algerian cities. Another success was Raayis's *Abnaa' al-Qasaba* (*The Casbah Sons*), first performed in Tunisia and Libya before being presented in Morocco. His play *al-Khaalidoon* (*The Immortals*), brought the armed struggle itself to the stage through narration by freedom fighters about their experiences during the war. It was performed in China and the Soviet Union in 1960 during a tour of forty-five days. Raayis (1921–75) was born in Algiers, had started his career as an actor, began directing and eventually turned to poetry and playwriting. He worked closely in his early days in the company of Qasanteeni and later on joined the Algerian Theatre Company. Imprisoned by colonial authorities, his work reflects the difficult experiences of his life. Some researchers, in studying his plays, which were written specifically for the Tunisian-based company, have noted their content and lively descriptions of the reality of the revolution and their portraits of its freedom fighters. As such they are seen as historical documents of the Algerian revolution. Nevertheless, it must be said that his scripts now also seem a bit extreme in their idealism, lack dramatic depth in their characterizations and, in their use of colloquial Arabic, lacked the spirituality of classical Arabic.

But other plays of a higher literary quality were also being written including *Masra' at-*

Tughaat (*The Death of Despots*, published 1959), by 'Abdallah Rukaibi and *at-Turaab* (*The Soil*), written by Abi al-'Id Doudou. Both were written in classical Arabic and could be read and played across the Arab world and they did indeed attract wide attention. Some local plays written in French and translated to Arabic were also performed by the National Liberation Front Company – 'Ind Ihmiraar al-Fajr (*Red the Dawn*), written by Asia Jabbaar and Walid Garn, directed by Mustapha Kateb and the Algerian entry in the 1969 Pan-African Festival held in Algiers; as well as *al-Juth-tha al-Mutawwaqa* (*The Encircled Corpse*), performed for the first time in Algerian colloquial Arabic under Jean-Marie Serreau during the Universal Expo in Brussels in 1958, and *al-Ajdaad Yazdadoun Daraawa* (*The Ancestors Redouble Their Ferocity*), both by Kateb Yacine. Both *al-Juth-tha al-Mutawwaqa* and *al-Ajdaad Yazdadoun Daraawa* are part of Yacine's work *Le Cercle des représailles* (*Circle of Reprisals*, 1959), which also includes a short farce *La Poudre d'intelligence* (*Intelligence Powder*) and a dramatic poem *Le Vautour* (*The Vulture*). Yacine's plays are all structurally tight and strong in characterization exhibiting a mixture of realism and symbolism in their portraits of a people. Among his important late plays, written in the Algerian dialect, are *Najma* (*The Star*) and *Mohammed* for ... *Khuth Haqeebatak* (*Mohammed ... Take Your Suitcase*).

After independence, the Algerian theatre continued to interact with the changing circumstances, particularly with the adoption of socialism as a national policy. In 1963, for example, a legislative decree known as the Decree of January 1963 was issued creating the Théâtre National Algérien and organizing theatrical activities throughout the country, a decree that seriously changed the operations of theatres in Algiers, Annaba, Constantine, Oran and Sidi-bel-Abbes. One of the clauses in the nationalization decree defined the function of the theatre in Algeria:

The theatre has become the property of the people and it will remain a weapon for their service. Our theatre today will express revolutionary realism and become a servant of the truth in its truest meaning. The theatre will fight against all negative manifestations that are contrary to the people's interests and will not be led by blind optimism or by any abstraction that does not interact with the revolutionary situation. It is not possible to

visualize a dramatic art without struggle, for without it individuals are rendered graceless and lifeless ... It is not logical that theatre be in the hands of private enterprise and this means whether it is inside the country or whether it is a theatre being welcomed from or dispatched abroad.

That same year, the National Liberation Front Theatre came back from its exile in Tunisia; its return was marked by an official change of name. From 1963 it was called the National Theatre Company of Algeria. First directed by Mohammed Budiyya, then by Mustafa Kaatib, the newly named National Theatre presented ten different productions during its first season in Algiers. In 1964, a national theatre school was established in Burj al-Kifaan with faculty drawn from other Arab countries. Eventually it produced a large number of artists who later joined the National Theatre. This school also sent groups of students outside the country for further specialized training.

The theatre community flourished over the next decade. Besides its many productions each year, the National Theatre organized and participated in numerous festivals which played a great role in acquainting Arab groups generally with one another and leading them to new levels of cooperation and greater awareness of new developments in the field. Among those festivals were the African Cultural Festival (first held in Dakar in 1966 and in Algiers in 1969); the Arab Dramatists' Conference, held in Damascus and other places; and the Timqaad Festival for Mediterranean Theatres, held yearly in Algeria since 1968. As well, many local festivals began including a national Amateur Theatre Festival, which was started in 1967 in Mustaghaanim.

Over the years of its existence, more and more foreign classics were seen at the National Theatre including works by Molière and Brecht translated into Arabic. The National Theatre continued to present plays of national importance, some set in Algeria, others set in such places as Vietnam and South Africa. It was this work which best confirmed the new Algerian theatre's identity and its revolutionary tendencies. Indeed, even the Cuban freedom fighter, Che Guevara, who visited Algeria in 1962, said, after attending one Algerian play at the National, 'I beheld the revolutionary theatre itself in the land of Algeria.' Indeed, there was a very healthy atmosphere in the arts at this time with freedom of expression guaranteed by governmental decrees and theatre artists playing a continuing and enhanced role in the overall development and advancement of society.

The plays of Ahmed 'Iyaad, better known as Ruwayshid, were typical of the kind of work Guevara and others were seeing in the 1960s, plays dealing with social issues from a revolutionary point of view, plays calling for a continuing challenge to the status quo. In his first stage play, *Hasan al-Tiro*, set during the Revolution, Ruwayshid explored the growing enthusiasm of average people for the revolution. In this play he has his protagonist tortured and imprisoned by colonial authorities, acts which lead him to the ranks of the freedom fighters.

Another such socially committed play by Ruwayshid was *al-Ghoula* (*The Ghoul*, 1966), a play about farm management after the colonists departed from Algeria. These farms, after they had been nationalized, came to be owned by Algerian peasants. The play criticized opportunism and self-interest. Ruwayshid's 1970 play *al-Bawwaaboun* (*The Doormen*) dealt with various social types and daily problems in a series of short scenes rich in excitement and suspense.

Alongside this socially critical trend in the theatre, 'Abd ur-Rahmaan Kaaki (b. 1934) was developing what came to be called 'heritage'

theatre and presenting new theatrical experiments. In his 'heritage' plays he tried to find artistic links with earlier periods and styles interconnecting them with more modern literary theatre. A native of Mustaghaanim, his first play was *132 Sana* (*132 Years*, 1962), his own history of Algeria and colonialism. He condensed that long period of time into a single concept – the Algerian family with its traditions, culture and values. Done in a populist format full of tales, roughly written poetry and local folklore presented through chants, dances and eulogies, the play attracted wide attention. Kaaki's second play, *Sha'b uth-Thulma* (*The People of Darkness*), written in the same style, was derived from the author's memories during the French occupation. His *Afriqiya Qabl al-'Aam Waahid* (*Africa Before the Year One*, 1963) placed Algeria, in the geographical and historical sense, into the centre of African history showing its various peoples as sharing the same common destiny and embodying the utterance of the African leader, Patrice Lumumba: 'Africa for Africans'.

By the early 1970s, Algeria began to experience profound political and economic changes. Through the early phase, the goal was to transform Algeria from a country with a consumer economy to one with a socialist economy, from an agrarian society to an industrial one. As an

Playwright Ahmed 'Iyaad, also known as Ruwayshid.

'Abd ur-Rahmaan Kaaki.

accompaniment to that, theatre groups began to flirt with socialist realism. One such was 'Abd ul-Qaadir 'Aloula (b. 1940), a playwright and director and later a manager of the National Theatre. 'Aloula attempted to derive some benefit from the writings of European playwrights, especially Brecht, Mayakowsky and Piscator. His play *al-Khubza* (*The Piece of Bread*) depicted the struggle between the working class and business owners leading to the workers' eventual victory. He wrote other plays of that type including *al-Maa'ida* (*The Dining Table*, 1972) and the *Hamaam Rabbai* (*God's Pigeons*, 1974). Other plays of note by him include *al-Ajwaad* (*The Generous*) and *al-Qawwal* (*The Praiser*). In reality, through his writing experience, 'Aloula was able to do away with many of the random elements that permeated the writing of plays and the process of directing them.

Decentralization became a key to government policy in the late 1970s with the National Theatre establishing regional branches in Oran, Annaba, Constantine and Sidi-bel-Abbes. Audiences continued to increase and the quality of writing improved as dramatists rejected socialist realism. Socially critical plays, however, continued to be dominant in the 1980s with the play *Juha Baa' Himaarahu* (*Juha Sold His Donkey*) by Nabeel Badraan and directed by Mustafa Kaatib in 1983 quite typical. Later representing Algeria at the Damascus Festival for Theatrical Arts (1984), it dealt with the misuse of privilege. This problem was also dealt with in 'Aloula's play *al-'Alaq* (*The Leech*, 1985).

Over the next decade, the National's programming began to shift its focus again inclining more towards the daily problems of individuals rather than the general problems of society as a whole. In 1985, the annual Professional Theatre Festival began offering both plays and seminars. During the second festival, fourteen plays were presented, the most noted of which was *Ghaabu al-Afkar* (*The Ideas Were Absent*), which dealt with the Algerian immigrants' situation in Europe and three seminars on theatrical problems and needs. At the same time, the first official Theatre Company for Children was established. This company of twelve began with a production of *ash-Shaatreen* (*The Clever Ones*).

The year 1987 saw the celebration of a quarter-century of Algerian independence. The celebrations included new performances by companies from across the country and abroad. The Third National Festival for Professional Theatre that year included several important plays – *ash-Shuhadaa' Ya'oudoun Hatha l-Usbou'* (*The Martyrs Are Returning This Week*) by Taahir Wataar and *al-Halzoun al-'Aneed* (*The Stubborn Snail*) by Rasheed Boujidra.

In the 1990s, Algeria, despite continuing social unrest, could boast of a range of theatre troupes working in a variety of styles – from the National Theatre to experimental groups – and a growing base of well-trained actors, directors and designers. Its writers remained committed to reflecting the national reality including the most serious problems that remained to be solved as the new millennium approached. As well, traditional forms were being looked at even more closely by avant-garde directors to see how they could be incorporated or utilized in new theatrical work.

Two trends could be seen in contemporary playwriting between 1985 and 1995 – the use of collective creation (a new theatrical experience in Algeria being employed by a number of groups) and the wholesale adapting of foreign plays to the Algerian and Arabic reality. This latter approach has sometimes been overdone to the point that nothing remained of the original play except its barest outlines. Even plays from other Arab countries have fallen victim to such handling, among them Tawfik al-Hakīm's Egyptian drama, *at-Ta'aam li-Kulli Fam* (*Food for Every Mouth*).

As for theatre schools, several have begun and then closed for lack of funds. The best known was Ma'had Burj al-Kifaan (Burj al-Kifaan Theatre Institute), a training school for theatre and dance established in 1964. With a training period of four years, this institute graduated its first group in 1969. In 1966, the Emotive Dance Company became part of the institute. The institute, however, closed in 1972. Madrasat al-Funoun ad-Draamiyya (School for Dramatic Arts) is among the later generation of schools, established in 1986 in the town of Burj Manaayil in central Algeria. Another is Madrasat al-Funoun ad-Draamiyya (School for Dramatic Arts) established in 1987 in Baatna, the capital of al-Awraas region. Besides offering training courses in theatrical arts and other subjects closely related to it, this school also offers training in music and dance.

The only attempt at creating a theatre magazine in the country was *al-Halaqa* (*The Ring*). It started in 1971 but published only three issues before it too ceased for lack of funds.

Abdallah El Rukaibi
Translated by Maha and Tony Chehade

Further Reading

Achour, Christian. *Dictionnaire des oeuvres algériennes en langue française* [Dictionary of Algerian works in French]. Paris: L'Harmattan, 1990.

'Aloula, Abd ul-Qaadir. *an-Nashaat al-Masrahi Fi al-Jazaa'ir* [Theatrical activity in Algeria]. Damascus: Ittihaad al-Kuttaab al-'Arab bi-Dimashq [The Arab Writers' Union in Damascus], 1982.

Arnaud, Jacqueline. 'Recherches sur la littérature algérienne d'expression française: le cas de Kateb Yacine' [Research into Algerian literature in French: the case of Kateb Yacine]. Thèse d'état, Université de Paris II, 1978.

Audisio, Gabriel. *Shurouqal-Masrah al-Jazaa'iri* [The dawn of the Algerian theatre]. Algiers, n.d.

Bachetarzi, Maheddine. *Memoirs*. 3 vols. Vol. I (1919–39), Algiers: Éditions Nationales Algériennes, 1968. Vol. II (1939–51) and Vol. III (1951–74), Algiers: Enterprise Nationale des Livres, 1968 and 1984.

Baffet, Roselyn. *Tradition théâtrale et modernité en Algérie* [Modern theatrical tradition in Algeria] Paris: L'Harmattan, 1985. 223 pp.

Baghli, Sid Ahmed. *Aspects of Algerian Cultural Policy*. Paris: UNESCO, 1978.

Bencheneb, R. 'Aspects du théâtre arabe en Algérie' [Aspects of Arab theatre in Algeria]. *L'Islam et l'Occident, Cahiers du Sud* (1947): 271–6.

——. 'Regards sur le théâtre algérien' [Looking at Algerian theatre]. *Revue de l'Occident Musulman et de la Méditerranée* 6 (1969): 23–9.

Boeglin, Jean-Marie. 'Revendication nationale' [National revindication]. *Partisans* 36 (1967).

Bradby, David. 'Genet, the Theatre and the Algerian War.' *Theatre Research International* 19 no. 3 (1994): 226–37.

Cordreaux, H. 'Le théâtre et publics algériens' [The Algerian theatre and public]. *Revue théâtrale* 31 (1956).

Cristea, George. 'Pre-Theatre: Rock Paintings and Engravings in Central Sahara'. *ASSAPH* [Studies in the Theatre] 7 (1991): 121–60.

Dejeux, Jean. *Djoh'a, hier et aujourd'hui* [Djoh'a, yesterday and today]. Sherbrooke: Éditions Naaman, 1978.

——. 'Le Théâtre'. *Maghreb: littératures de langue française*. Paris: Arcantère Éditions, 1993.

Djeghloul, Abdelkader. *L'Aurore du théâtre Algérien* [The dawn of Algerian theatre]. Oran: Université d'Oran Centre de Recherche et d'Information Documentaire en Sciences Sociales, 1982.

——. 'La naissance du théâtre' [The birth of theatre]. *Éléments d'historie culturelle algérienne*. Alger: Entreprise nationale du livre, 1984: 123–41.

Guseinova, D. *Alzhirskii teatr: ocherki istorii* [Algerian theatre: historical essays]. Moscow: Rossiysky In-t Iskusstvoznaniya, 1995. 140 pp.

Lanasri, Ahmed. 'Le théâtre'. In *La Littérature algérienne de l'entre-deux-guerres*. Paris: Éditions Publisud, 1995: 357–16.

Naylor, Phillip and Alf Andrew Heggoy. *Historical Dictionary of Algeria*. Metuchen, NJ: Scarecrow Press, 1994. 443 pp.

ar-Raa'i,'Ali. *al-Masrah Fi al-Watan al-'Arabi* [The theatre in the Arab world] 25. Kuwait: 'al-Majlis al-Watani lith-Thaqaafa Wa l-Funoun Wa l-Aadaab [National Council for Culture, Arts and Literature], 1980.

Ramadaani, Bou'laam. *al-Masrah al-Jazaa'iri Bayn al-Maadi Wa l-Haadir* [The Algerian theatre between yesterday and today]. Algeria: al-Mu'assasa al-Wataniyya lil-Kitaab [National Book Establishment], 1984.

Roth, Arlette. *Le Théâtre algérien de langue dialectale, 1926–1954* [Algerian dialectic theatre, 1926–1954]. Paris: François Maspero, 1967.

Siagh, Zohra. 'Le théâtre algérien, un aspect de la modernité?' [Algerian theatre: An aspect of modernity?]. *Écrivains Maghrébins et modernité textuelle*. Paris: L'Harmattan, 1994: 73–87.

Slyomovics, Susan. 'Les quatrièmes journées théâtrales Maghrébines' [The fourth theatre days in the Maghreb]. *Drama Review* 35 (summer 1991): 182–6.

Subyaan, Nasr un-Deen. 'Ittijahaat al-Masrah al-'Arabi Fi al-Jazaa'ir' [Arabic theatre trends in Algeria]. Master's thesis, College of Literature, University of Damascus, 1984.

Yakoub. 'Ahmed Bouffetout, la gamelle et les fourchettes avec' [Ahmed eat-it-all, with messkit and forks]. *L'Avant Scène Théâtre* 963 (1995): 1–38.

ANGLO-EGYPTIAN SUDAN

(see **SUDAN**)

ARAB REPUBLIC OF EGYPT

(see **EGYPT**)

BAHRAIN

(Overview)

An independent emirate in the Persian Gulf consisting of a small archipelago of thirty-three islands, only five of which are inhabited, Bahrain covers a total land area of 620 square kilometres (240 square miles). The country is home to 575,925 inhabitants (1995), 63 per cent of whom are Bahraini, 13 per cent Asian, 10 per cent Arabs from other areas, 8 per cent Iranians and 6 per cent others. Islam is the dominant religion with the Shiah form practised by 70 per cent of the population while the other 30 per cent follow Sunni beliefs. The official language is Arabic but English is widely spoken. In Arabic, Bahrain literally means 'two seas'. The principal islands are Bahrain, on which the capital city Manama is located, and Muharrq.

Though Bahrain is very small, it nevertheless has a history going back some five thousand years when the islands were the seat of the ancient civilization of Dilmun, founded during the Bronze Age and lasting in one form or another for over two thousand years. Dilmun is also a society whose name recurs regularly in Sumerian literature. The epic of *Gilgamesh*, for example, refers to Dilmun as holy and immortal. Dilmun also developed as an early centre of trade and commerce linking Mesopotamia with the Indus Valley. Its decline coincided directly with the fall of the Indus Valley civilization and the subsequent degeneration of trade between it and Mesopotamia.

Bahrain was one of the first territories outside the Arabian peninsula to accept Islam when, in AD 640, the Prophet Muhammad sent a letter to the ruler of Bahrain urging him to do so. Well governed and prosperous during this period and into the Middle Ages, the country again became an important trade route, this time between Iraq and India. It did, however, change hands often and became ensnared in various disagreements between warring Gulf sheikhs.

In 1487 the Omanis conquered Bahrain and built a fort whose ruins can still be viewed. In the late fifteenth century a Portuguese explorer wrote of both the quantity and quality of pearls to be found in the area and over the next hundred years the Portuguese used Bahrain as a way station. Bahrain came under Iranian control in the eighteenth century. In 1783 the Al-Khalifa dynasty – originating from Kuwait – helped re-establish Bahrain as an independent emirate and to the present day the dynasty's descendants continue to exercise influence in the country.

Beginning in 1861, Bahrain was forced to accept a series of treaties giving Britain control over its external affairs. British influence remained strong over the next half-century. The economic significance of the emirate increased when oil was discovered in commercial quantities in the early 1930s, the first discovery of oil on the Arab side of the Gulf. Coinciding with the collapse of the world pearl market, oil meant that Bahrain could remain financially secure which it did – under continuing British control – until independence in 1971.

Since 1973 the country has been a constitutional monarchy and has become increasingly prosperous from oil exportation income. These continuing revenues have also meant a major improvement in education and health-care standards. After the Iranian Shiite revolution in 1979, unrest grew among Bahrain's Shiites and in 1981 and 1985 the government reportedly foiled coup plots to stage a similar fundamentalist revolution in the emirate.

Culturally, as archeological discoveries indicate, the ancient inhabitants of Bahrain had a ritualistic religion meaning that the elements of a root theatre could be found here. Unfortunately there is very little information about its form. One of the few assumptions that can be made, however, is that the religion was a polytheistic paganism. The advent of Islam in the seventh century meant the new faith was widespread and the majority of Bahraini people were converted to it. Although the new faith did not completely lack rituals, it did not encourage drama and/or human representations. The tragic end of the grandson of the Prophet Muhammad and members of his family in the battle of Karbala on the Euphrates in Iraq, on the other hand, did inspire a kind of dramatic expression known as *ta'ziyah* (literally, mourning). Scholars now tend to regard this as a form of Islamic religious drama. In the first ten days of the Muslim month of Muharram the story of the martyrdom of Al-Husain is enacted in this style. Even now this tradition is still extant in some Shiite Muslim communities (see IRAQ for a detailed discussion of this form).

Other than *ta'ziyah*, the only other performance forms seen in Bahrain early on were puppet theatre and shadow plays, which were quite common from the Middle Ages to the eighteenth century and can still be seen on occasion. The Napoleonic expeditions to Egypt at the end of the eighteenth and beginning of the nineteenth centuries introduced European dramatic forms to the Arab world, forms which ultimately made their way to Bahrain.

In the early part of the twentieth century, the introduction of modern formal education paved the way for the use of such European-style drama in Bahraini schools. Later came the introduction of plays into the curriculum by Arab dramatists and still later came plays by Bahraini dramatists. This strong tradition of drama and theatre in schools has included the staging of plays by students and teachers.

Though the schools themselves produced and adapted mainly moral, historical and religious

Awal Theatre's production of Ebrahim Bu Hindi's *Soroor* directed by A. Rahman Barkat.

plays – primarily by Egyptian and Syrian authors – the idea of staging original plays also emerged within the classroom. It was in the 1950s that two schoolmasters and poets – Ibrahim Al'urayyedh and Abdul-Rahman Alma'awda – paved the way for the spread of theatrical arts in Bahrain. Both wrote poetic plays for their students, usually depicting historic figures and epochs in Islamic Arab history. Al'urayyedh wrote three plays – *Wa Mu'tasimah*, *Bayn Ad-Dawlatayn* and, in English, *William Tell*. The first two are extant, the first published in 1952 and the second written the following year but existing only in typescript. Copies of *William Tell* do not seem to have survived.

Alma'awda wrote seven poetic plays in all, each derived from incidents in Arab history. These plays were *Abdul-Rahman Ad-Dakhil*, *Ar-Rashid wa Charlemagne*, *Sayf Al-Dawleh*, *Al-Must'asim Bil-Lah*, *Jableh Bin Al-Abham*, *Al-'Ala' Al-Hadrami* and *Yawm Thi Qar*. None of these scripts is extant.

It was in the 1940s that clubs and literary societies began to show interest in theatre and dramatic literature. From these clubs grew

theatre groups, at first amateur in nature and intent but since the 1970s evolving to semi-professional status. Initially content to produce plays from the world repertoire in translation (among these were works by Shakespeare), they later began to produce plays by Egyptian and Syrian writers and still later by Bahrain writers in an attempt to create an indigenous dramatic movement. Along with this came adaptations of foreign works with local flavour done in the Bahrain vernacular.

Among writers whose work has been produced by these companies has been Aqil Sawar (b. 1946), Ali al-Sharqawi (b. 1948), Amin Saleh (b. 1949) and Yousef al-Hamdan (b. 1956). Sawar is a very popular realistic writer whose major works include *Al-Nawkhidha* (1985) and *Al-Baraha* (1990) while al-Sharqawi has made his reputation mostly in the field of children's theatre; his scripts have been produced widely both in and out of Bahrain. Saleh, who made his reputation as a novelist, first came to note as a dramatist with a rewriting of *Romeo and Juliet* under the title *Romeo al-Fareeg* in 1988. Among his important later plays have been *Al-Jutah* (1990), a comic look at capitalism, and *Ikhtitaf*

Awal Theatre's production of *Bint al Nokhatha* written by Aqil Sawar, directed by Abdulla Yousif.

(1993) about an airline hijacking. Al-Hamdan is an experimental dramatist as well as a respected academic critic and scholar. In 1990 he published a collection of his essays under the title *Al-Jathoum*.

The most active companies have been the Awal and Al-Jazira Theatres, two groups which have faced continuing government censorship by officials who see political purpose in virtually everything they do. While it is true that the intention of many writers and directors has been the correction of social problems, there is still a line between politics and art, a line that state censors have only rarely acknowledged. The result has been in most instances a refusal to license a script for performance.

The Awal Theatre was the first company to be established as an entity independent from a cultural society or art club. Founded in 1970 and registered as a not-for-profit institution, this group paved the way for a number of similar troupes with the same goals and activities. Based in Muharraq, the second largest island and town in Bahrain, its activities are mainly carried out in the capital city of Manama. The company depends on government subsidies for survival; being semi-professional, the group's actors, directors and designers devote their energies to the work during their leisure hours. Since its establishment, Awal has encouraged local playwriting by producing the work of a number of new playwrights. The company has also produced several Arab plays and adaptations from world dramatic literature. Its first production was *Kursi Ateeq* (1970), an original play written and directed by Mohammed Awad (b. 1935).

Al-Jazira Theatre was incorporated in 1971 with the bulk of its membership at that time consisting of former Awal actors and some members of the Al-Jazira Club. Similar to Awal, its members are also semi-professional. A number have trained at higher institutes of dramatic arts in other Arab countries, especially Kuwait.

These two companies stage regular seasons of plays in Bahrain. Both have taken part in dramatic festivals in the Arab world and have toured neighbouring Arab countries with their most successful works.

A third troupe of growing importance is the al-Sawari company, founded in 1991 by Abdullah al-Sa'wari (b. 1948). The group tends to present serious and/or experimental works and has received support from the government through the drama section of the Directorate of Culture and Arts of the Ministry of Information.

Awal Theatre's production of *Hadikat al Hayawan* directed by Jamal al-Gheilan.

Its work has introduced elements of Asian theatre to the country, especially techniques from *kathakali* theatre from India and *kabuki* from Japan. The group is as close as Bahrain has to a genuine experimental company.

There are also a number of private managements that stage commercial productions. Unlike the not-for-profit companies, the commercial groups receive no assistance or subsidies from the government.

As for playwriting, the influence of writers from other Arab states on the playwrights of Bahrain cannot be denied. Echoes of the Egyptian dramatist Ahmad Shawqi can be heard in the plays of both Al'urayyedh and Alma'awda. But the two dramatists who have probably most influenced Bahrain's theatre have been the Egyptian Tawfiq al-Hakīm and the Syrian Sa'dallah Wanous.

Contemporary Bahrain writers have also regularly derived their subject matter from the nation's history and current affairs. In most cases, colloquial Arabic is the main means of expression with the emphasis on social problems and daily realities. Many plays also try to make use of the Arab heritage specifically. Most of the

Al-Sawari Theatre's production of *The Darkness* by J.L. Hallway, directed by Mohammed Radwan.

Abdullah al-Sa'dawi's al-Sawari Theatre production of *Escurial*, by Michel De Ghelderode.

Scenes from al-Sawari Theatre's production of Salah A. Sabor's *Sacrifice*, directed by Abdullah al-Sa'dawi.

country's present writers are young men with solid academic backgrounds and literary training. At times they have succeeded in producing works that genuinely find an audience but most of these works have also been highly criticized, generally by those who do not see any value in theatrical production as a whole. It is argued that their plays are personal vehicles for abstract values or are too political. The controversy which has developed around such work has not always been healthy.

In the 1980s, a number of works began to be written specifically for children. Originally introduced in the Gulf by Kuwaiti troupes, it appealed greatly to young audiences, was a success financially, and attracted many imitators. These dramatists have utilized pantomime, fairytales, dance, music, song and farce elements. Subject matter for these productions is usually drawn from folklore, both Arabic and European.

Within the Gulf, along with its neighbour Kuwait, Bahrain has in the 1990s become an active entertainment centre with concerts, sporting and cultural events being seen regularly. These include performances by western pop acts, travelling ballet and opera troupes, shows by Arab musical stars, plays performed by international actors and exhibition sports matches. Such events are seen in the most modern facilities including a 4,000-seat indoor theatre and several outdoor arenas.

Mohammad A. al-Khozai

(See also **KUWAIT**)

Further Reading

Abdulla, Mohammad Hassan. *Al-Haraka al-Masrahiya Fi' l'Kuwait* [The theatre movement in Kuwait]. Kuwait City: Manshurat Masrah Alkhalij al-'Arabi, 1977.

——. *Al-Masrah al-Kuwaiti* [The Kuwaiti theatre]. Kuwait City: Dar al-Kutub ath-Thaqafiya, 1978.

——. *Al-Masrah al-Kuwaiti bayn al Khishiya war-Raja'* [The Kuwaiti theatre: between fear and hope]. Kuwait City: Dar al-Kutub ath-Thaqafiya, 1978.

——. *Al-Masrah Fi' l'Bahrayn Wa' l'Kuwait* [The theatre in Bahrain and Kuwait]. Kuwait City: Majallat Dirasat Alkhalij Wa' l'-Jazira al-'Arabiya, University of Kuwait, 1975.

——. *Saqr ar-Rushud*. Kuwait City: Majallat Dirasat Alkhalij Wa' l'Jazira al-'Arabiya, University of Kuwait, 1980.

——. *Saqr ar-Rushud Mubdi' ar-Ru'ya ath-Thaniya* [Saqr ar-Rushud the creator of the second thought]. Kuwait City: Manshurat Majallat Dirasat Alkhalij Wa' l'Jazira al-'Arabiya, 1980.

Az-Zayd, Khalid Su'ud. *Al-Masrah Fi' l'-Kuwait* [The theatre in Kuwait]. Kuwait City: al-Rubay'an, 1983.

Bahreèin: fidjeri chants de pêcheurs de perles [Bahrain: Fidjeri chants of the pearl divers]. [sound recording] France: Auvidis, 1992.

Ghulum, Ibrahim Abdulla. *Al-Masrah Wa' l'Taghyir al-Ijtima'i Fi' l'-Khalij al-Arabi* [The theatre and social change in the Arab Gulf]. Kuwait City: 'Alam al-Ma'rifa Magazine, 1986.

——. *Zawahir at-Tajriba al-Masrahiya Fi' l'Bahrayn* [The phenomenon of the theatre experiment in Bahrain]. Kuwait City: al-Rubay'an, 1982.

Haddad, Qasim. *Al-Masrah al Bahrayni: At-Tajriba Wa' l'Ufuq* [The Bahraini theatre: the experiment and the horizon]. Bahrain: Masrah Awal, 1980.

Al-Khattir, Mubarak. *Al-Masrah at-Tarikhi Fi' l'Bahrayn* [The historical theatre in Bahrain]. Bahrain: Ministry of Information, 1985.

Ar-Ra'i, Ali. *Al-Masrah Fi' l'Wattan al-'Arabi* [Theatre in the Arab nation]. Kuwait City: 'Alam al-Ma'rifa Magazine, 1980.

BRITISH SOMALILAND

(see **SOMALIA**)

COMOROS ISLANDS

(Overview)

Four major and several smaller islands located at the head of the Mozambique Channel in the Indian Ocean make up the tiny nation grouping of the Comoros Islands. The total land area is 2,250 square kilometres (900 square miles) divided among Njazidja (Grand Comore) 1,148 square kilometres (459 square miles); Nzwani (Anjouan) 424 square kilometres (169 square miles); Mahoré (Mayotte) 374 square kilometres (150 square miles) and Mwali (Mohéli) 290 square kilometres (116 square miles). Three islands – Grand Comore, Anjouan and Mohéli – make up the Federal Islamic Republic of the Comores, which has been independent since 1976, while the fourth island, Mayotte, is a French dependency. The population of the islands was estimated in 1995 to be 549,338. The capital, Moroni, is situated on Grand Comore.

Comorans are of African, Arab and Malagasy descent. Though French and Arab are official languages, the lingua franca is the Comoran variety of Swahili. Indeed, Comoran culture generally is very similar to Swahili culture as found along the African coast from Somalia to Mozambique. In terms of religion, Sunni Islam is practised by 86 per cent of the population and Roman Catholicism by the remaining 14 per cent.

Rival sultanates on the islands during the nineteenth century allowed France to establish a presence. In 1886 the Comoros Islands became a French protectorate and in 1912 France officially proclaimed them colonies. Until the 1960s the islands were more or less totally isolated from the world. France maintained a situation which forbade political organization and a local press. In December 1961, however, in response to increased demands from the people of the islands, a system of internal autonomy was set up.

Theatre in the Comoros Islands has not yet reached professional status. Performances are most often generated by amateur groups or students who are awaiting entrance to either an African or French university in Madagascar. The Alliance Franco-Comorienne brings together Comorans interested in adapting traditional stories, legends and fables, which are on the verge of extinction, for the modern stage. These amateur groups have performed plays from francophone Africa and classical French repertoires as well as Comoran plays in French that deal with social issues.

One such troupe works under the auspices of both the Alliance Franco-Comorienne and the Ministry of Culture, Youth and Sports. Les Enfants du Théâtre (Children of the Theatre) was established in 1988 under the artistic direction of Said Ali Mohamed. They work out of the Alliance Franco-Comorienne in Moroni on Grand Comore. Among their major performances have been *La Secrétaire particulière* by Jean Plya in 1990; *Le Droit d'aimer* (*The Rights of Love*) by Mahamoud Bacary in 1992; *De la chaire au trône* (*From the Pulpit to the Throne*) by Amadou Korie in 1993; *Le Règlement c'est le règlement* (*The Rules are the Rules*) by Sultan Chouzour and *Le Cri de l'espoir* (*Cry of Hope*) by Jean Pierre Gringoire Daogo in 1994; and *Moiceul* by the Ivoirian dramatist Bernard Dadié in 1995.

The Alliance Franco-Comorienne provides two performance spaces, at Moroni on Grand Comore and at Mutsamudu on Anjouan Island. The 300-seat theatre in Moroni presents national and international performances and is also used for seminars, official ceremonies, conferences and film screenings. In 1995 thirteen performances were held in the space.

The Alliance Franco-Comorienne de Mutsamudu has a seating capacity of between 400 and 500 places, depending on the stage configuration. Performances are held here only on an occasional basis and in 1995 four shows were staged. This space is also used for seminars and conferences.

Other spaces in Moroni include Al-Kamar, a 700-seat theatre that provides a space for various theatre performances; the 500-seat Palais du Peuple (The People's Palace) which hosts seminars, conferences and official ceremonies but has no programmed theatre performances; and the 300-seat Foyer des Jeunes de Foumbouni (Youth of Foumbouni Hall).

The Agence de Promotion et de Production Artistique (Agency for Artistic Promotion and Production) promotes artists in the fields of music, dance theatre and visual arts.

The Association pour le Progrès de l'Éducation et de la Culture (Association for the Progress of Education and Culture) in Mbeni (located in the prefecture of northeast Grand Comore) promotes language, culture, libraries, traditional dance and theatre.

Staff

Further Reading

Chamanga, Mohamed Ahmed. *Rois, femmes et djinns: contes de l'île Danjouan Comores* [Kings, women and spirits: stories from the Island of Danjouan Comoros]. Paris: Centre de recherche Océan Indien-Inalco, 1988.

Lambek, Michael. *Human Spirits: A Cultural Account of Trance in Mayotte*. Cambridge: Cambridge University Press, 1981.

Music of the Comoros Islands. [sound recording]. Recorded by Harriet and Martin Ottenheimer. New York: Folkways, 1982.

Rombi, Marie-Françoise and Mohamed Ahmed Chamanga. *Contes comoriens* [Comorian tales]. Paris: Conseil International de la langue français and Edicef, 1980. 139 pp.

DEMOCRATIC AND POPULAR REPUBLIC OF ALGERIA

(see **ALGERIA**)

DJIBOUTI

(Overview)

Located in northeastern Africa, Djibouti has long been at the crossroads of trade routes between Asia, the Arabian Gulf and Europe. Bordered to the north by Eritrea, to the west and southwest by Ethiopia and to the south by Somalia, and formerly known as French Somaliland, the country lies at the southern entrance of the Red Sea and the Suez Canal beyond. Within its 21,800 square kilometres (8,500 square miles) live approximately 580,000 people, 60 per cent of whom are Somali (Issa) and 35 per cent Afar. Long a major outpost of the French Foreign Legion in Africa, Djibouti's official languages are Arabic and

French but both Somali and Afar are widely spoken. More than 90 per cent of the population are Sunni Muslims and it can be fairly said that religion permeates every aspect of Djiboutian life and influences all relationships including each individual's relationship with nature.

From earliest times, the area was traversed by nomadic tribes. The Afars eventually settled in and around Ethiopia and the Issas in Somalia but both also settled uneasily in the land that would eventually become Djibouti. This is still the case in so far as these two groups are concerned.

Millennia before the coming of the Europeans, the rich oral traditions of these nomadic peoples – principally in poetry and songs handed down from generation to generation – were known in the region and beyond through trade with ancient Egypt, India and China.

The French came into the area in 1862, having acquired the right to settle there from the Afar Sultans of Obock in exchange for money and other goods. The Sultan of Tadoura made a similar agreement with the French in 1884. The construction of the capital town and port of Djibouti City began in 1888. According to the terms of a treaty signed between France and Ethiopia in 1897, Djibouti – then known as French Somaliland – was to be 'the official outlet for Ethiopian commerce' and to facilitate this a railway was built from Djibouti to Addis Ababa.

Following World War II, a series of anti-colonial demonstrations began to be seen in the territory and in 1951, the French government accepted a representative from Djibouti in the National Assembly. A formal Territorial Assembly was established in 1957. Hostility to French rule, however, continued and in 1958 one-quarter of the population voted against French interests in a national referendum. Over the next decade, political debate intensified and, in many cases, included arrests and the wholesale expulsion of anti-French Somalis. A referendum in 1967 then produced a vote of 60.4 per cent in favour of continued unity with France (nearly 40 per cent at that point being against the proposition). Riots followed the referendum and the United Nations in vain urged France to grant the territory independence.

At the beginning of the 1970s, the predominantly Somali African Popular Union joined with the predominantly Afar League for the Future and Order to become the African People's League for Independence, Djibouti's first inter-ethnic party. The decade also saw increasing turbulence and unrest in the colony, government resignations and, in 1976, the return of many who had been expelled. France finally granted Djibouti independence in 1977 and an inter-ethnic government was formed. Afars and Issas, however, have been fighting each other for control of the country ever since and French troops have retained a presence. With the high cost of continuing warfare, the government through the years has had to sustain itself and its programmes through continued support from France as well as aid from fellow members of the Arab League, particularly Saudi Arabia, Kuwait, Iraq and Libya.

Until 1972, when a national orthography was introduced, there was no written language in Djibouti. The strong Djibouti culture was sustained, therefore, primarily through oral transmission. Traditional Afar–Issa performance forms, for example, make extensive use of folklore, legends, songs, exchanges, riddles and allusion to folk tales. These devices serve to reinforce tribal solidarity by evoking past exploits.

Although Djiboutians use only a limited number of musical instruments, the Afars specifically have an extensive song repertoire which forms the basis of the overall Djiboutian performance tradition. Six of the most popular are the *kalluwalle*, *sadda*, *horra*, *tirtira*, *saare* and *kassow*. Singers traditionally perform the *kalluwalle* in a circle with a female oracle at the centre. Such songs involve statements of prowess and bravery. The *sadda* is sung primarily at weddings and public markets. Sexual propositions, compliments, playful slander and refusal are the basis of the song. *Horra* are songs heard at weddings, market and evening get-togethers and are sung by groups of men who boast of their accomplishments. *Tirtira* are war shouts performed as short interruptions of the *horra*. *Saare* are praise songs sung by a man. Some describe the beauty of his wife, others his bravery in battle. *Kassow* are challenge songs invoked if one man has a grievance against another.

European-style theatre productions began to be seen on a more or less regular basis in Djibouti in the 1950s with French influence the most obvious. Eventually enthusiastic amateurs moved from productions of French classic comedies to plays with elements of local satire by Djiboutian writers. Later original plays began to include social and political content, some using legends and folk tales in their commentary on such things as the ongoing national turbulence. Many of these early theatre groups were suspected by the ruling government of having connections to political parties and were, as a result, subjected to significant censorship and harassment. From 1967, however, there was more active encouragement of theatre activities by the government and more cultural facilities began to be made available.

Perhaps the best known Djibouti play is Hassan Sheikh Moumin's (b. 1930) drama, *Shabeelnaagood* (*Leopard Among the Women*, 1966), a play in sixteen scenes which, set in the 1960s, attacks the evils within contemporary Djiboutian society. Other plays of note staged after independence from France dealt with sovereignty, conscience, unity and peace. Early productions were done in French; performances since the 1980s are done mostly in Arabic, Afar and Somali.

In the late 1970s, Djiboutian theatre began to turn more to European techniques. The most active work came from the Théâtre des Salines Association, founded in 1977. It gained the support of French cultural agencies as well as national groups looking to escape from the traditional performance framework. Companies were encouraged particularly to explore the use of body in performance while dramatists focused on the changing nature of the society, liberation and education. The work attracted new audiences, especially young people and during the late 1980s and 1990s a number of professional and semi-professional companies, all based in Djibouti City began to appear. The most important of these is the Association des Comédiens Amateurs de Théâtre. Performing publicly in both French and Afar, the group, founded in 1990, stages both classical and contemporary works and, in its first year, even performed an AIDS awareness piece.

The Association Degaan, established in 1986, performs two to three times per year at the Maison des Jeunes de Hadj-Didek and at the Théâtre des Salines. The company has also toured productions to Yemen and Ethiopia. Performing in Somali, Degaan stages theatre, vocal and instrumental pieces as well as traditional dance.

Dinkara, also established in 1986, has a company of ten who jointly work as actors, directors, dancers, singers and musicians. They perform sketches, music and songs as well as occasional theatre-for-development pieces with governmental and United Nations' agencies. Working in Afar, French and English, the group has performed both within the country and in Ethiopia.

The five-member Troupe Artistique 4 Mars was begun by Miganeh Abdi and works out of the Maison des Jeunes Cité du Stade Palais du Peuple. In partnership with UNICEF it has presented work on themes of health, agriculture and fishing. The troupe performs an average of four shows per year and took its work to Libya in 1991.

The Association de la Jeunesse pour l'Évolution Culturelle (Youth Association for Cultural Evolution, established in 1987), is a group of about thirty actors, choreographers and designers mandated to work in the area of theatre for social action. Performing in French and Somali, it also works closely with the Ministry of Health and UNICEF to promote, among other campaigns, vaccination programmes.

In 1985 the first Festival National de Théâtre was held at the Centre National de la Promotion Culturelle et Artistique (National Centre for Cultural and Artistic Promotion) in Djibouti City. In 1994, Iris – a cultural support organization – co-sponsored with the Association for Culture, Communication and Development a festival of performing and visual arts. Six groups and musicians were included representing some 800 participants.

The first purpose-built theatre space in the country, Théâtre des Salines, was completed in 1964. Designed by a French architect, it is a 1,200-seat proscenium and is mainly used for national cultural events such as theatre and music festivals. The Palais du Peuple – a cultural centre – was established in 1994. About ten performances per year are seen at this 802-seat theatre which also has space for conferences and meetings. The Centre Culturel Français Arthur Rimbaud, a 266-seat theatre, was opened in 1995.

Between 1986 and 1991, 300 students participated in theatre workshops as part of the national education curriculum but a withdrawal of funding and a lack of human resources ultimately led to the programme's closure.

Staff

(See also SOMALIA)

Further Reading

Andrzejewski, B.W. 'Modern and Traditional Aspects of Somali Drama'. *Folklore in the Modern World* (1978): 87–101.

Bliese, Loren F. 'Afar Songs'. *Northeast African Studies* 4 no. 3 (1982–3): 51–76.

Morin, Didier. *Contes de Djibouti* [Tales from Djibouti]. Paris: Edicef, 1980. 170 pp.

Moumin, Hassan Sheikh. *Leopard Among the Women: Shabeelnaagood – A Somali Play*. Translated by B.W. Andrzejewski. London: Oxford University Press, 1974. 230 pp.

Schraeder, Peter J. *Djibouti: Bibliography*. Oxford: Clio Press, 1991.

DUBAI

(see **UNITED ARAB EMIRATES**)

EGYPT

The cultural capital of the Arab world and the cradle of one of the world's greatest civilizations, Egypt, situated in northeastern Africa south of the Mediterranean Sea, is bordered to the east by Israel and the Red Sea, to the south by Sudan and to the west by Libya. The country, officially known as the Arab Republic of Egypt (from 1958 to 1971 as the United Arab Republic), covers a total area of 1,001,500 square kilometres (400,600 square miles) and had a population estimated in 1995 at 62.3 million, 94 per cent of whom are Muslims.

Conquered by Arab invaders in the seventh century, Egypt's official language since that time has been Arabic. Egyptian Arabic, however, is distinct from that of other countries and, due in great measure to the country's domination of media such as film, radio and television, Egyptian Arabic has probably become the most recognizable and universal of the many Arabic dialects.

Although modern Egyptians are generically known as Arabs due to their language and Islamic traditions, the only truly Arabic group in the country is the Bedouins, the majority of whom remain tribal nomads living in isolated oases in the country's vast Sinai Desert. Other Egyptians are descended from eastern Hamitic stock while another important minority grouping is the Nubian people, who lived for thousands of years on their own land, Nuba, which stretched along the Nile from Upper Egypt in the south of the country to northern Sudan. With the construction of the high dam in the southern city of Aswan, however, and the creation of the artificial Lake Nasser in 1966, much ancient Nubian territory was flooded and many of ancient Nuba's stunning architectural traditions were lost.

Part of the Ottoman Empire in the eighteenth and nineteenth centuries, Egypt was occupied by the British in 1882. Under British control and influence for the next four decades, Egypt officially became a British protectorate with the advent of World War I in 1914 when the

Ottoman Empire aligned itself with the German forces. In 1922 Britain granted Egypt independence but during World War II the country's deserts became a battleground for British and German armies. After Gamal Abdel Nasser led a coup against ruling King Farouk and forced his abdication in 1953, Egypt became a republic. In 1954, with Nasser in power, the nation underwent a massive reorganization once again pursuing a policy at this point of pan-Arab socialism and developing closer ties with the Soviet Union.

Culturally, Egypt is a synthesis of its ancient history, its strong Islamic traditions, its colonial influences and its modern pan-Arab political and intellectual movements. As part of this cultural evolution has come the development of a western-style scripted theatre whose earliest manifestations date to the early part of the nineteenth century when Europeans again began to visit the country and European theatre companies began to tour in the region. Local groups emerged over the next fifty years and by the middle of the nineteenth century Egyptian musical theatre groups were offering short seasons in Cairo on a private and commercial basis, a tradition that continues to the present day.

Attempts to create a less commercial, more serious indigenous Egyptian theatre with plays by Egyptian dramatists date from the early part of the twentieth century. Sometimes supported by government agencies but mostly not, such initiatives began to receive official support after World War II and state involvement in the arts became national policy after 1952. Indeed, since then, the state – as in many Arab nations – has been actively involved in both the creation and development of a variety of cultural institutions and facilities ranging from a National Theatre Company to the Cairo Opera House, from a National Puppet Theatre to experimental theatres and a National Symphony Orchestra. Each of these has received significant financial support as have many smaller groups, including some from the alternative Free Theatre movement.

Over the twentieth century Egypt has witnessed the growth and international recognition of its literature – dramatic and non-dramatic – throughout the region, the Arab world generally and even internationally. Particularly noteworthy in this regard have been dramatist Tawfiq al-Hakīm (1899–1987) and novelist Najib Mahfuz (b. 1912), who won the Nobel Prize for Literature.

But Egyptian theatre has ancient roots as well,

توفيق الحكيم

Tawfiq al-Hakīm.

roots that go deeper than almost anywhere else in the world. The Pyramid Texts (2800 to 2400 BC with certain passages dating as much as a thousand years earlier) show scenes which we know were enacted depicting various actions through which the spirit must pass before entering the afterlife. Another famous historical example of the country's deep theatrical roots is the Abydos Passion Play – a communal performance event – which was enacted annually in the city of Abydos for nearly 2000 years (2500 BC to approximately 550 BC). The event, which lasted several days, marked the first day of spring with a massive re-enactment of the god Osiris's death and his ultimate resurrection after three days.

Even during Christian and early Islamic periods, quasi-dramatic performances continued to take place in Egypt. In one such theatricalized ritual, a young bride would be sacrificed in front of the entire community in celebration of the annual Nile flood. By the eighteenth century, shadow plays were among the country's most popular theatrical forms.

Other non-scripted but nevertheless theatrical populist forms included public storytelling, poetry reading and even chanting of the Quran. The *rawi* (narrator/storyteller) has also long been popular in all Egyptian communities for his ability to recall tales of the past through a solo enactment of both characters and situations. Such forms eventually developed less exalted offshoots including improvised comic sketches with bitingly satirical social criticism and occasional burlesque situations. By the late nineteenth century this type of comic sketch dominated public performance and on occasion the state was forced to step in to stop the coarsest type of ridicule. Also popular was the *samir* (evening chats with the central figures taking different sides) in which topics were debated including issues of a national or religious character. Such debates often took on epic and heroic characteristics.

In most of these instances, there was neither a stage nor a written dramatic text. The exception was occasionally found in an extremely simple form in the art of the shadow play which was improvised around a standard storyline most often involving the figures of ancient *karagöz*. It was Napoleon's visit to Egypt in 1798 which began interest in European forms and Napoleon later sent various French theatre troupes to play in Cairo. But it was Sheikh Rifaa Rafe al Tahtawi (1801–73) of Al Azhaz who is credited with pioneering the nineteenth-century Egyptian cultural renaissance within the country. Living in Paris during the 1820s and 1830s, he was struck by the public's great interest in theatre. As a result, he began to translate works of French classical theatre into Arabic and it was this French influence that was at the root of the mid-nineteenth century's new interest in dramatic form. Many such performances were attended enthusiastically by the country's aristocracy and upper-middle class. Because of such interest, the press also began to pay attention to the troupes, even listing the names of the artists, play titles and sometimes the subjects of the performances themselves, widening the base of interest further.

From 1885, amateur troupes and societies began to appear in Cairo and Alexandria presenting plays from the European repertoire that they themselves had translated. One of the longest lived of such groups was the Society for the Supporters of Acting, formed in 1912 by Mohammed Abdul Rahim and others interested in European culture. The first amateur group to study the art of acting on a methodological basis, the society's first production was a play based on the life of the British actor David Garrick. The company operated for the next forty years presenting one major show annually as well as giving workshops and lectures in schools. During its

existence, the troupe would boast many actors who would later go on to professional careers in the theatre. Among them were Abdul Rahman Rushdie (1881–1939), Mahmud Murad (1888–1925), Mahmud Taymur (1894–1973), Ismail Wahbi, Abdul Warith Assar (1894–1982) and Suliman Najib (1892–1955).

The early commercial shows with music (from about the 1870s) relied most heavily on a revue format – Franco-Arab songs, comic character sketches and broad farce routines. As these shows became more sophisticated they began to be centred in two sections of Cairo – Emad Al Din in central Cairo and Rud Al Faraj in the northern part of the city. In Emad Al Din, the shows proving most popular were musicals, melodramas and vaudevilles while in Rud Al Faraj comedy was the main attraction in open-air theatres with most shows liberally interspersed with songs and improvised routines by the popular comic stars. The audience would often engage in comic debate with the performers, the atmosphere ultimately being more nightclub-like than theatrical. Among the longest-running of the commercial companies have been the al-Kassar Troupe (1918–49), Ramsis Troupe (1923–43), Malak Opera Troupe, Ismail Yassin Troupe (1954–66), Tahiya Kariuka Troupe (1962–82) and al-Rihani Troupe (1916–79).

By the end of World War I, novelists and even poets began to look at theatrical art more seriously and began to utilize it both for new experiments in form and as another weapon in the growing struggle for independence and for defining the new Egyptian identity. Many of the early dramatists connected themselves to amateur, then semi-professional and then professional troupes which began to appear in the 1920s and 1930s. Among the most important of these new groups were the Troupe of Twenty founded in 1936 and the Vanguard Troupe (1942–5) which was also staging such plays in Arabic as *Faust* and *The Government Inspector*. By the 1950s, new plays and experiments could be seen almost every week in Cairo.

The early development of Egyptian dramatic literature is generally credited to Ya'qub Sannu (1839–1912), a Jewish journalist of strong liberal tendencies both intellectually and politically. A supporter of the Khedive Ismail, Sannu in 1870 formed the first 'national' theatre troupe (indeed, he called it the National Theatre), a company which would ultimately perform thirty-two plays, most written or adapted by him from European classics. The majority of these in their final form were satirical, short, simple in structure and used colloquial rather than classical Arabic. His best adaptations were of plays by Molière, Sheridan and Goldoni. In these plays Sannu – who also directed and acted in them – dealt with contemporary social issues. Despite his general support of the Khedive, however, Sannu's company was closed down by the government in 1872 because the Khedive felt that his plays were becoming a bit too critical of his government.

But clearly the art of scripted theatre had found fruitful soil in Egypt. Throughout the 1870s, despite the closure of Sannu's theatre, many Egyptians continued to attend theatrical performances. Among these were shows by visiting troupes from Damascus and Beirut led by artists such as Salim al-Naqqash and Soliman al-Qardahi.

The Damascan Ahmed Abu Khalil al-Qabbani (1833–1902) first came to Cairo to perform in 1884 (some two years after the beginning of the British occupation of Egypt) following the closure of his own theatre in Damascus by the Ottoman government. In Cairo he presented the first plays ever seen based on Arab and Islamic history as well as dramatizations of the tales from *The Thousand and One Nights*. Despite his originality, though, his plays were quite unsophisticated, often merely a transformation of the ancient tales into dialogue interspersed with songs. Al-Qabbani, however, had touched in his work important aspects of Arab culture, sources through which the Arab nation would come to know itself, its history and its literary heritage. He linked to older traditions of music, storytelling and poetry and was able to draw public attention to the significance and splendour of these older forms. Among the works of literature that al-Qabbani used to further anchor theatre to Arab culture were *Al Amier Mahmou, Nijl Shah Al Ajam* (*Prince Mahmoud the Shah's Son*), *Afifa* and *Antara Al Abassi*.

The play *Al Watan* (*The Homeland*) by Abdullah al-Nadim (1843–96) was the first dramatic success of real literary quality from this period, a time of growing national awareness, a time that witnessed the Orabi Revolution (1878–82), itself a battle for democracy, the elimination of Ottoman rule and the realization of economic reform. Expressionistic in style, this play – by a sheikh who was also a journalist and a spokesperson for the revolution – was an immediate success and was widely performed in the schools of Cairo and Alexandria, at gatherings of revolutionaries and in the coffee shops they frequented.

The last decade of the nineteenth century and the first decades of the twentieth saw an even stronger national response to colonialism. During this time, the history of Egyptian Pharaonic civilization began to be unearthed by archaeologists and became a further inspiration to go deeper into knowledge about these early Egyptian civilizations. Many nationalistic political, cultural and literary magazines along with new newspapers were begun at this point and major poets, authors and public speakers appeared calling on Egyptians to look back at their own history and ahead to an independent future. A whole new generation of Egyptian-born scholars emerged and the number of academics doing advanced studies abroad at this time – mainly in French and British universities – doubled.

An unprecedented upsurge in theatrical activity during the post-World War I period paralleled a growth in Egyptian middle-class society, now eager to participate in the cultural, political and economic spheres. During the 1920s, new theatrical troupes took the novel step of including playwrights, translators and adapters as well as musicians and designers in their companies. Perhaps most importantly, large audiences began to frequent the theatre and support dramatic art. Important new playwrights began to be produced and their works known. Among them of the period include Farah Antun (1874–1922), Ibrahim Ramzi (1885–1949) and Muhammad Taymur who all wrote plays in a variety of genres and showed a growing mastery of dramatic form. Further encouraging this growth were continuing tours to Cairo and Alexandria by foreign theatrical and musical troupes.

New and influential troupes were also formed during this period – led by the company of George Abyad (1880–1959) in 1912 which travelled across the Arab world and beyond; the troupe of Abdullah Okasha (1880–1942) in 1911; the comic revue troupe of Mustafa Amin; and Al Kumiedi Al Arabi (Arab Comedy Troupe) of Aziz Eid (1881–1942), director, actor and translator in 1915; troupe of singer Munira al-Mahdiya (1885–1965) in 1915; Najib al-Rihani Comic Troupe in 1916; the troupe of Abdul Rahman Rushdie in 1917; and the comic troupe of Amin Sidqi (d. 1944) and Ali al-Kassar (1885–1957), established in 1918.

The national resistance movement against British occupation that had begun after the Orabi Revolution escalated now under the leadership of a new generation of intellectuals, particularly those working in the fields of journalism, literature, law and religion. As well, knowledge of western culture increased. Massive new audiences were attracted to the national movements which were determined to represent all classes, professions and vocations. Literary and artistic creation was now to be put into the service of nationalism and a qualitative leap in the standards of culture became clear. The movement reached its peak in 1919 but continued unabated through the next decade, a period in which the press, public rhetoric and many types of literature developed, and music and popular songwriting spread.

George Abyad, however, was without doubt the star of stars. Studying theatre in France from 1904 to 1910, he arrived in Egypt in 1910 as director of a touring French company. Impressed by the changes taking place within the society and encouraged by the Minister of Education to form an Egyptian company, he agreed to stay and began his new career by staging plays translated mostly from French and English drama. It was due to him that many such classic works were introduced to the Arab world. Abyad also encouraged the creation of indigenous plays and had no problem when audiences and actors demanded that songs be included in the plays. Abyad's towering personality wielded an enormous influence – not only in Egypt but also in the other Arab countries he visited with his troupe – in encouraging young people to view acting as a respectable profession. In 1914, he joined forces with Salama Hijazi. Hijazi's singing and dancing skills complemented Abyad's dramatic skills and resulted in a company which achieved enormous critical and financial success. The troupe continued operating until 1932.

But there were other troupes of note working at this time as well in Cairo: the Ramsis Troupe (1923–43), Fatimah Rushdie Troupe (1927–34) and Actor's Union Troupe (1934). The Ramsis Troupe was formed by Yusuf Wahbi (1898–1982), the son of a pasha. Even as a young actor, Wahbi and his director, Aziz Eid, turned the company into one of the most theatrically admired and popular troupes of the period. Known for its realistic acting style, its imaginative direction and its often spectacular designs, the troupe turned away from exhausted historical plays and focused on socially rooted dramas and popular melodramas in Egyptian Arabic rather than classical Arabic. All were adapted so as to make comments on the problems of Egyptian society. The troupe disbanded

in 1943. Among its significant original scripts were *Rasputin*, *Al Dhab'ih* (*The Sacrifices*), *Kursi al Ietiraf* (*The Confessional*), *Bayumi Effendi*, *Al Qablah al Qatilah* (*The Kiss*), *Awlad al Fuqara* (*Children of the Poor*) and *Awlad al Dhawat* (*Children of the Upper Class*).

Wahbi's company marked another stage in the development of Egyptian theatre. Not only was he a major acting talent and a commanding presence but also he was a skilled manager who helped establish unprecedented traditions in the preparation and promotion of theatrical seasons and the organization of dramatic performances. In his theatre, audiences were urged to abide by basic rules of conduct during performances, which gave the troupe and the art a new respect and esteem and led to the general raising of the status of theatre in Egypt.

The Fatimah Rushdie Troupe, another jewel of the period, was formed by the actress Fatimah Rushdie (1909–96), one of the stars of the Ramsis Troupe, with the aid of Aziz Eid, who happened to be her husband. One of the first female stars of the Arab theatre and a gifted singer, her troupe presented an international repertoire including original musicals, several dramas written by the Turkish playwright Widad Urfi and plays written by the poet Ahmad Shawqi (1868–1932), pioneer of the Arabic verse play. The company included former performers from both the Ramsis Troupe and Okasha Troupe.

Until about 1915, short farces were often presented between acts of other shows, usually by small travelling companies that mixed songs with comic improvisations. Rarely were they taken seriously or even noticed by critics, dramatists or authorities. The comic theatre was given a new respect, however, when two gifted comic actors – Ali al-Kassar and Najib al-Rihani (1889–1949) – began to create independent pieces, eventually leading to the creation of their own troupe in 1916. During World War I, plays by these two actors became a popular alternative to the large number of historical plays that had been appearing.

Another major comic troupe – one which worked from 1916 until 1979 – was that of al-Rihani. He understood the importance of comedy as social criticism and used it to question new developments in culture and those middle-class attitudes which both produce and consume it. His plays put on stage many recognizable types: the 'struggling' Egyptian employee, the baffled bosses, the worker and the teacher. Many appeared in operettas he drew from *The Thousand and One Nights*. Al-Rihani evolved a form of critical social comedy, most of the incidents and themes in which he adapted skilfully from French farce. His later plays became deeper still, dealing with the problems facing Cairo society between the two world wars, particularly what he saw as the retreat of moral ideals and values in the face of the spread of materialist ambitions and moral dissolution. In verse adaptations done in collaboration with Badie Khairi (1893–1966), a writer of *zajal* (iambic verse), his plays revealed a strong social vision utilizing dialects, raising the standards of dramatic language and reflecting the many dimensions of Arab character.

A new National Troupe was begun with state support in 1935 under the direction of the poet Khalil Mutran, the first Egyptian troupe to be both established and financed by government. The National's first performance was Tawfiq al-Hakīm's *Ahl al-Kahf* (*Sleepers in the Cave*). A symbolist play, its central story was based on a tale from the Quran. This was followed with plays by Racine, Corneille, Shakespeare and other major European playwrights. Despite its artistic quality, however, the troupe, with its very literary base, was not a popular success. Most of the plays were simply beyond the grasp and interest of most theatregoers. Seven years later, the troupe was reformed and given an enlarged mandate that included musical theatre. Now called the Egyptian Troupe for Acting and Music, it presented mostly comedies and musicals.

The establishment of an Institute for Dramatic Art (later called the Higher Institute of Dramatic Arts) in Cairo in 1944 was another major factor in the evolution of the modern Egyptian theatre. Actors finally had a place to study and no longer needed to depend on intuitive talent alone. The institute became one of the major forces in the development of troupes within the theatre as a whole. From 1947, it produced the first of several generations of fine performers, directors, critics and designers. Forming groups all over the country, some began teaching in schools adding into the curriculum play production and eventually whole courses in dramatic literature. These graduates also affected the sister arts of radio and television as well as cinema.

It was Zaki Tulaymat (1895–1982), a director and for many years manager of the Egyptian Troupe for Acting and Music, who had begun lobbying for the development of such training as early as 1937. A graduate of the Paris Conservatoire, he ultimately became the first Dean of the Higher Institute of Dramatic Arts and, in 1950, he began the Modern Theatre Troupe which he limited to graduates of the Institute for Dramatic Art. This new and well-trained company sought to present translations of modern world drama and western classics, particularly those of Molière. The group also presented a number of original Egyptian plays including the premières of Muhamad Taymur's *Ibn Jala* and *Kadhib fi Kadhib* (*Lie Upon Lie*, 1952), Khalil al-Rahimi's *Dinshawi al Hamra* (*Red Dinshawi*, 1952), Mahmud Sha'ban and Anwar Fatah Allah's (1915–91) *Kifah al Shaab* (*Struggle of the People*, 1952), and 'Ali Ahmad Bakathir's *Musmar Juha* (*Juha's Nail*, 1951). Tulaymat had also established the concept of touring, playing in schools and community halls throughout the country.

Despite such personal efforts, however, the Egyptian theatre still lacked a base to make it a viable competitor with film in the 1950s. Locked into older western forms and methodologies in both playwriting and performance, it found itself unable to tackle issues of real interest to a broad public. At this time too, Egypt was full of dreams for a bright political and social future. The 1952 revolution had eliminated the monarchy and with it the notion of agricultural feudalism. National and political independence was assured and foreign domination in the economic field was being slowly curtailed. An emerging power among non-aligned nations, Egyptians saw essential reforms beginning to take place in many fields, reforms that were being felt by all classes of the society. Social justice was becoming more than just a slogan. New values and new social relationships were emerging across the country.

The establishment of the Modern Theatre Troupe gave rise to competition with the older company, the Egyptian Troupe for Acting and Music. But in 1953, the state decided that one strong troupe would be better than two struggling companies and merged the two groups under the name of the Modern Egyptian Troupe, the administration of which was handed over to Yusuf Wahbi. Wahbi, however, was not so interested in serious writing and though a number of original plays were produced, the reputation of the merged company fell further. By 1956, Wahbi stepped down as head of the troupe and was replaced by Ahmad Hamrush (b. 1922) who had been an officer in the 1952 revolution. Hamrush drew up more new plans for the company with the help of writers, academics and directors. The new vision sought to develop young talent, encourage indigenous playwriting and present the works of international dramatists whose works represented humanistic trends. In 1958, this company was renamed the National Theatre.

By the late 1950s and early 1960s, another generation of even more socially and artistically committed younger writers emerged. Among them Nu'man 'Ashur (1918–87), Yusuf Idris (1927–91), Alfred Faraj (b. 1929), Rashad Rushdi (1912–83), Fat'hi Radwan (1911–88), Lutfi al-Khuli (b. 1929), Sa'd al-Din Wahba (1925–97), Abdul al-Rahmani al-Sharqaw (1920–87); Mikhail Ruman (1927–73), Najib Surur (1932–78), Mahmud Diyab (1932–83), Salah Abd al-Sabur (1930–81), Ali Salim (b. 1936) and Mustafa Bahjat (1935–80). Their works excited a younger generation of intellectuals and artists and began to be embraced by ever larger segments of the society. Working right into the 1970s, these writers all had a fervent attachment to Egypt's historical past as well as to its political present. Interested as well in Egypt's role within the Arab world as a whole, they focused on both contemporary and long-term problems, celebrating both the anxieties and contradictions of the country along with its aspirations and achievements. The plays of these writers did not simply portray reality but were also aimed at reshaping it. Mingling realism and folk materials with symbolism, naturalism and expressionism, as well as epic forms with abstract forms, their works revealed clear European influences ranging from Ibsen and Chekhov to Pirandello, Sartre, Brecht and Ionesco.

Another strong impetus for the arts came in 1955 with the establishment of a governmental department for arts and literature under the scholar and writer Yihia Haqqi (b. 1905). One of the department's first acts was to form various committees to look into the state of theatre, film and music in the country and to propose means of supporting and improving them. In 1958, a Ministry of Culture and National Guidance was established which was to generally support culture as well as assist in arts training. It took as one of its major goals the dissemination of the arts to the widest possible population base. Under this Ministry, Institutes of Cinema and Ballet were founded and a Music Conservatory begun. The Institute of Dramatic Arts was also further strengthened. Students in all these fields were finally able to earn scholarships to complete their artistic studies abroad and on their return many played an important role in forming even newer theatrical troupes, especially during the 1960s.

From this point on, it is possible to divide the Egyptian theatre into two major stages – pre- and post-1967, with the year 1967, the year of the Egyptian defeat in the war with Israel, as a clear watershed. Looked at from the standpoint of dramatic output, it can be said that three major plays define the earlier period – al-Aydi al-Na'ima (Soft Hands) by Tawfiq al-Hakīm and two plays by Nu'man 'Ashur, al-Maghmatis (The Trick Cyclist, 1955) and il Nas illi Taht (The People Who Live Downstairs, 1956). These three works mark the real beginning of the socially critical play in Egypt and a new interest in theatrical performance. Built on the political and economic achievements of the post-1952 period, both the language and the conflict of the changing social classes were reflected in these works and other such plays by dramatists such as Lutfi al-Khuli who wrote al-Qadiyya (The Case, 1961) and Sa'd al-Din Wahba, author of two important plays, al-Sibinsa (The Guard's Van, 1962) and Kubri al-Namus (Mosquito Bridge, 1963). Along with continuing work from 'Ashur such as il Nas illi Fuq (The People Who Live Upstairs, 1957) and al-Hakīm in plays such as al-Safqa (The Deal, 1956) and Rihlah ila'l Ghad (Journey into the Future, 1957), the years leading up to 1967 were full of theatrical ferment and tremendous social energy.

The period of the 1967 war itself – the six months or so before and the six months after – saw these and other dramatists beginning to probe the many contradictions in Egyptian society, its negative social aspects and its manifestations of weakness and corruption whether in the family, the government or public organizations. This crucial period is characterized by both a social and intellectual conflict between revolutionary values on the one hand and social practices and the problems of applying them justly on the other. Questions were raised concerning social and political justice and the actual handling of the war. Among the important plays from this period were al-Hakīm's al-Sultan al-Ha'ir (The Sultan's Dilemma, 1960), 'Ashur's A'ilat al-Dughri (The Dughri Family, 1962), Rashad Rushdi's Rihla Kharij al-Sur (A Journey Outside the Wall, 1964), Alfred Faraj's Hallaq Baghdad (The Barber of Baghdad, 1963) and Sulayman al-Halabi (1964), Yusuf Idris's Sikkat al-Salama (The Road to Safety, 1965), Wahba's Bir al-Sillim (The Stairwell, 1966), Mahmud

Diyab's *al-Zawba'a* (*The Storm*, 1965), Mikhail Ruman's *al-Dukhkhan* (*Smoke*, 1962), Abdul al-Rahmani al-Sharqaw's *al-Fata Mahran* (*Mahran's Chivalry*, 1966) and Salah Abd al-Sabur's *Ma'sat al-Hallaj* (*The Tragedy of al-Hallaj*, 1965).

From the late 1960s to the mid-1970s, most of the serious plays focused on the 1967 war, reasons for the national defeat and ways to overcome its military, social and political consequences. Plays looked at the relationship between rulers and their people, royal interference and the nature of power. The issue of democracy versus totalitarian rule was also dealt with in several plays, the most important of which were Rushdi's *Baladi ya Baladi* (*My Beloved Country*, 1968) Ruman's *al-Ardhalji* (*The Petition Writer*, 1968), Wahba's *al-Masamir* (*Nails*, 1967) and *Ya Salam Sallim al-Heyta Bititkallim* (*Heaven Preserve Us, the Wall's Talking*, 1970), Ali Salim's *Kumidiya Udib: Inta illi Qatalt il-Wahsh* (*Comedy of Oedipus: You Killed the Monster*) and *Endama Zaharit al Afarit* (*What If I Were Seen*), Faraj's *Ali Janah al-Tabrizi wa Tabihu Quffa* (*Ali Janah al Tabriz and His Henchman Quffa*, 1968) and Al Sayid al-Shurbaji's *al-Biliatshu* (*The Harlequin*, 1969).

In this fertile period, plays dealt with a wide range of subjects – from the inevitability of the 1952 revolution to strong social criticism; and in a variety of styles – from realistic well-made plays to symbolist works, from folk-inspired pieces to meditative works dealing with profound philosophical and Arab issues. Even a number of modern verse plays appeared dealing with history, legends and fantasy. What unified the works of this period was a general desire not to speak directly and a profound but subtle sense of despair. The Egyptian theatre was clearly alive and well.

Writers of this generation – and theatre artists generally – wanted to deal directly with issues of personal and social justice, the right to resist oppression, the difficulty of adapting to social change and the need for ideals. In these plays, the individual would most often take on authority utilizing at times the traditional Arabic *rawi* and even Greek-style choruses and the use of Greek legends (the stories of Oedipus and the Oresteia for example).

The theatre since the late 1970s has, to a very large extent, continued these trends though the activities of the state troupes began to diminish from 1967 in both quantity and quality and new energies were brought in by the more than fifty Free Theatres that emerged during this period. Clearly, the 1967 defeat had tarnished the great dream of the establishment of a society of justice and prosperity, a power and a leader in the region. The state also began cutting public expenditures on the arts at this time with the monies saved going into military budgets. Even the state-supported National Circus was cut back.

The victory of the October 1973 war restored some of Egypt's lost honour, dignity and self-awareness but the economic open-door policy which followed led to the domination of consumer values over arts policy, the general lowering of artistic standards for a more populist vision. Private commercial troupes made a comeback of sorts at this time and attracted older audiences while the Free groups connected more directly to the young. Many stars of the theatre turned away from the stage almost entirely preferring to make films and popular television serials both in Egypt and in the oil-producing states of the region. During the 1970s as well, censorship became an issue with all plays suddenly having to get state approval.

The best plays of this period use a framework of legend and history to portray contemporary reality in an effort to avoid direct political expression. While some theatres were staging foreign works by Shakespeare, Racine, Chekhov and Strindberg to make their statements, others were finding new voices in the plays of Yussri al-Jindi (b. 1941), Fawzi Fahmi (b. 1938), Samir Sarhan (b. 1941) and Nabil Badran (b. 1941). The literary scholar and professor Muhamad Anani (b. 1939), early in his dramatic output, dealt critically and symbolically with issues of morals and social change. By the early 1980s, he was turning much more to folk materials to reflect contemporary issues in such works as *Mit Halawa* (1983) and *al-Ghurban* (*The Crows*, 1984). The latter play, written in verse, uses the crows as a symbol of despotism on the one hand and, on the other, as the aides of the ruler, as his harem and as his servants.

The critic, scholar and cultural animateur Samir Sarhan took as subjects for his best plays material from Arab history focusing on issues of governmental responsibility, democratic authority, moral and political responsibility and the psychological state of those who rule. Utilizing a very precise dramatic structure and language, he delved deep into the psychology of his characters. His most important play is the 1978 drama *Sitt al-Mulk* dealing with the moral and intellectual testing of a tyrant and based on Egyptian

Fardous Theatre's 1995 production of Linin al-Ramli's *Wagaa Demerr* (*Headache*).

Fahmy el Kholy's 1994 production of Samir Sarhan's *Sabah el Khier Ya Watan* (*Good Morning My Country*) at al-Hadith Theatre.

history. Yussri al-Jundi utilized folk materials and history in the best of his plays. Experimental in form, structure and language, his plays deal with false heroism and the problems of hesitant heroes. One of these works, *al-Yahudi al Ta'ih* (*The Wandering Jew*) looks at physical violence, fanaticism and the power of illusion.

Through the early 1980s a stronger infrastructure was being established, one which represented more effectively the country's artists and arts organizations. A number of specialized theatres were begun, focusing on such areas as children's theatre and touring. As the national economy expanded in the 1980s, new theatre buildings were again being built and old ones were finally being refurbished.

Since the mid-1980s the theatrical movement in Egypt has reflected the many changes that

accompanied the transformation of the country's economic system from state controlled to free market. As a result, the role of the commercial theatre has increased further. Perhaps in response, the Cairo International Festival for Experimental Theatre was established in 1988 to demonstrate that creativity was still an issue. That same year, the new Cairo Opera House was opened and by the 1990s state troupes were again presenting longer and longer seasons. In 1996, for example – the year that Cairo served as Regional Cultural Capital of the Arab world – thirty-eight new productions were seen in the capital along with some two hundred performances of variety shows, dance and circus events. Not counted in this number were the hundreds of commercial theatre performances going on as well.

Structure of the National Theatre Community

The Ministry of Culture through its Organization of Theatrical, Musical and Folk Arts (1960–71) has general responsibility for the operation of all state-supported arts companies. These include supervision of the National Theatre, Cairo Puppet Theatre, National Folk Arts Troupe, Music Theatre, Cairo Symphony and Cairo Chorale. All their performers are on permanent state salaries.

In addition to the many state troupes, Cairo has a large number of commercial theatres which present lighter theatrical fare at prices that can be substantially higher than those of the state theatres. There are approximately three commercial troupes for every theatre supported by the state with audiences for the commercial theatre running about eight times larger than those of the state-supported theatres.

There are also some fifty registered Free troupes which offer their own seasons and stage their own annual festival. These troupes receive little if any subsidy and range in status from professional to semi-professional to amateur groups.

Outside of Cairo, about one hundred theatres in total now exist in many of the country's twenty-six governorates. In many of these areas, the groups are still essentially non-professional operations offering shows on only an occasional basis. Some are affiliated with clubs, societies and universities. The governorates are also

visited on occasion by touring groups from the major cities.

One attempt at widening the base of theatre was the establishment of a touring group, the Popular Theatre, in 1947. Following the 1952 revolution, five branches of the company were set in operation, two to stage plays in the eight governorates of Upper Egypt and three in the governorates of Lower Egypt and the coastal cities. The experiment failed, however, as the actors refused to stay away from Cairo for extended periods.

In the 1960s, a series of cultural centres (cultural palaces) were established by the Ministry of Culture in the provinces with facilities suitable to receiving visiting troupes including performances by the Popular Theatre. Eventually provincial troupes were formed in the capital cities of each governate starting with Alexandria. Essentially non-professional or semi-professional operations, these companies are still given material and artistic aid by the Ministry of Culture, access to texts and directors as well as financial incentives to enable them to present two plays a year for thirty performances each. The shows are then offered free to the public. Through the late 1960s and 1970s, folk dance and folk music groups were established in the governorates.

The Cairo International Experimental Theatre Festival is held annually in early September.

During the festival, sixty to seventy plays from about thirty-five different countries are presented in about twenty locations in Cairo. Programmes are changed every second night. Seminars and meetings are held for the participants and the Egyptian theatre community.

Egypt boasts the oldest Arab theatre union – the Arab Artistic Syndicate which was established in 1955. There are also unions for theatre, music and film people and a General Union which links them together on major issues. A National Theatre Research Centre is involved in the collection of theatre materials and organizes regular exhibitions. Egypt is a member of the International Theatre Institute.

Artistic Profile

Companies

The country's oldest continuously operating company is the National Theatre, formed in 1953 as an amalgamation of the Egyptian Troupe for Acting and Music (founded 1942) and the Modern Theatre. Named the National Theatre in 1958, it has generally kept to a policy of staging indigenous plays, world classics and modern plays from the international repertoire. Working from Al Azbakia Theatre in Cairo, the company has staged works by virtually every major Egyptian dramatist including 'Ashur, Faraj, Idris, Rushdi, Wahba and al-Hakīm. Most of the company's directors have been Egyptians who had been trained or completed their studies abroad. Funded totally by the state, the National in 1998 had a resident company of a hundred and seventy-three people – ninety-two actors, eight directors, twenty-one designers and fifty-two administrators and staff.

The Pocket Theatre, founded by Saad Ardash (b. 1924), presented its first play in December 1962 – Samuel Beckett's *Endgame* – directed by Ardash. The production aroused controversy about the suitability of absurdist theatre for Egyptian society, particularly as the theatre's next production was Ionesco's *The Chairs*. The absurdist style nevertheless influenced a number of local dramatists including Tawfiq al-Hakīm who wrote *Ya Tali' al-Shajara* (*The Tree Climber*, 1962) in this style; it was presented by the Pocket Theatre in March 1964. Two other absurdist plays by Shawqi Abd al-Hakim (b. 1932) were also staged by the theatre – *Shafiqa wa Mitwalli* (1961) and *al-Mustakhabbi* (*What Is Hidden*, 1963) – plays inspired by the author's interest in Egyptian folk heritage.

The Pocket Theatre later expanded its repertoire by staging the first Egyptian translations of Chekhov, Brecht and Lorca. In the 1964–5 season Karam Mutawwa (1933–96) took over the theatre's management, put together a new company and staged Chekhov's *The Cherry Orchard* and Aristophanes' *The Frogs*. The following season the company staged works by Japanese, Italian and German dramatists as well as a new play by Najib Surer (1932–78), *Bahiya Khabirini*. The company was renamed the Vanguard Theatre in 1969 and a series of actor-directors took over its management, among them Ahmed Zaki (b. 1930), Ahmed Abdul Halim (b. 1931) and Samir al-Asfuri (b. 1937). The company has continued to operate into the 1990s presenting plays of an experimental nature, both indigenous and in translation including Peter Weiss's *Marat/Sade* which also exercised a significant influence on Egyptian dramatists.

In 1962, Cairo Television established three different troupes to help it fill its hours of transmission. Called Renaissance, Liberty and Peace, in their first season they presented four plays including one by Tawfiq al-Hakīm, *al-Ushsh al-Hadi'* (*The Peaceful Nest*). Others were based on well-known novels by Ihsan Abdul Qudus, Abdul al-Rahmani al-Sharqaw and Yussif al-Sebaei. In 1964, the three groups were expanded to ten divided into four branches – the Modern Theatre, Al Hakīm Theatre, Comic Theatre and World Theatre.

The Modern Theatre focused on plays by new dramatists while Al Hakīm Theatre specialized in works by leading Egyptian playwrights such as Rashad Rushdi, Lutfi al-Khuli, Mikhail Ruman, Najib Surer and Ali Salim as well as contemporary plays by international writers. The works of Ali Salim were particularly popular in the Comic Theatre for their sharp social criticism and strong political criticism, surpassing all standards to that time. Ultimately the World Theatre group ceased operations in 1967 since

Ahmed Zaki's 1969 production of Peter Weiss's *El Ghoul* (*The Lusitanian Bogey*) at the Pocket Theatre.

the most avant-garde new work was being done by the Pocket Theatre, international classics by the National Theatre and the most interesting contemporary works by Al Hakīm Theatre.

Other companies of note have included the Theatre Lights Trio, which operated from 1968 to 1995; the Art Theatre Troupe (founded in 1969 as Omar al-Khayyam troupe) and for many years under the direction of Jalal al-Sharqawi (b. 1935), later the dean of the Higher Institute for Dramatic Arts; the Egyptian Comedy Troupe formed in 1969 by Muhamad Awad (1932–97); the Art Studio Troupe formed in 1977 by Muhamad Subhi (b. 1949) which, for many years, had Linin al-Ramli (b. 1946) as its resident playwright; and the Nijime Troupe, founded in 1982 by the popular actor Muhamad Nijime.

A number of troupes have worked experimentally since the 1960s and 1970s. Among these have been the Abbas Ahmad Troupe in Suez, which has tried to incorporate such folk forms as the *samir* (communal chat) in its work, and the Audio Theatre of Intissar Abdul Fatah (b. 1953) which has looked into the use of sound as the base for theatre and has been influenced by some of the experiments of the Pole, Jerzy Grotowski.

When television entered the field of theatrical production in 1961, the commercial Saa Li Qalbak Troupe was taken on as television's Comedy Troupe. When television ceased supporting the group, the actors simply stepped back into live performance and, having established a major following on television, became even more popular than ever. Several actors in this company have become major stars.

A commercial company of note is the Troupe of United Artists, founded in 1966. One of the country's largest commercial operations, it performs in two large theatres in Cairo as well as in a large summer theatre in Alexandria. Most of its shows run for several years with Samir Khafaja (b. 1930) and Bahjat Qamar (1937–80) its resident dramatists.

A few words must be said here about Egyptian *mahbazhateya* (improvised comedy), which has a history going back to the thirteenth century. *Mahbazhateya* groups were widespread and they performed at a wide range of events from circuses to memorial celebrations, from national holidays to parties given by the wealthy. In 1815, Pellzoni, an Italian traveller, wrote about seeing two such comedies at a marriage celebration held in Shubra. In the

1830s, the Englishman Edward Lane wrote of such shows staged at a party held by Mohamed Ali on the occasion of the circumcision of one of his children. Lane's description of the shows appeared in his book *The Modern Egyptians* and his description was confirmed by the French traveller Gerard de Nirval who watched the same shows and described them in his book *A Trip to the East*.

Among the major modern comedians whose work reflected the improvisatory styles are Naguib el-Rehany, Fouad el-Mohandes (b. 1924) and Abdel Moneim Madbouly (b. 1922). Abdel el-Emam (b. 1940) took over from these earlier stars and enriched the private theatre sector with creations based on contemporary characters and social or political problems.

More literary inheritors of this tradition include the duo of playwright Linin al-Ramli and comedian and theatrical director Mohamed Sobhy. Starting their joint theatrical life with the play *El Fares* (*The Knight and the Prisoner*), a social comedy, they later formed their own troupe, Studio 80, which presented six successful comedies. Among them were *Inta Hor* (*You Are Free*, in 1983), *El Hammagy* (*The Barbarian*, 1985), *Weghet Nadhar* (*A Point of View*, 1991) and *Bel Arabi El Faseeh* (*In Plain Classical Arabic*, 1992).

Dramaturgy

Until the first decade of the twentieth century, the indigenous playwright was all but missing in the Egyptian theatre. With the exception of the plays of al-Qabbani, which were mostly drawn from *The Thousand and One Nights*, Arab and Islamic history, and three plays by Ismail Assim (1844–1919) in the 1890s, the great majority of plays that existed were translations from European classics by such dramatists as Sophocles, Shakespeare, Molière, Racine and Hugo. Foremost among the translators of these plays were Salim al-Naqqash, Najib al-Hadad (1867–99) and Muhamad Usman Jalal (1829–96) who adapted a number of plays by Molière into *zajal*, an iambic verse form.

But in the first two decades of the twentieth century came a new generation of writers who found real interest in the dramatic form. Foremost among them was Farah Antun who wrote *Masr al Jadidah wa Masr al Qadimah* (*New Egypt and Old Egypt*, 1913), the first play to tackle social problems. He later wrote *Salah al-Din wa Mamlakat Arushlim* (*Salah al-Din and the Kingdom of Jerusalem*, 1915), a play

about the Crusades from the Arab standpoint, and translated a number of classic works including *Oedipus Rex*, and five operettas for the Munira al-Mahdia Troupe.

Abbas Allam (1889–1949) wrote a number of social plays between the two world wars on the problems facing the Egyptian family – particularly divorce. The first of these was *Asrar al Qusur* (*Secrets of Palaces*, 1915). He also adapted and translated several farces and wrote one play about Arabs in Andalusia entitled *Abdul Rahman al Nassir*. His plays were performed by the Okasha Troupe, Victoria Moussa Troupe, Fatimah Rushdie Troupe and the National Troupe.

Muhammad Taymur, the pioneer of realism in Egyptian theatre, dealt in his plays *Al Usfur fil Qafass* (1918) and *Abdul Sattar Iffindi* (1918) with family problems such as the generation gap and the henpecked husband. In *Al Hawia* (*Identity*, 1921) he dealt with the problem of addiction. In *Al Ashra al Tayiba* (*The Good Ten*, 1918) he satirized the injustices of the Turkish viceroys in Egypt.

Ibrahim Ramzi focused many of the incidents in his plays on Egyptian and Arab history, particularly the Fatimid dynasty, including *Bint al Ikhshid*, *Al Hawari* and *Abtal al Mansura* (*Heroes of Mansura*). He also wrote several social plays such as *Jarkhat al Tifl* (*A Baby's Cry*). In total he translated and adapted seventeen European plays.

Other playwrights of note from this period include Ibrahim al Masri (1900–79), Antun Yazbak (1876–1933), Yunis al Qadi (1888–1969), Muhamad Abdul Qudus (1888–1969), Ahmad Zaki al Sayid and Farid Abu Hadid (1893–1967) who undertook the first experiment in translating into free verse. The poet Khalil Mutran (1872–1948) should be noted here for translating into Arabic (from French) a number of Shakespeare's plays.

The poet Ahmad Shawqi is credited as being the founder of the Arabic verse play. He wrote his first play *Ali Bik Al Kabir* (*Ali Bey the Great*) on Mameluke history in 1893, revising it in 1921. Between 1926 and 1932 he wrote a number of verse tragedies in the Romantic style – including *Masraa Kilyubatra* (*The Fall of Cleopatra*), *Qambiz* (*Cambyses*, 1931), *Majnun Layla* (*The Mad Lover of Layla*, 1931), '*Antara* (1932) and *Amirat al-Andalus* (*Princess of Andalusia*, 1932) – and two comedies, *Al-Sitt Huda* (*Lady Huda*) and *Al Bakhil* (*The Miser*).

Tawfiq al-Hakīm, without doubt the most important writer produced by the Egyptian theatre and perhaps by the entire Arab world, began his playwriting career in the 1930s. His work raised Arabic drama to the level of world literature and it is primarily because of al-Hakīm that the drama became an academically recognized literary form. His 1933 play *Ahl al Kahf* dealt with the finite qualities of humanity and was presented by the National Troupe as its inaugural performance in 1935. He later wrote a number of short plays which were published in the weekly newspaper *Akhbar al Yawm* between 1945 and 1949. His plays – *Shahrazad* (1943), *Barakassa aw Mushkilat al Hukm* (*Barakassa, Or the Problem of Ruling*), *Pygmalion* (1942), *Sulayman al-Hakim* (*Solomon the Wise*, 1943) and *Oedipus* (1949) – all dealt with the conflict between spirit and matter, humanity's conflict with the environment and fate. During the 1960s and 1970s he wrote a large number of plays with direct social and political relevance but he also wrote such humanist dramas as *Ya Tali' al-Shajara* (*The Tree Climber*) and *al-Ta'am li Kull Fam* (*Food for Every Mouth*, 1963), the former about art and material things and influenced by Theatre of the Absurd, the latter dealing with science and its human responsibilities. He wrote plays through the early 1970s at a furious pace, completing sixty before his death in 1987 at the age of 89. His most consistent themes include modernization (especially in the Arab world), government and its problems, and the duality of spirit and matter. Stylistically, his work ranged from the absurd to symbolism to realism.

A new generation of dramatists appeared in the 1940s following al-Hakīm's lead. Among them were the poet Aziz Abaza, Mahmud Taymur (1894–1973) – the younger brother of Muhammad Taymur – and 'Ali Ahmad Bakathir (1910–69), who came from Yemen and acquired Egyptian nationality in 1945 (*see also* YEMEN). Abaza followed more in the footsteps of Shawqi than al-Hakīm in his adherence to traditional rhymed verse, attention to verbal grandiloquence and rhetoric and dramatic lyricism. Abaza wrote ten plays between 1943 and 1963, seven of which were based on Arab history, dealing particularly with decisive periods and major historical turning points. His first play was *Qaiss wa Lubna* (*Qaiss and Lubna*, 1943), a well-known story of thwarted love. Other important plays of his which followed included *al-Abbasa* (1947), *Al-Nasir* (1949), *Shajarat al-Dur* (1951), *Ghurub al-Shams* (*Sunset*,1952), *Shahriyar* (1955), *Qafilat al-Nur* (*Caravan of Light*, 1959) and *Qaysar*

(1963), his version of the Julius Caesar story. He also wrote two contemporary plays, *Awraq al-Kharif* (*Autumn Leaves*, 1957) and *Zahra* (1969). Through his work, poetry and drama moved toward a closer union.

Mahmud Taymur was a novelist and short-story writer before he turned to playwriting. He wrote a number of one-act pieces and then turned to the full-length play creating fifteen works during the 1940s and 1950s. Working in a number of genres and styles, he wrote historical plays, plays based on legends and plays of contemporary social criticism. Mahmud Taymur's major historical plays include *Hawwa' al-Khalida* (*Eternal Eve*, 1945), *Al-Yawm Khamr* (*Wine Today*, 1945), *Ibn Jala* (1950), *Saqr Quraysh* (*The Hawk of Quraysh*, first performed in Tunis in 1955) and *Tariq al Andalus* (*Tariq of Andalusia*). His plays based on legend include *Uruss al-Nil* (*Bride of the Nile*, 1941) and *Ashtar min Iblis* (*Cleverer than Satan*, 1953) while his contemporary social plays include *Al Makh ba' 13* (*Air Raid Shelter 13*, 1941), *Qanabil* (*Bombs*, 1943), *Kadhib fi Kadhib* (*Lie After Lie*, 1951) and *al-Muzayyfun* (*The Falsifiers*, 1953). Taymur's style is characterized by elegant writing, characters with strong psychological motivations and a very sound dramatic structure.

'Ali Ahmad Bakathir was influenced in most of his plays by history, both ancient and modern. Yet these plays – *Ikhnato and Nefertiti* (1940) and *Harut and Marut* (1962) – also have a contemporary political level to them and are a response to contemporary political events. In his play *Al-Hakim Bi Amr Allah* (1948), for example, he deals with notions of self-importance as the play traces the life of an eccentric Fatimid Caliph who comes to believe that he is God. Bakathir deals with more contemporary political issues in *Ilah Isra'il* (*God of Israel*), *Shaab Allah al-Mokhtar* (*God's Chosen People*), *Shylock al Jadid* (*The New Shylock*), *Musmar Juha* (*The Nail of Juha*, 1951) and *'Imbraturiyah fil Nazaad* (*Empire on Auction*), the last an attack on Zionist and imperialist scheming. Among his social comedies are *Qutat wa Firan* (*Cats and Mice*) and *Julfadan Hanim* (*Lady Julfadan*, 1962). Writing almost exclusively in classical Arabic, his translation of Shakespeare's *Romeo and Juliet* was entirely written in free verse.

Abdul al-Rahmani al-Sharqaw, a poet and short-story writer and later chair of the Afro-Asian People's Solidarity Organization, was an innovator in the area of poetic drama. His play

Ma'sat Jamila (*The Tragedy of Jamila*, 1962) is the first original Egyptian play written in free verse though it is interspersed with lyrics and lengthy monologues. The play deals with the Algerian people and their sacrifices in the struggle against French colonialism as seen through the struggle of militant female fighter, Jamila. His later plays range from political dramas about contemporary Egypt and the Arab struggle generally to historical works about injustice, corruption and treachery. The tragedy *al-Fata Mahran* (*Mahran's Chivalry*) is generally agreed to be his best play. In it, he questions the revolutionary hero who deviates from the revolution to serve the emir.

Najib Surur, a director and actor, used the poetic drama to portray the epic struggle of the Egyptian people against feudalism in *Yassin wa Bahiya* (*Yassin and Bahiya*, 1964) and against imperialism and occupation forces in *Ah, ya leil ya Qamar* (*Oh Night, Oh Moon*, 1968). He deals with the factors that led to the defeat of 1967 and the frustration of the intellectual in *Qulu li Ain Al Shams* (*The Eye of the Sun*, 1973). His 1984 drama *Minein Ajib Nass* (*Where Can I Find the Right People*) deals with political corruption. His language is simple, colloquial, colourful and filled with dense suggestive imagery. He is generally considered to be a descendant of the Egyptian colloquial poets such as Badie Khairi and Bairam al Tunisi (d. 1961).

Salah Abdal-Sabur (1931–81) was one of the more innovative of theatrical poets. Influenced by T.S. Eliot, he wrote six plays, mostly characterized by symbolic realism. Sabur, both a critic and dramatist, focuses on the tragedy of vanquished individuals in his work. *Ma'sat al-Hallaj* (*The Tragedy of al-Hallaj*) deals with the dilemma of the intellectual when he turns from the word to action while *Layla wa'l Majnun* (*Layla and the Madman*, 1970) deals with the inability of the poet to take action. His major plays are strong and dramatically effective while his later work was obscure and experimental. His work is considered the most accomplished Arabic poetic drama to date. Other slightly later writers working in the genre of poetic drama include Shawqi Kamis (b. 1936), Mahran Al Sayid and Farouk Juweida.

At the same time as these men were looking at new poetic forms, many others were turning to more realistic genres. Nu'man 'Ashur, for example, wrote sixteen plays, most of them socially critical, using the realistic mode. His plays are a history of the Egyptian family from the 1940s through the 1980s and follow the movement of social classes during this period. By showing elements of family life and the conflicts between generations, he brings to light moral, intellectual and social relationships along with changes in societal values. These are the major themes in his early plays including *al-Maghmatis* (*The Trickcylist*), *il Nas illi Taht* (*The People Who Live Downstairs*), *il Nas illi Fuq* (*The People Who Live Upstairs*), *A'ilat al-Dughri* (*The Dughri Family*, 1963) and *Wabur al Tahin* (*The Flour Hill*, 1965). Starting with *Bilad Barra* (*Straight from Europe*, 1967) 'Ashur becomes concerned with observing the problems of the younger generation which had lost its attachment to the homeland and the effects of the economic open-door policy which began to corrupt the integrity of both family and society. Similar ideas can be seen in his plays *Burj al Madabigh* (*The Tower*, 1976), *Lebat al Zaman* (*The Toy*, 1983) and *Mulid wa Sahibihi Ghayib* (1985).

Yusuf Idris, a novelist and journalist, began his playwriting career by dealing with social and nationalist issues in his play *Jumhuriat Farahat* (*Farahat's Republic*, 1957), a one-act idealistic drama in which the values of justice and liberty prevail. He followed this the same year with *Malik al Coton* (*King of Cotton*), a play about a peasant's struggle against feudal values, and *Al Lahza al Harija* (*The Critical Moment*, 1958) about national resistance in Port Said in 1956. His later works change form as well as content striving for a vision of a new social system. *Al Farafir* (*The Lost Ones*, 1964) seeks to root itself in folk art, while in *Al Mahzala al Ardia* (*Earthy Comedy*, 1966) he turns to metaphysics and the relativity of truth. The play also focuses on the nature of ownership as the root of conflict. Two plays from the 1970s look at totalitarianism – *Al Mukhatatin* (*Stripped Bare*, 1970) and *Al Jins al Thalith* (*The Third Sex*, 1971), a play about a super-being and a new way of improving personal relationships. In all these works, Idris directs his fierce criticism and biting satire at modern society in a mix of abstractionism, surrealism and improvised comedy.

Alfred Faraj, another playwright of note, began his career as a critic and a writer of short stories. Utilizing Arab literary tradition generally as well as both ancient and modern Egyptian history, his first major success was with *The Thousand and One Nights*. His later full-length plays reveal a continuing search for political and social justice – *Suqut Farun* (*A*

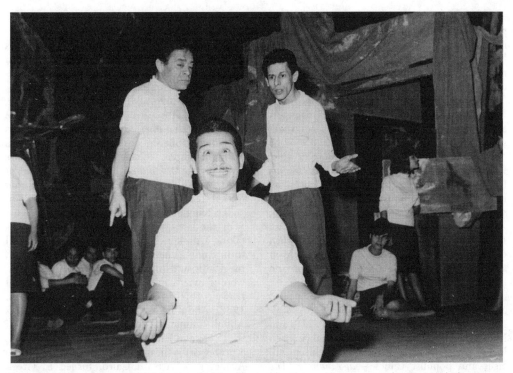

Al Farafir (*The Lost Ones*, 1964) by Yusuf Idris, directed by Karam Mutawwa at the National Theatre.

Pharaoh's Downfall, 1957), *Soliman al Halabi* (1965), *Al Zir Salim* (1967) and *Rassa'il Qadi Ashbilia* (*Messages from the Judge of Seville*, 1975). One of the few plays by Faraj in which justice does prevail is a comedy, *Hallaq Baghdad* (*The Barber of Baghdad*), in which the sultan arrives in time to set things right.

Another important dramatist is Rashad Rushdi, a professor of English literature, editor of several Egyptian literary magazines and one-time chair of the Academy of Arts. His plays focus on the inner truth of individuals as seen through the experiences and conflicts of the human psyche. Fate seems to pursue the individual in his plays through the present and into the future and cannot be avoided. These ideas are paramount in *al-Farasha* (*The Butterfly*), *Lu'bat al-Hubb* (*Love's Game*), *Rihla Kharij al-Sur* (*A Journey Outside the Wall*), *Khayal al-Zil* (*Shadow Theatre*, 1965), *Halawat Zaman* (*Sweetness of the Past*, 1967) and *Nur al Zalam* (*The Light of Darkness*, 1971). His plays became much more political and social in *Itfaraj ya Salam* (*See and Wonder*, 1966) and *Baladi ya Baladi* (*My Beloved Country*, 1968). The former portrays a confrontation between the people and despotic rulers during the age of the

Mameluks while the latter deals with human passivity in the face of invasion.

A one-time police officer who later turned to journalism and ultimately literature, playwright Sa'd al-Din Wahba ultimately occupied several leading positions in the Ministry of Culture and served as chair of the national film union. His early plays tend to focus on the question of who rules and how, the relation of the ruled to the ruler. Such themes are seen clearly in *Al Mahrussa* (*The Protected*, 1961), *al-Sibinssa* (*The Third Class*, 1963) and *Kubri al-Namus* (*Mosquito Bridge*, 1964). These works show the inevitability of the 1952 Revolution and the oppressiveness of the ruling class. *Sikkat al-Salama* (*The Road to Safety*, 1965) focuses on various social problems of the 1960s, particularly opportunism and corruption that threatened to stop the socialist advance while *Bir al-Sillim* (*The Stairwell*, 1966) portrays the splitting up of a family. *Saba Sawaqi* (1968) and *al-Masamir* (*Nails*, 1969) both deal with the 1967 war and its aftermath while *Al Ustaz* (*The Professor*, 1969) returns to the question of totalitarian rule.

Dramatist Mikhail Ruman was a professor of physics before turning to playwriting and expressionist form. His works focus on the plight of the contemporary Egyptian intellectual not content with society but unable to affect it. Hamdi, the hero of several of his plays, finds himself in constant conflict with corruption, laxness and bureaucracy as well as various forms of political and social oppression. In his first play, *al-Dukhkhan* (*Smoke*, 1962) we meet a frustrated intellectual striving to assert his will while in *Al Wafid* (*The Newcomer*, 1966) he deals with a revolt against totalitarian rule. Ruman's 1967 drama *Al Muar wa Al Ma'jur* (*The Borrowed and the Hired*) focuses on bureaucracy and administrative corruption with *al-Ardhalji* (*The Petition Writer*, 1968) looking at the falseness behind society's shining façades. *Laylat Masraa Guevara* (*The Night They Killed Guevara*, 1969), one of his last plays, looks at the confrontation between neo-colonialism and liberation movements.

Other playwrights of note from this period are Mahmud Diyab, Ali Salim, Shawqi Abd al-Hakim, Mustafa Mahmud (b. 1922) and Mustafa Bahjat. Diyab, early on a legal counsellor, deals in his early work with Egyptian villages and populist values – *al-Zawba'a* (*The Storm*) – while in his later work he takes a contemporary view of Arab history where the significance of victory is incomplete without social justice.

Ali Salim looks at questions of corruption within a framework of legend, fantasy and real-life events in such plays as *il Nas illi fi'l-Sama' l-Tamina* (*People of the Eighth Heaven*, 1966) and *Amaliyat Nuh* (*Noah's Journey*, 1975). He deals with political oppression and freedom of thought in plays such as *Kumidiya Udib: Inta illi Qatalt il-Wahsh* (*The Comedy of Oedipus: You Killed the Beast*) and *Bakalurius fi Hukm al Shu'ub* (*BA in Ruling Peoples*, 1979).

Another dramatist taking a non-realistic approach in his works is Shawqi Abd al-Hakim whose plays reveal a psychological expressionism rooted in folk forms – sayings, legends, verses and tales. His plays focus on fate and destiny using an internal conflict and a dialogue connected to dream and the unconscious. One of his best works is the drama *Al Aayian* (*The Sick One*, 1968) dealing with fate, truth, destiny and class conflict.

Mustafa Mahmud went from a career in medicine to a career as a full-time writer. Deeply immersed in Islamic studies, his plays have a philosophical bent. In *Al Shaytan Yaskun fi Beitina* (*Satan Lives in Our House*, 1976) he calls on a Sufi mystic to leave his philosophical isolation and participate in the building of the new society.

The last of the important 1960s and 1970s dramatists to be discussed here is Mustafa Bahjat, a mathematics professor whose best dramatic work was done between 1965 and 1975. Several of his plays are trials of the social system, challenges to those who rule. Influenced by the work of Eugène Ionesco and Samuel Beckett, his heroes confront the absurdity of life as well as the hidden forces which control them. In Bahjat's best plays – *Muhakamat Eilat Dabash* (*Trial of the Dabash Family*, 1971) and *Zumuruda* (1974) – dreams mingle with reality with the language being an eloquent classical Arabic.

By the late 1970s, Egyptian playwriting was taking a darker and slightly more experimental turn. Among the major dramatists writing into the 1980s and (in some cases) into the 1990s, were Fawzi Fahmi, Nabil Badran, Ra'fat al Duweiri (b. 1937), Abdul Aziz Hammouda (b. 1938), Abdul Ila al Salamuni (b. 1941), Mahfuz Abdul Rahman (b. 1932), Mohamed Salamawi (b. 1942) and Fat'hia al Assal (b. 1933). Fahmi, a professor of theatre and later president of the Academy of Arts in Cairo, turned to Greek legend for his first plays – Oedipus in *Awdat al Gha'ib* (*Return of Oedipus*, 1977) and Andromache in *Al Faris wal Assira* (*The Knight and the Prisoner*). Later turning to Arab history in *Lebat al Sultan* (*The Sultan's Game*, 1986), he looks at issues of exploitation while using *saja*, a classical rhymed verse. Nabil Badran's plays, particularly *Alam Ali Baba* (*The World of Ali Baba*, 1976) and *Juha Bae Himarihi* (*Juha Sold His Donkey*, 1985, a work based on *The Thousand and One Nights*), deal with the effect of political decisions on the masses. Ra'fat al Duweiri has been much more experimentally eclectic in his work dealing with Greek legend – *Leih . . . Leih* (*Why . . . Why*, 1984) – in his early work and to the existential absurd later on in *Wiladah Muteasirah* (*Difficult Birth*).

Abdul Aziz Hammouda, dean of the Faculty of Arts at Cairo University, turned to Pharaonic legend using non-Aristotelian forms as well as the Arabic *rawi* (narrative tradition). Relations between rulers and the ruled as seen from the viewpoint of the people is a basic issue in many of his plays: *Al Nass fi Tieba* (*The People of Thebes*, 1981), *Al Raha'in* (*The Hostages*, 1982), *Leilat al Kulunil al Akhira* (*The Colonel's Last Night*, 1983) and *Ibn al Balad* (*The Countryman*, 1987). This last play is about a populist leader who tries unsuccessfully to exploit his friendship with the ruler.

Abdul Aziz Hammouda's *Ibn al Balad* (*The Countryman*), directed in 1988 by Ahmed Zaki at the National Theatre.

Another writer dealing with issues of rulers and the ruled is Abdul Ila al Salamuni, a one-time professor of philosophy and later a government cultural employee. His play *Al Tha'r wa Mhlut al Adhab* (*Revenge and the Journey of Suffering*, 1982) uses the ancient Arab poet Imru' Al Qaiss as a symbol for those who are subjected to public pressure while his drama 'Rajul fil Qalan (*The Man in the Citadel*, 1987) deals with a ruler who by ignoring the will of the people loses his legitimacy.

The plays of Mahfuz Abdul Rahman use a unique type of dialogue, terse and direct, within what appears to be a traditional form. He deals with democracy and corruption in *Hafla Ala Al Khazuq* (*Party on a Spike*, 1983) and collusion and materialism in *Ariss li Bint al Sultan* (*A Husband for the Sultan's Daughter*, 1987). Mohamed Salamawi looks at social oppression and bureaucratic pressures in his best plays, among them *Itnein Taht al Ard* (*Two Underground*, 1987) and *Al-Ganzir* (*The Chain*, 1996). His plays tend toward an absurdist style.

One of the few female dramatists in the country is Fat'hia Al-'Assal (b. 1933) who began her dramatic career writing for television. Her most important plays are *Nisa' bila Aqnia*

(*Women Without Masks*, 1982) and *Sijn al-Nisa'* (*Women's Prison*, 1993) in which issues of female oppression are examined including the problem of fear of the response of the men around her.

Directors, Directing and Production Styles

Until the 1930s, trained directors did not exist and staging was generally left to the leading actor. In the late 1930s, Aziz Eid became the first autonomous director in the Egyptian theatre creating a new respect for the art among actors and audiences. Following him was the French-trained director Zaki Tulaymat, who was concerned in his productions with establishing a directorial methodology focusing on performance qualities including voice and gesture and proper research into character. An inspirational figure, he encouraged many young people to try their hands at staging plays and the best were sent abroad on scholarships returning home to assume the leadership of many theatres in the 1960s. Their influence was still being felt in the work of many directors in the 1990s.

Later Fatuh Nashati (1901–74) began a trend

Ahmad Abdul Halim's 1998 production of Alfred Faraj's *El Tayeb Wa El Shereer* (*The Good and the Bad*) at al-Hadith Theatre.

toward more autonomous work which would often dazzle audiences. Another director who trained abroad was Mahmoud al-Sabbaa (1911–89). Sabbaa learned his craft in England in the late 1930s and later worked for the Vanguard Theatre and Comic Theatre.

Starting after World War II came a generation of academically trained and artistically qualified directors, some of whom learned their skills in the west and some of whom were trained under professors of theatre in Egypt. This second generation is best represented by Nabil al-Alfi (b. 1926) and Hamdi Gheith (b. 1922) who both studied in France between 1949 and 1951.

Nabil al-Alfi's work leaned toward symbolism and among his most prominent works were Molière's *Don Juan*, al-Hakīm's *Isis* and Fahmi's *Lebat al Sultan*. Later a professor in the Higher Institute of Dramatic Arts, he was one of the first Egyptians to establish an effective methodology in this field. Gheith began his career working in a poetic style but eventually moved toward more and more abstraction.

The next generation of directors emerged in the 1960s and 1970s and can be divided into two groups. The first group – represented by Kamal Yassin (1922–87), Mohamed Abdul Aziz, Hungarian-trained Kamal Eid (b. 1932), French-trained Hussein Jumaa (b. 1925), Italian-trained Saad Ardash and Farouk al-Damardash (b. 1933) – represent a realistic trend with the stage considered as simply a segment of life and the theatre simply an attempt at imitating it. Ardash later began producing the plays of Brecht and moved into a more stylized approach to theatre.

The second group – Jalal al-Sharqawi (b. 1934) Italian-trained Karam Metawa (1934–97), British-trained Ahmed Zaki (b. 1930) and Ahmad Abdul Halim – focused on more innovative and modernistic approaches including total theatre, docu-drama, folkloric narrative and visual elements. For these directors, theatre was not simply the reproduction of life through art but the creation of another level of life, an independent reality. Metawa stood out for his total control over his productions and his directorial contribution to political theatre while Zaki, on his return from studying in England, managed the Puppet and Children's Theatre and later the Pocket Theatre. His work reflected an interest in the concept of 'total

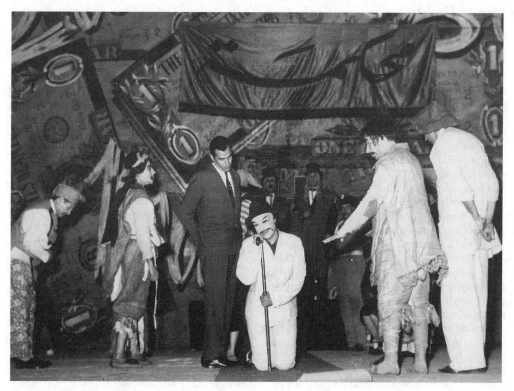

Saad Ardash's 1967 production of *The Good Person of Setzuan* at Al Hakīm Theatre.

theatre' including bare stage productions and an emphasis on the actor–audience relationship.

Fayez Halawah (b. 1932) wrote and directed his own plays in the private sector for his wife Taheya Karioka's troupe. His work generally reflected current political events and he was among the few directors to work within a framework of dramatic irony. Among those later directors who stood out were Samir El Asfoury (b. 1940), who used Egyptian and Arab heritage subjects in his work, and Abdel Rahman El Shafei (b. 1939) who in his search for folk roots used singers and musicians from the Egyptian countryside.

Serious acting methodology began just prior to World War I through the pioneering work of George Abyad, Abdul Rahman Rushdie and Yusuf Wahbi. Abyad regarded the actor's voice as all-important and worked with actors on developing a melodious delivery. His work was influenced by Arab oratory and the musicality of the French language. Rushdie, in contrast, stressed deep and heavy emotions while Wahbi

favoured absorption into the role following to a great extent the methodology of the French actor Constant Coquelin.

A new stage followed World War II when the ideas of the Russian director and teacher Konstantin Stanislavski began to become popular. First seen in American film acting in the late 1940s, the style became the basis for work at the Higher Institute for Dramatic Arts. Later, young Egyptian actors travelled abroad to study the Stanislavski system and brought the more subtle elements of it back to Egypt. In the 1960s, Brecht's theories of acting became equally popular.

From the 1970s on came an interest in still other approaches ranging from collective creation to the ideas of Grotowski. By the 1990s, it can be said that the Egyptian theatre was a mélange of styles representing virtually all the forms of acting and genres of drama that exist from the most realistic to the most exaggerated elements of musical-comedy.

Music Theatre
Dance Theatre

In 1869, shortly after the inauguration of the Suez Canal, the Khedive Ishmail, son of Ottoman-born Mohammed Ali, Ruler of Egypt, opened the first Cairo Opera House, a facility modelled on a similar facility in Vienna. With the opening of the Cairo Opera House came visiting performances by European theatre and music troupes from 1870.

Sheikh Salama Hijazi (1852–1917) was another early pioneer of the Egyptian musical theatre. A singer with a dramatic voice, he was an able composer and actor and quickly became the star of the commercial Iskandar Faraj Troupe, a company formed in 1891. In 1905, he started his own company, the Salama Hijazi Troupe. He composed several musical plays, encouraged the translation of foreign plays and staged many popular, high-budget extravaganzas.

Musical performances began connecting to the storyline in the 1920s and several musical theatre troupes began, among them the troupes of Abdullah Okasha, Sayyid Darwish (1892–1923), Munira al-Mahdiyyah (1884–1965), a female singer, and the Malak Opera

Troupe (1940–53). Okasha, a singer and actor in the Salama Hijazi Troupe, began his own troupe in 1911 as a commercial shareholding company called the Company for the Promotion of Arab Dramatic Art; in 1920 it built the Al Azbakiah Theatre, then called the Theatre of Al Azbakiah Gardens. His theatre took the novel step of employing major composers to create incidental dramatic music, among them Sayyid Darwish, Kamil al-Kholei, Daoud Hosni, Ibrahim Fawzi (1890–1952) and Zakaria Ahmad. The company operated until 1928.

The composer Sayyid Darwish had earlier formed his own troupe, the Sayid Darwish Troupe, which operated from 1921. An innovative composer and singer and a pioneer in the recognition of the validity of Arabic music, Darwish took original chants from the Ottoman era and turned them into theatrical compositions expressing human emotions, the daily cares of the people and even nationalist sentiments. Darwish was watered by the same spring from which the 1919 revolution burst: the search for an Egyptian identity, a re-examination of national character in all spheres of life and a resistance to foreign occupation.

Munira al-Mahdiyyah musical troupe operated between 1915 and 1934. Its founder was the most famous singer in the first quarter of the twentieth century and the first Muslim Egyptian woman to appear on a public stage. She was the star of her troupe and was both its best singer and actress. Between 1917 and 1919 she presented a number of European operas translated by Farah Antun and orchestrated by Kamil al-Kholei, among them *Carmen*, *Thaïs* and *Adina*.

Malak Opera Troupe was formed by another female singer and composer, Malak Muhamed (1902–84), in an effort to revive the musical theatre tradition during World War II. The troupe presented about thirty operettas, mostly composed by Malak Muhamed, in which she starred. Many of these included melodies and songs of deep emotion. Among the best of these original works were *Jawahir*, *Arus al Nil* (*Bride of the Nile*) and *Maisah*. The troupe also staged *Madame Butterfly* and *Faust*.

Ali al-Kassar later worked with the well-known writer and translator Amin Sidqi and until 1925 their troupe was known as the Sidqi-al-Kassar Company. When Sidqi split from it in 1925 al-Kassar ran it independently, presenting adapted musical farces until 1949. An outstanding comedian, al-Kassar throughout his career played the role of the Nubian – talkative, lively and impudent, the supporter of lovers, a kind of Arabic Harlequin. Among other important members of the troupe were Ratiba Rushdie, Aqila Ratib (b. 1915) and Hamid Mursi (1900–81).

The Musical Theatre began in 1960 and has produced a large number of operas and operettas in the years since. Its first two productions were both directed by Zaki Tulaymat – the operetta *Yawm al Qiyama* (*The Resurrection*) by Zakaria Ahmad and *Al Baruka* (*The Wig*) by Sayyid Darwish. The company has presented a range of translated operas and operettas including *The Merry Widow*. Among its most successful original musical performances have been *Mahr al Arussa* (*The Bride's Dowry*, 1964), *Hidiyat al Umr* (*The Gift of a Lifetime*, 1966), *Dunia al Pianullah* (*World of the Pianola*, 1975), *Leila min Alf Leila* (*A Night of a Thousand Nights*, 1977), *Misr Baladna* (*Egypt, Our Land*, 1978) and *Zaba'in Jahannam* (*Residents of Hell*, 1979).

After a long period of training under Soviet experts, the National Troupe of Folk Arts began its life in 1963–4 with a series of music and

Chandelier Dance (1993) performed by the Reda Folkloric Troupe at Cairo's Balloon Theatre.

dance performances. Since then it has presented annual seasons at Cairo's Balloon Theatre and at Alexandria's Great Theatre sharing both facilities with the Reda Folkloric Troupe which had been formed privately by the brothers Mahmud Rida (b. 1929) and Ali Rida (1926–93) in 1959. Both companies regularly tour within Egypt and across the region. The troupe is part of the folk arts sector of the Ministry of Tourism.

The Egyptian Modern Dance Theatre Company was founded in 1993 by the Lebanese choreographer Walid Aouni. Aouni had earlier trained with Maurice Béjart.

The Cairo Opera Ballet Company was founded in 1966 and has long been connected to the Higher Institute of Ballet. The company's first production – *The Fountain of Bakchisary* – was choreographed by the then director of the

Reda Dance Group, 1992.

Bolshoi Ballet, Leonid Labrovsky. Among major new works choreographed by Egyptian dancers have been *El-Somoud* (*Steadfastness*) by Abdel-Moneim Kamel about the 1967 war (restaged in 1973), Gamel Abdul-Rahim's *Isis and Osiris* (1984), Attia Sharara's *Egyptian Steps*, Youssri Selim's *Temple Music*, and Omar Khairat's *The Nile*. The company has toured widely playing in the former Soviet Union, Germany and France. Now based at the Cairo Opera House, it has a company of over fifty artists.

Theatre for Young Audiences
Puppet Theatre

Though a miniature puppet theatre was found in a tomb dating from the time of the pharaohs, though indigenous shadow plays can trace their Egyptian roots to the town of Fayoum in the sixteenth century and though the *karagöz* shadow theatre has a long history in Egypt, modern European-style puppet traditions do not have a very long history in the country. It was only in 1958, after the Romanian puppet theatre Tandarica played a short season in Cairo, that interest was spurred in such puppetry, mostly in relation to children's theatre. Two Romanian experts were subsequently recruited by the Ministry of Culture to train Egyptian puppeteers and to ultimately help form an Egyptian puppet theatre.

Puppetry of the Punchinello type was actually seen in Egypt much earlier having been brought with Ibn Danial from Iraq in the thirteenth century. Phantasmagoria scenes came with the trade caravans from Syria and Turkey and spread with the Turkish invasion of Egypt. Both were regularly seen among the shows of travelling artists in markets, squares and street corners. The Punchinello type was done as a form of glove and stick puppetry and was particularly popular in the nineteenth century.

The Romanian-trained Cairo Puppet Troupe

Icarus choreographed by Walid Aouni for the Egyptian Modern Dance Theatre Company, 1993.

began its life in 1959 with a short play entitled *Al Shatir Hassan* (*The Sweet Hassan*) by Salah Jahien (1930–86), a show inspired by *The Thousand and One Nights*. In 1960, the troupe performed in the World Puppet Festival in Bucharest and won an award for its production of *Al Leila Al Kabira* (*The Big Night*). In 1964, the Ministry of Culture created a 371-seat theatre for the troupe in central Cairo and the company has also toured widely. Now composed of more than a hundred people, the company has its own workshops. Performances are held eight to ten times per week, mostly for school groups.

Hossam Atta's 1994 production of Biram al Tunsi's *The Wonderful Well* at the Children's Theatre.

Puppets ultimately became an entry point for the development of an Egyptian children's theatre. In the 1990s children's theatre companies exist not only in Cairo but also in every one of the governorates. The first theatre to emerge in this field was the Children's Theatre, founded in 1964. In 1982, three other children's troupes were formed – the National Children's Theatre, Youth Theatre and Mobile Theatre.

Design

Until the late 1950s, design was not generally considered a key element in the theatrical experience. For the most part, basic design was done by the director with little thought given to symbolic or in many cases even realistic connection to text. The only exception to this was in operas where, at the Egyptian Opera House, design was considered a spectacular element and was usually given over to the control of an Italian designer or an Egyptian designer who had been trained in Italy.

Film and television design tended to be more realistic than stage design but it rarely went beyond the confines of a drawing room. When such designs were required theatres would hire film or television designers but the result was rarely effective. Too often the stage simply ended up filled with props that hindered the movements of the actors and which added nothing to the text.

By the late 1950s, however, a number of gifted artists interested in this area of theatrical art left the country to study design abroad. As they returned to Egypt in the early 1960s, their influence could be slowly felt in the new approaches they brought with them to scenic design. Among this first generation of Egyptian designers was Abdul Fatah al-Bialii (b. 1920), Salah Abdul Karim (1925–88), Ra'uf Abdul Hajid (1930–89) and Omar al-Nadji. At the same time, a number of those who had trained under Italian designers began to free themselves of adherence to the spectacular and began to develop their own design visions. Among the earliest of these were Sakina Muhamad Ali (b. 1933), Abdullah al-Ayuti (b. 1927) and Nuha Barada (b. 1942).

Others trained abroad brought other influences into their work. Among these were Ramzy Mostafa (b. 1926) who studied in the United States, Ahmed Ibrahim (b. 1925) who studied in France and was interested in new forms of realism in both sets and costumes, and Sabry Abdel Aziz (b. 1946) and Samir Hassan (b. 1938) who both studied in Russia and developed a more symbolist and expressionist trend.

The establishment of a department of design at the Higher Institute of Dramatic Arts and a recognition of this field at the Faculty of Fine and Applied Arts at Cairo University saw new generations of Egyptian-trained designers emerge in the decades since. Among the best of these have been Samir Ahmad (b. 1938), Nihad Bahjat, Abdul Moneim Karar (b. 1934), Fawzi al-Saadani (b. 1942), Zosar Marsuq (b. 1943), Majdi Rizq (b. 1939), Ashraf Naim and Muna al-Barudi (b. 1942).

Theatre Space and Architecture

The first theatre to be built in Cairo was the Opera House in 1869, a theatre which lasted until it burned down in 1971. The second was Al Azbakia Theatre which was built in 1871 and was replaced by the New Al Azbakia Theatre in 1920. It is this latter theatre, a proscenium stage house, which currently houses the National Theatre.

In 1922 the Mohamed Ali-Sayid Darwish Theatre was built, a facility used for many years both as a cinema and as a theatre. During the late 1950s and into the mid-1960s, the state turned a number of old cinema houses into legitimate theatres and many of these are still used. At the same time, it built a number of other

Cairo Opera House complex.

Mohamed Omer's 1997 production of *Hekmat Hanem* (*Lady Hekmet*) at the National Theatre.

proscenium spaces including Al Moqattam Theatre (the Floating Theatre), which is located on the banks of the Nile and holds 800, Cairo Puppet Theatre (built in 1964) which holds 371, and a small theatre in the Pharaonic Gardens which holds 100 and which was used by the Pocket Theatre between 1963 and 1969. In 1992, the Hanager Theatre, a traverse stage, was built. There are also a large number of outdoor theatres that are regularly used.

Training

In 1930, a Government Institute of Dramatic Art was opened in Cairo but it closed its doors a year later due to political opposition. It was replaced by a programme of lectures on dramatic art but even this was not supported and the lectures stopped after a single term. Nevertheless, the idea of a theatre school had been planted. In 1944, with the support of Taha Hussein (the dean of Arabic literary studies), director Zaki Tulaymat established the Institute of Dramatic Art (now known as the Higher Institute for Dramatic Arts). With Tulaymat as its first dean, a new generation of actors and intellectuals concerned with the history of the theatre and drama began to appear.

In 1947 a department for musical theatre was added and in 1959 another school operating at a university level called the Arts Academy was established with four-year degree programmes in theatre, music, ballet, Arabic music, folk arts, arts criticism and cinema. The academy offers degrees at the Master's and PhD levels.

There are design departments at the Fine Arts and Applied Arts Institutes. Several universities – including Cairo University, Ain Shams, Helwan and South of the Valley – now have drama departments and there is also one at the American University in Cairo.

Criticism, Scholarship and Publishing

Dramatic criticism began in Egypt as impressionistic writing by journalists unhampered by training and experience. The first critical writer to work from theory and experience was the dramatist Muhammad Taymur, who published a wide range of useful articles on plays and performers between 1917 and 1920 in the magazines *Al Manbar* (*The Lighthouse*) and *Al Sufur* (*Unveiled*). Nevertheless, criticism (or 'art journalism' as it was known then) remained limited to press reviews until at least the early 1940s yet it still had an influence on playwrights, adapters and translators as well as on directors, actors and theatrical producers.

The first specialized magazine on theatre in Egypt was called *Theatre* and was edited by Abdul Majid Hilmi during 1925–7. Muhamad al-Tabei, a leading journalist who frequently travelled to Europe, started his own specialty theatre magazines in the 1930s, *Rose al-Yusuf* and *Akhir Saa* (*Latest News*).

Academic influence began to be felt in the 1940s when cultural magazines and even publishing houses began showing interest in European dramatic literature, particularly in French existential dramas by Jean-Paul Sartre and Molière's comedies. Many of these were translated by Muhamad Mandur Awad. One of Mandur's colleagues, Muhamad Ghuneimi Hilal began writing modern dramatic theory based on these and other western works and it was through these efforts that departments of Arabic language and literature throughout Egypt began to include dramatic literature in their studies. Turning toward modern literature in general, Egyptian universities eventually began to reorient their curricula in this direction eventually graduating a number of distinguished scholars in the field.

Among them was Abdul Qadir al-Qutt who produced the first Egyptian translations of Shakespeare and became the leading expert on Shakespearian text and performance. During the 1940s, two other academicians – Luwis Awad and Ali al-Raei – went to Britain to further their studies in this growing field, which was dominated by the critical ideas of George Bernard

Shaw and T.S. Eliot. Awad's early work was purely theoretical including the first Egyptian translation of Horace's *Ars Poetica* to which he also wrote an important introduction. He later wrote at length on trends in European drama in the 1950s and 1960s including the new plays of John Osborne and Arnold Wesker, the British and French absurdists and other experimental writers. His writings greatly influenced Egyptian dramatists during this period. Ali al-Raei published studies of Shaw and the theory of drama and his work had a more direct influence on dramatists such as Tawfiq al-Hakīm, Alfred Faraj and Sa'd al-Din Wahba. His influence on the theatre continued to increase when he later became head of the governmental theatre organization.

Ahmad Rushdie Salih and Abdul Fatah al-Barudi, two slightly later critics, both studied literature and drama at university and in the Higher Institute for Dramatic Art and subsequently worked as journalists. Salih was primarily interested in the folk connections of literature, performance, music and dramatic form. Barudi's work was more methodological and he urged writers and directors to stay with established methodological bases to ensure effective relations between performer and audience. Through the 1940s, Barudi edited the theatre criticism section of the magazine *Al Thaqafa*. A third critic of note who began to write in the late 1950s was Rashad Rushdi, also a playwright. Chair of the department of English literature at Cairo University, his approach to criticism was based on his belief that neither text nor performance should begin with any preconceived models but should evolve from the needs of the work itself. His writings also showed a keen interest in language and psychological dimension of character.

Egyptian dramatic criticism in this early generation of specialized critics clearly revolved within the orbit of western approaches and theories. In the next decades, this approach would shift to more indigenous modes and from an interest primarily in dramatic literature to an interest in theatrical forms. Leaders in these new approaches were Fuad Dawara, Raja' al-Naqqash and Baha' Tahir. Dawara took a societal and realistic approach to his criticism connecting the dramatic work to events going on within the country and insisting on its social significance. Al-Naqqash too looked for social significance in the work with particular interest in performance, plotting and even design elements. Tahir, while also seeking a social connec-tion, looked most closely at the work of the director as the true master of the theatrical event.

Critics in the late 1960s and 1970s extended these ideas with a variety of new approaches ranging from a total disinterest in dramatic literature (Safinaz Kazim) to a disinterest in social commitment (Amir Iskander and Farouk Abdul Qadir) to a concern with audience reception (Jalal al-Ishri). All, however, sought connections to the indigenous in both performance and script while remaining extremely open to new ideas from abroad ranging from Brechtian *Verfremdungseffekt* and the epic to the Poor Theatre concepts of the Pole Jerzy Grotowski, from the ideas of 'empty space' of Peter Brook to the interest in the establishment of a modern canon espoused by scholars such as Eric Bentley and John Gassner.

Joining with this generation of working critics were a number of playwrights and academics who both wrote and lectured on the need to evolve an Egyptian-based dramatic literature and a theatre rooted in Arabic theatrical form. Among these were Abdul Aziz Hammouda, Samir Sarhan, Muhamad Anani, Fawzi Fahmi, Farouk Abdul Wahab and Nihad Suliha. They extended the work of the theatre critics and connected back to the ideas of Muhamad Mandur Awad and Rashad Rushdi. All helped in the struggle to find an artistic and intellectual identity for the Egyptian theatre. At this time, another scholar-critic, Ibrahim Hamada, with many of these same goals in mind, compiled and published a useful dictionary of dramatic and theatrical terminology in Arabic.

Abdul Aziz Hammouda
with Ahmed Zaki, Samir Awad, Shawky
Kamis, Ahmed Abdel Hameed and
Sami Khashaba

Further Reading

Abdel Wahab, Farouk. *Modern Egyptian Drama: An Anthology*. Minneapolis, MN: Bibliotheca Islamica, 1974. 493 pp.

Abyad, Soad. *George Abyad* [in Arabic]. Cairo: Egyptian Book Organization, 1970.

Abou-Saif, Laila. 'The Theatre of Naguib al-Rihaani: The Development of Comedy in Egypt'. Dissertation, University of Illinois, 1968.

el-Alem, Mahmoud Amin. *Tawfiq al-Hakīm: Intellect and Artist* [in Arabic]. Cairo: Egyptian Book Organization, 1982.

el-Alemay, Adel. *The Zar Ritual and Ritual*

Theatre [in Arabic]. Cairo: Egyptian Book Organization, 1993.

Armbrust, Walter. *Mass Culture and Modernism in Egypt*. New York: Cambridge University Press, 1996. 275 pp.

el-Ashry, Ahmed. *The Hero in the Theatre of the Sixties* [in Arabic]. Cairo: Egyptian Book Organization, 1992.

el-Ashry, Gala. *Theatre: Mother of the Arts* [in Arabic]. Cairo: Egyptian Book Organization, n.d.

Astre, G.A. 'Le théâtre philosophique de Tawfiq al-Hakīm' [The philosophical theatre of Tawfiq al-Hakīm]. *Critique* 66 (1952): 934–45.

Awad, Ramsis. *Bibliographic Encyclopedia of the Egyptian Theatre* [in Arabic]. Cairo: Egyptian Book Organization, n.d.

Badaur, Muhammad Mustafa. *Modern Arabic Drama in Egypt*. Cambridge: Cambridge University Press, 1987. 246 pp.

Bebars, Ahmed Samir. *The Arab Theatre in the Nineteenth Century* [in Arabic]. Cairo: Egyptian Book Organization, 1985.

Brown, Irving. 'The Effervescent Egyptian Theatre'. *Theatre Annual* 21 (1964): 57–68.

Dawara, Fouad. *The Theatre of Tawfiq al-Hakīm* [in Arabic]. 2 vols. Cairo: Egyptian Book Organization, 1984 and 1986.

Dawood, Abdel Ghany. *Zaki Tulaymat* [in Arabic]. Cairo: Egyptian Book Organization, 1997.

Egyptian One-Act Plays. Translated by Denys Johnson-Davies. Pueblo, CO: Passeggiata Press and London: Heinemann, 1981.

Ethman, Ahmed. *Classical Sources of the Theatre of Tawfiq al-Hakīm* [in Arabic]. Cairo: Harib, 1978.

Gad, Leila R. 'The Puppet Theatre in Cairo'. *World Theatre* 14 no. 5 (September–October 1965): 452–3.

Ghany, Mostafa Abdel. *Egyptian Theatre in the Eighties* [in Arabic]. Cairo: Egyptian Book Organization, 1984.

al-Hakīm, Tawfiq. *Theatrical Form* [in Arabic]. Cairo: Egyptian Book Organization, 1968.

Hamada, Ibrahim. *The Shadow Play and the Ibn Daniel Plays*. Cairo: Egyptian Book Organization, 1961.

Hammouda, Abdel Aziz. *The Political Theatre* [in Arabic]. Cairo: Egyptian Book Organization, 1971.

Ismail, Said Ali. *History of the Egyptian Theatre in the Nineteenth Century* [in Arabic]. Cairo: Egyptian Book Organization, 1997.

Kader, Farouk Abdul. *The Rise and Fall of the Egyptian Theatre* [in Arabic]. Cairo: Egyptian Book Organization, n.d.

Khamis, Shawqi. *Children's Theatre* [in Arabic]. Cairo: Egyptian Book Organization, 1995.

Khashaba, Sami. *Contemporary Theatrical Issues* [in Arabic]. Cairo: Dar El Maarif, n.d.

Landau, Jack M. 'On the Beginnings of Theatre in Egypt'. *Hamizrah Hehadash* 2 (summer 1951): 389–91.

——. 'Les théâtres et mystères' [Theatres and mysteries]. *L'Amour de l'Art* (n.d.).

——. *Studies in the Arab Theatre and Cinema* [English and Arabic]. Cairo: Egyptian Book Organization and Philadelphia: University of Pennsylvania Press, 1958.

al-Lozy, Mahmoud, 'Censoring the Censor: The Politics of Satire in Nu'man 'Ashur's *Sima Awanta*'. *Theater Three* (fall 1989): 31–46.

Metawie, Hani A. 'Egyptianizing Theater in Egypt: A Descriptive and Critical Examination of the Clash Between a Quest for Authenticity and a Tendency to Assimilate Western Meta-Theater.' Dissertation, Florida State University, 1985. 361 pp.

Mikkawy, Abdal Ghaffar. 'Neue Wege Agyptischen Theaters' [New style Egyptian theatres]. *Orient* no. 1 (April 1965): 15–19.

Moatty, Mohammed Abdel. 'Il teatro egiziono contemporaneo tra la cultura araba e quella europea' [Contemporary Egyptian theatre between Arabic and European cultures]. *Teatro Oriente/Occidente* (1986): 377–86.

Moreh, Shmuel. 'Hamahazai hamikri Tawfiq al-Hakīm' [Tawfiq al-Hakīm: Egyptian playwright]. *Bamah* 20 nos. 101–2 (1985): 88–95.

Moussa, Fatma, ed. *A Dictionary of the Theatre* [in Arabic]. 5 parts. Cairo: Egyptian Book Organization, 1995–8.

Munir, Samy. *The Egyptian Theatre After World War II* [in Arabic]. Cairo: Egyptian Book Organization, 1978.

'New Cairo Opera House'. *Prism Quarterly of Egyptian Culture* 11 (January–March 1985): 2–4.

Nieuwkerke, Karin van. *A Trade Like Any Other: Female Singers and Dancers in Egypt*. Austin, TX: University of Texas Press, 1995. 226 pp.

Papadopoulo, A. 'La saison théâtrale au Caire' [Theatre season in Cairo]. *Revue de Caire* no. 19 (April 1956): 325–38.

Raghib, Nabil. *Alfred Faraj's Theatre Language* [in Arabic]. Cairo: Egyptian Book Organization, 1985.

——. *Nu'man 'Ashur's Theatre Art* [in Arabic]. Cairo: Egyptian Book Organization, 1982.

——. *Rashad Rushdi's Dramatic Art* [in Arabic]. Cairo: Egyptian Book Organization, 1987.

——. *The Theatre of Social Transformations* [in Arabic]. Cairo: Egyptian Book Organization, 1990.

Ramadan, Abdel M. 'Egypt's Theatre Is International'. *UN World* 5 (March 1951): 61–2.

el-Refai, Mohamed. *Palestine and the Egyptian Theatre* [in Arabic]. Cairo: Egyptian Book Organization, 1995.

——. *A Wagon Called Theatre* [in Arabic]. Cairo: Egyptian Book Organization, 1997.

Sadgrove, Philip. *The Egyptian Theatre in the Nineteenth Century: 1799–1882.* Reading, Berkshire: Ithaca Press and Centre for Middle Eastern and Islamic Studies, University of Durham, 1996. 214 pp.

Sakhoukh, Ahmed. *Egyptian Theatre at the Crossroads* [in Arabic]. Cairo: Egyptian Book Organization, 1995.

Sarhan, Samir. 'The Zar Beat'. *The Drama Review* 25 (winter 1981): 19–24.

Soleiha, Nehad. *Egyptian Theatre* [in Arabic]. Cairo: Egyptian Book Organization, 1993.

——. *Theatre: Between Art and Intellect* [in Arabic]. Cairo: Egyptian Book Organization, 1985.

Starkey, Paul. 'Tawfik al-Hakīm: Leading Playwright of the Arab World'. *Theater Three* (fall 1989): 21–30.

Yalourakis, M. 'Le théâtre égyptien'. *Nea Hestia* (1953).

Zaki, Ahmed. *On Directing* [in Arabic]. Cairo: Egyptian Book Organization, 1978.

——. *The Theatre: A Face and A Mask* [in Arabic]. Cairo: Egyptian Book Organization, 1988.

FEDERAL ISLAMIC REPUBLIC OF THE COMORES

(see **COMOROS ISLANDS**)

FRENCH SOMALILAND

(see **DJIBOUTI**)

FUJAIRAH

(see UNITED ARAB EMIRATES)

HASHEMITE KINGDOM OF THE JORDAN

(see JORDAN)

IRAN

(Asia Volume)

IRAQ

One of the world's most ancient civilizations – connected historically to Sumer and Babylon – modern Iraq shares borders with Turkey to the north, Iran to the east, the Arab Gulf, Kuwait and Saudi Arabia to the south, and Jordan and Syria to the west. Covering an area of 438,300 square kilometres (167,000 square miles), 95 per cent of Iraq's population adheres to some form of Islam with Shiites making up about 60 per cent of the Muslim community and Kurds, who represent close to 19 per cent of the population, and other Arabs making up the rest. The total population in 1995 was about 21.5 million. Arabic is the official language and the first language of about three-quarters of the population with Kurdish the official language in several governorates in the Kurdish region. The national capital is Baghdad.

In the years prior to World War I, Iraq was part of the Ottoman Empire. During the war it was invaded by Britain and in 1920 became a British Mandate. Local unrest, however, resulted in various uprisings. In 1921, Iraq – under the rule of Emir Faisal – became quasi-independent with full independence coming eleven years later. Following Emir Faisal's death in 1933, his son King Ghazi I took power and in 1936 formed an alliance with several other Arab nations. During World War II, Iraq was again occupied by the British but after the war the pro-British government was overthrown and a new government came to power under Abd al-Karim Kassem. In 1963 political turmoil led to five years of civil war between Iraqi Arabs and the country's Kurdish minority. A new government was formed by Ahmed Hasan al-Bakr, who led the country until 1979 when Saddam Hussein became president.

In 1980 Saddam's armies invaded Iran, setting off a conflict that lasted eight years. In 1990, Iraq invaded neighbouring Kuwait, claiming historical sovereignty over this smaller neighbour. United Nations forces, led by the United States, attacked Iraq and, during an intense six-week period, caused significant damage to the country. In 1991 a cease-fire was established and Iraqi forces withdrew from Kuwait. Nevertheless Iraq found itself for most of the 1990s under UN sanctions, which led to political and cultural isolation from much of the international community and which severely hurt the economy, medical services and, not least, the country's theatre and cultural infrastructure.

Iraq's culture historically includes various types of public performances involving poetry, storytelling, dance and music and, in literary terms, dates back to the year 2 BC, the genesis of the nation's most famous cultural creation, the epic poem *Gilgamesh*, a work that is considered the equivalent of Homer's *Iliad* and *Odyssey*. This epic and other religious poetry was recited during holidays and festivals, planting and harvest time, and was linked to invocations and prayers relating to such essential industries as sheep-shearing, and prayers for fertility and victory in war. Such events were performative rather than performance phenomena, events that people participated in to assuage the gods, priests and kings.

Even after Iraq's conversion to Islam in the seventh and eighth centuries, storytellers and poets continued to wander the region bringing news and story-songs with their tales of adventure. Always immensely popular, this art – *al-qaskhoun* or *al-hakawati* (storytelling) – was performed in public, often in market-places. In its later forms, the storyteller would be placed on a raised stand and, with a cane in his hand, would be able to look down on his large audience who would be seated all around him on the ground. More than merely narrating his tale, the storyteller would change his voice for different characters, using the cane for sound effects. Widespread during the Abbasid periods, such performances can still be seen in some Iraqi villages.

By the late thirteenth and early fourteenth centuries, other forms of performance began to emerge. One such was *khayal al-zhil* (shadow theatre), an art first practised here by Ibn Daaniyaal al-Mawsili (d. 1311). A native of the Iraqi city of Nineveh, he grew up in Egypt during the time of the Mamluks where he probably first encountered this art which was then mostly referred to by its Turkish name – *karagöz*. The word and the form became widespread during the Ottoman occupation with such shows attended by all levels of society, including women (women attended mostly during the holy month of Ramadan).

Another entertainment was *as-samaajaat*, a term that can be roughly translated as uncouth jesters. First seen in the courts during holidays, it was a particular favourite during the reign of Khalif al-Mutawakkil. In such performances, groups of masked jesters would be brought before the Khalif to present comic routines. Some were exceedingly bold to the point of rudeness. At the same time that they began to perform for a wider public, they began to be seen less often in court, ostensibly for security reasons.

Even more popular was the art of *as-saakhir* (the mocker). Widespread during the Mongol occupation of Iraq in the thirteenth century, such mockery was seen as a way to render Mongol behaviour a source of laughter and derision through imitation of gestures and actions in front of non-Mongol audiences. This form continued to be practised well into the Ottoman era. Indeed, it may even have preceded the appearance of the shadow theatre which seems to have been brought to Iraq from the Far East, perhaps with the arrival of the Mongols.

One of the most significant events in Muslim history is the martyrdom of al-Hussein bin 'Ali, an event that led to the creation of still another performative form – the distinctive lamentation rituals called *al-maraathi*. Relating the historical clash between al-Hussein and Yazeed bin Mu'aawiya which ended with al-Hussein's death, *al-maraathi*, written much later and not necessarily in the same style as it is known today, became an integral part of the Islamic tradition of lamentations, which are passed from generation to generation. Such events can be seen in many Islamic countries. (See also IRAN for a more detailed examination of this subject.)

It was during the Ottoman period in the early nineteenth century that western-style literary theatre first began to be seen in Iraq, mostly in schools. Attracted to the form, local amateurs began to stage their own small productions at clubs and eventually began to stage short original plays. The year 1880 is generally agreed to be when the first Iraqi-written play was created. Written by the poet Hanna Habash, this first script was composed of three one-act plays, *Aadam Wa Hawwa'* (*Adam and Eve*), *Yousuf al-Hasan* and *Toubiyya*. The first play by an Iraqi writer to be printed was *Lateef Wa Houshaaba* (*Lateef and Houshaaba*), an adaptation of a French original by Na'oum Fathalla Sammaar in 1892. Other early plays and adaptations from this same period include *Naboukhath Nassar* (*Nebuchadnezzar*) written by the Reverend Hermiz Nersu and presented on the stage of the Clerical School in al-Mawsil in 1888; *Istish-haad Maarterisyous* (*The Martyrdom of Marterisius*) translated into Arabic by the teacher Saleem Hassoun and printed in 1902; *Sha'ou*, a play written by Saleem Hassoun and printed in 1905; *Selestra*, adapted from the Turkish by Muhyiddeen Khayyaat; *Jaan Daark* (*Joan of Arc*) performed in al-Mawsil and Baghdad in 1909; *Wafaa' al-'Arab* (*The Loyalty of the Arabs*) written by Antoine al-Jameel and printed in 1909; *al-Baree' al-Maqtoul* (*The Murdered Innocent*) written in 1911; and *Liwajh Allaah al-Kareem* (*For God's Sake*) written by Hanna Rassaam and Habeeb Yousef and presented in Baghdad in 1912.

Most of the playwrights mentioned were well versed in foreign languages and were residents of al-Mawsil, where it was easier to get in touch with the European world through Turkey and Syria. These early playwrights were in this sense transferring to Iraq what they saw and read about from the west. For most, the religious aspects of their plays were the centres, a way to blend evangelism and entertainment. The period they worked in – from about 1880 to 1921 – may be considered the blocks on which others later built a more mature edifice.

During the post-World War I years and the replacement of the Ottoman occupation by that of the British, such a literary theatre became part of a new cultural language and one of the means through which Iraqis were able to vent criticism and opposition. During this time as well, a number of small British and Indian theatre companies played in Baghdad becoming models for local acting and writing. Most of the original plays of the period were nationalistic in nature, stirring national pride and recalling historic Arab glories, achievements, battles and heroes. Most were written in classical Arabic which was considered more appropriate for high ideals and deep feelings than the colloquial Arabic used every day. Such plays were done between about 1900 and 1921 in private clubs and at such venues as the Dominican Sons School, Apostolic Delegate School and Sham'oun as-Safa School in the city of al-Mawsil, the Industrial School, the Public Park, the Chaldaean School, at the Military Theatre in the Basaateen area and on the stages of open-air movie houses.

Among the earliest to stage plays at the social clubs was the Nouri Fattah Group, established in 1919. Its only play was *an-Nu'maan bin al-Munthir* which was presented on the stage of the movie house Olympia. Initially, the theatre

attracted intellectuals and members of the more educated social classes who again saw theatre as a means to discuss social issues with a wider public. Eventually short plays began to be seen even in movie houses between films. Most were done for entertainment but some were staged for more serious purposes – moral guidance or social criticism. Such sketches – including comedies that were often little more than buffoonery done by amateurish entertainers – could be seen in such venues as late as the end of World War II. By that time, the public had seen enough British and Indian touring theatre to know that they wanted something more.

More and more Iraqi clubs began to allocate major portions of their programmes for theatrical and other artistic activities during the 1920s and 1930s. Among the many early groups of note were Jam'iyyat at-Tamtheel al-'Arabi (Arab Acting Society) established in 1922; Firqat Muntada at-Tah-theeb (Good Behaviour Club Company) established in 1923; al-Firqa at-Tamtheeliyya al-Wataniyya (National Acting Company) established in 1927 by Haqqi ash-Shibli; al-Firqa al-'Asriyya at-Tamtheeliyya (Modern Acting Company) established in 1929 and headed by Mohieddine Mohammed; al-Firqat al-'Arabiyya lit-Tamtheel (Arab Company for Acting) established in 1934 and headed by Yahya Faayiq; Firqat Ansaar il-Fann at-Tamtheeliyya (Acting Company for Art Supporters) established in 1934 and headed by 'Abdalla al-Azzawi; and Firqat Babil lit-Tamtheel (Babel Acting Company) established and headed by Mahmoud Shawkat. Artistic activities were not limited to Baghdad, but extended to other Iraqi cities such as Basrah and al-Mawsil.

In the 1930s as well, a number of Iraqi artists had begun to study theatre abroad and on their return tried to establish more complex models. Training institutions began to be set up by 1940 and a kind of historical documentary theatre emerged.

During the war, the Ministry of Labour and Social Affairs issued an edict to all active companies that scripts for the first time had to be submitted to the ministry for approval before they could be staged. The government continued to watch the various activities of theatre, however, even after the war allowing certain artists to continue their activities (even offering them special privileges), while preventing others from having theatre careers at all. The only exception to the censorship rules were in schools whose plays did not have to be approved in advance. By 1947, however, the government began to require even schools to apply for production permits.

In the late 1940s Haqqi ash-Shibli was named head of the Fine Arts Institute in Baghdad and his influence on theatre training and theatre practice over the next decades was enormous. First came a new interest in realistic theatre brought about by an understanding of the ideas of Stanislavski. This led to a movement aimed at adapting plays from the international repertoire to Iraqi reality. Second came a new interest in national folk traditions. Added to this were an increasing number of visits to Baghdad by Arab theatre groups from abroad.

The theatre at this time was also changing social habits. During the Ottoman regime, for example, men and women were segregated when they went to public events with certain times or spaces only for men and others only for women (who also had to be veiled). By the 1930s, thanks to the influence of the clubs and the many new theatre groups, integrated performances began to be seen.

Post-war Iraq underwent even greater social and political changes as the economy became more industrialized and as agriculture became more mechanized. On the cultural level, the theatre became more and more political and arts periodicals began to appear appealing to the new culture-minded intellectuals. Labour and social movements also became active in the process, and groups began to offer performances in spaces owned by labour unions and labour-oriented clubs.

The 1958 Revolution brought the monarchy to an end and established Iraq as a republic; ten years later, the 1968 Revolution established Iraq as a modern nation-state. Both these revolutions utilized theatre. The first provided for the simple establishment of many semi-professional and professional theatre companies; the second provided theatre workers, artists and companies with an infrastructure as well as appropriate buildings, financial support and assistance.

The tremendous growth of the theatre in the 1970s and through the early 1980s was built on these important roots. When the country found itself at war with Iran through much of the 1980s and cut off from much of the international theatre community during the 1990s, theatre activities were also negatively affected. An evaluation of these two decades will require a greater distance in time than the present survey is able to afford.

Structure of the National Theatre Community

During the early 1980s, more than a dozen regularly producing theatre groups were in operation in Iraq. The wars since have limited those numbers and affected their ability to perform. Even so, a number of points can be made about Iraq's theatre.

The majority of theatrical activities in the country has traditionally been government supported and, to some extent, government controlled. This said, the quality of the relationship between the government and the theatre has been reasonably positive. Indeed, the reality of Iraqi theatre even in the 1990s shows a wide variety of artistic approaches, a large number of state-supported 'official' theatrical companies, the production of many foreign plays each year, and the existence of branches of the Baghdad-based al-Firqa al-Qawmiyya lit-Tamtheel (National Theatre Company) in smaller cities such as Basrah, Nineveh, Baabil and Karbala.

Beginning in 1968, festivals became an active part of the Iraqi theatre; some sponsored by theatres themselves and others sponsored by government agencies. The School Theatre Festival, which has been held by the Ministry of Education since 1969, is in the late 1990s the largest national festival with regional competitions preceding the national finals each year.

A number of rural theatrical companies came into being in the 1970s; these are now supported by the Ministry of Agriculture, which sponsors a Festival of Rural Theatre every five years.

In 1977, Iraq's six universities and the Artistic Institutions Establishment held a symposium aimed at upgrading student artistic activities. The outcome of this symposium was a university festival that was held for the first time in 1978. The next year the country's first Labour Theatrical Festival was held with the participation of twelve labour unions.

In 1984, two more festivals were begun, the first by the Fine Arts Institute in Baghdad and the second by the Theatre Club, a subsidiary of the Cinema and Theatre Institute. In 1985, the Artists Union held its own festival. Another annual festival, the Baghdad Festival of Arab theatre, began in 1985, and now operates under the auspices of the state's Cinema and Theatre Department.

The Iraqi Theatre Centre of the International Theatre Institute is an umbrella organization for many of these national activities and has added in some events of its own including the celebration of World Theatre Day. The Iraqi Theatre Centre offers financial support to theatre companies and sponsors workshops in such areas as playwriting, directing, design and lighting.

There is an Iraqi Actors' Union which ensures artists' salaries and working conditions including financial support after retirement.

Artistic Profile
Music Theatre
Dance Theatre

Companies

The oldest still operating Iraqi theatre company is Firqat al-Masrah ash-Sha'bi (Popular Theatre Company) which began its operations in 1948 under 'Abd ul-Kareem Haadi and 'Abd ul-Qaadir Tawfiq. Its first production was an Arabic version of a play by the French dramatist Sardou called here *Shuhadaa' al-Wataniyya* (*The Martyrs of Nationalism*) and co-directed by Ibraheem Jalal (b. 1923) and 'Abd ul-Jabbaar Tawfiq Wali. The company through the years has presented a wide range of works from the international and Arabic-language repertoire including Henrik Ibsen's *Bayt ad-Dumya* (*The Doll's House*), Tawfiq al-Hakīm's *al-Lis* (*The Thief*) and *as-Saa'a al-Akheera* (*The Last Hour*) by the Romanian playwright Mikhail Sebastian.

The largest and most highly subsidized company is al-Firqa al-Qawmiyya lit-Tamtheel (National Theatre Company) which was established on a professional basis in 1968 under the Cinema and Theatre Department of the Ministry of Culture and Information. Producing a wide range of dramatic styles by playwrights from around the world, the National has had major success with the works of Bertolt Brecht, Albert Camus, Eugene O'Neill, Aleksei Arbuzov and, among Arab playwrights, Alfred Faraj, Sa'dallah Wanous, Salaah 'Abd us-Sabour and Mahmud Diyab. Among Iraqi playwrights, the company's most successful productions were of works by Qassim Mohammed, 'Aadil Kadhim, Yousif al-A'ni, Sa'doun al-'Ubaydi, Taha Saalim, Nour ud-Deen Faaris, 'Ali ash-Shawk, Nadhim Hikmat and 'Abdalla Hasan. The National has toured to countries such as Egypt, Syria, Libya, Kuwait, Tunisia, Algeria and Morocco and has presented several children's plays. Based in Baghdad, it has two large and relatively well equipped theatre halls – al-Masrah al-Watani (National Theatre) and Masrah ar-Rasheed (Rasheed Theatre).

Firqat al-Masrah al-Fanni al-Hadith (Modern Artistic Theatre Company) was started in 1965 by Ibraheem Jalal as an offshoot of the Modern Theatre Company which he had started in 1952. Yousif al-A'ni later took over the company as director, leading actor and resident playwright and it is al-'Ani's name that has been most closely related to it between the 1970s and 1990s. Keenly interested in developing new audiences for the theatre, the company has focused on plays with particular social relevance to Iraq, wherever those plays may come from. Among the important foreign dramatists produced by the company have been Molière, Chekhov, Gorki and Cocteau while among Iraqi playwrights of note have been, aside from al-'Ani, Nadhim Hikmat, Qassim Mohammed, Khaleel al-Qaysi and Taha Saalim.

Firqat Ittihaad al-Fannaaneen (Artist Federation Company) was established in 1967 and in the 1990s was being run by the playwright and actor Taha Saalim. Beginning with a group of young university graduates, the group's early work showed much promise but it proved difficult to keep the company together and it ceased operating for several years after which it re-started but without the same energy and excitement. Some of the group's important early work included Nour ud-Deen Faaris's *al-Bayt*

Founders of the modern Iraqi theatre: Ibraheem Jalal (left) and Haqqi ash-Shibli.

al-Jadeed (*The New House*) and several plays by Taha Saalim – al-Koura (*The Ball*), *Ward Juhannami* (*Hellish Roses*) and al-Baqara al-Haloub (*The Milk Cow*).

At the end of the 1950s, Firqat Masrah 14 Tammouz lit-Tamtheel (July 14 Acting Theatre Company) emerged under the name Firqat al-Fajr al-Jadeed (New Dawn Company). During the 1960s, this company became active in radio and television, ceased its stage operations for a number of years, and then resumed under its present name. Another group of note is Firqat Masrah al-Yawm (Today Theatre Company) established in 1969. The group is still operating and until early 1998 was being run by Ja'far 'Ali, a teacher at the Fine Arts Academy. Tending toward the avant-garde, the group has staged a number of successful works by Nour ud-Deen Faaris. Among them, *The Stranger*, al-'Atash Wa l-Qadiyya (*Thirst and the Cause*), al-Yunbou' (*The Fountainhead*) and 'Arous bil-Mazaad (*The Auction Bride*). The company also presented a number of plays by the Iraqi playwright Muhieddeen Zankana, and by foreign playwrights such as Edward Albee, Pirandello, Aleksei Arbuzov and Anton Chekov.

Other Baghdad companies of note include Firqat al-'Iraaq al-Masrahiyya (Iraqi Theatrical Company), Firqat Baghdaad (Baghdad Company), Firqat Baabil (Babil Company), Firqat Diyali (Diyali Company) and Firqat Masrah ar-Risaala (Message Theatre Company).

Outside the capital, Firqat Salaar lit-Tamtheel (Salaar Acting Company), founded in 1984, is without doubt the most distinguished Kurdish theatre in northern Iraq. It is named after its founder, the actor Ahmad Salaar, a graduate of the Fine Arts Academy in Baghdad who has also been a teacher in the Fine Arts Institute in Sulaymaaniyya province. Other provincial companies of note include Firqat ar-Ruwwaad (Pioneers Company) in Nineveh Province, and Firqat al-Masrah al-Kurdi at-Talee'i (Kurdish Avant-Garde Theatre Company) and Firqat al-Funoun al-Kurdiyya al-Hadeetha (Kurdish Modern Arts Company) in Arbil Province.

Dramaturgy

Sulaymaan Ghazaala (1853–1929) is generally agreed to be Iraq's first playwright of note. Born in Baghdad, he studied medicine in Paris where he lived from 1880 until 1886. He later practised as a doctor in various centres in Turkey, Syria, Armenia, Libya and eventually Iraq. In 1923 he was elected to the Constituent Assembly and later to Parliament. But though his profession was medicine his passion was theatre and he wrote a number of plays important in the development of the genre. Among them were *Lahjat ul-Abtaal* (*The Way Heroes Talk*), the first Iraqi play written in verse and whose published versions went through two printed editions in 1911, *'Ali Khoja* (1913), and *al-Haq Wa l-'Adaala* (*Right and Justice*, 1929), also written in verse. All of his plays could be described as socio-political and comment freely on contemporary issues. Besides his plays, he wrote seventeen books ranging from economics to sociology.

Another playwright of note from this early period was Mousa ash-Shaabendar (b. 1899) who wrote several plays under his pen-name, 'Alwaan Abou Sharaara. Educated in Baghdad and Switzerland where he obtained his doctorate in political science in 1930, his best known play was *Waheeda* (*Alone*, 1930). As interesting as the play is as a piece of realistic writing, equally interesting is the play's introduction, which is considered one of the seminal documents on dramatic writing in Iraq.

Another early writer is Yahya Qaaf ush-Shaikh 'Abd ul-Waahid (1900–66). A graduate of the Teachers' College in Baghdad, he started his work in theatre in the public school system and eventually began working as an actor joining the Arab Acting House Company in 1923. In 1924, he wrote the play *Fat-h Misr* (*The Conquest of Egypt*), which was published in 1925. A year later he wrote *al-Qaadisiyya Aw Sa'd Bin Abi Waqqaas* (*The Qaadisiyya Battle or Sa'd Bin Abi Waqqaas*), a historical play in five acts, which was not published until 1935. One of the Iraqi theatre's pioneers in utilizing theatre for social purposes, he often wrote about the need to eradicate illiteracy. Art for him was a weapon to be used in the battle for intellectual advancement.

The last of the pioneers to be dealt with here is Safaa' Mustafa, born in Baghdad in 1913. Following his university studies in Germany, first in music and then in theatre, he returned to Baghdad in 1936 and became a member of the National Theatre Company. Among the many plays that he wrote were *Haatha Mujrimukum* (*This Is Your Criminal*, c.1936), *'Aalam Jadeed* (*A New World*), *al-Watan Wa l-Bayt* (*Home*

and Country, 1944), *'Antar lil-Ajaar* (*'Antar for Rent*), *Taalib Min al-Janoub* (*A Student from the South*) and *Catherine* (printed 1938).

Taha Saalim (b. 1920) studied at the Fine Arts Institute in Baghdad and began working as a playwright and actor with the Modern Theatre Company in Baghdad. In the 1960s, he helped found Firqat Ittihaad al-Fannaaneen (Federation of Artists Company). Among his many important plays are *Fawaanees* (*Lanterns*), *Qarandal*, *al-Koura* (*The Ball*), *Tantal, Ma Ma'qoula* (*It Is Not Possible*) and *al-Baqara al-Haloub* (*The Milk Cow*).

Khaalid ash-Shawwaaf represents a kind of mid-point in the development of Iraqi playwriting. Born in Baghdad in 1924, he graduated from the College of Law in 1949 and practised law until 1958. In governmental institutions, he occupied various positions including general manager of the Cultural Department in the Ministry of Culture and Information and deputy manager of the Cinema and Theatre Agency. A noted free-verse poet, he published several verse plays including *Shamsu* in 1952, *al-Aswaar* (*The Ramparts*) in 1956 and *az-Zaytouna* (*The Olive Tree*) in 1986. The subject of many studies, ash-Shawwaaf's plays are based on the well-made-play tradition.

More modern still is the work of dramatist Yousif al-A'ni (b. 1927). A practising lawyer early in his career, he later headed the first Iraqi State Establishment for Cinema and Theatre in 1960. Most of his plays have been done by the Modern Theatre Company in Baghdad which he also ran for many years. One of the strongest literary voices in the theatre from the 1950s to the 1980s, he created a series of articulate and powerful plays looking at issues of social import. Writing both allegorically and realistically, his plays have included figures such as the 'political prisoner', the 'labourer' and the 'son of the people'. Among his best plays have been *Ra's ash-Shaleela* (*The Tip of the Thread*), *Aani Ummak Ya Shaakir* (*I Am Your Mother Oh Shaakir*) and *Fulous ad-Dawa* (*The Money for Medicine*). During the 1960s, he wrote *al-Muftaah* (*The Key*) and *al-Kharaaba* (*The Wreck*), two plays which moved away from his earlier realism. His late plays were again realistic – *ash-Shari'a* (*Waterhole*) and *al-Khaan* (*The Inn*). Al-A'ni was heavily influenced by the modern German theatre especially by the plays of Bertolt Brecht.

Sa'doun al-'Ubaydi was born in al-'Amaara in 1935. After obtaining a degree in acting and directing at the Fine Arts Institute, he moved to

Kassem Mohamed's production of *Zeenet El Nissa* (*The Prettiest Woman*) by Yousif al-A'ni at al-Hadith Theatre.

London where he received his diploma in acting-directing from the Guildhall Institute in 1962. Returning to become a director at the National Theatre Company and later heading the Theatre Branch of the Artists' Union, he was a co-founder of the Baghdad Artistic Theatre Company and the Message Theatre. Specializing as both writer and director in folk forms, he staged many of his own plays including *al-Ashqiyaa'* (*The Wretched*) and *al-Bidaaya* (*The Beginning*, 1986). Some of his early plays – *al-Ashqiyaa'* (*The Wretched*) and *Jismaan Fi*

Mathalla Waahida (*Two Bodies Under One Umbrella*) – were published in a 1962 collection and four others were published in *Arba' Masrahiyyat* in 1986.

'Adil Kadhim (b. 1939) made his début as a dramatist in 1966 with *at-Toufaan* (*The Flood*). He followed this work with *Tammouz Yaqra' an-Naqous* (*July Tolls the Bell*), *al-Hisaar* (*The Siege*) and *al-Mawt Wa l-Qadiyya* (*Death and the Cause*). Translated into several languages, his plays are tightly structured and tend to have folk themes.

Muhieddeen Zankana (b. 1940) graduated with a degree in Arabic from the University of Baghdad in 1962. A teacher and a writer of short stories, novels, essays and literary studies, his first stage play was *As-Sirr* (*The Secret*, 1968), a tightly woven political play. Other plays of note include *Al-Jarraa'* (*The Exhorter*, 1970); *as-Sou'aal* (*The Question*, 1975), a play later performed in Tunisia, Egypt and Kuwait; *al-Yamaama* (*The Pigeon*); *Fi ar-Rub' ar-Raabi' Min al-Qarn al-'Ishreen* (*In the Fourth Quarter of the Twentieth Century*); *Yahduth Haatha* (*This Happens*) based on a story by the Turkish writer 'Azeez Yasineen; and *al-Lu'ba al-Hajariyya* (*The Stone Toy*, 1982). All these plays were written in classical Arabic. The only play that he wrote in colloquial Arabic was *al-Ijaaza* (*The Vacation*, 1977). Realistic plays for the most part, his works focus on such unusual subjects as humans and their art.

Directors, Directing and Production Styles

Haqqi ash-Shibli (1903–85), an actor, director and outstanding theatre administrator, profoundly influenced the earliest professional theatrical generations in the country. The first person to be granted a fellowship for the study of theatre outside Iraq, he studied in Europe and on his return he was appointed director of oratory for national schools and in the early 1940s established and headed the Acting Division at the Fine Arts Institute in Baghdad. At the institute, through the 1940s and 1950s he trained hundreds of artists who propagated the idea of theatrical art from one end of the country to the other. A founder of the National Theatre Company, he also acted in the first Iraqi film in 1946. General manager of the Cinema and Theatre Agency, he later served as head of the Artists' Union. In 1973, he was honoured as a pioneer of Arab theatre at the Carthage Festival.

Yahya Faa'iq (1913–83) was a founder of Firqat Ma Bayn an-Nahrayn (Mesopotamian Company), the Arab Acting Company and Republican Theatre Company (1958). Directing in a cinematic style – a style he called the fourth dimension – he once said 'it is the utilization of the cinema technique on the stage that typifies my work. It displays emotions as well as backgrounds of characters and events in a clearly understood manner and it helps actors to communicate.'

Ibraheem Jalal graduated from the Fine Arts Institute in 1945 and was one of the founders of the Artistic Theatre Company in 1952. Later studying in Italy and in the United States (Chicago Art Institute), he became a teacher at the Fine Arts Academy in Baghdad on his return to Iraq. His directing style is an amalgam of two artistic schools, Stanslavski's and Brecht's, and part of his importance lies in his many theoretical essays attempting to explain the interplay of the two styles. Among his important productions have been *Aani Ummak Ya Shaakir* (*I Am Your Mother Oh Shaakir*) by Yousuf al-'Ani, *at-Toufaan* (*The Flood*, 1966) by 'Aadil Kadhim, *Fawaanees* (*Lanterns*, 1966) by Taha Saalim, an adaptation based on Brecht's play *Puntila* called *al-Bayk Wa s-Saayik* (*The Bey and the Driver*, 1973), *Maqaamaat Abi l-Ward* (*The Assemblies of Abi al-Ward*, 1977) by 'Aadil Kadhim, *Rihlat as-Suhoun at-Taa'ira* (*The Journey of the Flying Saucers*) by Karl Filtelsinger and *al-Malhama ash-Sha'biyya* (*The Folk Epic*) by Qassim Mohammed. Jalal also worked in the United Arab Emirates, at the Theatre Division of the Fine Arts Academy in Baghdad and had headed the Iraqi Artists' Union.

Ja'far as-Sa'di (b. 1922), one of the founders of al-Firqa ash-Sha'biyya lit-Tamtheel (Popular Acting Company), studied directing at the Chicago Art Institute in the United States, worked as a teacher in the Fine Arts Institute and then at the Fine Arts Academy. Essentially a realistic director, as-Sa'di directed plays in many styles and from many periods ranging from Chekhov to Shakespeare to Sophocles.

Badri Hassoun Fareed (b. 1927) is another Iraqi director who studied in Chicago (Goodman Theatre and the University of Chicago). Later heading the directing programme at the Fine Arts Academy, he was a founder of the Vanguard Youth Company in 1959. In his directing style, Fareed emphasized the importance of the actor. A playwright as well, he has written most of his own plays in colloquial Arabic and has often directed them.

Ibraheem Jalal's 1973 production of the Brecht adaptation of *al-Bayk Wa s-Saayik* (*The Bey and the Driver*).

One of the masters in directorial and acting training, his major productions have included plays by Ibsen, Chekhov, Casona and Racine.

Sami Abd al-Hameed (b. 1928) graduated from both the Fine Arts Institute and the College of Law in Baghdad. Later studying at the Royal Academy of Dramatic Arts in London, he went on to obtain his Master's degree from the University of Oregon. A former head of the Theatre Division at the Fine Arts Academy and head of the Iraqi Artists' Union and Federation of Arab Dramatists, al-Hameed helped to anchor the Iraqi theatre to a theoretical as well as an artistic foundation. In his approach to directing, he combined the classical with a popular and folk-oriented spirit. He directed a range of important productions from Shakespeare (*Lear, Hamlet* and *Merchant of Venice*) to Camus, Tennessee Williams (*The Glass Menagerie*) and Sophocles' *Antigone*. For the National Theatre Company, he staged Taha Saalim's *Qarandal* in 1971, Fouad at-Takrali's *Malhamat Kilkaamish* (*The Epic of Gilgamesh*) in 1978, *Tareeq al-Majd* (*The Road to Glory*) in 1983 and *as-Sakhra* (*The Rock*), Betti's *Jazeerat al-Maa'iz* (*Crime on Goat Island*) and *Bayt*

Bernarda Alba (*The House of Bernarda Alba*), *Odeeb Malikan* (*Oedipus the King*) and Yousif al-A'ni's *al-Muftaah* (*The Key*).

Playwright-director Qassim Mohammed (b. 1935), whose plays have been widely produced in the Arab world, graduated from the Fine Arts Institute and then studied at the GITIS Institute in Moscow. His theatrical approach both as playwright and director is based on the use of folk material. Among his own plays, one can see this clearly in works such as *Tayr as-Sa'd* (*The Bird of Luck*), *as-Sabi al-Khashabi* (*The Wooden Boy*), *Majaalis at-Turaath* (*The Heritage Gatherings*), *Risaalat at-Tayr* (*The Bird's Message*) and *Hikaayat al-'Atash Wa l-Ard Wa n-Naas* (*The Story of the Thirst, Land and People*).

Muhsin al-Azzawi (b. 1939) was trained at the Theatre Division of the Fine Arts Institute, at the Dramatic Arts Academy in Prague and received his PhD from the Garlis University in Czechoslovakia. In 1975, he helped establish Firqat ash-Shu'la lit-Tamtheel (Torch Acting Company) and later the National Theatre Company where he directed many plays by Iraqi playwrights, including works by 'Ali ash-Shawk, 'Abdalla Hasan, Qassim Mohammed and 'Aadil Kadhim. Known for his social awareness, his

Iraqi stage director Qassim Mohammed.

Sami Abd al-Hameed in *Speak Up Stone*, a play about the Palestinian *intifada*.

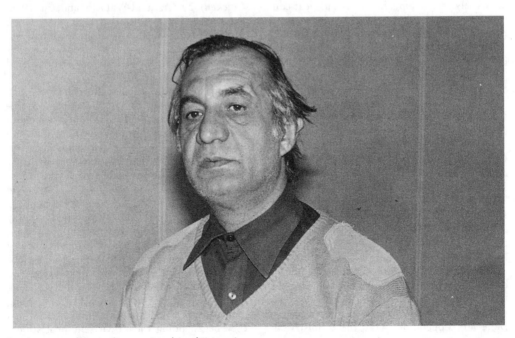

Iraqi actor and stage director Mushin al-Azzawi.

productions combine the strange and the real intermingled with a sense of comedy.

'Awni Karroumi (b. 1945) graduated from the Fine Arts Institute in 1965 and the Fine Arts Academy in 1969. In 1972, he received his PhD in political science from Humboldt University in the former Democratic Republic of Germany. Among the many plays he directed in Iraq were Camus's *Kalikula* (*Caligula*), *al-Maseeh Yuslab* *Min Jadeed* (*Jesus Is Being Crucified Again*), *Rithaa' Uour* (*The Lamentation of Ur*) and Brecht's *Galileo*. Karroumi has published several books including *Ittijahaat Wa Tabee'at al-Masrah al-'Arabi Wa l-'Iraaqi* (*The Nature of and Approaches to the Arab and Iraqi Theatre*) and *Turuq Tadrees at-Tamtheel* (*Methods of Teaching Acting*).

Theatre for Young Audiences
Puppet Theatre

Before the 1950s, many writers tried their hands at creating children's plays and some actually succeeded quite well including 'Isa 'Azmi, Ra'ouf al-Khateeb and 'Abd us-Sattaar al-Qaragoli. After the 1950s, a more specialized group of writers emerged who focused almost exclusively on either school theatre or plays for young audiences.

The most distinguished children's dramatist in the country has been 'Abd ul-Qaadir Raheem (b. 1932). His plays were written in a style that mixed romanticism and realism using a simplified classical Arabic. Satiric, critical and immensely entertaining, his work had clear educational, moral and social objectives. Inspired by folk tales and classic stories such as *The Thousand and One Nights*, he wrote and directed more than a dozen plays starting in the 1950s including *Ista 'Abd Innhu Akhi Wa Sadeeqi* (*Mr 'Abd, He Is My Brother and Friend*, 1953), *Ameer al-Alwaan* (*The Prince of Colours*, 1953), *Hallaaq Baghdaad* (*The Barber of Baghdad*, 1954), *Ana Wa l-Himaar Aw 'Aaqibat at-Tama'* (*The Donkey and I or the Outcome of Greed*, 1955), *Usfour Barada* (*The Bird of Barada*, 1956), *Abou l-Qaasim at-Tanbouri* (1957), *Hikaayat as-Sayyaad 'Aashour* (*The Tale of the Fisherman 'Aashour*, 1965), and *Madeenat az-Zujaaj* (*The Glass City*, 1986). In 1975 he won a national playwriting prize for his school play *Haay Shlown Warta* (*Oh What a Dilemma*).

The National Theatre Company, funded directly by the central government, has since the late 1960s presented one children's play each year as part of its regular season programming. Done in cooperation with the Ministry of Education and with subsidized prices, such pro-ductions have attracted well-known writers and some have been major successes. One such was *Tayr as-Sa'd* (*The Lucky Bird*, 1970), adapted and directed by Qassim Mohammed, who followed this with *as-Sabi al-Khashabi*, an adaptation of *Pinocchio*. Among Mohammed's other successes for children have been *Sirr al-Kanz* (*The Secret of the Treasure*) and *Rihlat as-Sagheer Wa Safrat al-Maseer* (1981) based on Saint-Exupéry's *The Little Prince*.

The Public Agency for Radio and Television tried its hand in this field when it presented in 1975 *ad-Dajaaja ash-Shaatira* (*The Clever Chicken*) by 'Azza al-Wahaab and, in 1976, *Sabaah ul-Khayr Ayyatuha as-Sa'aada* (*Good Morning Happiness*) by Farouq Salloum and Saami 'Abbaas. Its success kept children's theatre on television at least on an occasional basis for the next decade.

Puppetry – other than shadow theatre which was discussed in the opening historical section – was actually seen on television before being presented on the stage in Iraq. Anwar Hayraan and Taariq ar-Rabee'i were the first to introduce this art form on television in 1956 and by 1961 'Azza 'Abd al-Wahaab had a successful television series, *Imrahou Ya Sighaar* (*Have Fun Little Ones*), in which he used glove-puppets. From 1968 until 1985, Iraq was visited by many Belgian, Polish and German puppet companies, which increased interest in theatrical puppetry still further. Al-Wahaab was able to convince the General Federation of Iraqi Women to support and organize a puppetry training session, which was attended by twenty young women over a seven-week period after which they began doing their own semi-professional puppet shows.

In 1985, the first of many puppet programmes was staged at the Children's Museum of Antiquities. Using glove-puppets, these shows dramatized historical tales.

Besides the experiences of these various artists in the capital, several attempts were made by puppeteers in the provinces. The most successful one was in Karbala by 'Alaa' al-'Ubaydi. His endeavours received the support of the Education Agency which regarded his puppetry performance as a learning instrument for students as well as entertainment for the general public.

Design
Theatre Space and Architecture
Training

Design has been an increasingly important element in the country's various training institutions but during the 1980s and 1990s was not a major element in Iraqi theatre.

Many small stages exist across the country but few have the facilities necessary to qualify them as major theatres. Among the major spaces in the country are the National Theatre's large proscenium house and an Italian-style theatre at the Fine Arts Academy.

In the area of training, the most important early name is that of Haqqi ash-Shibli, the actor and director, who, after studying in France, returned to help found the acting division of the National Fine Arts Institute in Baghdad (the Fine Arts Institute itself was inaugurated in 1940 under the name Ma'had al-Mouseeqa al-'Iraaqi – Iraqi Music Institute). Determined that other students should have the same kind of opportunities afforded to him, he was largely responsible for a steady increase in the number of the Fine Arts Institute's graduates who were

A scene from *Abu El Tayeb El Mutanaby* by Ibraheem Jalal.

ultimately sent abroad on study grants to such places as Britain, the United States, Italy and, from 1958, the Soviet Union, Czechoslovakia, Hungary, Romania and the German Democratic Republic among other countries.

After completing a five-year programme, graduates in theatre are given the institute's Art Diploma, which allows them to be hired as actors or theatre teachers. In 1961, the institute added a section for advanced theatre and design, Akadamiyyat al-Funoun al-Jameela al-'Ulya (Advanced Fine Arts Academy), whose purpose is to produce graduate teachers in these areas. In 1964, this section graduated its first eleven students, both male and female.

Productions at the institute are open to the public and have included plays by Shakespeare, Molière, Chekhov, Ahmad Shawqi, Tawfiq al-Hakīm and others from the European, American, and Arabic theatre. From the 1970s, the work of Iraqi playwrights was also being seen along with children's theatre and mime. From 1984, the institute began its own annual theatre festival, open to the general public.

In 1977, the Ministry of Education opened branches of this institute in other parts of the country including Basrah, the second largest city in Iraq; in al-Mawsil (1979) and in as-Sulaymaaniyya (1980).

In 1967, a Fine Arts Academy was carved out of the Fine Arts Institute and attached to the University of Baghdad. Two years later, the academy began offering a Master's degree in acting and directing; in 1979, it opened a section for radio, television and design. Shortly thereafter, it opened a section for arts education offering training for teachers in theatre and the plastic arts. After four years at the academy, students are granted Bachelor of Arts degrees and the highest ranking students have the right to be offered scholarships to complete further advanced studies in Iraq or abroad. In the early 1990s, a doctoral programme was added.

Other training institutions have emerged as well. In 1960, the Cinema and Theatre Institute was established under Maslahat as-Sinema Wa-l-Masrah (Cinema and Theatre Authority) with Yousif al-A'ni as its first general manager. In 1968, its name was changed to al-Mu'assasa l-'Aamma lis-Sinema Wa l-Masrah (State Cinema and Theatre Department). With branches across the country (including one attached to the National Theatre Company) in such provincial cities as Basrah, al-Mawsil and al-Hilla, one can now study design, dramatic literature and theatre history. The latter section, called the Centre for Research in Theatre and Film Studies, publishes essays through its monthly magazine, *Cinema Wa Masrah* (*Cinema and Theatre*). It includes a unit for manuscripts, photographs and vocal records.

Criticism, Scholarship and Publishing

The earliest theatre criticism in the country dates to the 1920s and 1930s and was essentially journalistic in nature. It was only after the first group of trained artists returned from abroad after completing their studies that criticism took on a deeper tone and moved away from simple description. The new criticism took on a more social tone looking into the relationship of theatre to society. More than anything these writings were general cultural essays with social and educative objectives. At its best, such theatrical criticism could be found in *Majallat Funoun* (*Arts Magazine*) of the period, a platform for Iraqi art in general and theatrical art in particular.

A second phase began after the July Revolution in 1958 and continued in its development until the mid-1960s. Criticism in this phase also started from a journalistic base, but with a much greater understanding of theatrical values, presentation and directing skills, in addition to a wider cultural awareness. The critical writings in this phase affected, as they developed, audiences, the artistic process as a whole, and the structure of the critical essay itself. A major essay on dramatic literature by Salaah Khaalis and published in 1954, as a preface to the play *Ra's ash-Shaleela* (*The Tip of the Thread*), was perhaps the first critical essay to combine artistic awareness with progressive political thinking. Arguing that theatrical development often accompanies the growth of a new social class, the essay was widely read and debated.

A third phase started in the mid-1960s marked by the publication of a book connecting theatre and history. Entitled *al-Haraka al-Masrahiyya Fi l-'Iraaq* (*The Theatrical Movement in Iraq*, 1965), it was written by Ahmad Fiyyaad al-Mufraji (b. 1936) and was the first book to look at the whole of Iraqi theatre development, an actual field survey of the activities of theatrical companies put into a historical and sociological context. A second book of note appeared shortly thereafter, *al-Masrah al-'Iraaqi Fi 'Aam 1967* (*The Iraqi Theatre in 1967*) by Badri Hassoun Fareed, focusing on a year the author considered as a watershed in the history of the Iraqi theatre. A third book on the same subject, *Wajhan li-Wajh* (*Face to Face*, 1967) by Yaseen al-Nusair (b. 1941) was the only book to include studies on all contemporary Iraqi stage presentations of the year.

Among the most useful other books was *at-Tareeq Wa l-Hudoud* (*The Path and the Limits*, 1977) by Yousef 'Abd ul-Maseeh Tharwat (b. 1921), which included essays on contemporary theatre archetypes, a general survey of Iraqi plays and their intellectual traditions, world theatre and major dramatists. Another book of note was 'Ali Muzaahim 'Abbaas's (b. 1940) *Salaaman Ayyuha l-Masrahiyyoun* (*Greetings Oh Dramatists*, 1985), which dealt with some of the artistic and intellectual phenomena in the general progression of the country's theatrical movement during this period.

A number of perceptive critics emerged from this period. Of these, the most important have been Mohammed Mubaarak (b. 1939), a graduate in English literature from the University of Baghdad whose best book is *Diraasaat Naqdiyya* (*Critical Studies*, 1975), Yaseen al-Nusair and Ahmad Fiyyaad al-Mufraji, the latter author of a range of critical books including *Masaadir Diraasat al-Masrah Fi l'Iraaq* (*Sources for Theatrical Studies in Iraq*, 1979). He was the most committed Iraqi man of letters in documenting the general cultural movement.

Yousef 'Abd ul-Maseeh Tharwat is an analyst of dramatic form and author of *Tashreeh al-Masrahiyya* (*Anatomy of the Play*), *Ma'aalim ad-Draama Fi l-'Asr al-Hadeeth* (*Characteristics of Drama in the Modern Age*) and *Diraasaat Fi al-Masrah al-Mu'aasir* (*Studies on the Contemporary Theatre*). 'Abd ul-Ilaah Kamaal ud-Deen (b. 1942) is the author of many books on the socialist theatre. Jameel at-Takreeti (b. 1930), possessor of a doctorate in literary theory from the University of Moscow, has published a number of academic studies and critical essays on the history of theatre such as *Qiraa'a Wa Ta'ammulaat Fi l-Masrah al-Ighreeqi* (*Readings and Meditations on the Greek Theatre*).

Other notable books include *al-Masrahiyya al-'Arabiyya Fi l-'Iraaq* (*The Arabic Stage Play in Iraq*) by 'Ali az-Zubaydi, a collection of lectures including one chapter on Iraqi plays written in verse and another on the origins of the theatre in Iraq through the Ottoman regime; *al-Masrahiyya al-'Arabiyya Fi l-'Iraaq 'Aam 1971* (*The Arabic Stage Play in Iraq in 1971*) by 'Umar at-Taalib, which traces the development of Iraqi plays from inception to 1971; *Hisaad al-Masrah Fi Ninewa 1880–1971* (*The Theatrical Harvest in Nineveh 1880–1971*) by Khidr Jum'a Hasan, a survey of theatrical activities in Nineveh from 1880 to 1971; *Azamat an-Nas al-Masrahi* (*The Dramatic-Text Crisis*) by 'Ali Muzaahim 'Abbaas, looking at the dearth of good locally written stage plays in Iraq; *Masrah at-Tifl Fi l-'Iraaq* (*The Children's Theatre in Iraq*) by Hasaballa Yahya; and *al-Masrah al-Madrasi Fi l-'Iraaq* (*School Theatre in Iraq*) by Thaamir Mahdi.

Ahmad Fiyyaad al-Mufraji, Sami Abd al-Hameed, 'Abd ul-Ilaah Kamaal ud-Deen, 'Ali Muzaahim 'Abbaas, Yaseen al-Nusair and Yousuf al-'Ani
Translated by Maha and Tony Chehade

Further Reading

'Abbaas, 'Ali Muzaahim. *Salaaman Ayyuha l-Masrahiyyoun* [Greetings oh dramatists]. Baghdad: Wa'i l-'Ummaal Press, 1985.

Carruthers, Ian. 'Julius Caesar in Iraq'. *Australasian Drama Studies* 15–16 (October 1989–April 1990): 59–69.

Fareed, Badri Hassoun. *al-Masrah al-'Iraaqi Fi 'Aam 1967* [The Iraqi theatre in 1967]. Baghdad: 1968.

Al-Hadethy, Waleed Hassan. 'Educational Theatre In Iraq: Elementary and Secondary Levels, Late Nineteenth Century to 1985'. PhD dissertation, University of Colorado, 1986. 399 pp.

al-Hameed, Sami Abd. 'Afkaar Hawl ad-Dikor Wa l-Ikhraaj al-Masrahi' [Thoughts on theatrical décor and direction]. *al-Muthaqqaf al-'Arabi Magazine* 11 (Baghdad 1974).

——. 'al-Isaala Wa t-Tajdeed Fi l-Masrah al-'Iraaqi' [Originality and renewal in the Iraqi theatre]. *al-Muthaqqaf al-'Arabi Magazine* 1 (Baghdad 1971).

——. 'al-Komeedya Fi l-Masrah al-'Iraaqi'

[Comedy in the Iraqi theatre]. *al-Akadami Magazine* 1 (Baghdad 1971).

———. 'Tajribati Fi t-Tamtheel Wa l-Ikhraaj' [My experience in acting and directing]. *al-Aqlaam Magazine* 6 (Baghdad 1980).

———. 'Tatawwur ath-Thihniyya al-Ikhraajiyya Fi l-Masrah al-'Iraaqi' [The development of the directing mental set in the Iraqi theatre]. *al-Aqlaam Magazine* 3–4 (Baghdad 1987).

Hasan, Khidr Jum'a. *Hisaad al-Masrah Fi Ninewa 1880–1971* [The theatrical harvest in Nineveh 1880–1971]. al-Mawsil: al-Jumhour Press, 1972.

al-Jaadir, 'Abd al-Mun'im. *Min Tareekh an-Nahda l-Fanniyya Fi l-'Iraaq al-Hadeeth* [From the history of the modern artistic renaissance in Iraq]. Baghdad: Baghdad Press, 1950.

al-Jazaa'iri, Mohammed. 'al-Masrah al-'Iraaqi Wa l-Marhala ar-Raahina' [The Iraqi theatre and the current phase]. *Aafaaq 'Arabiyya Magazine* 1 (September 1976).

Kamaleddin, Abdul Ilah. 'The Arabian Nights and the Iraqi Theatre'. *Gilgamesh: A Journal of Modern Iraqi Arts* (summer 1990): 59–63.

———. 'The Role of the Youth in Iraqi Theatre'. *Gilgamesh: A Journal of Modern Iraqi Arts* 4 (1989): 77–81.

Karroumi, 'Awni. 'Tajribati Fi l-Masrah' [My theatrical experience]. *al-Aqlaam Magazine* 6 (Baghdad 1980).

Lee, Du-Hyon. 'Pyonghwawa munhwawa sarangui chugje' [A festival of peace, culture and love]. *Korean Culture and Arts Bi-monthly* 114 (November 1987): 60–2.

Al-Mafraji, Ahmad Fayadah, ed. *A View of Children's Theatre In Iraq*. Baghdad: State Organization for Theatre and Cinema, 1978.

Mahdi, Thaamir. 'al-Fi'l Wa l-Wujoud Fi Masrahiyyat *al-Bayt al-Jadeed* li-Nour ud-Deen Faaris' [Action and existence in the play *The New House* by Nour ud-Deen Faaris]. *al-Muthaqqaf al-'Arabi Magazine* (June 1974).

———. 'Muqaddima Fi sh-Shi'r Wa l-Masrah' [An introduction to poetry and the theatre]. *al-Masrah Was-Sinema Magazine* 1 (November 1970).

Metwali, Mohammed Hanaa. 'Teatr cieni i Ibn Danijal' [Shadow puppets and Ibn Danijal]. *Dialog* 29 (April 1984): 120–6.

al-Mufraji, Ahmad Fiyyaad. 'Bidaayaat al-Masrah Fi l-'Iraaq' [Beginnings of the Iraqi theatre]. *al-Masrah Was-Sinema Magazine* 6 (Baghdad 1972).

———. *Haqqi ash-Shibli Raa'id al-Masrah al-'Iraaqi* [Haqqi ash-Shibli the Iraqi theatre pioneer]. Baghdad: Twaini Press, 1985.

———. 'Haqqi ash-Shibli: Thikrayaat Fi l-Fann Wa l-Hayaat' [Haqqi ash-Shibli: memories about art and life]. Addendum of the *al-Jumhouriyya Magazine* (Baghdad 1980).

———. *al-Haraka al-Masrahiyya Fi l-'Iraaq* [The theatrical movement in Iraq]. Baghdad: ash-Sha'b Press, 1965.

———. 'al-Hayaat al-Masrahiyya Fi l-'Iraaq' [Theatrical life in Iraq]. *al-Masrah Was-Sinema Magazine* 1 (Baghdad 1982).

———. *Masaadir Diraasat al-Masrah Fi l-'Iraaq* [Sources for theatrical studies in Iraq]. Baghdad, 1979.

———. *Masrah at-Tifl Fi l-'Iraaq* [The children's theatre in Iraq]. Baghdad, 1978.

———. *Masrah Fi l-'Iraaq* [The theatre in Iraq]. Baghdad, 1987.

———. 'Min Taareekh Masrah at-Tifl Fi l-'Iraaq' [From the history of the children's theatre in Iraq]. *al-Masrah Was-Sinema Magazine* 12 (Baghdad 1974).

Naseef, Jameel. 'al-Masrahiyya al-'Iraaqiyya Wa l-'Ilaaqa Bayn al-Mawdou' Wa l-Habka' [The Iraqi stage play and the relation between the subject and the plot]. *al-Masrah Was-Sinema Magazine* 3 (Baghdad 1970).

Nouri, Sabaah. 'an-Nashaat al-Masrahi Fi l-'Iraaq' [Theatrical activity in Iraq]. *al-Aqlaam Magazine* 12 (Baghdad 1970).

al-Nusair, Yaseen. 'ad-Dikor Fi l-Masrahiyya al-'Iraaqiyya' [The Iraqi theatrical décor]. *al-Masrah Was-Sinema Magazine* 11 (Baghdad 1974).

———. 'The Beginning of a New Stage in Theatre'. *Gilgamesh: A Journal of Modern Iraqi Arts* (spring 1990): 75–81.

———. 'Thalaath Namaathij Min al-Ikhraaj al-Masrahi al-Mahalli' [Three types of local theatrical direction]. *al-Masrah Was-Sinema Magazine* 10 (Baghdad 1974).

———. 'Wajhan li-Wajh [Face to face]. Baghdad: Daar as-Saa'a Press, 1967.

ar-Raa'i, 'Ali. 'al-Masrah Fi l-Watan al-'Arabi' [Theatre in the Arab homeland]. *'Aalam al-Ma'rifa Magazine* (Kuwait 1979).

Research Section of the Cinema and Theatre Public Institution. *al-Masrah al-'Iraaqi al-Yawm* [The Iraqi theatre today]. (Baghdad 1978).

ash-Shawwaaf, Khaalid. 'Tajribati Fi Kitaabat al-Masrahiyya ash-Shi'riyya' [My experience in writing plays in verse]. *al-Aqlaam Magazine* 22 (Baghdad 1987).

al-Taalib, 'Umar. 'Athar al-Masrah al-'Arabi 'Ala l-Masrah al-'Iraaqi [The influence of the Arab theatre on the Iraqi theatre]. *al-Masrah Was-Sinema Magazine* 12 (Baghdad 1974).

———. *al-Masrahiyya al-'Arabiyya Fi l-'Iraaq 'Aam 1971* [The Arabic stage play in Iraq in 1971]. Baghdad: an-Nu'maan Press, 1971.

Tharwat, Yousef 'Abd ul-Maseeh. 'al-Masrah al-

'Iraaqi Fi Yawm al-Masrah al-'Aalami' [The Iraqi theatre during the world theatre day]. *al-Masrah Was-Sinema Magazine* 2 (Baghdad 1970).

——. *at-Tareeq Wa l-Hudoud* [The path and the limits]. Baghdad: Ministry of Information, 1977.

al-Tikarli, Fouad. 'The Dreams Game'. *Gilgamesh: A Journal of Modern Iraqi Arts* 1–2 (1997): 43–8.

at-Tu'ma, Saaleh Jawaad. *Bibliografia al-Adab al-Masrahi al-'Arabi al-Hadeeth* [Bibliography of modern Arabic theatre literature]. (Baghdad 1969).

Yahya, Hasaballa. 'Towards New Values in the Iraqi Theatre'. *Gilgamesh: A Journal of Modern Iraqi Arts* 3 (1989): 55–9.

az-Zubaydi, 'Ali. *al-Masrahiyya al-'Arabiyya Fi l-'Iraaq* [The Arabic stage play in Iraq]. Cairo: Arab Research and Studies Institute and the Arab League, 1966.

ISLAMIC REPUBLIC OF MAURITANIA

(see **MAURITANIA**)

ISRAEL

(Europe Volume)

ITALIAN SOMALILAND

(see **SOMALIA**)

JIBUTI

(see **DJIBOUTI**)

JORDAN

A Middle Eastern kingdom, which for many centuries was part of the Roman and later the Ottoman empires, Jordan, on the Gulf of Aqaba north of the Red Sea, is bounded by Syria to the north, Israel and Palestine to the west, Iraq to the east and Saudi Arabia to the south. Covering a land area of some 89,000 square kilometres (over 34,000 square miles), the country's 4.4 million people (1997) are almost all of Arab origin and 95 per cent are Muslim. Amman is the capital and Arabic the official language, with English widely spoken and French a third language.

Jordan's modern history dates back to 1921 when the Emirate of Transjordan was established as a self-governing territory in the British sphere of influence. Full autonomy came in 1923 with Prince Abdullah as the country's ruler. In 1946 Abdullah was proclaimed King of the independent Hashemite Kingdom of Jordan, and four years later lands on the West Bank of the Jordan River (including the eastern part of Jerusalem) formally became part of the state. In 1952, Abdullah's grandson, Hussein ibn Talal, became the new king, and was still ruling in 1998.

In 1967, as a result of the Six Day War with Israel, some 6,600 square kilometres of the West Bank, including Jerusalem, were occupied by Israel, sending a large number of refugees across the Jordan River and tens of thousands of others deeper into Jordan. Jordan tried to solve this refugee problem by working closely with the United States, which was trying to broker a peace agreement in the Middle East, and with the Palestine Liberation Organization (PLO) which was attempting to win back Palestinian lands. Tensions between Jordan and the PLO reached a head in 1971 when the PLO was officially expelled from the country. Political problems continued for Jordan during the Gulf War (1991), however, when the government found itself supporting United Nations measures condemning Iraq's invasion of Kuwait while also trying not to offend its much larger neighbour.

As for western-style theatre, there was none before 1918. But there were Al-hakawati (storytellers) from Damascus and Jerusalem who inspired the roving poets who sang their tales as they played the rababa, a traditional musical instrument. According to al-Masrah fil-Urdun (Theatre in Jordan, 1981) a study done for the Association of Jordanian Theatre Professionals by Abdullateef Shamma and Ahmad Sheqem, it was in 1918 that an Arab Catholic priest named Anton al-Heehi came to Jordan from Bethlehem and began an Arab Catholic Youth Society with as one of its objectives being the teaching of the art of stage acting. Along with Father Zakaria al-Shomaly, who had come from Baitsahour in Palestine, they offered a number of theatrical performances. In the 1920s (according to an essay by Rox al-'Uzaizi in 1978 that appeared in the Ministry of Youth and Culture magazine Funoun) they staged a production of Hamlet with their students.

Other than this and similar amateur undertakings and experiments over the next two decades, literary theatre in Jordan remained a mainly academic endeavour until the late 1940s when community cultural clubs began to appear along the lines of those in Palestine. In 1947 the Cultural Co-operation Club staged one of the first Arab dramas to be seen in the country, Mahmud Taymur's Egyptian play Suhad. Such simple performances took place in cinemas,

The Death of Thebes by Fawanees Theatre Group

church halls or even private homes. Shakespeare and Molière were two of the writers whose works were most often produced.

These performances were looked upon as dubious at best. Not only was the script style curious but also in such productions all roles were played by men. Indeed, performances for male and female audiences had to take place on different days.

The first appearance of a woman on stage in the country did not occur until the early 1960s, marking the beginning of the modern Jordanian theatre movement. With the establishment of Jordan University in 1963 came a fresh group of students eager to learn about new forms and styles, the forerunner of a general cultural movement aimed at bringing to Jordan a more modern intellectual sensibility.

The first Jordanian to study theatre was Hani' Snobir, who returned to the country in 1963 to work with a group of enthusiastic students of the Jordan University to stage Robert Thomas's *The Trap*; this attracted wide attention and started discussions about the importance of

Sawsan Darwazeh's 1991 production of *Decoration of the Ankle Bracelet In the Triangle of Time*.

strengthening theatre in the university's cultural life. Among the plays later staged by the students was *I Want to Kill*, by Tawfiq al-Hakīm, in 1965.

That same year the Ministry of Information sponsored a formal meeting bringing together for the first time under government sponsorship many of those working in the area of theatre. The result was the setting up of the Department of Culture and Arts in the Ministry. From this came the creation of Usrat al-Masrah al-Urduni, the first professional theatre body in Jordan (the members of which were the students who started their theatre activities in 1963 at Jordan University). This group presented two theatre seasons of translated western plays which unfortunately did not connect to audiences. Both public involvement and attendance were minimal.

The Six Day War of 1967 and the loss of Jordanian territory left the country in a state of shock. A production of John Steinbeck's *The Moon Is Down* later that year was staged by the group and effectively captured the national

mood. This was followed by Sartre's *No Exit* (*Huis Clos*) which also captured the national frustration and finally brought audiences to the theatre.

Over the next few years, Usrat al-Masrah al-Urduni would present a continuing range of foreign scripts – many of them, however, with little connection to anything local – including plays by Shaw, Ibsen, Molière and Wilde, most of which were directed by Snobir. The group admitted that its overall task of trying to generate new theatre audiences would have been made easier if other groups had emerged. However, because there were no others working at such a level, this group's seasons had to be diverse and multifaceted. Despite the importance of the group as a model for Jordan's theatre, it never really found a way to connect with or to reflect specifically Jordanian issues through its evolving art.

In 1969 the first Damascus Theatre Festival took place in Syria and companies came to it from across the Arab world. Jordan was repre-

Jordanian Theatre Family's production of *The Moon Is Down*.

sented by Usrat al-Masrah al-Urduni's production of a Spanish play in Arabic, *Boat Without a Fisherman*, by Casona. The group quickly realized that continuing to stage foreign plays would to a very great extent keep it out of step with theatre developments in other Arab countries. Clearly it needed to produce Arab plays. This was done when it produced two specially commissioned short plays, *The Key* and *The Locusts* by the Jordanian short-story writer Jamal Abu Hamdan, at the second Damascus Theatre Festival.

Though the group closed down in 1971, a new generation of trained theatre people emerged and a number of young dramatists started writing on Jordanian issues and attracting a new local public. Official support rose and fell depending on who was running the Department of Culture and Arts.

The early 1970s saw energy turned toward the many individual theatrical initiatives going on at Jordan University. Directors such as Ahmad Qawadri and Hatim as-Sayed had presented their first productions on campus and begun attracting new audiences and participants. Other groups emerged, such as Amoun 74 founded by Suheil Elias. Presenting a major new annual production over the next four years, two directed by Elias and two directed by Jamil Awad, the company's history was highlighted by Jamil Awad's production of *ash-Shahadeen* (*The Beggars*, 1977) adapted from Jamal Hamdan's play. One of the first to be produced by a private group, the production attracted wide audiences and much debate. Yet audiences were still relatively small and the group ceased operation in 1978.

During this same period a Ministry of Culture and Youth was created which employed several theatre directors. Now, with the support of the

Fawanees Theatre Group's 1992 production of *Gilgamesh*.

Fawanees Theatre Group's production of *Au el Fawanees at the Bottom of Siksak*.

government, there was pronounced progress in the development of the theatre movement. The Association of Jordanian Theatre Professionals was established shortly thereafter, determined to create an infrastructure upon which a professional theatre could be built in Jordan, and between 1977 and 1981 there was a pronounced rise in the quality and quantity of theatre activities. Unfortunately, internecine struggles for control quickly paralysed theatrical activities again both public and private. On the positive side, a department of theatre was opened at Yarmouk University in Irbid in the north of Jordan, which helped to diminish the foreign nature of theatre activities and women began to be drawn to theatre with less traditional resistance.

One of the Department of Culture and Arts' major productions at this time was the 1979 drama *Rasoul min Qaryat Tamira lil Istifham an Masa'lat al-Harb was-Salam* (*A Messenger from the Village of Tamira Sent to Inquire about the Matter of War and Peace*) by the Egyptian dramatist Mahmud Diyab. Adapted and directed by Hatim as-Sayed, this production engaged the audiences with its handling of sensitive topical issues relating to the Arab–Israeli struggle and the many moves that were being made to defuse the resistance against the occupation.

Another breakthrough came with the creation in the early 1980s of the Royal Cultural Centre in Amman. Until then, virtually all productions had taken place on the stage of the Department of Culture and Arts (now the Usama Mashini Theatre) or at the Samir Refa'i Auditorium at Jordan University. Nevertheless, though theatrical activities were beginning to be seen as socially acceptable and those working in the theatre were no longer looked on with contempt, most still had to work in television or other jobs to make a living. Government support was

Department of Culture and Arts' 1979 production of *A Messenger From the Village of Tamira Sent To Inquire About the Matter of War and Peace*, directed by Hatim as-Sayed.

Fawanees Theatre Group's 1982 production of *Dum Dum Tak* based on Brecht's *Master Puntila and His Man Matti*.

modest, there were no professional unions for theatre and those working in it had no social security or labour rights. Because of this, by the early 1980s, theatre was once again more or less inactive in the country.

Yet another start occurred at the end of 1982 when another new theatre group emerged presenting well-known plays from abroad, including the work of Bertolt Brecht. In its Founding Manifesto, the new Fawanees (Lanterns) Theatre described Jordan's then current situation in a series of strong metaphors:

> Extreme cold and pitch-black darkness. . . . seeking one who can, with his eye and the eye of his intuition, cut through the darkness and see through the webs of time; who can see how bodies can be transformed into motionless representations; houses into cold, dark tombs; streets into mere lines, black and empty; trees into branches, broken and silent. Thus the sound of silence rings out. There is not a single human voice, only cold freezing everything.

It was in its way a call for not just theatre but a new kind of theatre, one committed to social action and social change.

Fawanees's first production was an adaptation of Brecht's *Master Puntila and His Man Matti*, an attempt by its director to link the country's future to specific social and class issues. The first private group to take such a specific approach, the company was able to create a climate of intense enthusiasm which not only benefited its own work but also encouraged other groups to try their hand at theatre. In 1984, the Fawanees group took an unorthodox version of *Hamlet* to the Rabat Theatre Festival. The importance of the production lay in its search for a new scenographic style utilizing colour, light and silence. Fawanees also utilized musicians on stage, pushing the flow forward with original theatrical scores, while mocking and commenting on the action through recognizable local tunes.

During the 1990s, productions continued to emerge irregularly from three main sources: the Department of Culture and Arts, small groups

Fawanees Theatre Group's 1984 production of *Hamlet*.

Popular Theatre Group's production of *The Ash Girl*.

Wafa Qusous' puppet production of *Tales From My Grandmother's Chest*.

following the style and approach of the Fawanees Theatre, and productions done at Yarmouk University. Still today none of the people involved earns a salary, and rehearsals are held around work commitments. Even the Fawanees, which had as many as forty people connected with its work at various times, has said that its mission can only be to try and increase 'the continuing growth and social acceptance' of theatre in the country.

As for Drama-in-Education it was introduced in the 1980s in some private schools to help young people learn through drama and gain confidence, self-awareness, and creative expression. By the mid-1990s, a national training program in Theatre-in-Education was established and was providing public school teachers with the training needed to use drama and theatre in their teaching. This national programme also toured state schools in the kingdom, presenting plays and conducting workshops with the students and teachers discussing behavioural, social and other issues.

The country's major performing arts festival is the Jerash Festival for Culture and Arts, begun in 1981 by Yarmouk University. Over the years the festival has become a meeting point for Arab and international performing artists and has helped develop a new audience for opera, modern dance, ballet, classical music and literary theatre. Performances at this festival have regularly used ancient Roman sites in the city of Jerash north of Amman.

The Ministry of Culture also sponsors its own festival every year. The Fawanees Theatre started the Amman Theatre Festival in 1994, the first in the Arab world to be organized without direct financing or intervention of government. This festival has become a successful international meeting point for independent theatre groups from around the Arab world.

Zein Ghanma and Nader Omran

Further Reading

Document on the First National Conference of Culture. Amman: University of Jordan, 1985.

The Fawanees Theatre: al-Bayan at-Ta'sisi [Founding manifesto]. Amman, 1984.

Hawari, Bashir. *Dirasat* [Studies]. Amman: Jordanian Book League, 1980.

Shamma, Abdullateef and Ahmad Sheqem. *al-Masrah fil-Urdun* [Theatre in Jordan]. Amman: Jordanian Theatre Professionals Association, 1981.

al-'Uzaizi, Rox. *Funun* [Arts magazine]. Amman: Ministry of Youth and Culture, 1978.

KUWAIT

(Overview)

An independent state located at the head of the Persian Gulf, Kuwait is – per capita – one of the world's richest nations. Bordered on the south by Saudi Arabia and to the north and northwest by Iraq, Kuwait was at the centre of a war between Iraq and a UN force led by the United States in 1990–1 when Iraq, in defiance of the United Nations Security Council, annexed the country and declared it Iraq's nineteenth province. In 1991 Kuwait's autonomy was restored.

With just over 1.8 million people in 1995 living in an area of 17,820 square kilometres (6,880 square miles), Kuwait's population is 45 per cent Arab-Kuwaiti and 35 per cent other Arabs from neighbouring countries. Minorities include 9 per cent from south Asia, 4 per cent Iranians and 7 per cent others including many Pakistanis and Indians. Islam is the predominant religion with 45 per cent of the population following the Sunni sect. Kuwait's official language is Arabic; English and French are used for commerce and other languages, mainly Farsi and Urdu, are also spoken.

Kuwait's history is rooted around its capital, the city of Kuwait, which was settled in the early seventeenth century and known as Kadhima. An emirate of the Utoob Arab clan, Kuwait was never ruled by Ottoman Turks, although it cooperated with the Ottomans, particularly Medhat Basha after his visit to Kuwait. In 1938, after the discovery of oil in the country, British presence in Kuwaiti affairs increased, and the country became a British protectorate. In 1961 Kuwait became an independent country. The first constitution and national assembly were created in 1963. In 1997 Kuwait was officially a constitutional monarchy led by Crown Prince and Prime Minister Sheikh Sa'ad al-Abdullah as-Salim al-Sabah and Emir Sheikh Jabir Ahmad al-Jabir al-Sabah. A founding member of the oil-producing cartel OPEC, Kuwait joined the United Nations in 1963. During the 1980s, as war raged between Iran and Iraq, Kuwait suffered from the bombing by both sides. The long-standing territorial claims by Iraq on Kuwait were renewed after the Iran–Iraq conflict and led to the invasion by Iraq in 1990. The invasion was condemned by both the United Nations Security Council and the Arab League, who supported the Kuwaiti people and their legal government. The liberation of the country caused a major ecological disaster when some 600 oil wells were set alight in Kuwait. By early 1992 the burning oilwells had been extinguished and Kuwait was again moving toward rebuilding the country as well as its culture.

During the British colonial period Kuwait saw the emergence of a nationalist movement that sought to build a Kuwaiti culture separate from both the British and from other Arab states. The country's earliest performative traditions stem from an oral folklore that has its roots in epic tales, stories and songs, poetry, riddles and proverbs. Developing in the coastal *al-maqahi al-sha'biya* (coffee-houses), such stories were an immensely popular form of entertainment and can be seen as a form of indigenous theatre. In an attempt to collect these stories and help protect this oral tradition, Kuwait established a Folklore Preservation Centre in 1957 to record and classify Kuwaiti folklore to ensure that it remained a living art. In 1982 the study of such folklore was formally introduced into the education curriculum.

Further support for the folk arts came in 1974

Hassan Yakoup Ali's *Lovers of Habiba* directed by Fuad Al Shatti.

when the National Council for Culture, Arts and Letters was established to work in the area of cultural planning, promotion and development. The council also assumes responsibility for disseminating culture generally including the fine arts and works toward the preservation and study of national heritage through cultural exchanges on both an inter-Arab and international level.

Another of the country's performative traditions involves folk dance with a number of folklore troupes performing regularly. The majority of these receive annual financial support from the government. In addition, Kuwait Television has formed its own Kuwait Television Folklore Troupe which has presented performances of popular dances at various international festivals.

In 1984 a conference was held at the Arab Gulf States Folklore Centre in Dawha, Qatar to discuss methodologies of collecting and documenting folk dance and music. In 1991, with the cooperation of UNESCO, the Folklore Centre established an archive of visual and sound recordings and a bibliography of studies conducted by both Arab and international scholars.

Among the most recognized of Kuwaiti dances is the traditional *ardah*, which blends agility and manipulation with the use of a sword. Done to the communal rhythm of drums, tambourines and poetic singing, the *ardah* attracts large audiences throughout the country. Other dances of note include the *samri*, *khamari* and *tanboura*. All are performed at family gatherings, social occasions and wedding celebrations. Special songs and dances accompany the various chores performed on ships, another important element in Persian Gulf cultures. The most famous of the Kuwaiti sea songs are *Al-Dawari*, *Al-Holo* and *Al-Singhari*.

Theatrical activities in Kuwait began as early as the 1920s when the first spoken dramas proved popular. However, it was not until 1956 that the first regular theatre group, Al-Sha'bi Group, was founded. Other groups followed including the Al-Arabi Group (1961), Arab Gulf Group (1962) and Kuwaiti Group (1965). These four, known as 'Domestic Theatre Groups', are all state subsidized. By the 1990s, Kuwait had a number of private theatre groups as well as longstanding amateur groups such as the Kuwaiti Players (founded 1957), who have their own theatre space.

A scene from the Kuwaiti production *Recalling of Life*.

Tawfiq al-Hakīm's *Judge of the Tribe* directed in Kuwait by Muhammad Khodre.

The 1960s saw the emergence of a group of remarkable theatre practitioners in all disciplines of dramatic work – writing, production and acting. They, with many others, made significant contributions to the establishment of modern theatre in Kuwait. Abd al-Aziz al-Surayy's plays, for instance, have been produced in many Arab countries. His best known play is *Dā'al al-īk* (*The Cock Is Lost*), a social drama about an English-educated Kuwaiti searching for his Arab roots. Among the well-known directors are Fuad Al Shatti, Muhammad Khodre and Munqiz al-Suray.

Saqr al-Rushud (*c.*1944–78) is another Kuwaiti playwright of note. After obtaining a degree in commerce and economics from Kuwait University he became interested in drama and subsequently wrote and directed several plays. Profoundly influenced by both Abd al-Aziz al-Surayyi and western theatre, he used problems of modern life – the clash between deep-rooted philosophies towards women versus more progressive, modern attitudes, for example – as material for his work. His best known plays include *I and Fate* (1964), *The Big Fang* (1965), *The Barricade* (1966) and his widely acclaimed *The Mud* (1965).

Waleed al-Rikaib (b. 1954) is the editor of the cultural section of *Al-Amil* review, a journal of general union workers in Kuwait, as well as the author of one play, *Attachés to a Boxed City*.

Training for the theatre profession has been carried out since 1964 at the Institute for Dramatic Studies which in 1973 became the Higher Institute for Theatrical Arts, funded by the Kuwaiti government. The first graduates from the Higher Institute for Theatrical Arts – both men and women – completed their studies in 1977. Many of the graduates have assumed positions in the Ministries of Information and Culture (where much cultural animation takes place) or have taken up employment in other regions of the Gulf. The institute holds a cultural festival at the end of every academic year at which plays are publicly staged. These include works from both Arab and world literature.

In 1982, Kuwait University introduced the first course in the Gulf region on folk literature as part of its studies in Arab languages. In 1986 a course on folkloric anthropology was added by the department of sociology. In 1984 the Kuwait Foundation for Scientific Progress dedicated its major award to the study of Arab and, more specifically, Kuwaiti folklore, further

Hassan Yakoup Ali's *For a Handful of Dinars* directed by Fuad Al Shatti.

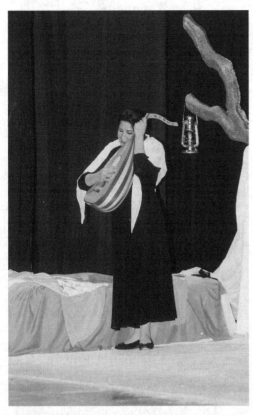

The Kuwaiti drama *Trench of Invasion*.

emphasizing the importance of research in this area.

The Kuwait theatrical movement is represented in the General Union of Arab Artists and the Arab Dramatists' Union. It is also a member of the International Theatre Institute. The country issues a monthly publication entitled *From World Drama* that translates international plays. More than 400 plays have been translated in this series from various countries.

Staff
with Fuad Al Shatti

(See also **BAHRAIN**)

Further Reading

Dasgupta, Gautam. 'The Eyes of War'. *Performing Arts Journal* 13 (1991).

Davis, Eric and Nicolas Gavrielides. 'Statecraft, Historical Memory, and Popular Culture in Iraq and Kuwait'. *Statecraft in the Middle East: Oil, Historical Memory and Popular Culture*. Miami: Florida International University Press, 1991. 274 pp.

Dukhi, Yusuf Farhan. *al-aghani al-kuwaytiya* [Kuwaiti songs]. Qatar: Arab Gulf States Folklore Centre, 1984. 503 pp.

Good Morning Kuwait by M. al-Rashoud, directed by Munqiz al-Suray.

Gröesl, B. and H. Gube. 'Das Kuwait Conference Centre' [The Kuwait Conference Centre]. *Bühnentechnische Rundschau* 83 (1989): 13–17.

Kamal, Safwat. *madkhal fi-dirasat al-fulklur al-kuwayti* [An introduction to the study of Kuwait folklore]. Kuwait City: Ministry of Information, 1973.

al-Najjar, Muhammad Rajab, ed. *al-ghatawi aw al-alghaz al-sha'biya fi-l-kuwayt wa usuluha fi-l-turath al-sha'bi* [al-Ghatawi or Kuwaiti oral folk riddles and their origins in folk culture]. Kuwait City: al-Rubay'an , 1985.

——. *mu'jam al-alghaz al-sha'biya fi-l-kuwayt* [The encyclopedia of Kuwaiti folk riddles]. Qatar: Arab Gulf Folklore Centre, 1985.

al-Nuri, Abdallah. *al-'amthal al-darija fi-l-kuwayt* [Common proverbs in Kuwait]. 2 vols. Beirut: Qalfat Press, 1976.

Scarce, Jennifer M. *The Evolution of Culture in Kuwait*. Edinburgh: Her Majesty's Stationery Office, 1985.

al-Shamlan, Sayf Marzuq. *al-al'ab al-sha'biya al-kuwaytiya* [Kuwaiti folk games]. Beirut: Dar I'lam al-Fikr, 1970.

LEBANON

The former centre of Middle East banking, Lebanon, with an area of only 10,450 square kilometres (4,000 square miles) lies on the Mediterranean Sea bounded on the north and east by Syria and on the south and southeast by Israel. One of the first Arab countries to gain political independence during the modern period (from France in 1943), Lebanon now has a parliamentary and democratic system of government. Although its resident population is about 3.5 million (no official census has been held since 1932), some 6 million Lebanese emigrants live in other parts of the world, with particularly large communities being found in France, Canada, the United States, Brazil, other parts of the Middle East and in a number of African countries.

Lebanon's national capital is Beirut and the country's official languages are Arabic and French. English, Armenian and Kurdish are widely spoken. Some 70 per cent of the population are Muslims with most of the remaining 30 per cent Christians. A founding member of the League of Arab States and the United Nations, Lebanon played an important role in the drafting of the Universal Declaration of Human Rights.

Historically, Lebanon has roots that reach back into antiquity. Indeed, there are some seventy or so mentions of the country in the Old Testament. Lebanon was known as the home of the Phoenician people who, among others, were at one time the masters of the Mediterranean Sea and who, with purple sails, roamed far and wide. Among famed ancient Phoenician cities were Jubayl (Byblos), Sayda (Sidon) and Sur (Tyre). Lebanon was mentioned by Greek poets and dramatists such as Homer and Euripides, the latter saying in his play *The Bacchae*, 'The land shimmers with the aroma of milk, wine and the nectar of flowers rising as the fumes of the incense of Lebanon.'

Throughout its history, Lebanon has been overrun by larger nations including the ancient Egyptians, Hyksos, Hittites, Assyrians and Chaldeans. The Persians ruled the land from 539 BC to 333 BC and when the Persian Empire fell under the onslaught of Alexander the Great, the Greeks took control, ruling Lebanon from 333 BC to 64 BC. During this period of Greek rule, trade flourished and cultural and intellectual life advanced, paving the way for an intermixing of eastern and western civilizations and giving birth to what became known as Hellenic civilization. The Greeks were followed by the Romans who dominated Lebanon from 64 BC to AD 635, a period distinguished by a general prosperity in industries such as farming, lumber trading and textiles. It has been recorded that when one of the Roman emperors visited Byblos, he enjoyed living in the city and not only enjoyed discussions about the goddess 'Ashtarout (Astarte), but also performed an act of worship for her. The Romans, it should be noted, did not tamper with the rights and privileges enjoyed by major Phoenician cities.

The year 1098 marked the start of the Christian Crusades, which lasted almost two centuries, finally ending in 1291. Through this long period of war, much interaction – intellectual as well as bellicose – took place between *al-faranja* (the European foreigners) and those Muslims living in the east. Such interaction even led to bilateral economic exchanges. After the Crusades, Lebanon was ruled by the Mamluks whose reign ended in 1516, when they were defeated by the Ottoman Turks. During the Ottoman era, Lebanon was divided into several principalities. The Ottomans remained in Lebanon for more than four centuries, their control ending only after World War I. During those centuries and especially during the rule of Jamaal Pasha, the Lebanese people experienced severe forms of tyranny and injustice. Simple hunger caused the death of thousands, and the threat of starvation sent thousands of others outside the country to seek asylum. During that same period, 60 per cent of Lebanese forests fell to the axe. In that atmosphere, calls for Arab independence and freedom from Ottoman rule became intense.

In 1918, Ottoman control ended and colonial control passed to the French. In 1922, however, the Lebanese were allowed to replace French Administrators with an elected Parliament. By 1939, however – the outbreak of World War II – the French High Commissioner had to declare martial law, suspend the constitution, dissolve Parliament and limit the authority of the country's president because of the continuing independence movement. In 1943, following rioting and a general strike, the French government, in agreement with Britain, proclaimed Lebanon's complete independence.

With the resumption of constitutional life in Lebanon, elections for a new Parliament were held and a (Maronite) Christian, ash-Shaikh Bishaara al-Khouri, was elected as President of the Republic. He in turn approved the nomination of a Sunni Muslim, Riyaad as-Solh, as Prime Minister. Periods of cooperation between the two major religious communities have alternated ever since with periods of tension. Civil war finally broke out in 1975 but was declared over in 1989 with the signing of the Ta'if Accord. By the end of the war, the country was in shambles and most of the 1990s was spent trying to put the pieces back together again.

Theatrically the country has an equally long and complicated past. Perhaps the oldest of Lebanese theatre forms is connected to the many Adonis and Astarte celebrations, among the first forms to depict stories from Phoenician mythology. These celebrations recount in music, dance and story the profound love of Adonis and Astarte. According to this specific part of the legend, Adonis, while hunting, was attacked by a beast and killed leaving his lover inconsolable. While his blood reddened the waters of Nahr Ibraheem (Ibraheem River), Astarte cried bitterly and ultimately went into an extended mourning for him. It was that loss of true love which was remembered each spring by Phoenician women, who would sing heart-rending laments. The tradition (along with other Semitic and Greek myths) was used – particu-

larly in the middle decades of the twentieth century – as the basis for plays.

Such events, part of the national mythology, connect with other equally well known folk and religious celebrations. Examples can be found in *khayal al-zhil* (shadow theatre), in the continuing popularity of *al-hakawati* (the storyteller), and in the performances of sharp and satirical monologues. All these have connected and converged with Lebanon's complicated theatre traditions over the centuries, sometimes being reflected in literary ways and sometimes in forms of celebration.

Other major forms – *al-hakawati* and *khayal al-zhil* being simply the best known – provided the theatre with even more stylistic considerations both in terms of genres and subjects. These forms inspired many modern directors to experiment with such things as audience participation as they tried to incorporate into their work elements of those celebratory events found in birth rites, *halaqaat az-zaar* (spiritualist seances), weddings and funerals. All these are part of the theatrical atmosphere that the modern Lebanese theatre benefited from and which playwrights and directors have made use of in their stage work.

Khayal al-zhil generally follows but could also predate Ottoman traditions – a collection of comic scenes performed behind a large white screen by figures cut out of leather. The light source is directed from behind resulting in the projection of shadows onto the screen. The master puppeteer stands behind the screen speaking for all the characters, and sometimes narrating events. Such shows often parallel and comment on contemporary issues. In other examples, the shows are politically or sexually frank. Known in Beirut and environs from about the eighteenth century as *karagöz*, it was particularly popular in large cities including Sidon and Tyre. The venues for shadow theatres were most often popular cafés, and it reached a large working-class audience. Shadow theatre productions, one of the most accessible forms of recreation in Beirut in the time before cinema, radio and television, would tour with companies from Beirut playing in Damascus (Syria) and vice versa.

Older, equally popular and also influencing modern theatre practice has been the art of *al-hakawati*. A revered community figure, *al-hakawati* would perform in popular cafés ringed by listeners who came to hear the adventures of Arab and foreign heroes. One of the most famous adventures was called *Qissat 'Antar*

(*The Story of Antar*) and was built around the life of this Arab horseman and poet who lived between AD 525 and 615. One of the few poets whose writings hang on the draperies covering the *ka'abah* in Mecca (Holy of Holies shrine), he was known for his love for his cousin 'Abla for whom he fought many battles. The stories of his life were always seen as a sort of literary dessert in evening gatherings throughout the Arab world. Audiences exhibited strong reactions during the narration and would often divide into groups, each supporting different characters. Other biographical tales that were part of the repertoire included the story of *al-Malik ath-Thaahir* (*ath-Thaahir the King*) and *Sayf Bin Dhi Yazin*.

The storyteller's function went beyond the simple act of narration, often encompassing a range of stories, virtually acting them out as a one-person stage show. These would include poetry recitations and the mimicking of well-known personalities. *Al-hakawati* would use props as needed.

Also popular were monologists. *Al-Monoloj* (the monologue) in the Arab world tends to be satirical and is usually frankly critical of particular social and political situations. With or without musical accompaniment, the monologues might also include jokes and poetry. Introduced to Lebanon by Egyptian monologists, this art became particularly popular in cafés and restaurants in the 1930s. By the 1950s, however, it was seen only on rare occasions. Among the famous stars of this genre were Omar az-Z'inni, a popular poet whose work was often memorized and recited at parties, Yahya al-Lababeedi, Daowoud Qaranou' and Yousef Husni.

Another traditional theatricalized style is the *'Ashourah* (Ashura), a religious ceremony celebrated by Shiite Muslims. During these celebrations, participants re-enact the story of the sufferings and pains endured by al-Husain Bin 'Ali and the tragedy of his martyrdom in the city of Karbala. A religious theatre, these rites include all the main features of theatrical presentations – prepared scripts, actors, props, period costumes and a specially erected stage which would be surrounded by an eager audience ready not only to watch but also to participate in the proceedings.

In Lebanon, these religious celebrations are connected to the Shiite and Alawi *ta'ziyeh* (see also IRAN) and were apparently brought by Iranian Shiites to southern Lebanon. Still seen in Mantaqat an-Nabatiyya (the Nabatiyya area),

they acquired a form whose dramatic momentum was clearly derived from religion. These celebrations feature semi-simulated sword blows to people's heads which draw blood as a good omen and in emulation of the bleeding of al-Husain, the Shiite Muslim martyr.

One can view certain Lebanese Christian celebrations in a similar light: Palm Sunday and Eid Barbara (Barbara celebration, or Hallowe'en), in which participants wear masks and roam around the city, town or village visiting houses, singing songs and demanding treats. Another celebration is Eid al-'Adhra' Mariyam (Virgin Mary Festival) which is accompanied by processions and the singing of hymns.

The Lebanese past is rich in such folk forms and many more can still be found at weddings, holiday events and community celebrations. One such is *haflaat az-zajal*, a type of competitive poetry in which two or more poets try to prove who can perform best. It is done on its own but more often at occasions such as weddings and private parties. This art is particularly popular in Lebanon and the ability to perform extempore is a prime requisite for those interested in working in the field.

A more literary form of theatre – leaving out the influence of the ancient Greeks – re-emerged in Lebanon in the nineteenth century when French and Italian troupes visited the region. Their performances were seen by many from Lebanon including the businessman Marun al-Naqqash (1817–55). Born in Sidon, al-Naqqash moved with his parents to Beirut, where he became fluent in French, English, Italian and Turkish. As an adult he travelled to France and Italy on business. It is believed he encountered Italian dramatic forms, particularly opera, which he found immensely appealing.

After returning home, he wrote his first play in Arabic and called it *al-Bakhil* (*The Miser*). Although of the same name as Molière's original, *L'Avare*, the play was significantly different, however, as a close reading of the two scripts will confirm. Those wishing to ignore the significance of this event argued that it was simply a translation or adaptation. Those wishing to credit al-Naqqash with being the first to write an Arabic-language play in this region have recognized the uniqueness of this production in which he, members of his family and merchant friends participated as actors when it was performed in his house in Beirut at the end of 1847. The production – rightfully considered the starting point for the emergence of Arabic language theatre in this area – remained for many at the time simply one more foreign amateur presentation since its availability was limited to a specific group of people and not to the public at large. Nevertheless, *The Miser* was a scripted play about more or less average people rather than an epic saga or folk tale and, created in Arabic by an Arabic-speaking group of actors, and it marked a major change in indigenous performance history.

In 1850, al-Naqqash wrote another play, *Abu' l-Hasan al-Mughaffal* (*Abu' l-Hasan the Fool*), which he also presented at his house, and to which he invited an elite group of Ottoman statesmen who happened to be in Beirut at the time. The British traveller, David Urquhart, described al-Naqqash's stage and setting:

It was erected in front of the house in the manner that we are careful to emulate in our theatres: a door in the middle with two apertures above and two windows on the side. At the end of the courtyard was the backstage area, near which were the side doors. The stage was placed in the centre, the audience sat facing the stage and the hall was shaded by ship sails.

Urquhart described the performance:

The acting was hesitant and the singing was bad, but the direction, technically speaking, was quite successful, pointing out the playwright's potential talents as well as proving that the Arab spirit could certainly be awakened and moved.

Al-Hasoud as-Saleet (*The Insolent Envier*), the third stage play that al-Naqqash wrote, was presented in Beirut in 1853. He composed music for each play, a stylistic device that is still seen in the Arab theatre. His nephew, Salim al-Naqqash, who continued this work in Egypt, later said that his uncle had introduced theatre in the Arabic language to this part of the world.

Marun al-Naqqash believed that theatre's major role was to uncover social problems. He often stressed basic morality in his plays or in the special speeches he wrote to introduce them. In his first pre-play speech (Beirut, 1869), he spoke of theatrical art generally, emphasizing that the theatre's mission was to link artistic enjoyment to precepts that refine character: 'for through such theatre, people's shortcomings will be bared allowing the discerning to learn a lesson and be wary.' Such moral aims long remained the goal for Lebanese playwrights.

Marun al-Naqqash's contributions to modern Arabic theatre were major and his theatrical presentations remained for decades a yardstick against which one could measure the quality of Arab theatre. As well, the pursuit of a career as a dramatist or a theatre artist after al-Naqqash became something socially acceptable. Even his brother Nicola (1825–94) wrote two plays while his nephew Salim along with Adeeb Ishaaq began a theatrical company that moved to Egypt in 1876. That company presented several plays at the Zeezna Theatre in Alexandria. When it ceased operating, it divided into two newer companies: Firqat Yousef al-Khayyat (Yousef al-Khayyat's Company), which remained active from 1877 until 1895, and Firqat Sulaimaan al-Qirdaahi (Sulaimaan al-Qirdaahi's Company), which operated from 1882 to 1895. Under the wing of those two companies, a number of other Arab theatre artists came to note including George Abyad, a Lebanese-Egyptian, and the Egyptian Salaama Hijaazi.

By the end of the nineteenth century, several Lebanese-Egyptian companies had been formed offering performances, respectively, in Beirut, Cairo and Alexandria. A number of Lebanese dramatists moved to Egypt at this time where they found more fertile soil. But early in the twentieth century religious authorities decided to challenge the new art as antithetical to Islam. As a result of this and of the Urabi Revolt, the royal patronage which the Khedive Ishmail (then the ruler of Egypt) had long accorded to the arts and sciences generally and to Arabic theatre in particular came to an end. This said, he still allowed visits to Egypt by European companies.

Such religious attacks had much earlier taken place in Syria and Lebanon when Ottoman authorities and local religious figures banded together to discourage all performing art forms. By the reign of Sultan Abd al-Hamid (1876–1910), Ottoman authorities, determined to show their power, imposed measures which led to even greater influence by *al-mashaayikh al-muslimeen* (Muslim religious figures) who suddenly felt free to attack theatre people for being immoral, degenerate and negligent towards Islamic principles. Besides increased censorship and the banning of certain newspapers, all attempts at criticism of the regime or expression of independent thought in theatrical form was considered reason enough for continuing investigation.

Those at the start of careers at that time found themselves totally unable to earn a living in the theatre while those in mid-career found doors suddenly shut to them. As a consequence, during the 1870s and 1880s, Lebanese and Syrian artists and intellectuals began to emigrate en masse to Egypt where the general atmosphere, at that time, was freer and more independent.

Lebanese–Egyptian theatrical cooperation reached an advanced stage at this time with a relatively large number of companies from Egypt coming to Lebanon and vice versa. Nevertheless, the actual process of establishing and developing companies came to differ significantly in the two countries. In Lebanon this meant that the next generation of writers and actors set out to create theatre companies and to produce plays utilizing subjects derived from history, religion and contemporary social problems. Beirut became the focal point for most of the activities and, under the direction of this next generation of artists, groups slowly emerged and construction began on new theatres.

During this next period writers and directors also began to tap historical and literary sources from which they derived themes and plots for their plays. A modern Arab renaissance period resulted (between about 1898 and 1939) in which there was such a marked degree of increasing interest in Arab history that a variety of nationalistic sentiments were also awakened. Virtually all Arab artists at this time sought to recall the past glory of the Arab nation as a whole and tried to find examples of courage, heroism and high moral character. The first to realize the importance and value of this heritage were poets and it was they who were responsible for the first important plays including *Salaah ud-Deen al-Ayyoubi* (*Saladin*). Dealing with a famous military commander and ruler, the play focused on Saladin's exploits in battle against the Crusaders. Another play, *as-Samaw'al* by Father Khaleel Iddi, was similar to *Saladin*, in that it too dealt with the life of an Arab personality known for his courage and loyalty – Imru'u al-Qays. The most famous of the many plays about this poet and statesman was Adeeb Lahoud's *Imru'u al-Qays*.

Many plays were also written about Yousef Karam, a Lebanese Christian hero who struggled against the Ottoman presence in Lebanon. The best known play about him was written by Father Hanna Tannous. Indeed, the presence of the Ottomans in Lebanon along with the injustices and brutalities they committed were ripe subjects for plays. Among the most acclaimed have been *Jamaal Baasha Fi Lubnaan* (*Jamaal*

Pasha in Lebanon) by Father Butrus al-Ashqar and *Lubnaan 'Ala al-Masrah* (*Lebanon on the Stage*) by Adeeb Lahoud.

Romantic subjects too began to abound at this time. In an earlier time, Arab writers depicted profound emotions in melodious and refined poems. With this as inspiration, Lebanese playwrights in the first decades of the twentieth century explored emotion in their writings drawing on well-known romantic subjects in their desire to present love as a human spiritual ideal. Shakespeare's *Romeo and Juliet* was translated into Arabic several times during this period, audiences obviously enthralled by the idea of someone sacrificing himself for his beloved. It should be noted that love at this time meant a spiritual relationship between two lovers, something to be defended from the temptations of wealth and betrayal.

By the 1940s, romantic plays began to change in nature, benefiting from the new-found freedom following independence. Some playwrights – Abdalla Hushayma for one, in his play *al-Khayr Wa sh-Sharr* (*The Good and Evil*) – were determined to explore all aspects of love more openly than ever before. Some even dealt with relatively risqué subject matter such as adultery, attributing its causes to a wife's weakness or her tendency towards liberality as in Yousef al-Qaadi's play *az-Zawja al-Mutamarrida* (*The Rebellious Wife*). What is surprising looking back on this play is its suggestion that the wife's adultery was actually caused by the husband's questionable love.

Perhaps the most famous of the romantic plays was *Majnun Layla* (*Mad about Layla*), a subject about which more than one play was written. The most important playwright to write a play on this subject was Maroun 'Abboud, a well-known Lebanese man of letters. In his 1912 play, the leading characters represent the famous Arab lovers, Qays and Layla, who had lived in the Arabian peninsula during the second half of the seventh century. In the story, the father's despotism is the main obstacle to the realization of the lovers' happiness.

Also popular were religious plays written by men of the cloth of all clerical ranks. Most simply propagated the faith retelling stories from the Old Testament and the Gospels. Some clerics even wrote plays about other clergymen, such as *al-Batriyark Jubrael Hajoula ash-Shaheed* (*Patriarch Gabriel Hajoula the Martyr*) by Hanna Tannous, *Rifqa* by Pierre Rufaayil, *Maar Ifraam* (*Saint Ifraam*) by George Saqqaal al-Halabi and *Majaa'at Lubnaan Wa l-Mutraan*

Antoine 'Areeda al-Bishirraawi (*The Famine in Lebanon and Archbishop Antoine 'Areeda al-Bishirraawi*) by Father Gabriel as-Sirr 'Ali.

The story of the Virgin Mary was a subject for more than one early Lebanese play – the best probably being *Intiqaal al-'Adhra* (*The Virgin's Ascension*, 1936) by the Reverend Yousef Baheet. Bishop Yousef al-Haayik wrote several scripts which stand out, including *al-Qiddeesa Jaan Daark* (*Saint Joan of Arc*), *Jazaa' Ka's Maa' Baarid* (*Reward for a Cold Cup of Water*) and *al-Ghaaliyaat ath-Thalaath* (*The Precious Three*), the last being set in Rome in AD 272 during the reign of Emperor Orlean the Persecutor. In this play, three Christian women are sentenced to be thrown to the lions but are eventually saved by their faith.

In 1945, inspired by the tenets of the Muslim religion, Shaikh 'Umar Sabra wrote *Islaam 'Umar* (*The Conversion of 'Umar to Islam*), which was presented on the stage of a school belonging to al-Maqaasid al-Khayriyya al-Bayrutiyya (the Maqaasid Charity in Beirut). This was an exception, though, since theatrical activities in Islamic schools are not generally encouraged because of wariness concerning the art of acting.

Along with these plays – all based around Arab virtues – came a number of plays dealing with social issues such as family problems, young people and western cultural influence. New types of stage characters came to be seen such as *al-walad al-mutafarnij* (the Europeanized boy), *al-fataat al-mutafallita al-mutaaliba biqadar akbar mina l-hurriyya* (the liberal girl demanding more freedom), *ash-shaab as-sikkeer* (the inebriate youth), *al-muqaamir* (the gambler), *al-mar'a al-khaa'ina* (the adulteress) and *ar-rajul al-intihaazi* (the opportunist). Alongside these, other more positive characters also appeared such as *al-um al-faadila* (the virtuous mother), *al-muwaatin al-ghayour 'ala 'aadaatih wa taqaleedih* (the citizen who is zealous for his customs and traditions), *al-fataat al-mutahassina* (the chaste girl) and *al-fallaah al-mutamassik bi-ardih* (the peasant who clings to his land). All these were woven together in stories that combined urban customs and village traditions. The city was seen as the centre of problems while the village was seen as the symbol for truthfulness, openness, love of the land, and as the guardian of national moral values.

These ideas were best reflected in plays such as *Ghareebun Haatha* (*This Is Strange*) and *al-Intiqaam* (*The Revenge*) by Fareed Mudawwar,

'Aasifa Fi Bayt (*A Storm in a House*) and *'Aasifa Fi Qarya* (*A Storm in a Village*) by 'Abdalla Hushayma, *Mathaalim al-Hayaat* (*Life's Injustices*) by Edwaar ad-Dahdaah and *al-'Aashiq ash-Shaarid* (*The Distracted Lover*) by Joseph al-Ghareeb. The last two plays were performed many times by many companies.

Michael Nu'aymi, a well-known writer of the time, published a play called *al-Abaa' Wa l-Banoun* (*Fathers and Sons*, 1917), about the relationship between children and parents. The play shows how parents interfere in the selection of husbands for their daughters and wives for their sons. Additionally, this play demonstrates the role and influence of the feudal landowner in the form of the stage character known as *al-Bek*. What is particularly noteworthy here is the author's use of colloquial Arabic for certain characters.

The 1940s and 1950s saw a waning of interest in Arab historical and cultural subjects and the appearance of an even larger number of plays which dealt with various social problems. Of special importance seemed to be the blind desire by young people to emulate western lifestyles. Among the many dramatists looking at this issue were Fareed Mudawwar, 'Abdalla Hushayma, Yousef Younis and Sa'eed Taqiyyuddeen. The last was famed for his critical and satiric writings.

Few political plays were seen prior to independence, a situation brought about by the close monitoring of the arts by first the Ottoman and then the French colonial authorities. The first moves to speak out came in the 1920s, paralleling the establishment of the Lebanese Communist Party in 1924. In 1936, two other political parties were established – the Lebanese Phalangist Party with a Christian base led by Pierre al-Jumayyil, and the Syrian National Social Party, which was led by Antoun Sa'aadi, who called for unification of a Greater Syria. The following year, 'Adnaan al-Hakeem established the Najaada Party, an Islamic group oriented towards Arab nationalism. Despite the spread of these political organizations and their influence on society, the theatre remained quite insulated from direct political involvement and none of the parties included policies toward or even sought useful propaganda from theatre groups.

Schools and universities, especially those that were established by foreign Christian missions in Lebanon, formed by this time a sort of continuing laboratory for theatrical experimentation which mirrored to some extent a growing professional movement. They not only adopted theatre as an activity, but also built stages and encouraged their students to delve into theatre as an art form. Many professors at this time took it upon themselves to write and translate plays as well as to train students in acting. They also offered private off-campus theatre companies an opportunity to perform on their stages. The most important in this regard was the American University of Beirut and that of Saint Joseph University, a French-language Jesuit institution (see section on **Training**).

From the 1940s on, attempts were made to consistently utilize a more colloquial form of Arabic on the stage, a movement which connected to attempts by actors to break away from classical stage plays and the grand manner of acting. By the early 1960s, theatrical language had changed significantly and by the 1990s, classical literary Arabic language was seldom heard on the Lebanese stage.

The 1950s, on the other hand, was a kind of middle phase, a calm after the activity of the previous two decades and a calm before the activities that would take place in the early 1970s. A number of reasons have been advanced for this: the passing away of many of the century's pioneer actors and playwrights, the curtailment of many scholastic theatrical activities, the arrival of the modern cinema with its more realistic techniques and the collapse of old theatre styles after their first encounters with modern concepts brought from the west by new Lebanese theatre people.

As a result, the 1950s was a period in which theatrical activities lost their intensity and energy and began playing a rather indistinct role in the search for a national cultural identity. This loss of forward movement was exploited by cultural Francophile protagonists led by the École des Lettres (French Advanced Literature School) in Beirut which opened a theatre in one of the wings of the Conte de Shaila Sports Palace and another on its campus. The campus theatre was administered by the École des Lettres and the theatre's operation was handled by the school's teachers and students with the participation of several Lebanese and French theatre people including George Heritier, Henry Khayyat, Jaques Mettra (who staged the first Beckett and Ionesco works seen in Lebanon), Michel Corvin (a French scholar who directed the theatrical studies section at the École des Lettres until the 1970s), Marc Henri Mainguy, Cécile Janis and Alan Plisson. Besides presenting plays in French, the College Acting Centre, a

subsidiary of the École des Lettres, operated as a theatrical laboratory for western avant-garde theatre.

The year 1960 marked the beginning of a real revolution in the Lebanese theatre largely inspired by western acting and directing techniques. The two pioneers of this movement were Antoine Multaqa and Mouneer Abu Dibs. The former studied philosophy and psychology and did a lot of amateur theatre in his home town of Waadi Shahrour, a village not far from Beirut. In 1953, he both acted in and directed Shakespeare's *Macbeth* at the Jesuit University. Abu Dibs, for his part, had worked at a French television station in Paris when he decided to return to Lebanon to participate in the efforts of the newly born Lebanese television station. He particularly wanted to see plays on television and, since locally written programmes were quite rare at the time, he started out using mostly foreign scripts. With their interests merging, Abu Dibs and Multaqa agreed to present *Macbeth* on television in 1960. That was followed by other plays and later that same year together they established a School of Modern Theatre and a new company called Firqat al-Masrah al-Hadeeth. Its early productions included *Odeeb al-Malik* (*Oedipus the King*) by Sophocles, *Macbeth* by Shakespeare, *ath-Thubaab* (*The Flies*) by Sartre and *al-Malik Yamout* (*The King Is Dying*) by Ionesco. The company, according to its founders, sought to express the essential human spirit in a ritualistic form.

When the two men separated some years later, Abu Dibs continued such experiments. By 1970, he began writing his own plays. Among them were *at-Toufaan* (*The Flood*, 1970), *Gubraan* (*Gibran*, 1972), *Yasou'* (*Jesus*, 1973) and *Thilaal* (*Shadows*, 1974). At the beginning of the war in Lebanon in 1975, he went to France where he established a new company with French actors creating a production at the Odeon Theatre in Paris in 1978. In 1990, he returned to Lebanon and resumed his activities. One of his productions in 1996 exhibited a continuation of his earlier style.

Antoine Multaqa for his part remained with Abu Dibs for only a year, after which he left to establish another company, Halaqat al-Masrah al-Lubnaani (Lebanese Ring Theatre). Multaqa's view of actors differed from that of Abu Dibs, who believed that an actor was a means to a larger concept. For Multaqa, the actor was the centre of the theatre. Multaqa's work with the actor was divided into two parts: theory and practice. He required of the actor a sound grounding in science and culture. Everyone who worked with him had to study subjects such as theatre theory and human psychology. His work also concentrated on the physical. As with Abu Dibs, Multaqa's work also used improvisation.

Halaqat al-Masrah al-Lubnaani presented Shakespeare's *Macbeth* in 1962 and (in 1963) *Jareema Wa 'Iqaab* (*Crime and Punishment*) by Dostoevsky. In 1964, the company participated in the Nancy Festival in France. Multaqa subsequently created his own theatre space in the Ashrafiyya district of Beirut in an old movie house. He inaugurated the theatre with an adaptation of Kleist's German comedy *al-Ibreeq al-Maksour* (*The Broken Jug*).

Multaqa began in 1971 the Storyteller's Theatre which rejected the picture frame stage almost entirely, working instead with the audience seated on two or more sides. His model was the presentational style of *al-hakawati* and some public religious celebrations. He ultimately cleared the stage of most props and visual elements replacing them with symbolic elements that would allow the spectators to use their own imaginations. Multaqa sought to borrow a dimension from folk culture – the concept of the public square – to emphasize the idea that there are communal traditions to be followed.

Multaqa worked throughout these years with his wife Lateefa Multaqa. In her own right, she had a distinguished role in the Lebanese theatrical movement directing, adapting and acting in many plays. She taught courses in acting at the Fine Arts Institute, a department of the Lebanese University which had been established in 1965 as a result of her husband's efforts.

During the 1960s and into the early 1970s, the concept of playwright in Lebanon also experienced profound changes. From a writer of a literary text, the playwright slowly became a script engineer. That is, the playwright changed from a man of letters to a text shaper who worked closely with actors and directors, from a solitary individual to a group participant. Some worked well within that framework; others did not. Among those who flourished in this changed format was 'Isaam Mahfouth, author-dramaturge for such plays as *az-Zinzalakht* (*The Chinaberry Tree*) and *ad-Diktatour* (*The Dictator*); Remon Jbaara, author-dramaturge of *li-Tamut Desdemona* (*Let Desdemona Die*) and *Taht Ri'aayat Zakkour* (*Under Zakkour's Care*); and Mouneer Abu Dibs, author-director of the trilogy *at-Toufaan* (*The Flood*), *Yasou'* (*Jesus*) and *Gubraan* (*Gibran*).

During these years as well, scriptwriting generally went through three different phases. Due to their overlapping occurrence in time, they cannot easily be defined by decades or years, but they can easily be defined by parameters of form. These three phases are translation, adaptation/Lebanonization and authorship.

The modern translation phase came about because directors and actors found themselves without scripts of interest to produce. As a result, they did as their predecessors did and resorted to the western cultural heritage. Most young directors and actors, for example, were amazed by the richness of the Shakespearian legacy when they discovered it as their predecessors had done before them. In the literary work of Dostoevsky and Camus, they found deep spiritual and philosophical elements that conformed to the eastern mentality and stimulated innovations in acting and directing. They were equally fascinated by the strangeness of Theatre of the Absurd and began producing the works of Ionesco and Beckett. These were real gambles for them since the theatre itself was not on such firm ground and their audiences were not even used to literary theatre. Through such work, though, they were reconnecting local culture to that of the west.

Among those involved in this work in the 1960s and 1970s were Unsi l-Hajj and Adonis and 'Isaam Mahfouth; Unsi l-Hajj translated works by Shakespeare (*The Comedy of Errors*, 1963), Ionesco (*Exit the King*, 1965), Dürrenmatt (*Romulus the Great*, 1965), Camus (*The Just*, 1967), Brecht (*The Exception and the Rule*, 1968) and Arrabal (*A Celebration for a Murdered Negro*, 1968). Adonis translated Goethe's *Faust* in 1968 and Büchner's *Danton's Death* in 1970, while 'Isaam Mahfouth translated Beckett's *Waiting for Godot* in 1967.

At that point, theatre critics among others began to confront the issue of whether theatre should be seen as a high literary art or theatre as a popular art, an art connected somehow to Lebanese reality. The decision for most lay somewhere between these two approaches. One first step in this regard was the discarding of classical Arabic on the stage and replacing it with colloquial Arabic. Such a transformation went beyond the question of language in many cases resulting in the adapting of scripts to Lebanese realities. Known as 'Lebanonization', such attempts sought to impart a Lebanese identity, in language and content, on each production. Such a movement formed a first step

Jalaal Khouri's 1962 production of Beckett's *Waiting for Godot*.

toward the writing of national plays by local dramatists. The measure of the success of a 'Lebanonized' script was generally judged by how close it was able to connect to Lebanese audiences. Such a treatment was given to plays as far afield as Ben Jonson's *Volpone* and Kleist's *The Broken Jug*. Nizaar Miqaati and 'Afeef Radwaan also 'Lebanonized' several plays by French comedy writers such as Labiche and Feydeau. Even Gogol's *The Government Inspector* received such treatment.

Doubtlessly, the Arab–Israeli war of 1967, which ended with an Arab retreat on the Egyptian, Syrian and Jordanian fronts, had a great effect on everyone in this part of the world. The educated and the cultured sought to reflect and express larger communal concerns and plays commenting on the war and its aftermath began to appear. All Arab governments were exposed to public discontent. The new realities were painful, so much so that they could not be ignored or put aside. Innumerable productions began to appear dealing with the causes and consequences of the war. Most expressed bitterness, gloominess and frustration and most contained painful indictments against the Arab world as a whole for being submissive towards incompetent and bumbling leaders.

A new language also slowly developed which added social, political and intellectual levels to aesthetic ones. The proximity of the theatre to daily events began to provide people with a genuine echo of their daily concerns. The play *ad-Diktatour* (*The Dictator*), for example, frankly criticized the military leadership and military regimes suggesting that their real interest was simply maintaining power. In 1970, Ya'qoub ash-Shidraawi directed *A'rib Ma Yali* (*Parse the Following*), which was a play written in verse criticizing the fragmentation of the Arab world and its inability to find collective solutions to fundamental issues such as the Palestinian problem.

Henry Haamaati wrote *Majdaloun* at this time, a play directed by Nidaal al-Ashqar and Roger 'Assaaf. Authorities, however, ordered the production to be stopped. In his play, Haamaati created a quick and sometimes violent dialogue between people and government. A realistic portrayal of life in the town of Majdaloun, the play focused on the crisis in daily living conditions, the struggle between the older and the newer generations and the political contradictions among the rebels, Palestinian armed fighters, ruling political authority and the Israeli enemy.

Jalaal Khouri, in his play *Jeha in the Villages Facing the Enemy*, attacked the kind of defeatism exhibited in the border areas of southern Lebanon. Directed by Jalaal Khouri and performed in Beirut, the play's protagonist, Jeha, was naïve, simple and apolitical. When forced to face an enemy armed with the latest technical and military tools the results became predictable.

'Isaam Mahfouth's play *Limaatha . . . (Why . . .)* was another accusatory political work in which three characters representing aspects of Arab nationalism are studied: Sirhan Sirhan, who assassinated Senator Robert Kennedy in the United States in 1968; Antoun Sa'aadi, who established and led the Syrian National Social Party; and Farajalla l-Hilu, a noted communist in the 1960s, who was tortured to death in a Syrian prison. Mahfouth said that he chose his three characters because 'the first one represented individualism, the second represented nationalism and the third internationalism. Death was the common denominator for all of them.'

> I wanted, as many others did, to condemn those who merely observe by juxtaposing them against those who fought for causes. I wanted to awaken reactions. . . . I wanted to induce a sense of shame and, by a palpable shock, to scour the rust off the revolutionary slogans that, by their useless repetition, alienated people . . . individuals and groups, rebels and rebellion, what is and what must be in this backward part of the world.

Mohammed al-Maghout also dealt with similar issues in two of his plays: *al-Marsilyaaz al-'Arabi (The Arab Marseillaise)* and *al-Muharrij (The Clown)*. In the second play, he compared and contrasted past Arab glories with the present backwardness, and connected this fall to a western invasion of Arab-Islamic thought.

In 1971, Shakeeb Khouri adapted Orwell's *Animal Farm* into a play called *Jamhouriyyat al-Hayawaanaat (The Animal Republic)*. The play dealt with and actually attacked Arab military regimes, especially those that came to power in the name of socialism and ended up by betraying ideals and the public interest. *The Animal Republic* was a cry against dictatorship and a call for democracy as the best means for governing.

In 1972, Remon Jbaara wrote *Taht Ri'aayat Zakkour (Under Zakkour's Care)*, a play which dealt with war, sacrifice and militarism. Jbaara utilized a bitterly sarcastic language, his

characters living somewhere between derision and suffering. Similar to absurdist works, his play was not pegged to a specific time and place. The accusations were again directed towards the military regimes with the commander in this case captivated by a halo of greatness.

During this period, the most performed play in the country was *as-Sitaara (The Curtain)* by Rida Kabreet and directed by Michel Nab'a. This play, first presented in 1972, was more optimistic than most of those already mentioned for, although it dug up and exposed the reasons for the fall of the Arab individual, it also suggested that there was hope. At the end of the play, a child is to be born who will change the situation and instigate a revolution at all levels.

The period between 1960 and 1975 was part of a larger cultural movement in which promoted artists tried to cross disciplines. Poets translated plays that were then designed by major artists for productions that included actors, dancers and musicians.

In 1975, however, the movement forward in the country's performing and literary arts, simply stopped. Lebanon was stricken by civil war, in which many internal and external forces participated. Virtually destroying the country at this time and decimating the country's theatres, it was a war which saw the Lebanese divided against one another along both religious and political lines. As a result, many left the country or moved to safer ground within the country.

Beirut was itself divided into an eastern sector, which was predominantly Christian, and a western sector that was mostly Muslim. Actors were scattered and universities were redivided by these two basic communities. Work stopped for nearly five years.

By the 1980s, however, new theatre spaces had begun to be established by new groups, especially in the Christian areas outside Beirut. Among these were the Château Trianon Theatre, the Athenée Theatre and George the Fifth Theatre. Along with others established in West Beirut, all began to operate quietly whenever war conditions allowed.

The civil war lasted until about 1990. During these fifteen years little new work was done aside from the occasional light comedy. As a result, however, a new interest in what could be called modern vaudeville emerged – evenings of sketches, songs and dance. The war also affected play production. Those groups and individuals who owned theatre spaces became intensely interested in quick profits. The comedies began to attract a new type of spectator whose modest

Antoine Moultaka's 1987 production of Dürrenmatt's *The Visit*, Beirut.

taste began to dominate theatre life. At the same time, with economic conditions deteriorating daily, theatre rentals increased and ticket prices had to be raised. This resulted in the exclusion from the theatre of not only the poor but also middle-class audiences. A new audience emerged which wanted from the theatre only easy laughs. By the mid-1990s there were virtually no serious or experimental theatres in the country.

As the 1990s drew to a close, however, a new theatrical movement was again in the process of beginning, started by veteran directors and enthusiastic young people. Among such new groups were the City Theatre headed by Nidaal al-Ashqar and the Beirut Theatre. Both began to offer high quality productions and were planning, as part of their programming, to bring foreign companies to Lebanon to help the theatre community catch up on what it has missed during the long war years.

Structure of the National Theatre Community

The war between 1975 and 1990 all but destroyed any national theatrical infrastructure. Indeed, Lebanese theatre since its inception was primarily established and operated by interested individuals as private enterprises and state subsidy is all but unknown. The country has neither a national theatre building nor a national company. The country's major international theatrical event has traditionally been the Balbeck Festival. There are no unions or other national theatrical agencies.

Artistic Profile

Companies

Beirut's first regularly producing theatre companies date to the second half of the nineteenth century when groups started playing seasons in the capital, then went on tour to other cities in the country and eventually on tours as far away as Egypt. By the turn of the twentieth century, however, the numbers of such companies dwindled until, by the 1920s, regularly producing groups became a rarity. Thanks to a growing movement toward nationalism, theatre started to revive in the late 1920s; in the 1930s a whole new generation of theatre groups began to be established once again.

The most important of the companies established during that decade were the Firqat al-Ittihaad al-Masrahi (Theatrical Federation Company) created by 'Isa an-Nahhaas in 1938; Jam'iyyat at-Tamtheel Wa r-Riyaada (Society for Acting and Sports) begun by Mohammed Shaamil; Jam'iyyat Tarqiyat at-Tamtheel al-Adabi (Society for Improving Literary Acting), also established by Mohammed Shaamil; Firqat Qadmous (Qadmous Company) started by Joseph al-Ghareeb in 1939; Jam'iyyat al-Adab at-Tamtheeli (Literary Acting Society) started by Michel Haaroun in 1939; and Firqat al-Opera al-Lubnaaniyya (Lebanese Opera Company) started by Sou'aad Kareem in 1939.

This expansion continued into the 1940s with the establishment of Firqat 'Abd al-Hafeez al-Mahmasaani ('Abd al-Hafeez al-Mahmasaani Company) established in 1941; al-Firqa al-Lubnaaniyya lil-Masrah Wa s-Seenama Wal-Ithaa'a (Lebanese Company for the Theatre, Cinema and Radio) established by Yousef al-Qaadi and Saami al-Qaadi in 1943; Firqat an-Nahda al-Fanniyya (Artistic Renaissance Company), also established by Yousef al-Qaadi in 1944; Firqat al-Arz al-Fanniyya (Artistic Cedar Company) established by Michel Taabit, Lucien Harb and George Qaa'i in 1945; Firqat at-Tathqeef al-Watani lil-Museeqa Wa t-Tamtheel (National Education Company for Music and Acting) established by Saami al-Qaadi in 1946; and Firqat Lubnaan lit-Tamtheel al'Arabi (Lebanese Company for Acting in Arabic) established by Pierre Rufaayil in 1949.

Among the significant companies established during the 1950s were Firqat al-Yaqtha al-Fanniyya lil-Museeqa Wa t-Tamtheel (Artistic Awakening Company for Music and Acting) established by Saami al-Qaadi in 1950, and Firqat ash-Shu'la al-Lubnaaniyya (Lebanese Flame Company) established by 'Ali Shamsuddeen in 1952.

Most of these companies produced translations of English and French plays and only occasionally original works by Arabic-language playwrights. The work was ultimately more valuable in literary terms than it was in theatrical innovation. Acting techniques were copied from touring actors from abroad and from early film acting. Though the techniques of theatrical pioneers, such as George Abyad, were still fresh in their memories, the acting generally was skewed towards unnatural gestures and vocal exaggeration. Indeed, the playwright Sa'eed Taqiyyuddeen said of this type of work:

> Generally speaking, our acting is artificial. Some overdo hand gestures so much that one might imagine them to be fencing, or an actor might be in a love scene yet, physically, seem to be wailing and lamenting. How many solemn and sad speeches were transformed into derisive mockery by an actor's stony delivery and immovable demeanor as if he were completely detached from whatever was happening around him.

During the 1950s, as a direct result of western theatrical influences that began to infiltrate the Lebanese theatre, attempts were made to make acting technique more natural.

New companies of note established in the 1960s included Firqat al-Masrah al-Hadeeth (Modern Theatre Company) in 1960 headed by Mouneer Abu Dibs; Halaqat al-Masrah al-Lubnaani (Lebanese Theatre Ring) established in 1961 and headed by Antoine Multaqa; Firqat al-Masrah al-Hur (Free Theatre Company) established in 1965 and run by André Jid'awn and Madonna Ghaazi; Firqat Muhtarifee Bayrout lil-Masrah (Beirut Professional Theatre company) established in 1968 under the dual management of Nidaal al-Ashqar and Roger 'Assaaf; Firqat Hamaazkiyyeen (Hamaazkiyyeen Company), an Armenian theatrical company managed by George Sarkisian, and Firqat Gulbenkian (Gulbenkian Company), an Armenian venture managed by Berge Vazilian.

Firqat al-Masrah al-Hur set out to be a populist theatre and moved from one area of Beirut to another presenting its shows in factories, cinemas and schools. Among the plays it staged were works by O'Neill, Ben Jonson and Goldoni.

Al-Masrah al-Watani (National Theatre) was a private venture established in central Beirut in 1965 by the popular actor Hasan 'Alaa'uddeen (d. 1975), known to most Lebanese from television as Shoushou. As the new company's leading actor, Shoushou assumed the role of a naïve young boy, poor, not-too-bright and wearing old worn-out clothes. The character became famous all across Lebanese society. Shoushou worked closely with director Nizaar Miqaati, Roger 'Assaaf and Berge Vazilian. Most of the group's early shows were European comedies in Arabic adaptations. He regularly added songs to his plays, often dispensed with the original endings and wrote his own, which often enabled him to comment on current events.

Another group of note at this time was Firqat Muhtaraf Bayrout lil-Masrah (Beirut Workshop Theatre Company) which began in 1968 and encouraged group authorship and collective direction. Its models were the Workshop at Stratford East which had been started in England by Joan Littlewood, the Open Theatre of Joseph Chaikin and the Living Theatre of Julian Beck and Judith Malina. Run by Roger 'Assaaf and Nidaal al-Ashqar, the company tried to affect society through critical commentary and populist techniques involving music and movement.

In 1979 Roger 'Assaaf left to establish another group which he called Firqat Masrah al-Hakawati (Storyteller's Theatre Company) with the stated objective of connecting to Arab traditions. The work of this company was also collective in manner. The group sought its inspiration in Arabic cultural heritage and historical styles seeking out stories that could be adapted to conform to their evolving performance methods, methods which included narrative models. Using as its base the art of storytelling, a distanced type of theatre emerged that is almost Brechtian in its nature. Its most successful show was *Hikaayaat Min Sanat 1936* (*Stories from the Year 1936*).

Firqat al-Masrah al-Lubnaani lid-Draama (Lebanese Drama Theatre Company) was begun in 1966 by Michel Khattaar to stimulate theatrical activities in schools. The company also sought to encourage playwrights by publishing their work and later began a theatre magazine. His group staged works that ranged from the Bengal dramatist Rabindranath Tagore and the Egyptian playwright Tawfik al-Hakīm to Racine. Khattaar later taught at the University Centre for Drama Studies, a subdivision of the French Advanced Literature College, where he directed several plays in French including *The New Tenant* by Ionesco, *Talab Zawaaj* (*A Marriage Proposal*) by Chekhov, and *Georges Dindin* by Molière. Khattaar has written a number of plays for children. In 1996, he established the Centre for Artistic and Artisan Creativity in north Beirut where he has again presented a number of plays for children.

Other groups active between the late 1970s and 1990s, groups which throw a direct light on the contemporary theatre in the country, are discussed in the opening historical section.

Dramaturgy

Lebanon's first modern playwrights began working in the nineteenth century. Pioneers in this then new art, they included Salim al-Bustaani, Ibraheem al-Ahdab, Najib al-Hadad and Farah Antun.

Al-Bustaani (1848–84) belonged to a literary family famed for its contributions to poetry and fiction. He started his career by translating European classics (including Shakespeare) into Arabic. Al-Ahdab (1826–91) was born in Tripoli, northern Lebanon. One of the pioneers of the national literary renaissance, he wrote, translated or adapted some twenty plays. His writings were inspired by and derived from Arab history. The most famous of his plays were *al-Mu'tamid Bin 'Iyaad, Wilaada Bint al-Mustakfi Ma'a l-Wazeer Ibn Zaydoun* (*Wilaada the Daughter of al-Mustakfi with the Minister Ibn Zaydoun*), *'Abd us-Salaam, Abu n-Nuwwaas Ma' Jinaan Jaariyat Thaqeef* (*Abu n-Nuwwaas with Jinaan the Thaqeef Slave*), *Majnoun Layla* (*Mad About Layla*) based on popular mythology, and *Jameel Wa Buthayna* (*Jameel and Buthayna*).

Al-Hadad (1867–99) wrote sixteen stage plays, some of which were translations or adaptations while others were his own creations. His translated plays were *as-Sayyid* (*El Cid*) and *Seena* (*Cinna*) by Corneille, *Ifijeeni* (*Iphigénie*) by Racine and *at-Tabeeb Raghman 'Anhu* (*Le Médecin malgré lui/A Doctor in Spite of Himself*) by Molière. One of his own plays that he derived from pre-Islamic Arab history, *Intiqaam al-Badawi* (*The Bedouin's Revenge*), was a tragedy that went beyond the theoretical boundaries of classicism because its characters had unique psychological traits. Another play, *Salaah ud-Deen al-Ayyoubi*, was derived from Arab military history. Najeeb's adaptations included *Romeo and Juliet* by Shakespeare, *Hernani* by Victor Hugo and *Ghadre Wa Hub* (*Perfidy and Love*) by Schiller.

Many Lebanese dramatists of this period lived and worked mostly in Egypt, for example Yousef al-Khayyaat (fl. 1877–95), Sulaimaan al-Qirdaahi (fl. 1882–1909), Iskandar Farah (fl. 1891–1909) and, perhaps the most famous of all, Farah Antun (1874–1922). Antun, born in northern Lebanon, emigrated just after the turn of the century to Egypt where he started his literary activities by writing about social issues. A journalist as well as a novelist, poet and playwright, he translated many works. In 1906, he travelled to the United States and on his return began a new publication called *Majallat al-Jaami'a* (*The University Magazine*). The most important of his own plays were *Masr al-Jadeeda Wa Masr al-Qadeema* (*The New Egypt and the Old Egypt*), which he wrote in 1913, *Salaah ud-Deen Aw Fat-h Baab al-Maqdis* (*Saladin or the Conquest of Jerusalem*), which he wrote in 1914, *Abu l-Hawl Yataharrak* (*The Sphinx Moves*) and *Banaat ash-Shawaari' Wa Banaat al-Khudour* (*Street Girls and Boudoir Girls*). Antun's stage plays were regularly performed in both Lebanon and Egypt.

Father Hanna Tannous (1866–1946) was a priest, teacher of literature and poet who wrote thirty-seven religious, historical and eloquent nationalistic plays, many for his students as acting exercises. Among the best known are *Malik ad-Dayaamees* (*The King of the Dayamees*, 1901), *Shuhadaa' Najraan* (*The Martyrs of Najraan*, 1903), *al-Batal al-Majhoul* (*The Unknown Hero*, 1906) and *Yousef Bek Karam* (1913). Reverend Hanna derived his subjects from Arab and Lebanese history and the social and religious reality of the time.

Sa'eed Taqiyyuddeen (1885–1961), another playwright who began his work in the early decades of the twentieth century, wrote five popular satires and later became active in politics. In his theatre work he advocated that women be allowed to perform on stage, one of the first Arab theatre people to take up this cause. His major plays include *Lawla l-Muhaami* (*Were It Not for the Lawyer*), *Hafnat Reeh* (*A Handful of Wind*), *Nukhb al-'Adouw* (*A Toast for the Enemy*), *al-Manbouth* (*The Outcast*) and *Qudiya al-Amr* (*It Is Finished*). These plays were all performed in Beirut.

Reverend Yousef al-Haayik (1885–1961) was

another clergyman and educator and probably the most prolific Lebanese dramatist with some forty plays to his credit. He used the theatre as a means for evangelization and for the purification of souls. Among his plays are *al-Malik an-Nu'maan* (*Nu'maan the King*), *'Aaqibat ath-Thulm* (*The Aftermath of Injustice*), *Da'd Ameerat Ghassaan* (*Da'd the Ghassaani Princess*), *Jazaa' Ka's Maa' Baarid* (*Reward for a Cold Cup of Water*), *Sirr al-Ameer al-Hazeen* (*The Secret of the Sad Prince*), *al-Qiddeesa Alisaabaat* (*Elizabeth the Saint*) and *Jaan Daark* (*Joan of Arc*). His works are still performed in Christian schools.

Another name of note is the philosopher-poet Kahlil Gibran, who wrote several short plays, each with a philosophical and sentimental bent.

Adeeb Lahoud (1885–1946) was a teacher and an educator. In 1916, he was appointed director of Arabic Language Studies in the Ottoman Office in the Jubayl (Byblos) region. It was during this time that he began writing plays such as *Lubnaan 'Ala al-Masrah* (*Lebanon on the Stage*), a play dealing with the sufferings that the Lebanese endured under the Ottomans during World War I; *Al-Fataat al-Mafqouda* (*The Lost Girl*), a play that dealt with a dispute between two Arab leaders; *Ash-Shahaama Wa sh-Sharaf* (*Magnanimity and Honor*), a play derived from Persian history; *Barbara ash-Shaheeda* (*Barbara the Martyr*), a religious play; and *Imru'u al-Qays*. Lahoud's two daughters appeared on stage during the 1920s.

More contemporary dramatists are discussed in the opening historical section.

Directors, Directing and Production Styles

George Abyad (1880–1959), among the best Arab actor-directors of his time, was born in Beirut, studied in Paris at the Conservatoire, and began his career in Beirut before moving to Egypt. For the most part, he performed only in French (even in Egypt) though he encouraged writing and adapting foreign plays into colloquial Arabic. Among his major performances were *Macbeth* and *Othello* by Shakespeare. Abyad was a force in Arab world theatre generally and Egyptian-Lebanese theatre well into the 1940s and 1950s.

Among the more contemporary directors is Shakeeb Khouri, a pioneer in the modern theatre movement. He began his career in 1957; when television was introduced into Lebanon in 1959, he was among the first to work in this new medium directing a series of plays ranging from literary adaptations to plays by Schiller. Khouri studied theatre at the Royal Academy of Dramatic Art in London and many Lebanese francophiles looked down on his Anglo-Saxon education, but he insisted that he found the Anglo-Saxon civilization equal to that of the Franco-Latin. In the 1970s he began staging the plays of absurdist writers including Beckett and Ionesco.

In his later work, Khouri reached a distinctive ritualism in form, from which he derived cinematographic features. Khouri's play *Cabaret*, which he wrote and directed in 1972, portrayed the onset of human submission to the machine, a situation that led to an overwhelming yearning for life in the rural villages. In his play *al-Fakh Aw al-Qiddaas al-Aswad* (*The Trap or the Black Mass*), which he wrote and directed in 1975, Khouri relates the story of a man who discards his own culture, a situation that could lead only to death. Religious questions also come into his work, introduced as an irresistible force and an invisible magic power.

Remon Jbaara, another director of note, has written that theatrical work is composed of three elements: sound, which includes vocal, musical and word effects; silence, which is the complement of sound; and movement. He defines his theatre as being the presence of the actor and the audience first of all and a place for literature only second. His theatre is a mixture of surrealism and absurdity and, therefore, deeply tragic. His theatre is non-mimetic. Indeed, he says that realistic theatre is trivial, evil and the enemy of real art. Jbaara's plays and productions delve into the labyrinth of the absurd, retreat back into an eastern sensibility and ultimately return to family and fringes of religious faith. One of the constants in Jbaara's theatre is authority. He considers the human animal to be between two authorities – one representing universal laws and the other representing earthly ones. Jbaara's theatre is a categorical cry of refusal and a rebellion against everything. He neither refutes nor agrees that his theatre is political and argues that theatre must be neither a political platform nor a series of manifestos.

Jalaal Khouri, another notable director, grew up in a Marxist ambience (his father was an enthusiastic communist), which had an effect on his education. He later became very fond of surrealistic poetry, the literary works of James Joyce, and Aragon, but he found difficulty in reconciling his understanding of Marxism and his artistic knowledge. It was only when he

became familiar with Brecht that Khouri found a way to blend form and content. However, fitting Brecht to the Lebanese reality was not easy for a direct political openness was somewhat dangerous. Khouri, however, kept a balance between ideology and aesthetics. He adapted a number of Brecht's plays to Arab reality. His play, *ar-Rafeeq Sij'aan* (*Comrade Sij'aan*), was presented in East Germany in 1980 at the Volkstheater Rostock; it was Khouri's best production to date, an example of the contradictions between totalitarianism and the individual. The ideological struggle here is between imperialism and communism, between two rural families.

Another of his plays – which he also directed – was *Jeha Fi l-Qura al-Amaamiyya* (*Jeha in the Villages Facing the Enemy*). The Jeha stories are popular in a number of Middle Eastern countries and probably originated in the Konya area of Turkey. Jeha is a young man known for his clever anecdotes. In this work, Khouri pits Arab archaism against Israeli pragmatism and rationality. The first part of the play deals with local

Director Jalaal Khouri.

Jalaal Khouri's 1980 production of *ar-Rafeeq Sij'aan* at the Volkstheater Rostock, former East Germany.

Antoine Moultaka's production of *L'Émigrée de Brisbane* by Georges Schéhadé at the Francophonie Festival, Paris, 1990.

problems, specifically a conflict between charcoal makers and their managers. The second part pivots around an encounter between Jeha and a group of Israeli military administrators.

In dealing with the modern theatrical movement in Lebanon, it is not possible to ignore the major contribution of a director of Armenian origin, Berge Vazilian, one of the prime movers in the establishment of an Armenian theatre in Lebanon, following that community's exodus from Turkey to escape persecution early in the twentieth century. Vazilian has exhibited a dis-

tinctive directing technique, especially in comedies, and tries to create a balance between vaudeville and literary theatre. In one of his productions he included a group of poems, some surrealistic and others fantastic or simply eccentric. He transformed the poems into visual tableaux through colour, light, sound and movement as well as singing, pantomime and music. His work has added a special dimension to both the Lebanese and the Arab theatre.

Other contemporary directors of note are discussed in the opening historical section.

Music Theatre

Music and movement have long been a part of Arab festivals and celebrations but it was not until the 1950s that a formal musical theatre emerged in Lebanon. Known as *al-masrah al-ghinaa'i* (singing theatre), such shows included song and dance and were often built around folk tales, jokes and anecdotes. Such materials have

long inspired poets, writers and masters of music, especially those materials that were related to demons, fiends, criminals and highwaymen. Such folk tales formed a tapestry of rich materials that not only fed people's imagination across the ages, but also left their imprints on the more modern musical theatre in Lebanon.

Many modern musicals had their premières on the Near East Broadcasting Station (radio), which was established in Beirut in 1953. Yahya al-Lababeedi and Tufeeq al-Baasha created most of the early productions working with director Sabri ash-Shareef. Shareef later directed most of the musicals created by the Rahbaani brothers and Fayrouz. The station also hired a number of poets to compose dialogues in *zajal* (vernacular verse), which was most suitable for singing.

In 1949, a meeting between Sabri ash-Shareef and the Rahbaani brothers led to the production of a collection of musical sketches starring the composer and comedian, Filemon Wihbi, whose tunes had been not only widely known, but also sung by the best vocalists in the Arab world. At that point, the Rahbaani brothers established al-Firqa ash-Sha'biyya al-Lubnaaniyya (Lebanese Folkloric Company), among whose objectives was the revival of a populist theatre returning Lebanese songs to their original identity and maintaining a special sense of the Middle Eastern spirit.

The brothers, 'Aasi ar-Rahbaani (1921–86) and Mansour ar-Rahbaani (b. 1923), were first attracted to music as children and they studied it under the guidance of the French musician Bertrand Rebouillard. Later joining the National Conservatoire, they played for fun in nightclubs where they revived the older musical tradition. So popular did this music become that their songs began to be played on Arab radio stations and eventually became top sellers. The singer who popularized most of their songs was Fayrouz, 'Aasi ar-Rahbaani's wife, whose fame was later to extend far beyond the borders of Lebanon.

In this style, the Rahbaani brothers created twenty-five musicals which could be divided into three groups. The first was distinguished by its Lebanese village atmosphere, customs, traditions and folklore. The most important musical shows in this style were *Mawsim al-'Izz* (*The Seasons of Glory*, 1960), *Jisr il-Qamar* (*The Moon's Bridge*, 1962) and *Bayya' il-Khawaatim* (*The Ring Peddler*, 1964). The second group included historical and epic works such as

Ayyaam Fakhr ud-Deen (*Fakhr ud-Deen's Era*, 1966), the story of a famous Lebanese prince who ruled in the seventeenth century and was known for his wisdom, sophistication and nationalism; *Jibaal as-Sawwaan* (*The Granite Mountains*, 1969) the story of a people's struggle to rid themselves of their country's occupiers; and *Petra*, a play about the history of Jordan. The third group of shows dealt with urban events. The most successful of this group were *Haala Wa l-Malik* (*Haala and the King*, 1967), *ash-Shakhs* (*The Person*, 1968), *Sah in-Nawm* (*Good Morning*, 1970) and *Ya'eesh Ya'eesh* (*Long Live Long Life*, 1971).

The most important phenomenon in the rural works was the portrayal of the common Lebanese man, a peasant well-rooted in the land. Love, in the Rahbaani show, was full of innocence and naïvete. The success of these shows had as much to do with nostalgia for the land as anything else.

During the course of a half-century, the Rahbaanis' theatre was able to create a new genre in Lebanon and a rich body of work whose essence included genuinely Lebanese spiritual and intellectual elements. Fayrouz not only influenced their style but also ensured popular success. The Rahbaanis' theatre helped to define this cultural period and to give Lebanon a musical artistic identity.

Others who produced musical shows in Lebanon included Romeo Lahoud and the Anwaar Company. Lahoud presented several operettas during the Balbeck Festivals and in theatres in Beirut during the 1970s. His work differed from that of the Rahbaanis in that it was more blatantly commercial and had less of a thematic sense. His shows were built around costumes, sets, music and dance.

Firqat al-Anwaar (Anwaar Company) was established in 1959 by Sa'eed Frayha, a noted journalist and publisher. The most famous of its offerings was *al-Mawaasim* (*The Seasons*), which was an ensemble of several dance tableaux tied together by a simple story. It was presented in Beirut and in several Arab and European capitals.

Dance Theatre

Lebanon's dance heritage is deeply rooted. Perhaps the oldest form is *raqsat ad-dabki*, a kind of foot-stamping dance seen in various folk celebrations. It remains the base for many contemporary on-stage dance styles. It is a dance done by country people rather than those in the city and is used sometimes to express a sense of collective unity as indicated by a close shoulder-to-shoulder stance and hand-in-hand clasp as the dancers rhythmically step forward and back and then side-to-side while intermittently stamping their feet.

Among the various types of the *dabki* dance are *ad-Dabki l-Biddawiyya* (Bedouin Dabki) introduced by migrating bedouins and distinguished by its long monotone chanting (similar to the chants of the cameleer in the desert) and *ad-Dabki l-ʿAskariyya* (Military Dabki) which is distinguished by its strict, military-like dance steps.

The *dabki* used to be customarily danced during celebrations, weddings, parties and national festivals. Some *dabki* dances are performed by men alone as a kind of display of manliness and to show off in front of the women. The lead dancer's position in the *dabki* is always to the right of the dancing group, whereas a beginner stands on the left. The dance could be danced in public squares or even on the roofs of houses. Through the years, its performance was extended to theatres where it became an indispensable component of all staged shows.

Doubtlessly, the Lebanese dance theatre is greatly indebted, in its origin and development, to the *dabki*, which was its major source of inspiration. In Lebanon, many companies which called themselves folk dance companies, used a mixture of modern dance and the *dabki* in their repertoires. Among early choreographers were Marwaan and Wadeeʿa Jarraar, who worked in the late 1950s and throughout the 1960s.

By the 1970s companies sought new forms in an effort to free their dances from the parameters of the traditional folk steps and movements. One of those that succeeded was the Caracalla Company, which was established by Abdul Halim Caracalla. The creator of one of the first real dance theatres in the Arab world, his company took material from both Arab and Lebanese traditions and restructured it based on modern dance techniques. A student of folkloric studies in Dijon (France), he later studied Martha Graham's technique at the London Contemporary Dance Theatre from which he received his Master's degree.

Caracalla's first major choreographic work was done at the International Balbeck Festival. In Osaka, (Japan), he presented a programme called *Lubnaan ʿIbr at-Taarikh* (*Lebanon Across History*), which highlighted his search for identity, an endeavour that has been his mark from the beginning. Since then, his company has toured widely. In 1992, the Caracalla Company staged a major Shakespearian-inspired production *Hulm Laylat Sharq* (*An Eastern Night Dream*). The group's Heritage Research Centre also gathers items pertaining to heritage: customs, traditions and musical standards.

As for western-style ballet, the pioneer in the country was Georgette Jbaara in the 1960s. A student of ballet in Egypt, she received a scholarship from the Yugoslav Embassy in Beirut to continue her studies in Yugoslavia, where she strengthened her skills in Russian technique. Returning home, she established al-Madrasa al-Lubnaaniyya lil-Baalé (Lebanese Ballet School) in Beirut. From the beginning of her work, she sought to link western ballet with a Middle Eastern spirit whether in the dances she created or through the use of local music by noted composers.

In 1966 she presented her first show and in 1972 she produced a dance interpretation of a play by the British dramatist Edward Bond under the title *Khitaan al-Luʿba* (*The Toy's Threads*). Throughout her career she worked regularly as a choreographer with such directors as Shakeeb Khouri and Mouneer Abu Dibs. Among these were shows for children, *Waiting for Godot, Man of La Mancha* and *Hamlet*. Her most famous dance roles were in *Coppélia, Les Sylphides, La Belle au Bois Dormant* and *Swan Lake*. Throughout her career she has also worked to give women an opportunity to express themselves through dance.

European-style mime is a new theatrical genre in Lebanon. Early experiments began to be seen in the late 1950s and early 1960s at festivals. More serious experiments began with the efforts of dramatist Maurice Maʿlouf who, after completing his specialized theatrical studies in England, returned to Lebanon in the late 1960s as an actor and director. His first major production was *Fadʿus*, a work about a man who migrates from his rural village to the city where he is confronted with more modern ways of living, with less human personal relationships and with new moral codes. A later production of note was *Farhat 'Arees* (*The Bridegroom's Joy*) in which he dealt with the concept of universal order as seen through the life of a traffic cop.

The onset of the 1975 war in Lebanon curtailed but did not put a stop to Ma'louf's activities, for he was still able to continue his teaching of mime at the Lebanese University. Some of his graduates followed in his footsteps, the most noted being Faa'iq Humaysi who has presented several of his own shows in Lebanon and other Arab countries and teaches this art in the theatre division of the Lebanese University.

Theatre for Young Audiences
Puppet Theatre

In Lebanon, the puppet theatre's origins derive from that of the shadow theatre and the *karagöz*, which were well known in the major Lebanese cities such as Beirut, Taraablus (Tripoli) and Sayda (Sidon). Shadow-puppets were made of leather, cardboard or cloth. Further details on the background of shadow theatre in Lebanon can be found in the opening historical section.

Marionette theatre is a much more recent phenomenon. Beginning in the early twentieth century in Lebanese schools, it took a professional turn around 1960 when a French marionettist named Tarabeau, who was previously active in the puppet theatre in Egypt, presented several puppet performances on Lebanese television which itself had been established only the previous year.

Tarabeau's marionette presentations encouraged Faakhouri (d. 1997) to establish a theatre which he first named Masrah ad-Duma al-Mutaharrika (Moving Doll Theatre) but later renamed Um Toufeeq (Toufeeq's Mother) and finally settling on the name Um Nabeel (Nabeel's Mother). Some of the songs performed by Faakhouri's company became quite popular and were sung by almost every Lebanese child at the time. Kifaah, Faakhouri's son, later joined the company as did his sister Jinaah. All three regularly participated in the various presentations of their father's company. Eventually, Faakhouri established his company at Beirut University College where they presented performances on Saturdays and Sundays.

Faakhouri derived his musical stories from Lebanese and foreign folklore.

Other puppeteers continued to emerge in the 1970s and again in the 1990s. Among them were Ghaazi Makdaashi, who studied in Bulgaria and later started a group called as-Sanaabil (Spikes of Grain); Kareem Dakroub, who specialized in Russian-style performances and who manufactured his own puppets; and Ahmed Qa'bour, who also composed musical scores. Dakroub experimented with the Japanese *bunraku*. Among Dakroub's major shows were *Tanbouri Laabis Haafi* (*Tanbouri Forgot His Shoes*, 1992) and *Shou Saar bi-Kafr Minkhaar* (*What Happened in Kafr Minkhaar*, 1992); *Lawnu bi-La Lawn* (*Its Colour Is Colourless*, 1994) and *Shatti Ya Dinyi Sisaan* (*O Let It Rain Baby Chicks*, 1997).

Another person active in the field was Najla Jraysaati Khouri, who in the 1990s combined marionettes with the art of shadow theatre. Her company, Sundouq al-Firji (The Peep Show), presented in this style a production that attracted much attention, *Hikaayat al-'Anza al-'Annouziya* (*The Tale of Goatee the Goat*).

Two theatres for young audiences in the country use puppets on occasion – the Children's Theatre and the Modern Child Theatre Company. The government's Educational Centre for Guidance and Research, a section of the Ministry of Education, proposed in the late 1990s a programme of courses on theatre that would be in the official curriculum at both schools and universities.

Design
Theatre Space and Architecture

The first European-style proscenium theatre space in Beirut was the Masrah Zahrat Souriyya (Syrian Flower Theatre) built in 1904 by the Jam'iyyat Ihyaa' at-Tamtheel al-'Arabi (Society for the Revitalization of Arab Acting). Headed by Patrou Pawli, Masrah Zahrat Souriyya presented Shakespeare's *Hamlet* as its first production. Subsequently many major Cairo-based companies (including the Lebanese-born George Abyad and his company and the Ameen 'Atalla Company) performed on its stage. In 1922, the theatre was converted into a cinema though it continued to be used for plays. It was ultimately destroyed by fire.

Almost as old was Masrah al-Kristaal (Crystal Theatre). Partly destroyed during World War I, it was rebuilt to standards that placed it on a par with the best theatres in the Arab world. It included 41 luxurious seat boxes and 420 seats and loges. Used by many Lebanese and Egyptian theatrical companies, it was popular with foreign groups of the time. In 1923, this theatre was converted into a cinema.

The major theatre from the late 1930s was Masrah Faarouq (Farouq Theatre) Started as a nightclub, it was soon transformed into a theatre by its owner 'Ali al-'Arees who named it, at first, the Naadia Theatre after his wife. Not long after that, it was renamed the Farouq Theatre after King Farouq of Egypt. When King Farouq was deposed in 1952 the theatre's name was changed to at-Tahreer (Liberation) Theatre. It was destroyed during the civil war.

At-Tiyatro al-Kabeer, built in 1925, is best known by its French name, the Grand Théâtre. Playing an important role between the 1930s and 1940s, the Grand Théâtre was equipped with special machinery for moving sets and backdrops for quick scene changes. This theatre also had a series of traps and a curtain that, when needed, could divide the stage area into two halves. Its internal space was designed to resemble European opera houses and had good acoustics, an unimpeded stage view and comfort. The Grand Théâtre was used by numerous Lebanese companies during the 1930s and 1940s, and by many famous Egyptian and foreign companies including the Comédie-Française.

Other large theatres that have been destroyed or turned into cinemas through the years include the Chef-d'oeuvre (Masterpiece) Theatre, which is now a cinema, and the Corsal, which was destroyed. One of the few remaining older small spaces is Masrah al-Kristaal.

The Empire Hall, established in 1920, provided both a stage for play performances and a screen for films. The Egyptian Theatrical Company of Fatimah Rushdie performed several times in this theatre. The Parisiana Theatre, located to the east of Martyr Square in the centre of Beirut, in its heyday was able to compete favourably with the great theatres of Beirut. At first famous as a café, a stage was later built on its roof. Two other old Beirut theatres are the Basta Theatre and the Tiriaton.

One of Lebanon's only theatres in the round was created by 'Ali al-'Arees in 1941 near the eastern limits of Beirut. However, due to military events during World War II, the French Mandate Authorities confiscated the theatre and used it as a storage facility for weapons.

Training
Criticism, Scholarship and Publishing

The American University of Beirut initiated its theatrical activities and was one of the main sources of literary theatre during the early decades of the century. Various student groups presented a range of shows in Daniel Bliss Hall, built in 1900. These included productions of Shakespeare starting with *Julius Caesar* in 1903, *Hamlet* in 1904, and *Othello* and *Macbeth* in 1905. A new space was built in 1913 under the direction of Robert Halden West, a space that was ultimately known as West Hall. Early plays done in Arabic and presented in West Hall included Elias Fayyaad's *Bayn Narayn* (*Between a Rock and a Hard Place*, 1925), Sa'eed Taqiyyuddeen's *Qudiya l-Amr* (*It Is Done*, 1926), and Anees al-Khouri al-Maqdisi's *Aal al-Humayraa'* (*The Humayraa' Family*, 1930). Used by campus and other theatre groups through the decades, West Hall found itself part of the modern theatre movement in the country in the 1960s and 1970s.

Saint Joseph University was established by the Jesuits in Beirut in 1874 and initiated its theatrical activities shortly thereafter. In 1882, a student group presented the Arabic play *Hukm Herodus 'Ala Waladayh* (*The Judgement of Herod on His Two Sons*). Theatrical performances were generally presented at the end of the scholastic year; particularly active were professors such as Najeeb Hubayqa and the Revd Hanna Tannous.

At the turn of the century at Saint Joseph's, an organization was established that came to be known as the Literary Assembly, a gathering that included a group of professors and alumni who were interested in cultural activities in general. Starting in 1901, the members of the Literary Assembly presented a play in Arabic, an activity that was repeated many times until World War I. The most important of the plays presented were *ar-Rasheed Wa l-Baraakima* (*ar-Rasheed and the Barmakids*, 1903), *al-Haarith* (1904) and *Bir Wa 'Uqouq* (*Loyalty and Ingratitude*, 1908).

By 1928, the Literary Assembly had resumed its theatrical activities including discussions on theatrical arts generally including the fundamentals of the art of writing plays. In the minutes of one of their meetings, the following was recorded:

> It is imperative to pay special attention to the subject, the division of a play into acts, compliance with prevailing circumstances and the showing of good taste, in addition to selecting a suitable non-radical subject that is both condensed and elaborate, well-knit, leading to a conclusion and depicting events that are both close to reality and believable.

Presenting a stage play at the end of each school year became a practice adopted by most schools, including those run by Christian monasteries and American and French missionaries in Lebanon from the mid-nineteenth century. The theatre was considered then as an educational and character-refining instrument. The most famous of those schools were al-Madrasa al-Batrakiyya (Patriarch's School, established 1873), Madrasat al-Hikma (Wisdom School, established 1874), Madrasat al-Maqaasid al-Khayriyya al-Islaamiyya (Islamic Maqaasid Charity School, established 1878) and Madrasat Zahrat al-Ihsaan (Flower of Charity School, established 1880).

The School of Modern Theatre was begun by Mouneer Abu Dibs and Antoine Multaqa in the early 1960s with the support of the Balbeck Festival. The festival allocated to the school an old building which became its base of operations. The school's activities, managed by Abu Dibs, Multaqa and his wife Lateefa, attracted many of the young generation who were interested in acting. Some of those who attended that school later became famous on the Lebanese stage.

Abu Dibs, as a teacher of theatre, long said that his work was based on the 'dialectics of the visible' and the 'hidden interplay between the mystic eastern spirit that is inclined towards magic and the new theatre emerging in Europe.' For him, theatre connected to larger issues and was a communication that could affect society. The method is live contact – the actor, light and shapes, colour, gesture, sound. To achieve this work, the actor needed to learn both technique and humility. The word too he saw as a symbol with its own physical presence different from a word in any other literary form. The merging of all these elements became the theatrical work for him and it was this idea he sought to communicate to his students.

Multaqaa and Abu Dibs along with Raymond Jbaara and Shakeeb Khouri were collectively responsible for the establishment in 1965 of a theatre division at the Lebanese University. Connected to the Fine Arts Institute, it included applied acting as well as theory and, in its early years, was similar to the school earlier established by Multaqa for the Lebanese Ring Theatre. As with everything else connected to the university, the war affected the programme's direction and changed its makeup considerably.

Nabil Abu Murad
Translated by Maha and Tony Chehade

Further Reading

Abdel-Nour, Jabbour. *Étude sur la poésie dialectale au Liban* [Studies in the dialectic poetry of Lebanon]. Beirut: Lebanese University, 1996.

Abu Murad, Nabil. *al-Akhawaan Rahbaani, Hayaat Wa Marsah, Khasaa'is al-Kitaaba ad-*

Draamiyya [The Rahbaani brothers, life and theatre, attributes of writing for drama]. Beirut: Amjaad Publishing 1990.

——. *al-Masrah Fi Lubnaan: Maraahilahu, Anwaa'ahu, Qadaayaah (1975–1990)* [The theatre in Lebanon: its phases, types and issues (1975–1990)]. Beirut, 1997.

Botitsiva, Tamara Alexandra. *Alf 'Aam Wa 'Aam 'Ala l-Masrah al-'Arabi* [The Arab theatre's one thousand and one years]. Beirut: al-Faraabi Publishing, 1981.

Dagher, Yousef As'ad. *Mu'jam al-Masrahiyyaat al-'Arabiyya Wa l-Mu'arraba* [Dictionary of Arabic and Arabicized theatrical plays]. Baghdad: Iraqi Ministry of Culture and Fine Arts, 1978.

'Irsaan, 'Ali 'Uqla. *ath-Thawaahir al-Masrahiyya 'Ind al-'Arab* [Arab theatrical phenomena]. Tripoli, Libya, 1983.

Mahfouth, 'Isaam. *Masrahi Wa l-Masrah* [A dramatist and the theatre]. Beirut: 2002 Publishing, 1966.

Al-Masrah Fi Lubnaan [The theatre in Lebanon]: *A documentary publication*. Beirut: Ministry of Culture and Higher Education.

Mu'tamar as-Sinema Wa th-Thaqaafa al-'Arabiyya [The cinema and the Arab culture conference]: Roundtable lectures under the auspices and supervision of UNESCO. Arab Liaison Centre for Cinema and Television, Beirut, November 1963 and 1964.

Najm, Mohammed Yousef. *Najeeb Haddaad*. Beirut: ath-Thaqaafa Publishing, 1966.

——. *al-Masrahiyya Fi al-Adab al-'Arabi l-Hadeeth (1847–1914)* [The theatrical play in modern Arabic literature (1847–1914)]. Beirut: ath-Thaqaafa Publishing, 1967.

Sa'd, Faarouq. *Khayal al-Zhil al-'Arabi* [The Arab shadow theatre]. Beirut: al-Matbou'aat lit-Tawzee' Wa n-Nashr, 1993.

Salaamé, Ghassane, *Le Théâtre politique au Liban (1968–1973)* [Political theatre in Lebanon (1968–1973)]. Beirut: Dar al-Mashreq, 1986.

As-Sawda, Yousef. *Taareekh Lubnaan al-Hadaari* [The history of Lebanese civilization]. Beirut: an-Nahaar Publishing, 1972.

Shaoul, Paul. *al-Masrah al-'Arabi al-Hadeeth (1976–1989)* [The modern Arabic theatre (1976–1989)]. Beirut: Riyaad Najeeb ar-Rayyis Publications, 1989.

LIBYA

Officially the Socialist People's Libyan Arab Jamahiriya, Libya is a north African country situated on the Mediterranean coast, covering 1,775,500 square kilometres (685,520 square miles). Bordered by Tunisia and Algeria to the west, by the Mediterranean to the north, Sudan to the southeast, Niger and Chad to the south, and Egypt to the east, Libya's social structure is still based around tribal units. The Berbers, the largest ethnic group, while still existing independently in certain parts of the country, have been largely assimilated into the country's more broadly based Arab culture.

In 1995 the country's population was estimated at 5.2 million, 92 per cent of whom were ethnically Berber/Arab with the remaining population made up of Greeks, Maltese, Italians, Egyptians, Pakistanis, Turks, Indians and Tunisians. Although Arabic is the official language, Italian and English are widely understood in major cities. In addition, some Berbers still speak their original Hamitic language. The vast majority of Libyans are Sunni Muslim (97 per cent) while the remaining 3 per cent are Christian. Tripoli is the country's capital.

The territories of modern Libya were first united under the Ottoman Turks in the sixteenth century. In the eighteenth century, the Karamanli dynasty was established in Tripoli, ruling for 120 years during which the territories of Libya were further consolidated. The Ottomans regained control of the area in 1835.

By the end of the nineteenth century, Islam had become dominant and became an influential political as well as religious force. In 1911 Italy invaded Ottoman-controlled Libya and the Turkish sultan was forced to relinquish all rights to the area leaving the country as an Italian colony. Tripoli was captured by the British during World War II and western occupation forces remained there through the war. After the war, the Allies permitted the Libyans to form an independent state led by King Idris I and in 1953 the country became a member of the Arab League. Oil was discovered in 1959, effectively transforming the country from a poor desert sheikhdom into an oil-rich monarchy.

In 1969, Colonel Muammar al-Qaddafi led a coup which deposed the king and Libya became a socialist-fundamentalist country. As leader, Qaddafi launched a cultural and social revolution that blended religious fundamentalism with Arab nationalism. By the late 1990s, Libya was in theory a *jamahiriya* (people's democracy) governed by the various tribal units through local councils. In fact, Libya was and is still ruled by the military and governed by a sole political party, the Arab Socialist Union.

During the 1980s, Libya's government severed virtually all ties with the west and challenged the influence of the United States in particular in the Arab region while at the same time manifesting strong support for the cause of Palestinian Arabs and guerrilla movements in Africa and around the world. By the late 1980s, Libya found itself isolated by much of the world community; through the 1990s, Qaddafi has tried to mend diplomatic relations especially with neighbouring countries.

Though Libya has seen the rise and fall of many sophisticated civilizations, it has maintained generally isolationist policies through the centuries and, as a result, while it has preserved certain folk traditions in storytelling, music and dance, it has not developed a literary theatre or a theatre with a European-style mimetic tradition. In addition, such activity is severely limited by the fundamentalist orientation of its Islamic leaders and the government.

The Libya National Folk Dance Group, based in Tripoli, is one of the few formal arts organizations in the country. Founded in 1963, group members come from various areas and represent diverse folk traditions. The group has toured internationally and by the mid-1980s had fifty-five dancers whose work expressed life in village and desert communities through changing rhythms and flowing body movements.

One dance not in the repertoire of the group is the *hagallah* dance – a traditional Libyan form, now almost extinct – is a coming-of-age celebration for a *hagallah* (young girl). The dancer dances alone with her head and face fully covered with a scarf, in front of a line of men, called *kefafeen*, who clap and chant in unison as the dancer performs steady, rhythmic side-to-side and up-and-down movements while taking very small steps. She holds either a small stick or a handkerchief in her hands. The men chant about how she is growing up and will soon be a beautiful woman. The dancer may stop in front of one young man and hand him the other end of the scarf or stick, while she dances around it. He might then offer her a bracelet as a sort of 'proposal'. This ritual proposal is not binding as the young man she stops in front of might be her brother.

Occasionally, a professional dancer was hired to perform this dance, in which case she would choose the leader of the *kefafeen* with whom to dance. After dancing with the stick or scarf, she would kneel and mime taking off her bracelets. The *kefafeen* would then mime giving her an additional bracelet or two. The bracelets would all then be put back on.

A girl or woman performing the *hagallah* wears a simple dress with long sleeves, with a wide, muffler-like heavy fabric wrapped around her hips. Additionally, the dancer wears a peplum skirt, with a buffer under the top part of the peplum to make it move more visibly.

Musical instruments are specific to regional traditions in Libya. Most dances are accompanied by the same basic instruments across the country such as drums, fiddles, larger stringed instruments, metal ideophones such as spoons and bagpipes. Rhythm, melody and scale vary. Such songs and dances tell stories of life in the desert. Often the tune is in the form of a lamentation.

Staff

Further Reading

El-Giernazi, Fawzi. *The Tawarig People and Folk Dances of Southern Libya*. Ottawa: Jerusalem International Publishing House, 1984. 72 pp.

MAURITANIA

(Overview)

Located in northwest Africa, the Islamic Republic of Mauritania links Arabic north Africa and sub-Saharan Africa and is, in this sense, very much a multiracial nation. Bounded on the north by the western Sahara and Algeria, on the east by Mali, on the south by Mali and Sénégal and on the west by the Atlantic Ocean, the country has a land area of 1,030,700 square kilometres (397,950 square miles) with more than 90 per cent of the population living in the southernmost quarter. The national capital is Nouakchott.

The population of Mauritania (1995 estimate) was 2.26 million, the majority being Moors of mixed Arab-Berber and Sudanic ancestry who speak Hassaniyah, an Arabic-based dialect. Many still lead a nomadic existence. The minority Black population is composed mostly of Sooninke people who migrated to this region following the collapse of the ancient Wagadu Empire (modern-day Ghana), the Pulaari who are dispersed throughout the south, and the Wolof who live in the vicinity of Rosso in coastal southwestern Mauritania. Tensions have long existed between the Arab and Black communities with Blacks arguing that the government has been consciously trying to exclude and marginalize them politically and culturally. In 1989 a bloody revolution broke out resulting not only in many deaths on both sides but also in the deportation or exile of over 100,000 Blacks to Sénégal and Mali while Arab Mauritanians left those countries and returned home. At the same time many young people studying abroad found themselves unable to return from African, European and North American institutions for political reasons. Rising domestic pressures and interna-

tional criticism of its human rights record ultimately forced the government to implement a new, more liberal constitution and in 1991 opposition parties were allowed for the first time.

In theatrical terms, the roots of national performance art are essentially oral and can be found in stories, legends, historical and communal celebrations and familial rites of passage. These roots are shared by both the majority and the minority cultures in the overall development of music, poetry, dance, movement and the still popular stagings of short, satiric, improvised sketches. The great poet and fiery humourist Hammam Faal has produced many such works in this latter style and a number have been broadcast on radio. Among other writers working in this style (and in recent decades in more scripted forms) are Hamet Koyate, a bilingual Arabic-Sooninke writer, Guelaye Fall, who works in Pulaar, and Youssouf Gueye Tene, a Pulaar writer whose most important pieces are *Death in Oualata Prison* and *The Exiles of Goumel* (published in the Nouvelles Éditions Africaines series in France).

Of interest here is the indigenous notion of *lehmar* (imitation), a word also used to describe a person who imitates. Used here in a satiric way, *lehmar* has allowed commentators – as close as one gets to actors in this tradition – to hold aberrant social behaviour up to ridicule whether the behaviour comes from a prince and his attendants, a group of shepherds or just a crowd of average people. The imitation or *lehmar* can be innovative and imaginative in the same way that an actor can be. In his comments, the *lehmar* uses words, movement and emotions. Whatever is done, the goal is emotional release and amusement. The *lehmar* builds his stories on questionable behaviour and, by observing social reality challenges it and gives it back to his society in a new form which, when done well, can stimulate real appreciation. This form goes back far in time, long before anyone called it theatre. From the beginning it used stories and dialogue. Though not a play as such and without a formal stage or designed setting (although specific costumes and even wigs are occasionally worn) and though the *lehmar* is not 'acting' in the European sense, the *lehmar* and the art are still alive and making connections with the people.

Dance and music-related forms exist as well. *Lebaat el dabous* (Pin Game), for example, is a danced competition between two teams of men. Begun by the singing of songs (usually by women) and the playing of such popular Mauritanian musical instruments as the *ardeen* (played by women), the *tidinet* or drums (played by men), the teams consecutively present specific dances. Sticks are used in the dances to represent everything from canes to swords. Also extremely popular, *lebaat el dabous* always attracts a large audience. Like the *lehmar*, this form provides psychological release and a cleansing of the

psyche after a hard day's work. Such forms have represented the pinnacle of indigenous art for centuries, perhaps for millennia.

It was not until the mid-1950s that Mauritanians tried their own hands at western-style entertainment. By that time, dramatic literature had become part of the school curriculum and the production of plays was a natural extension of school studies. Outside of schools, local writers began to write for the form and early plays, coming around the time of independence, were filled with national enthusiasm and discussions of such things as communism and pan-Arab nationalism. The subjects eventually became more socially critical touching on such sensitive issues as bribery, nepotism and even divorce.

In 1958 the company El Keikoutya – a group which boldly included both men and women in its numbers – began working in Nouakchott with Hammam Faal as its leading actor. Eventually the group toured its original productions, mostly satires which attracted wide attention. Both the community and the government saw such work as an extension of the *lehmar* tradition and as such it seemed socially acceptable. This company's work through the mid-

The pioneer of the modern Mauritanian theatre movement, actor and poet Hammam Faal.

Production of *The Kingdom of One Mind*, 1991.

1960s very much shaped the development of theatre in Mauritania and served as a model for a number of other groups which emerged, played for a time and then ceased operation. One of the longest lived of these was the Korian Troupe, which made profound connections in its work with theatre groups in the Arab world.

Plays at this stage were often collectively written and many others were collectively signed for the protection of particular individuals involved in their creation. Two which stood out in the late 1960s were *Ahmad Walad Eida* and *El Sheikh Maa El Eineen*, both dealing with incidents in Mauritanian history and both reflecting the intense nationalism of the period. Other plays examined such issues as the Palestinian question. Audiences were drawn to these plays not only for their theatrical qualities but also for their frank and controversial content.

By the early 1970s, various government agencies began to support performances by making available to the groups performance spaces and by helping to establish annual and regional theatre festivals. Also sponsored were a number of national conferences on the theatre with

particular emphasis on potentially greater governmental involvement and sponsorship. The government along with various foreign agencies had already led the way in this regard by sponsoring visits to the capital of troupes from France and Egypt, performances which set a standard that local groups sought to match.

Particularly popular among local audiences was another style that included theatre elements, the Concert Party, a traditional African evening involving songs, dances and sketches. Many Mauritanian dramatists, in fact, started out by writing satirical sketches and working in this form. By the 1970s, even Concert Parties were dealing with social issues with some pieces written in classical Arabic (previously most Concert Parties were done only in Hassaniyah). Such quasi-dramatic texts were often written by well-known figures in the community and often satirized others who were equally well known.

From such sketch writing came a number of attempts at what can be called pedagogical theatre or theatre for social action. Sometimes sponsored by government agencies and other times sponsored by community organizations, short pieces handled such issues as hygiene and the need for education. Some of these shows were built around traditional events such as harvest celebrations or marriage rites.

In 1985, theatre activity in the country was deemed to be popular enough to ask each state to sponsor a student play at a festival for National Youth Year. It was from this dramatic focus that a whole new generation participated in theatre or saw theatre for the first time. Through the late 1980s and into the 1990s, more than a dozen new, generally non-professional groups emerged, nine in the capital. Unlike the Concert Party performers, these groups sought fully developed scripts and insisted on regular rehearsals and formal performances. Among the most important of these groups were El Resala (The Message), El Morabeon (The Captives), Diloul (originally from the province of Tiarat), Chi Ilouh Vehl (Here and There) which ceased operation in 1992 and Shabab El Moheet (The Ocean of Youth). Many of the new companies produced local plays which questioned the general drift of the society, particularly Mauritania's rapid urbanization and move away from traditional nomadic culture. Probably the most important play to come out of this period was a version of *La Legende de Wagadu* (in English called *The Legend of Wagadu as Seen By Siya Yatabare*), a feminist retelling by the sociologist Moussa Diagana of the well-known tale which juxtaposed traditional faith with personal acquisitiveness. The play was staged by the Théâtre de l'Espoir with help from the French Cultural Centre and directed by Patrick La Mauff. The play, vaguely reminiscent of the Antigone story and involving a debunking of traditional power, later played successfully at the Festival des Francophonies in Limoges, (France) and was published in English in a collection of francophone African plays by the Ubu Repertory in New York.

In 1988 the Ministry of Culture inaugurated a national theatre, El Masrah El Kawmi, and funded extended training sessions for its new company of actors (chosen from all the existing groups). The government also brought in a group of experts in areas such as movement and music. Working with a company of fifteen, El Masrah El Kawmi's first major production was *Al Looba* (*The Game*) by Mohammed Fal Wahad Abd el-Rahman (b. 1956), a landmark play which looked at traditional Bedouin society and the role of local shamans. Staged by the country's best known director, Badr Aldin Walad Obeed (b. 1962), a Palestinian whose family moved to Mauritania when he was 13, *Al*

Mohamden Weld Abdalla, Abdallah Weld Ubeid and Bint Wahab Nabat Shamad in *The Engagement Party*, 1994.

Looba attracted wide attention for both its subject matter and its use of this still relatively new genre. The author, a graduate of universities in Morocco and Syria, had been for a number of years director of the Museums Division in the Ministry of Culture. Following the success of this play, he was acknowledged as the premier playwright in the country.

The creation of the national theatre spurred other groups as well. From those who remained or who did not want to join El Masrah El Kawmi came a second important company, the Shankit Troupe, formed in 1989 by El Walee Walad El Sheikh Yeeb. Working with a nucleus of thirty-six artists, the troupe's goal was as serious and as professionally focused as the National's. Its first production, *Thakafaa Lel Beea* (*Selling the Culture*) by Mostafa Ahmad Ghoneem, connected culture and capitalism and was staged at the new Youth Hall in the capital. The group's second major production was a play by el-Rahman, *Bareek Al Samgh* (*The Glowing Gum*), which won a national prize when it was staged at the National Youth

The Glowing Gum, 1990.

Festival by the group's director Alkhalil Walad Mohamed Saleh. The production marked a real move forward in national theatrical sophistication and theatrical appreciation by audiences.

Working outside the Arab mainstream for the country's Black communities have been two troupes of note – Compagnie Foppu, founded in 1991 and dealing quite often with problems of illiteracy, and the Troupe Yillenkaré, part of the Sooninke community and connected to the Mauritanian Association for the Promotion of the Sooninke Language and Culture in Nouakchott. In operation since 1977, both the association and the Troupe Yillenkaré have been involved in cultural and artistic activities aimed at drawing attention to Sooninke issues and popularizing and promoting these issues through literature and art. Plays staged by the Troupe Yillenkaré (several of which have been published by Éditions l'Harmattan in Paris) include *Wagadu Biida* (1983), *Ji Xooro* (1984), *Daraama* (1993), *The False Judge* (1995), *The Towers* (1996), *The Émigré* (1996) and *Return to Terror* (1997).

Through the early 1990s, about six plays per year were being staged in the capital, a number never before reached; virtually all were sold out. The new theatrical art was also making an impact on the related fields of poetry and fiction with novelists and poets suddenly becoming interested in the form.

Still, theatre had to depend for its survival on the contributions, financial and otherwise, of its own artists. Government support remained almost non-existent through the 1990s and the theatre was not seen as commercial enough to generate interest from the private sector. The most a group could expect from the government was the donation of a performance space for a short period of time. Box-office revenues were also negligible even for successful shows with ticket prices reaching a high of less than US$1, about the price of a pack of good cigarettes and often the same or less than a ticket to a film. As a result, actors, in even the country's major troupes, have never been paid. All performances require entertainment licences which means going though a government approval process. To supplement their meagre incomes, a number of groups regularly tour, sometimes travelling on foot to various locations for lack of transport or money.

Critic and playwright Mohamed El Hassan Weld Mohamad El Mostafa.

In the early 1990s, Mauritanian artists were, however, finally able to obtain government grants to study theatre abroad, most often in Tunisia and occasionally in France. There is also now a National Artists' Union open to all theatre people. Since 1994, plays created specifically for children have been seen at the National Centre; like most facilities, this is not a theatre but rather a series of open spaces which, by adding chairs and raised platforms, can be turned into very modestly equipped theatres.

Mohamed El Hassan Weld Mohamad El Mostafa
Translated by Christine Henein

Further Reading

Anthologie de musique maure [Anthology of Mauritanian music]. [sound recording]. Paris: Ocora, 1982.

Belvaude, Catherine. *Ouverture sur la littérature en Mauritanie: tradition orale, écriture, témoignages* [Introduction to literature in Mauritania: oral, written and testimonial traditions]. Paris: L'Harmattan, 1989. 152 pp.

Ould Hamody, Mohamed Said. *Bibliographie générale de la Mauritanie*. [General bibliography of Mauritania]. Nouakchott: Centre culturel français de Nouakchott and Paris: Sepia, 1995. 580 pp.

MAYOTTE

(see **COMOROS ISLANDS**)

MOROCCO

(Overview)

A country of strong contradictions and a rich and varied cultural heritage, Morocco is located in northwestern Africa, part of the Grand Maghreb, and bounded by the Mediterranean Sea to the north, the Atlantic Ocean to the west, by Algeria to the east and southeast and by Mauritania to the south. Morocco has a land area of approximately 446,550 square kilometres (172,400 square miles) including the Spanish territories of Ceuta and Melilla. The Moroccan population of 29.2 million is almost entirely ethnically Arab-Berber and follows Sunni Muslim teachings. Berber or Amazigh languages are becoming more important in the region as a movement is underway to have the languages taught. Arabic, the official language, was brought to the area by invaders in the seventh century. In addition to Arabic, French is widely used in business, government and post-primary education. Morocco's capital is Rabat and, in the summer, Tangier.

Throughout its history, Morocco has felt the influence of many cultures. Excavations have unearthed elements of Phoenician, Hellenic, Carthaginian, Andalusian and Roman civilizations. During the late Roman Empire, Christianity made its way into the region as had Judaism before it but from the seventh century, Arab influences affected the area most profoundly. From 1912 until independence in 1956, Morocco was divided into two protectorates one French and one Spanish. From the 1920s, an active underground existed seeking independence, a goal finally achieved when Mohammad V established an independent monarchy and absolute power was consolidated by his successor, King Hassan II. In 1975, in cooperation with Mauritania, Morocco claimed the potentially rich oil-producing region of the Spanish Sahara. Mauritania pulled out in 1979, however, in response to guerrilla opposition, leaving the area totally under Moroccan control.

In the 1990s, it can be said with some accuracy, two types of modern theatre exist within the country – national (comprised of amateur, university and professional) and visiting (Arab, Asian and European, especially French). Amateur theatre is independent in contrast to professional theatre whose repertoire and even the future of those participating is dictated by the state. According to Abdelwahed Ouzri, in *Le Théâtre au Maroc: structures et tendances*, there are five companies structured in affiliation with a public institution: the Troupe de la Radio created in the 1940s, Troupe al Ma'mora, an extension of the Moroccan theatre troupe created by French theatre expert André Voisin, the Troupe du Théâtre National (formed in 1974), the Troupe du Petit Masque and the Troupe Seddiki. University theatre, especially from Qarawiyine, Fes, Meknes and Casablanca, is equally important to the country; a University Theatre Festival is held in Casablanca every year.

However, Morocco's modern theatre is only one small aspect of the country's theatre life as a whole, a theatre life much more deeply rooted in traditional modes involving music and dance. Indeed, culturally and historically, African and Arabic folk-based arts and traditions easily predominate over western-style theatre activities. This influence can be seen and heard particularly in local dances and music. Throughout the twentieth century, moreover, traditional forms have been further mixed with western traditions, particularly those of France and Spain.

Such cultural transfers are a two-way process. Andalusian music and song, for example, seem to have their roots in Morocco from where they were brought into Muslim Spain. Later to flourish in Moorish courts throughout the Iberian peninsula, such music is still popular in the north of Morocco where new pieces are still composed and played on stringed instruments with melodies sung in either classical Arabic or the Arabic Andalusian dialect. Such music can also be heard at the beginning of important ceremonial occasions. Berber music, on the other hand, has been more influenced by African musical forms, most Berber songs being accompanied by the *bendir* (an instrument shaped like a large tambourine and resonating like one but in actuality a drum).

Morocco dance traditions are equally varied and range from the provocative and erotic *guedra* (literally meaning 'cooking pot') dance to more staid Arabic dances. The *guedra* is found in the southern regions and is performed exclusively by women; the dancers wear black garments and dark veils completely covering their bodies. The entire dance is performed in a kneeling position with an emphasis on the movements of hands, arms and snapping of fingers. It reaches its climax when the dancers 'collapse' on the floor. Known to some as a seduction dance, it is now rarely seen except when it is staged for foreign visitors. Other folk dances include the *ahouach* and *ahaidous*, both originating in the Atlas valleys. The *ahouach* is performed by both men and women. Wearing sparkling coloured robes, they move shoulder to shoulder in a circle to music played on the *bendir* by male musicians who sit in the centre. In other versions, circles of men and women alternate to the rhythm of the *bendir* and the words of poetic songs.

The *dekka*, another non-religious dance, is performed to an orchestra of diverse drums, while the *ghaïta* is a battle dance culminating in the firing of rifles. The *gnawa* is a drumming/chanting dance of African origin, while the *houara* (originally from near Agadir) is performed by women spinning wildly into a human whirlwind in a circle of men. Other well-known folk dances include the *tata*, a wedding dance, the *taskiouine*, a war dance performed by men, and the *tissint*, a dagger dance performed by both sexes wearing indigo-coloured costumes. Other dances are done for Sufi religious purposes, such as the *aissawa* which incorporates snake-charmers and music-induced trances, performed by members of the Sidi Aissa sect.

An appreciation of these dances and musical forms, together with some understanding of the role of traditional poetry and storytelling in their performance, are essential towards acquiring a real sense of the history and richness of Moroccan theatrical forms. Otherwise, the non-Moroccan observer may take away a distorted impression of western theatre forms as practised by a limited few in Morocco. Clearly Moroccan theatrical taste has developed from and been cultivated by both western and local influences interacting over a long period. In looking at the country's cultural history, the scholar Najib al-Oafy in his *Jadal al-Quera* (*Literary Debates*, p. 87) has observed that,

those who are interested in the theatre must agree that Morocco, as other Arab countries, has known a variety of theatre forms and had practiced them even before the winds of the European Renaissance and certainly before colonialism . . . and its cultural constructions. The theatre is a celebratory art and from an anthropological point of view is doubtless instinctive and is realized in many forms and through many emotions in which reality and legend, rationality and imagination, consciousness and unconsciousness are rooted.

Before the advent of Islam, for instance, acting – the core of theatrical art – was popular in Moroccan society, probably through the country's many contacts with Greek and Roman culture. Morocco, in fact, had been the subject of several Roman military invasions, and Rome's cultural influence is still evident in the many ancient ruins of Roman theatre buildings throughout the country.

In his study of Arab theatre, *The Itinerant Theatre Festival in the Arab World*, Osman al-Ka'aak says that:

Acting was well-known in the ancient world. It originally came from India. Juba the Second (in his history of theatre) wrote of the different varieties. Non-mimetic acting – either as part of religious ritual tradition (in India) or connected to religion in the ancient Greek style – always included poetry, dance or a combination of movement and visual representations intended to influence or propitiate the gods. It also included bizarre comic portraits used to mock well-known public figures and to show their faults. Even non-Romans saw and acted in Roman-style theatres and even produced the plays of the Roman writer Terence. Several extant theatre buildings in north Africa are concrete proof that non-Romans enjoyed theatrical art.

The Roman theatres, for the most part, fell into disuse after the coming of Islam, a fact that implies only that the theatre is a communal art and needs public support. Such support was transferred at this time to other forms of public 'theatrical' activity ranging from the displays of artifacts and people at the many weekly markets to annual communal celebrations such as al-Mawsem (literally, 'the season') which were often tied to harvest cycles; public events such as weddings and community games can also be included.

What Islam had done was to replace Roman-style theatre with other types of public spectacle which fulfilled psychological needs that in other lands were met only via aspects of theatre. Public prayer was one such experience. Performed in a purpose-built space (the mosque), such public gatherings reached their highest and most theatrical level in the annual Hadj (pilgrimage to Mecca) in which hundreds of thousands of people publicly expressed their faith. Such demonstrations, of course, had celebrants, audiences and carefully structured scenarios all including intellectual argument, songs and chants (the latter day equivalents of the Greek dithyramb).

From such public events other forms of celebration emerged such as Mawkeb al-Shumu' (Candle Caravan) in the city of Sala, a festival involving the carrying of candles two metres long weighing some thirty kilograms each. Al-Mawludeya (The Birth), another theatricalized religious festival, is celebrated on the occasion of the birth of the Prophet Muhammad. Held in mosques and even private houses, it involves group song and allows each participant an opportunity to show the importance of The Messenger. All these performances are redeemed by Sunni Muslims because they fall into the category of *bid'a* (misleading innovation). Sultan al-Tulba (The Student Sultan) is another theatrical celebration, lasting an entire week. Celebrated in the city of Fes, it is primarily a charade in which a student is given the power of a sultan for seven days. In this student kingdom, reality yields to imagination and the life-force is celebrated: a spring festival, everyone is a participant and enjoys the joke. But when the seventh night is over, the sultan must relinquish his throne. If the mock sultan and his aides dally, they are beaten. Sidi Al-Katfy is a public celebration performed by workers in Rabat. A commentary of sorts on mystic assemblies and rituals, it involves a group of twelve people who assemble their audience around them in a circle. Its goal is to satirize well-known individuals in the city.

The *halqa* (circle) is a centuries-old performance style that has traditionally been carried out in public squares and market-places. Animated by a storyteller through tale and mime and often sung to music, the *halqa* can best be thought of as an interactive performance taking place between the performer/storyteller and the spectators, who become 'actors' in turn as they are invited to act out certain segments of the performance with the *halqa* performer. Myths, religious stories and popular tales make up the repertory. A few props or accessories are used, such as a cane, box or rug. Abdelwahed Ouzri

Actress, playwright, director Fatima Chebchoub performing a one-woman halqa entitled *Moulat Sserr* in which she portrays eighteen different characters in nine Moroccan dialects.
Photo: Debbie Folaron

states that 'it is the only theatre in the world where spectators pay after or during the performance, and not before'.

The *bsate* was common under King Mohammed ben Abdellah (1757–90). It was an occasion, under the guise of 'performance', to present complaints and denunciations before the king, against the unjust acts carried out by local officials. The performance usually consisted of short and humorous farces. The main character was 'buhu' in the north and 'al M'siyyah' in the south.

All these forms of alternative theatre art were in existence in Morocco long before the arrival of the Spanish and the French with their more formal and less communal literary theatre. When such shows appeared in Morocco (among the earliest plays were Spanish-language works performed in the city of Tetouan in the 1860s; indeed, a theatre was built there by the Spanish around that time and Theatre Cervantes was

built in the city of Tangier in 1913) they were presented by the colonials for the colonials; obviously, audiences could not have been very large for these Spanish-language productions. When the French arrived, they too introduced literary theatre with several productions of classics and comedies (Molière was particularly popular among colonial communities). The first French theatre building was al-Masrah al-Balady (Public Theatre) built in Casablanca in 1922; the second was al-Masrah al-Balady (Public Theatre) in the city of al-Jadida.

Early experiments in this western formal theatrical style by Moroccans themselves took place in western-style schools, specifically the Fes High School, which staged a dramatization of the novel *Salah al-Din al-Ayyoby* by Najib Haddad prior to World War I. Salah al-Din al-Ayyoby is the Muslim hero of the Crusades. According to scholars taking into account the Spanish occupation, the first Moroccan text for the stage, *Ahl al Kahf*, was written in 1920 by Abazakour and acted in the same year by his troupe of students and teachers. By 1921, according to Muhammad Dawood, an original Moroccan play called *al-Zawch* (*The Bird*) was staged at a school in Tetouan. An article written in 1946 for the magazine *Majalat al-Anwar* (*The Light*, 3: p. 7) claimed that the first non-scholastic theatre group which committed itself to doing western-style plays in the country was founded that year by Muhammed Zaghary in Fes. Called Jawq al-Tamtheel (Acting Company), its creation was soon followed by another formed by Haj Mokhtar Abd-al-Salam al-Mathry, by a third in Rabat under the management of al-Sayed al-Yazeedy and by a fourth in Tangier – Jame'yat al-Helal (Crescent Society).

The first professional Arab-language theatre company to visit Morocco was that of the Egyptian stage star Muhammad Ezz el-Din, who in 1923 toured the region with an adaptation of *Salah al-Din al-Ayyoby*. The production attracted widespread attention. Following his successful visit, other Arab theatre companies added Morocco to their touring schedules including in 1923 a Tunisian troupe directed by Chadli ben Friha and Egypt al-Firqa al-Mokhtalaqua (Blended Company) which visited Morocco in 1924 with the support of the city of Fes. Among its members were Abd-al-Razzaq Kerbaka, Hasan Banan and his wife Aliaa', Rafool and his Syrian wife. Several members of this company decided to remain in Marrakesh including Hasan Banan, who formed a company mainly committed to producing satirical works that played successfully for several years in Jenan El-Harty (Shakroon, pp. 36–7).

By 1950, the government felt positive enough about theatrical activities to pay for the advice of the French theatre expert, André Voisin. He was assisted by two Moroccan animateurs, Tahar Ouaaziz and Abdessamad Kenfaoui. 'I saw myself as something of a cultural animateur,' Voisin was later quoted as saying (Hassan al-Mani'ee, p. 60). 'Certainly the amateur groups I saw in schools, clubs and scouting organizations had no real sense of performance style. All I could do was speak with them and offer workshops.'

Voisin stayed in Morocco from 1950 to 1956 and visited the entire country on foot so as to become familiar with the traditions, customs and rituals. He established workshops on theatrical performance and tried to link them to Moroccan popular culture. Under his direction, the Moroccan Theatre Troupe performed an adaptation of Molière's *Fourberies de Scapin* (*Amayal Joha*) and a collective creation, *Les Balayeurs*, at the Festival de Paris in 1956, just after Moroccan independence. The performance was a huge success. After Voisin's departure from Morocco he left behind students who would later develop careers in theatre: Tayeb al-Seddiki, Ahmed Tayeb L'Alj, Mohammed Said Affifi, Larbi Doughmi and Fatima Regragui.

Within five or six years, many of those who had participated in these activities organized even more independent groups as the politics in the country became steadily more liberalized. Among the groups established in the 1950s were Masrah al-Tali'aa (Avant-garde Theatre) in Fes, al-Masrah al-Tala'ee (Growing Theatre) in Casablanca, al Masrah al-Haie (Living Theatre) in Asfi, and al-Masrah al-Faqui (Poor Theatre) and Masrah al-Mokhtabar (Critical Theatre) in Casablanca.

Then in 1954, the founding of al-Ma'moura (National Theatre) marked the début of the country first professional theatre, many of its pioneering members having come from a company formed by the Moroccan Broadcasting Company in 1949. Al-Ma'moura was considered the 'glory' of Moroccan theatre during the 1950s and 1960s. Sadly though, after repeating the same work in the same style for some twenty years, al-Ma'moura was forced to close down in 1974 when audiences stopped coming and when subsidies were withdrawn. One year later, the Ministry of Youth and Sports tried to re-establish the company with a new perspective. It had

one major success: the experimental *al-Ein Wa al-Kholkhal* (*The Eye and the Anklet*), by Ahmad al-Iraqi, Abd-El-Salam al-Habib and Abdel Karim Berchid, directed by al-Husseini al-Marini and al-Arabi Belsheb. Despite the success of the play at the Arab Youth Festival in Tripoli, Libya, in 1975, the company was again closed down.

The same fate befell Tayeb al-Seddiki Masrah Annass (People's Theatre) which was forced to close in 1985, also for lack of support. Formed in 1974, two very successful productions were *Diouane Sidi Abderrahman al Majdoub* (based on the life and work of the popular poet al Majdoub, directed and performed while the troupe was still under the auspices of the Municipal Theatre of Casablanca) and *Maqqamat Badi Zamane al Hamadani* (based on the early Arab poet al-Hamadani, famous for his *maqamas*; it was created and performed in 1971), the latter having enjoying much acclaim throughout the Arab world. Its last show was *Kitab al-Imta' Wa Moanassa* (*The Book of Pleasure and Entertainment*) by al-Tawhidy. Al-Seddiki himself has long been considered one of the most visibly important personalities in the history of Moroccan theatre, especially during the 1960s and 1970s. He directed the Municipal Theatre of Casablanca from 1965 to 1977 in additional to translating and adapting a significant number of works for performance in Morocco. He also experimented with the *halqa* in his own creations.

In the programme for the first production of the National company, Muhammad al-Haddad, a well-known writer from Tangier, later to become one of the period's more important dramatists, wrote: 'In the absence of national playwrights, the theatres of the country should take a special look at writings by novelists which can be dramatized. Hopefully serious works will be attempted and not just comedies even though they too can be useful in pointing out social problems in the country' (quoted in *The Moroccan Arts Magazine*: p. 89).

One of the few writers who had earlier proved himself adept as a dramatist was Muhammad al-Quorry (sometimes called al-Faqeeh al-Quorry, 1897–1937), an established poet who found the theatre an exciting way to reach audiences. As early as the 1930s, he had publicly attacked colonialism in his work, suggesting that its real motivation was the eradication of the Moroccan character. Punished for his views, compelled to leave the country for extended periods of time, condemned to perpetual forced labour in 1936 and finally tortured to death by the French administration, his death was a cause for national mourning. His plays are filled with nationalistic passion. Among them is the drama *al-Awseya'e (The Guardians), Ilmo we Nataïjouho (Science and its Outcome), al-Yatim al-Mohmal (The Forgotten Orphan)* and *al-Mothri al-Azeem (The Wealthy)*.

Another writer of note who turned to the theatre late in his career was Abd-El-Wahid al-Shawy (b. 1911), a journalist from Fes. Coming from a well-established family, he began his career as an actor and later turned to directing and eventually script writing. Among his many plays in the 1940s and 1950s were *Awaidouna Fi al-Zawaj (Our Marriage Habits), Quif Ayyoha al-Mottaham (Stop Thief!), Asdeqoun Am Losoos (Friends or Robbers), Ayna al-Ehsane (Where Is Kindness?), Nahno Atfal De'aaff (We Are Weak Children), Halqat al-Malahi (The Circle of Fun), al-Makr Wa al-Kheda'e (Betrayal and Cunning), Majnoon Iradatihi (The Madness of His Will), Monajat al-Sekkir (Talking to the Drunk), al-Motafarnej (Pretending To Be Foreign), Be Al-Elm Yantafy al-Fasad (Through Knowledge the Lie Will Disappear), Yatim al-Saharae (The Orphan of the Desert)* and *Fayn Dwak Ya Mrid (Where is Your Medication O Sick One?)*. Only a few of these scripts were published.

Al-Mahdy al-Mani'i was another writer and actor from this period. Many of his best works were adaptations which he used to focus on questions of colonialism. Among these were several Molière adaptations including *Tartuffe* (prevented from being staged by colonial authorities but subsequently printed in book form) and *al-Bakhil (L'Avare* or *The Miser)*. Other prominent playwrights included Muhammad Ben al-Sheikh al-Osmany, author of the historic play *al-Roshdo Ba'd al-Ghaie (Guidance After Loss)*; Abd-El-Khaleq al-Torees (b. 1910), one of the leaders of the patriotic movement in Morocco and author of the early play *Entisar al-Haqq Be El-Batel (The Victory of the Truth via Falsehood*, 1933); and Muhammed Zaghary, author of *Entisar al-Baraah (Victory of Innocence)*, who was also a popular actor famous for playing women's roles before women were permitted on stage.

Perhaps the country's foremost dramatist is Abd-Allah Shakroon. Starting out his career working as an actor and director in radio and television, he eventually turned to script writing. His early plays were in Moroccan Arabic (the dialectic) rather than Fusha (classic) Arabic that

had been used previously. His best work is based on close, graphic observation of day-to-day life of ordinary Moroccans. His social criticism is more subtle but equally clear and firmly rooted in Islamic/Arabic thought and beliefs. Among his most important plays are *al-Waqe'a (The Event), Awlad al-A'aqera (Sons of the Sterile), Ishaq (Isaac), Kanza Bent al-Jiran (Kanza, the Daughter of the Neighbour), Eshkoun El-li Khayr (The Complaint of the Good), Ebn Dareej (Son of Dareej), Haroun al-Rasheed Haret al-Jabry (The Isle of al-Jabry), Irth al-Bakhil (The Heritage of the Stingy), al-Hasood (The Envier), Khawla al-Khaledoun (The Immortals), Urwa Wa A'afraa' (Urwa and A'afraa'), Emra'a A'alema (A Knowledgeable Woman), al-Mostada'afoun (The Weak)* and *Maso'oda Wa Mubarak (Maso'oda and Mubarak)*.

If adaptation of novels by the first wave of Moroccan playwrights is to be regarded as the foundation of the modern Moroccan theatre, a fresh impetus emerged in the 1960s and 1970s when a new wave of dramatists explored celebratory, traditional forms in an attempt to create links between western dramatic art and Arabic traditions. Many plays written from the 1970s on are in fact based on folk tales, myth, magic and legends. Influenced by social changes in France particularly and Europe more generally, these works were free in form, angry in content and experimental in style. Among the important names attached to this period are directors and writers such as Nabil Lahlou, Muhammad al-Kakhat, Muhammad Shahraman, Abd-El-Salam al-Habib, Radwan Ehdadu, Ahmad el-Iraqi, Muhammad Meskin, Youssof Fadel, Abdel Karim Berchid, Hoory al-Hussien, Sa'd-Allah Abd el-Majeed, Saïd Sam'aly, Muhammad al-Batooly, Muhammad al-Nakroush, Abdesshen El Haddad, Abdessham Chraibi, Abdelkader al-Badawi, Said Saddiki, Mohamed Timud, Ahmed Tayeb L'Alj, Abdessamad Lkenfawi, Mohamed Hasan Ljoundi, Ahmed LBasri, Brahim Lwazzani, Mohamed Warda, Elmeskini Essohir, Farid Ben Mbarek, Abdellatif El La'bi and Abd-Allah al-Mesabehy.

Perhaps the only principle that most of these artists agreed upon was that theatre had to be created in the language of the people rather than written in a literary style. Most earlier Moroccan writing had been done in Fusha (formal/classical Arabic). By the late 1960s and 1970s the vernacular had crept into the works of writers such as Ahmad al-Taieb al-Alaj and the radio plays of Shakroon. By the end of the 1970s, with a general rising interest in Arab heritage, a split began to emerge, with some groups working only in Fusha and others (such as al-Badawi Company and al-Wafa'a Company in Marrakesh) focusing almost exclusively on the local dialect. There were also poetic plays produced (by Allal Thami Lkhieri, Hassan Triberq and Allal Lfassi) and even a few productions in the French language by Nabil Lahlou and Abdellatif El La'bi. Some plays can be found in which both French and Arabic appear, reflecting still other aspects of social reality, especially Jewish plays in the French Cultural Centres.

The 1970s witnessed another new phenomenon – the appearance of monodramas or single-actor plays called *al-masrah al-fardi*. Whether this was done for artistic or economic reasons (or both) is difficult to say with certainty, but clearly the form has definite, identifiable links with the time-honoured Arabic storytelling traditions including *al-rawi*, *al-hakawati* and *al-halqa*. By 1977 these one-person plays had become so popular that a national festival of one-person plays was held in Rabat.

Throughout the late 1970s, many theatre groups felt a need to publish manifestos articulating their theatre beliefs and goals. Al-Ihtifaliyya (Celebration Theatre), established by Abdelkrim Berrechid along with Abderrahman Benzidane, Touria Jabrane, Abdelouaheb Aydoubia, Mohammed Batouli and Tayeb al-Seddiki (who was the first one to break away from the group) was the first to issue such a manifesto in 1976. An artistic collective, their manifesto states:

> We believe in refocusing an Arab theatre that has lost sight of its goals. There are too many different directions being followed right now and the lack of a clear direction leads to no direction and leaves us as a people submissive to imperialism and pulls us from our own needs and history. We must give the Arab people and the Arab theatre a clear identity, an identity linked to Arab reality.

The company Sa'ad-Allah Abd-El-Majeed took a more Grotowskian approach to its work arguing for a 'poor theatre' based on the presence of the actor as opposed to technological effects. The manifesto of Masrah al-Marhala (Milestone Theatre) was written by Hourri al-Hussein and argued for a new type of language in the theatre, one that could connect to social reality and its attendant political, social and economic aspects.

Ahmad al-Tayyeb al-A'alj (b. 1928), a playwright and adapter, an actor, poet and musician, attracted a following for the skilful blend of folk tales and songs in his plays. In fact, he went so far as to employ his art to express an alternative reality. Born in Fes, his most important plays are *Fi Tarik, Diwan Didi Abderrahman El Majdoub, La Bataille de Zellaqa* (*The Battle of Zellaqa*), *Maqamat Badia Ezzamane el Hamadani, Essefoud, La Légende du pauvre* (*The Legend of the Poor Man*), *Le Livre des délectations et du plaisir partagé* (*The Book of Delights and Shared Pleasures*), *Le Dîner de gala* (*Gala Dinner*), *Les Sept grains de beauté* (*Seven Beauty Spots*), *al-Mohtaref* (*The Professional*), *al-Shaheed* (*The Martyr*), *Halib al-Deyouf* (*Milk of the Guests*), *al-Ard Wa al-Diab* (*The Land and the Wolves*), *al-Sa'ad* (*The Happiness*), *Hadda Bouchaïb al-Yanasib* (*The Lottery*), *Khafif al-Shasheya* (*The Light of the Cloth*), *al-Na'ora, al-Nashba, Qady al-Halaqa* (*The Judge of the Circle*), *al-Shareka* (*The Company*), *Sdaft Hammady* (*Hammady's Button*), *Mallak al-Dewayra* (*The Owner of the Little Home*), *al-Bolgha al-Mashoora* (*The Magic Shoe*) and *al-Rashwa Nashwa* (*Bribery is a Pleasure*).

Other theatres and individual artists took different views in their work. Abdelkadir al-Badawi, a playwright, actor, director and theatre manager with the independent Ferqat al-A'hd al-Jadeed (New Generation Company), a group started in 1956, wrote a series of more populist working-class plays. His was a theatre of protest against social oppression and social ills. Among them *al-A'amel al-Matroud* (*The Fired Worker*), *Rayat al-Elm* (*The Flag of Science*), *al-Madlomoun* (*The Oppressed*), *Kefah al-Ommal* (*The Struggle of the Workers*), *Ummi al-Tahira* (*My Mother the Pure*), *al-Mo'allem Za'bool* (*Chief Za'bool*), *Kefah al-Jaza'er* (*The Struggle of Algeria*), *Yad al-Sharr* (*The Hand of Evil*), *al-Tather* (*The Cleansing*), *Ghita, al-A'ateloun* (*The Unemployed*), *al-Maslaha al-A'amma* (*The Public Interest*), *al-Hareboun* (*The Fugitives*), *al-Nowaqeseya, Fi Entidar al-Qitar* (*Waiting for the Train*), *al-Guerba Fi al-Mizan* (*Depression in the Scale*) and *Bouyout Men Zojaj* (*Houses of Glass*).

The generation of Moroccan theatre *aficionados* that emerged by the 1980s were more objective in their pursuits than their predecessors. They wanted to pursue careers in theatre and were determined to create a theatre industry. Their main concern was to write viable scripts and set up regular production units based in

MOROCCO

their home cities, but they were also committed to touring at home and abroad. This contemporary theatre was touched with the soul of experimentation along with national commitment.

Among the most influential of this later generation has been Nabil Lahlou (b. 1945), an actor, writer and director who has directed and acted in both Rabat and Paris. Lahlou got his theatrical start in Fes with the Howat al-Masrah (Amateurs of the Theatre) company. In 1965 he directed his first play al-Sa'aa (The Watch) by Muhammad Taymoud. He left to study theatre in France but returned to Morocco and in 1970 joined al-Qena' al-Sagheer (Small Mask) company. His innovative production of al-Salahef (The Turtles) was considered a breakthrough in both subject matter and style.

Another dramatist of note from the 1980s is Muhammad Taymoud himself, a playwright and director famous for his theatre of body language, as in Hibal Khouyout Sha'arr (Threads, Strings, and Hair). In his work the actor is at the centre of space and experience. Striving to create a mystical surrounding, he utilizes disassociated voices and chanting to connect on an unconscious level with his audience. His major plays include al-Diah al-Lami'ah (The Shining Shoes), Alf Lila Wa Lila (A Thousand Nights and a Night), Sala Lmae (The Water Was Liquidated), al-Zaghnana, Urss al-Dib (Wedding of the Wolf) and Mawkeb al-Sou'yane (The Caravan of the Seekers).

Muhammad al-Kakhat, actor, writer, director and professor, must also be remembered in this group. An experimental writer, his theatre, Les Amateurs du Théâtre à Fes, depends on the representation of inner human desires through the use of physical symbols and bold designs, lighting and acoustic effects. Of his plays the best known are Beshar al-Khayr (Herald of the Good), al-Nowa'eer, Beghal al-Tahona (Mules of the Grinder) and al-Mortajala al-Jadida (The New Inventor). These plays are characterized by their use of a pared-down language and their willingness to explore the 'forbidden' and the 'unspoken' in order to reach and purge the soul through magic and ritual. His group is able to work through the university infrastructure.

Two other playwrights of note from this era are Radwan Ehdado (b. 1941) and Abd-El-Salam al-Habib. Ehdado, from Tetouan, is best known for his work with the Literary Theatre company in Tetouan. His most successful plays are al-Damm (The Blood), al-Ard Wa al-Zaytoun (The Land and the Olives, 1976) directed by Abd-El-Wahed al-Shattat, and Fi

Entidar Zaman al-Jenoun (Waiting for the Time of Madness, 1980) directed by Abd-El-Aziz al-Naserey. Al-Habib's breakthrough play was Mout Esmoh al-Tamarrod (A Death Named Rebellion) performed by the Ferqat al-Tali'eaa (Front Company) in Fes.

Muhammad Balheesy (b. 1951), an actor and director, has long been associated with the Ferqat al-Liwaa' al-Masrahy (General Theatre Company) in Taza. In his work, he employs popular music and utilizes heritage styles. As a result, his plays are often lively celebrations with traditional costumes, jewellery, dancing, singing and chanting. Among his most successful works in this style have been Maqam al-Nour (The Standing Light), Bab al-Donia (The Door of Life) and al-Mansee (The Forgotten), all written by him; Salef Rhounja, al-Serjan Wa al-Mizan (The Saddles and the Scale) and Urss al-Atlas (The Wedding of Atlas) by Abdelkrim Berrechid; and Saleh Wa Maslouh (Good and Mended) and Janaiziyat al-A'arass (The Wedding Funeral) by Abd-El-Haqq al-Zerwally.

Muhammad Meskin is a playwright from the city of Oujda, in eastern Morocco, whose most important works include Niroun al-Safeer al-Motajawoel (Niroun the Wandering Ambassador), Trajedia al-Sayff al-Khashaby (The Tragedy of the Wooden Sword), Usber Ya Ayoub (Be Patient Ayoub), Emra'aa Wa Qamees Wa Zaghareed (A Woman, A Shirt and Cries of Joy), al-Nazeef (The Bleeding) and Mehrajan al-Mahabeel (Festival of Fools).

Muhammad Shahraman is another playwright well known for plays in which colloquial and literary language and literature meet. Muhammad Zohayr has said of his work 'Shahraman combines the music of public song and the strong language of Marrakeshi slang. His scripts celebrate both languages and excite through their wide weaves, their circles, their ability to go below the surface.'

Another notable contributor to the contemporary theatre is Yahya Bo-Dalal, an experimental theatre director who brings together the literary and the scenographic. His work depends on technology to a great extent as well as on games and elements from the circus, politics, commedia dell'arte and acrobatics. He works with the body and on the body. The plays he produces are all written by Muhammad Meskin and are performed by only one company, al-Masrah al-Ummaly (Workers' Theatre) in Oujda.

Al-Meskini al-Sagheer began his career as a poet but eventually gravitated toward playwriting. Among other achievements, he established

175

al-Madina (*The City*), a literary magazine with a strong theatre component. Historic and heritage symbols are prevalent in his work, but principally as masks which act as mouthpieces for social commentary. Of his numerous plays, the most widely known are *Modakkirat Rajol Ya'rifohom Jayyedan* (*The Autobiography of a Man Who Knows Them Well*), *al-Ka'as al-Akhira Ya Saiyedaty* (*The Last Glass O' My Lady*), *al-Embrator* (*The Emperor*) and *al Jondo Almthal* (*The Exemplary Soldier*).

One of the more unusual artists in Morocco is al-Tammy Janah who is best known for his movement theatre and love of body painting. His company, al-Ferqa al-Ehtifalleya Lel-Fenoun al-Derammeya (Celebrative Company for the Dramatic Arts) is built around the physical body which dominates all and makes use of masks, colours and objects. He has, however, written only one play to date.

Le Théâtre d'Aujourd'hui (Theatre for Today) was formed in 1987 by Abdelwahed Ouzri and the actress Touria Jabrane to practise many of these plays.

University theatre was especially significant during the 1960s, according to Ouzri, when it was established through the Union National des Étudiants Marocains (UNEM) aided by the poet Abdellatif Laabi and the director Farid Ben M'barek. The UNEM was outlawed in 1973 and cultural and artistic activities were forbidden within university settings. In 1988, Hassan Smili (of Ben Msick University in Casablanca) launched the Festival International de Théâtre Universitaire à Casablanca (FITUC) and theatre workshops; this was followed by another initiative by Abdellatif Chadli of the University of Meknes. He organized a national festival of university theatre in 1993. FITUC continues to host Moroccan and international university troupes on an annual basis.

Theatre for young audiences in Morocco goes back to the early 1960s when a number of companies were established, funded by the Ministry of Youth and Sports. Despite much activity through the years, though, few original scripts have emerged with most being adaptations of popular children stories. The first such group was, according to Hasan al-Mani'ee, The Dolls' Theatre, an offshoot of the Moroccan Theatre Company, founded in 1959. By 1987, the movement had advanced far enough for Rabat to host a National Festival of Children's Theatre. A study centre for children's art was established that same year. Called the National University of Children, it took as its mandate the expansion

of educational and artistic consciousness via children's theatre; the organizing of local groups and activities; acting as a lobby group for children's theatre; and the planning of children's theatre festivals on pan-Arabic, African and international levels.

Didactic and moralistic, Moroccan children's theatre is typified by plays like *al-Bayt al-Jadeed* (*The New House*) by Ben al-Amin Abd el-Salam, which aims to develop a seriousness of spirit in children and argues a need for children to make good use of their time and to organize their work. The genre utilizes recognizable folk characters such as Joha, Alaa El-Din, Hdidan, Ali Baba, Sinbad, *karagöz* figures and animal fable characters. Animals also figure prominently in plays such as *al-Sarsar Wa al-Namla* (*The Cockroach and the Ant*), *al-Tha'alab al-Ta'aer* (*The Flying Fox*), *al-Sayyad Wa al-Samaka al-Dahabeya* (*The Fisher and the Golden Fish*) and *Mohakamat al-Sa'alab* (*Trial of the Fox*). These plays also fully exploit theatrical resources such as songs, masks and dance. One of the major figures in the field is Najib Ghelal who, after studies in Paris, established with his French wife, Patina Masse, a theatre company called al-Meshkal (Kaleidoscope).

There are a number of puppet theatres ranging from the shadow theatre of *karagöz* to marionettes. The major groups are Sondoq al-Furaja (Viewing Box), the Fadely Brothers, the Puppet Company of the Ministry of Youth and Sports and Puppet Company of the Ministry of Cultural Affairs.

On the level of infrastructure, theatre practitioners in Morocco do not belong to any formal organizations, unions or associations and, as a result, the theatre remains without a unified voice. In the late 1970s, a national union for theatre practitioners was established, but it did not last long. On those few occasions when government support has been given, it carried with it many bureaucratic constraints. There are, nevertheless, two ministries with responsibility for theatre and its advancement – the Ministry of Youth and Sports and Ministry of Cultural Affairs. The first is mandated to supervise the large number of amateur groups while the second is principally concerned with the affairs of the professional theatre.

In 1986, the Institut Supérieur d'art dramatique et d'animation culturelle (ISADAC, Higher Institute for Theatre Arts and Cultural Activity) opened under the management of director and critic Ahmad Badry. The Ministry of Youth and Sports also offers theatre courses on a workshop

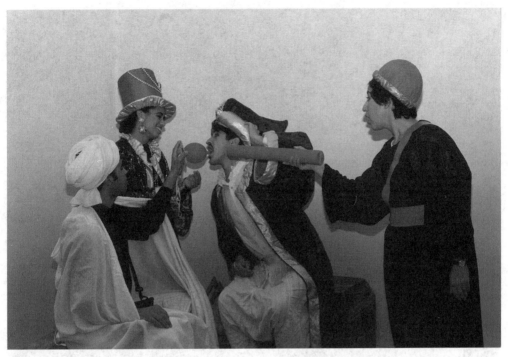

A scene from the comic halqa *Almatmora* performed by Fatima Chebchoub (right) and selected students, in Meknes, 1997.
Photo: Debbie Folaron

basis with additional training opportunities provided by the National Music Institute in Rabat and the National Institute in Casablanca, which has two acting departments, one Arabic and the other French. There is also a department of Arabic acting in Casablanca sponsored by the Ministry of Cultural Affairs. Many Moroccan students study in European institutes of theatre arts.

A Moroccan Centre for Theatre Research (CMRD) was established in 1953 under the auspices of the Association of Youth and Sports. After independence, supervision of the centre was assigned to al-Ma'moura Company. Throughout the 1990s, the CMRD did a limited number of studies.

As for theatre buildings, Morocco inherited a group of theatres from the colonial era and they are still in use since they have all the necessary equipment. Only one new theatre has been built in Morocco since the 1960s, the Muhammad al-Khaames V National Theatre in Rabat in 1962. Open-air theatres are numerous, however. Among the best known are Masrah al-Hebool (Theatre of Elhboul) in Meknes, Masrah Thaleth Mars (The Third of March Theatre) in al-Khmysat, Masrah Sidi Bo-Zayd (Sidi Bo-Zayd Theatre) in al-Jadida

and Masrah al-Hawa'a al-Talq (Open-Air Theatre) in Agadir.

In the late 1980s, the government decided to allot one per cent of community budgets to the building of local cultural centres, complete with theatres, with additional funds earmarked for the sponsorship of artists. It was also recommended that each economic region would establish and fund two theatre companies. In the late 1990s the outcome of this initiative was still unclear.

On the academic front, the first important study of theatre in Morocco appeared in 1974 – a university thesis by Hasan al-Mani'ee (later published in book form) called *Abhath Fi al-Masrah al-Maghraby* (*Research into the Moroccan Theatre*). He subsequently wrote five more books on the subject. Following this pioneering work, Abd-El-Rahman Ben Zeidan published a number of critical studies including *Men Qadaya al-Masrah al-Maghraby* (*The Case for the Moroccan Theatre*), *al-Muqawama Fi al-Masrah al-Maghraby* (*Colonial Resistance in the Moroccan Theatre*), *Kitabat al-Takrees Wa al-Taghieer Fi al-Masrah al-Maghraby* (*The Writing of Devotion and the Changing Moroccan Theatre*) and *As'elat al-Masrah al-Araby* (*Questions of Arabic Theatre*).

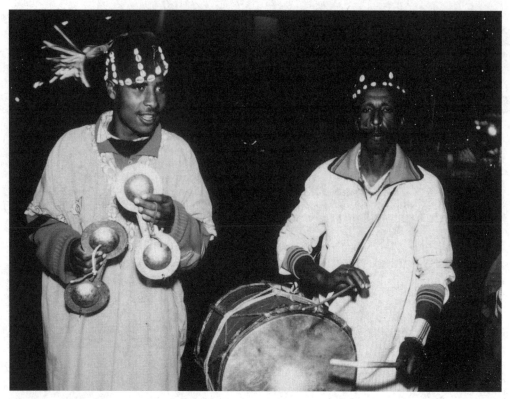

Street performers at the Marrakesh market.
Photo: Benoit Aquin, CIDA

Muhammad Adeeb al-Sellawy has published two books of note – *al-Masrah al-Maghraby Men Ayna Wa Ela Ayna* (*The Moroccan Theatre: From Where to Where?*, 1975) and *al-Ehtifaleya Fi al-Masrah al-Maghraby al-Hadith* (*Celebration in the New Moroccan Theatre*, 1975). Another scholar Esa Yakan wrote a series of useful articles about the Moroccan theatre later collected into a book entitled *al-Tansheet Bewasetat al-Masrah Be El-Maghreb* (*The Theatrical Movement in Morocco*, 1976), a fundamental and essential reference for anyone wishing to understand theatre development in Morocco.

More specific studies have been conducted on both individual cities and their theatres in terms of development and genre. Among the best titles are a study of Marrakesh theatre by Abd-Allah al-Ma'awey, a writer and director; *Aseela Society and its Theatre*, by Mostafa Abd-El-Salam al-Mahmah, an historic study of the theatre movement in the city of Aseela; and al-Mahmah *A History of Children's Theatre in Morocco*, the first work to examine this genre.

Other scholarly studies have been published by Azzddine Bounnit, Mostafa Ramdani, Salem Guindi, Hassan Bahrawi and Hassan Lyonssfi.

Specialized theatre magazines have all lasted only an issue or two. Among these were *al-Qessa Wa al-Masrah* (*Story Writing and Theatre*) and *Resalat al-Fann* (*The Art Message*), both published in the 1960s; *al-Masrah al-Maghriby* (*The Moroccan Theatre*) published in Marrakesh in 1974; and *al-Lewaa' al-Masrahy* (*The Theatre Leader*) published by the Theatre Leader Company in Fes and edited by the actor Muhammad Aadel in 1979. One theatre newspaper also existed for a short time, *al-Ta'asis* (*The Establishment*).

Abdelkrim Berrechid
Translated by Khaled F. Refai

Further Reading

al-Andalosey, Zakeya Ebad. 'Helaly Abd-El-Wahed, Sa'ad-Allah Abd-El-Majeed, Nasr-al-

Din al-Tohamy, al-Masrah al-Thaleth Bayna al-Madmoun Wa al-Shakl' [The third theatre: a study in the establishment of a youth theatre]. *Mejallat al-Madina* [The City Magazine] 6 (June 1981).

Ben Zeidan, Abd-El-Rahman. 'As'elat al-Masrah al-Araby' [Some questions of the Arabic theatre]. *Selselat al-Derasat al-Naqdeia* [Critical Studies] 7. Casablanca: Dar al-Thaqafa [The Culture House] 1987.

——. *Nahwo Kitaba Jadida Ala al-Kitaba al-Masraheya al-Maghrebeia* [Towards a new form of Moroccan theatre writing]. n.d.

Berrechid, Abdelkrim, 'Bayan al-Masrah al-Ehtifaly' [Manifesto of the celebrative theatre]. *Jaridat al-Elm* [The Science Magazine] 310 (23 April 1976).

——. 'al-Malameh al-Asasseya Li-El-Ekhraj al-Masrahy Fi al-Maghreb' [Directing theatre in Morocco: basic principles]. *Mejallat al-Madina* 6 (1981).

Cantin, Chantal. 'Creating theatre in Morocco: an interview with Fatima Chebchoub'. *Australasian Drama Studies* 27 (October 1995): 63–9.

Chebchoub, Fatima. 'The Female Artist in Morocco: With References to Actresses'. *Australasian Drama Studies* 27 (October 1995): 53–62.

'Connaissance du théâtre Marocain' [Understanding Moroccan theatre]. *Europe Revue Littéraire Mensuelle* 602–3 (1972): 158–62.

Ehdado, Radwan, 'Maserat Masrah al-Howah Be-El-Shamal Qabl al-Esteqlal' [Navigating the amateur theatre in the north before independence]. *Majalat al-Fenoon* [The Arts Magazine] (November 1979).

Ersan, Aly Oqla. *al-Zawaher al-Masraheia End al-Arab* [Theatre phenomena within the Arab world]. Tripoli: al-Monsha'aa al-Aamma Lel Nashr (General Foundation for Publishing), n.d.

al-Ka'aak, Osman. *Mahrajan al-Masrah al-Arabi al-Motanaqqell* [The itinerant theatre festival in the Arab world]. Rabat, 1984.

Kapchan, Deborah A. *Gender on the Market: Moroccan Women and the Revoicing of Tradition*. Philadelphia: University of Pennsylvania Press, 1996.

——. 'Hybrid Genres, Performed Subjectivities: The Revoicing of Public Oratory in the Moroccan Marketplace'. *Women and Performance: A Journal of Feminist Theory* 7–8 no. 2/1 (1995): 53–85.

al-Kettany, Zien-al-Aabedin. 'al-Marhoom Abd-El-Wahed al-Shawy: Ra'ed al-Nahda al-Fanneyya Be El-Maghreb' [The Apology of Abd-El-Wahed al-Shawy, the pioneer of the artistic renaissance in Morocco]. *Majalat al-Fenoon* [Moroccan Arts Magazine] 2, n.d.

Louassini, Zouhir. *La identidad del Teatro Marroqui* [The identity of Moroccan theatre]. Granada: Grupo de Investigaçion Estudios Arabes Contemporaneos, 1992.

Majalat al-Anwar [The Light Magazine] 3 (1946).

al-Mani'ee, Hasan. *Abhath Fi al-Masrah al-Maghraby* [Research into the Moroccan theatre]. Rabat: Matba'aa Sawt Meknas [The Voice of Meknas Printing House], n.d.

al-Oafy, Najib. *Jadal al-Quera* [Literary debates]. *Contemporary Moroccan Innovation*, Rabat: Dar al-Nashr al-Maghrabeia, n.d.

Ouzri, Abdelwahed. *Le Théâtre au Maroc: structures et tendances* [The theatre in Morocco: structures and trends]. Casablanca: Éditions Toubkal, 1997.

al-Sa'eh, al-Hasan. 'Tareekh al-Masrah al-Maghraby' [The history of Maghreb theatre]. *Majalat al-Fenoon* [The Arts Magazine] 5–6 (1974).

Salloum, Habeeb. 'Morocco Fantastic Folkloric Dance'. *Al Jadid* 2 no. 9 (July 1996).

al-Sellawy, Muhammad Adeeb. 'al-Ehtifaleya Fi al-Masrah al-Maghraby al-Hadith' [Celebration in the new Moroccan theatre]. In *al-Mawsoo'aa al-Saghira* [The compact encyclopaedia]. Baghdad, n.d.

Shakroon, Abd-Allah. 'Tatawwor al-Masrah al-Maghraby Qabl al-Esteqlal Wa Ba' adaho' [The development of the Moroccan theatre before and after independence]. *Jaridat al-Elm* [The Science Magazine] (1956).

——. 'Le Théâtre marocain passé et présent' [Moroccan theatre past and present]. *Premières Mondiales* 32 (1963).

al-Shawy, Abd-El-Wahed. 'Taqallob al-Fan al-Masrahy Be el-Maghreb' [The shaky theatre of Morocco]. *Jaridat al-Sa'ada* [The Happiness Newspaper] 29 (1933).

Soussi, Jamal. 'Le Théâtre au Maroc de 1912 á 1956: le théâtre au Maroc sous le protectorat' [The theatre in Morocco from 1912 to 1956: theatre in Morocco under the protectorate]. PhD dissertation, Université de Paris III, 1984. 99 pp.

al-Torris, Abd-El-Khaleq. *Entesar al-Haqq Be El-Batel* [The victory of truth by falsehood]. Tetouan: al-Matba'aa al-Mahdeya [Mahdeya Print House], 1933.

MUSQAT

(see **OMAN**)

NORTH YEMEN

(see **YEMEN**)

OMAN

(Overview)

A 4,000-year-old sultanate on the east coast of the Arabian peninsula which was opened to general tourism only in the 1990s, Oman is bordered by the Gulf of Oman and the United Arab Emirates to the north and northwest, Saudi Arabia to the west and Yemen to the southwest. With a land area of 212,460 square kilometres (82,030 square miles), the country's population was 2.18 million (1996) of which some 750,000 were expatriate workers – mainly Indians, Pakistanis and East Africans. The capital is Musqat.

Oman is a Muslim society which follows the Ibadi tradition, probably the least known group within that religious community. As many as 80 per cent of Omanis are Ibadis with the remainder mainly Sunni or Shiah.

Conquered by the Persian King Cyrus in 536 BC, it was later invaded by what is now Iraq, the Mongols and then the Persians again. Islamic since the seventh century AD, Oman – that is mainly the city of Musqat and its surrounding areas – came under Portuguese control in 1507 and the Portuguese remained there until 1650. Re-establishing their own autonomy at that time, Omani traders eventually extended their influence as far south as the African island of Zanzibar. Briefly under Persian control again between 1741 and 1749, Oman signed a treaty of friendship with Britain in 1798 but retained its independence and its own far-flung empire, controlling territories as far away as Mombasa and operating trading posts up and down the African coast. At its height, the empire also controlled portions of what are now India and Pakistan. Omanis refer to their country as being among the oldest of the independent Arab states.

Internal power struggles between the country's coastal regions (governed by Hindu sultans) and the interior (ruled by Muslim imams) occurred during the nineteenth century and well into the twentieth. Between 1932 and 1970, Sultan Said bin Taimur, a reclusive and repressive ruler, controlled Oman. In 1970 his son, the British-educated Qabus bin Said (b. 1942) overthrew him and embarked upon an ambitious modernization programme funded by the country's large oil reserves, which did not begin to be exploited until 1967, late by Gulf standards. In 1976 an Omani Ministry of National Heritage and Culture was established. Five years later, the country was a founding member of the Gulf Cooperation Council.

Unlike Saudi Arabia, where women cannot work with men or drive and there are no elections, Oman now has several women in the partially elected Consultative Council. Tolerance and equality for both sexes is based in the country's new Basic Law scheduled to come into full effect in the year 2000.

Like most Arab countries, Oman has a long history of storytelling, dance and music but not a very long history of European-style literary theatre. Indeed, the literary theatre was not even seen until the 1950s. In the 1990s, it was still considered something exotic and primarily for intellectuals. As such, no professional community had yet emerged.

It is difficult to identify the beginnings of this modern kind of theatre practice because few written documents are available. What does exist is based primarily on anecdotal evidence. Most, in fact, is based on the testimonies of older people recalling childhood memories about their school activities in and around

181

Musqat. Traditionally, that is prior to 1970, there were only three schools – all Saidi Schools – in Oman. The largest and most prestigious was the Saidi School in Musqat which was established in 1940. The first to follow a non-Quranic education system when modernization came in, this school is the most prestigious in the country, has produced many people who went on to run the country's government and is the school of choice for most Omanis. The second school was the Saidi School in Salalah (southern region), established in 1951 while the third was the Saidi School in Matrah, established in 1959.

According to a book called *Hints*, published by the Ministry of Education, Training and Youth in 1985, the Saidi School in Musqat had an enclosed courtyard used for major celebrations and end-of-year events. It was apparently at some of the latter that scripted plays were seen for the first time. Many of these end-of-year events were attended by government officials, by the foreign community and by parents; they were one of the social highlights of the Omani calendar.

A teacher from the period, Ahmed Salem, recalled in an interview for this article, that:

At the end of every school year celebrations were held at which short dramatizations of school texts – many of them of Egyptian and Lebanese origin – were presented. Some were comic in nature. I remember doing a presentation based on being miserly. Such shows were presented annually from at least 1949 when I joined the staff and continued up to the time I left the school in 1969. Throughout that period the presentation of these short plays was supervised by the teachers on an alternating basis.

Tawfik Aziz, the school's principal between 1956 and 1973, recalled that at the end-of-year celebrations

the dramatizations were done in Fusha, the standard Arabic, with a few done in English. Most came from school texts. Of these, I remember the Lebanese book *Al Mrooj* which took about ten or fifteen minutes. I became the supervisor of the theatre activities when I arrived at the school. Because we had no stage, we pushed desks together and covered them with fabric. We also connected two classrooms together so that the entrance could be used as backstage areas. The audience sat in the inner courtyard. The topics of those plays were religious mostly with some about

society or history. Some used comic situations. The audience often included high government officials in the Sultanate and even people from the British Consulate. This celebration was quite official because the end-of-year at the Saidi School was the only such recognized annual event organized at that time in the country.

The actor Ridha Abdul-Latif, later a prominent member of the Domestic Club Theatre, recalled similar theatre experiments at the Saidi School in Matrah. The highlight for him was in 1960 when a ninety-minute work was presented called *Saqr Kuraish* (*Kuraish's Eagle*).

From 1970 the doors of such schools were thrown open to all Omani students and new facilities were built in all cities and villages in the country. By the end of 1987, 696 co-ed schools were in existence compared with the three that taught boys only before modernization. Theatre activities had become a continuing part of the education system by the mid-1990s with theatre specialists available for almost every region of the country. Indeed, by the 1990s one could see productions of plays by Molière, Shakespeare and even the Egyptian dramatist Tawfiq al-Hakīm.

From the schools, theatre grew in popularity in the early 1970s to the point that the country's many social clubs began to add in amateur theatre groups. During this period as well, many young people left the country for advanced studies in the United Arab Emirates and to attend universities in Cairo and Beirut where they were exposed to newer styles of theatre and more advanced theatre movements. On their return home, they used the club theatre groups to stage the kinds of shows they had been seeing abroad. Those who attended as well as those who participated – both men and women – joined in enthusiastically. Particularly important in this regard were the activities during the 1970s at two Musqat clubs – the Domestic Club and the Oman Club. By the 1980s, such activities had been seen all across the country.

Mohammed Bin Elias Bin Faqir, Ridha Abdul-Latif and his brother Amin Abdul-Latif (who studied at the Higher Institute for Theatre Arts in Cairo) were among the early members of the Domestic Club and their names rank high in the club's and the country's theatre history.

Shows at these clubs were usually quite short with five or six pieces presented in one summer evening. The 1971 shows by the Domestic Club were composed of several original pieces including *The Return of Shanjoub*, a play by Mussa Jaafar who also directed it; two pieces written and produced by Ridha Abdul-Latif – *The Madness of the Brain* (co-written by Hussein Yousef) and *Between Culture and Triviality*; *The End of Time* by Ridha Abdul-Hakīm; *The Justice Council* by Tawfiq al-Hakīm; and *al-Nar wa'l-Zaytun* (*Fire and Olives*) by Alfred Faraj.

In 1972 the Club evenings included *Between Wrong and Right* by Mussa Jaafar; *Socrates* by Ridha Abdul-Latif, a play about the trial of Socrates; *The Complaints of the Community* by Mohammed Bin Elias Faqir, a social comedy; *Wholesale Doctor*, a comedy by Mussa Jaafar; *The White Bed*, an allegorical social comedy; *The Dervishes*, a social comedy; and a children's musical *The Heroic Horseman*, based on the Moroccan play *Alf Lila wa Lila* (*The Thousand and One Nights*).

In 1973 the Club presented the comedy-drama *Suicide of Truth* by Amin Abdul-Latif; *The Female Slave*, an adaptation based on the Egyptian play *Throat Block* by Sa'd al-Din Wahba; *People Have Misjudged Me* by Mahmoud Shahdad, the first play to include an Omani actress; *The Insane Are Living in Luxury* by Mohammed Elias Faqir, a social comedy; and *The Fatigue* by Ridha Abdul-Latif, a two-part play written as an allegory which was subsequently presented in Cairo and Beirut.

In 1974 the Club presented the social drama *The Duty and the Rope* by Hussein Abdul-Latif; *Socialization Coffeehouse* by Mohammed Elias Faqir; *Oh Sea, Your Time Is Easy*, a realistic drama written by Mussa Jaafar; and *The Love and Land Song* with a cast of fifty written, directed, designed and choreographed by Jaafar.

In 1975 the Club presented another Jaafar work, the realistic drama *From Life*; the poetic *Love Tablets* by Amin Abdul-Latif; and *Samba* by Ridha Abdul-Latif. All of the Club's 1975 productions were recorded by Oman Television and remain in the national television archives as well as those of the Domestic Club. These recordings reveal both the nature of the plays as well as the level of production of the company. In 1976 the Club presented another of Jaafar's social dramas, *All That Talk Hurts the Head*; *The Inhabited Home* by Mohammed Elias Faqir; and the musical drama *Forgiveness* by Amin Abdul-Latif, which was also recorded for television.

After 1976 the Domestic Club presented only occasional productions and within two or three years, as its key members left for job or educa-

tional opportunities, the group stopped producing altogether.

At the same time as the Club's theatre activities diminished, the Domestic Club itself moved into an area of Musqat which was at a distance from its traditional public. Ironically, the new space contained something the original members had been in need of for many years: an indoor, air-conditioned theatre with lighting facilities. The pioneers had long been working in an open courtyard and missed out on this new opportunity.

The only book about the company, *Theatre in the Domestic Club*, an archival volume, says that as many as 2,500 people saw the most popular shows. The book also points out that audiences were segregated by sex, with two performances usually for men and one for women.

One other social club of note, the Oman Club, also produced on a similar basis during the 1970s; it was from this group that the television and radio star Salih Shweired first gained attention. Unfortunately, there is virtually no documentation for productions by this group.

By the end of the 1970s few productions were seen at all in Oman at the clubs. In an attempt to encourage theatre activities, the Ministry of Education, Training and Youth began a series of festivals for young people. Best Play awards were given for plays written by people under 25 and awards were given for best productions both regionally and nationally. Such events were important in the overall theatrical development of the country.

By the mid-1980s, Club productions had begun to be seen again. Among the most important was the Nahdha Club's 1984 production of *The Crusher of Thieves*, a full-length children's play with music written and staged by Abd-Elkarim Bin Ali Bin Jawad. Performed at the Women's Association Theatre, it was later recorded and broadcast on national television. Another production of note was the Abri Club's (a group from the Zahiry region) *A Pause in the Situation* done at the Ministry of National Heritage and Culture theatre.

Perhaps the most important group to emerge in the 1980s was the Youth Theatre founded in 1980 by a number of young people concerned with improving the situation of theatre in the country. Appealing for support to the Ministry of Information and Youth – which was in charge of youth clubs – the loosely knit group convinced the ministry to bring in an expert from another country to help move things forward. A director from the United Arab Emirates, Mustafa Hashish, was recruited.

Under his direction, the Omani Youth Theatre was formed on a non-professional basis in Musqat. Affiliated to the ministry, the company's first production was Shakespeare's *The Merchant of Venice*, a controversial choice. Not only was the play complex and challenging theatrically, but also it dealt with social and religious issues that Omanis were not accustomed to seeing dealt with in a public way. As well, three women were in the cast. But the ministry supported the production and helped the group to find a suitable space in which to rehearse.

For the performances themselves, the group rented the Continental Theatre in Musqat. Lighting and sound were borrowed from Omani Television. During rehearsals other experts had been brought in to improve the group's skills in acting, again paid for by the ministry. The production featured unprecedented technical support – designers, make-up artists, a stage manager and technicians. The show was an immense success and set the stage for the development of an ongoing and ultimately more professional theatrical community. After a six-month rehearsal period, the production was staged under the auspices of the country's tenth anniversary of modernization celebrations (18 November, 1980).

For its second production, the group was urged to present an Omani play or, at least, an Arab play. Because no Omani play was deemed suitable, the group chose the latter route and the play was then adapted to Omani reality – *Aylat Al-Dughri* (*The Family of Al-Dughri*) by the Egyptian dramatist Nu'man 'Ashur. The play was a social drama with some comic situations.

One writer whose work was ultimately seen on a regular basis at the Youth Theatre was Mansour Makawi, an Egyptian who first came to Oman in the late 1970s when he had been commissioned to help Omani writers learn the art of adaptation. He stayed and wrote a number of plays himself based on Omani reality. In 1982, he wrote *The Homeland*, an historical epic about the Omani struggle against the Portuguese. It was also the first historical theatrical work about Oman. In 1983 he wrote two plays – *Al-Rayah* (*The Flag*) about the heroism and piety of the Omani Imam Warith Bin Kaab Al-Kharoosy, and *The Migrating Bird* about the life of the Omani singer and artist Salem Bin Rashid Al-Souary. *The Migrating Bird* was staged by Mohammed Bin Saeed al-Shanfary, one of the first Omanis to have real training in theatre and a man who was by 1984 the director of the Youth Theatre.

That same year Makawi offered the Youth Theatre a new play written in a populist style that has come to be called country drama. Entitled *Al-Tawa* (*The Well*), it is about irrigation but despite success and its use of Omani Arabic it was not felt to be totally accurate in its portrayal of Omani society. In 1985 the Youth Theatre staged Makawi's *Al-Mahar* (*The Dowry*). Directed by Mohammed al-Shanfari, the play mixed the old Arabian folk tale *Anter and Ablah* with a modern realistic incident relating to dowry demands. The production required huge resources for design, make-up and cast. Despite this, however, *The Dowry* was a success and became the first Omani play to be performed in other regions of the country, being seen in Salalah in the southern region, Nazwi in the interior region and Soor (Tyre) in the eastern region.

Two other Youth Theatre productions of note are the children's play *Naam Aqwiya* (*Yes, We Are Strong*) by Ibrahim Shaarawy and an adaptation of Tawfiq al-Hakīm's *Urid an-Aqtul* (*I Want to Kill*) produced and published in 1987 by Abd-Elkarim Bin Ali Bin Jawad under the title of *I Want to Understand*.

Mansour Makawi's last play in Oman was *Strange* in 1986. It was staged that year by Mohammed al-Shanfari. Dealing with greed and the conversion of society, it was a model for social drama followed by many other Omani writers in the years since.

The year 1987 was an important one for the Youth Theatre. The company participated in the Second Youth Theatre Festival organized by the Cooperation Council of the Arab Gulf States with a musical play called *The Ship Is Still Stopping*, written and produced by Abd-Elkarim Bin Ali Bin Jawad. In the same year, Mohammed Al-Shanfari wrote and produced *Alfaar* (*The Mouse*), a play dealing with marriage and ownership. The Youth Theatre also presented that year *Al-Khabaz* (*The Baker*) by Abd-Elkarim Bin Ali Bin Jawad about the damaging influence of rumour in society.

For all its contributions, however, the Youth Theatre was still working in the 1990s without an adequate hall and as a youth cultural activity rather than as a specialized theatrical activity. Most of its members were still employees of government ministries. Productions attracted a public but even so they remained more a curiosity than anything else because they were limited to only a few days of performance each year.

Nevertheless, independent troupes are emerging. Known as domestic troupes, the first was established in 1987 – the Awakening Troupe. The company's first show was *The Major Awakening* and its second show was *The Treasure*, a play that later became part of the school curriculum. In 1988, a second company appeared – Majan (Free), a group established by the older members of the Youth Theatre. Both these troupes are determined to attract a wider public.

In the mid-1990s, their determination was rewarded on one level: the Ministry of National Heritage and Culture accepted the idea of establishing two cultural centres for the country, one in Musqat and another in Salalah. Both these centres will contain theatre spaces with basic lighting and sound equipment.

Unfortunately, despite these attempts, theatre in the 1990s in Oman remains a marginal activity. Training is still all but non-existent and performance spaces are really much better for lectures than plays. Only three clubs even have stages suitable for performances – the Oman and Domestic Clubs in Musqat and the Nasr Club in the southern region. Few Omanis seem interested or have the skills to develop a truly professional new generation.

Abd-Elkarim Bin Ali Bin Jawad
Translated by Yacob Idris

Further Reading

Anthony, John Duke. *Historical and Cultural Dictionary of the Sultanate of Oman and the Emirates of Eastern Arabia*. Metuchen, NJ: Scarecrow Press, 1976.

Excerpts from Omani History. Oman: Ministry of Education, Training and Youth, 1985.

Johnstone, Thomas Muir, 'Folklore and Folk Literature in Oman and Socatra'. *Arabian Studies* 1 (1974): 7–23.

——. 'Folk tales and Folklore of Dhofar'. *Journal of Omani Studies* 6 (1983): 123–6.

Oman: arts traditionels du sultanat d'Oman [Oman: traditional arts of the Sultanate of Oman]. [sound recording]. Ivry, France: Auvidis, 1993.

Shawqi, Yusuf. *Dictionary of Traditional Music in Oman*. Translated and expanded by Dieter Christensen. Wilhelmshaven: F. Noetzel, 1994. 224 pp.

Theatre in the Domestic Club. Oman: Domestic Club, 1977.

The Youth Theatre Publications. Texts for the plays performed by the Youth Theatre. Includes *Fatigue* and *The Suicide of Truth*.

PALESTINE

(Overview)

Palestine is a country which, while non-existent on any current political map, has remained very much alive for its people, who often refer to it as a country in exile. The geographic area considered as Palestine has varied since ancient times, and covers what is now the modern state of Israel plus the West Bank area bordered by the Jordan River and that section of the Sinai called the Gaza Strip. Part of the Turkish Ottoman Empire from the Middle Ages to the nineteenth century, and under a British mandate for the first half of the twentieth, Palestine's struggle for recognition of its people's political rights, including statehood, has made this country-without-a-country a continuing flashpoint for tensions in the Middle East since the late 1920s.

Historically, Palestine's geographical location at the crossroads of trade routes linking the continents of Africa, Asia and Europe allowed it to become a melting pot of various cultures and influences, and the sanctified grounds of three major monotheistic faiths – Judaism, Christianity and Islam. It has been a battleground for some of the region's most powerful civilizations and states: Assyrian, Pharaonic, Greek, Roman, Persian, Arab and European among others.

By the twentieth century, Palestine's population was a mixture of Muslim, Christian and Jewish. Immediately following World War I, which dislodged the Ottoman Empire, the country was placed under a British mandate, and began to see a steady immigration of European and Russian Jews known as Zionists bent on the creation of a Jewish state in Palestine. During that period, tensions mounted and steadily became more violent and unmanageable as the divide widened into a political,

economic and cultural chasm between the Arab and Jewish communities. In 1947, the United Nations partitioned Palestine into a Jewish state and an Arab state. By mid-1948, the Jewish state – Israel – came into being, leading to armed struggle between Israel and its Arab neighbours. Many Palestinians, as a result of the fighting, ended up as refugees in the West Bank, Gaza, Lebanon, Syria, Jordan and Egypt, with others moving even further from the region. Another war in 1967 brought the West Bank and Gaza areas and the many Palestinians there under direct Israeli occupation.

From 1964, Palestinian independence came to be led by an amalgam of groups generally working together under the name of the Palestine Liberation Organization (PLO) with Yasser Arafat its long-time leader. Sometimes military and sometimes purely political, the PLO has tried during this period to act as a centre for the Palestinian diaspora. On several occasions, this took the form of populist actions, one of the most intense and longest lasting being the *intifada* (uprising) which began in 1987 and lasted for years as a protest against Israeli military occupation. Involving a range of protests from boycotts and strikes to demonstrations and stone-throwing incidents to even greater acts of violence in its latter stages, the *intifada* among other things led to long discussions between the PLO and the Israeli government and, in 1993, to the signing of the Oslo Accords, an agreement on Palestinian autonomy in the Gaza Strip and parts of the West Bank. Although the Palestinians insisted that this was only a first step towards the long-awaited establishment of a new Palestinian state (a state already declared by the PLO), the final status of the West Bank and Gaza and of the Palestinian refugees still remained to be negotiated late in 1998.

Until a final settlement was reached, most Palestinians – and there were as many as 4.5 million of them according to some estimates – remained officially stateless. It is this diaspora, along with nearly 1 million Palestinian Arabs who ultimately acquired Israeli citizenship and remained under Israeli rule in Haifa, Jaffa, Nazareth and the Galilee villages, and another million or so who found citizenship and livelihoods in other countries around the world, who make up the people and the idea of Palestine approaching the year 2000.

As for Palestinian culture generally and theatre specifically, both must be examined as part of a very wide historical context. The dismemberment of the geographic and political entity of Palestine in 1948, an event called by the Arab community the *nakba* (catastrophe), and the subsequent dispossession of millions of people, created a large wound in the Palestinian sense of identity. Over the next decades, however, culture in its many forms – from popular communal activities to specific literary and performing arts activities – fast became one of the Palestinian people's main unifying forces, significantly helping to keep the far-flung community together. At the same time, Palestinian poetry, theatre and music became highly politicized, affirming the political aspirations of the Palestinian people and protesting against the difficult daily living experiences of the community. While such cultural activity has been ongoing in a general sense, it has suffered from a lack of specific continuity meaning that specific artists and groups would surface for a time and then disappear, sometimes being driven into exile, sometimes surfacing somewhere else. This phenomenon has seriously affected the development of Palestinian theatre which, like all theatres, requires some form of stable environment.

Adding to the difficulty of articulating a specific Palestinian theatre is the fact that such massive population movements have meant that texts and records of a whole generation have been destroyed or made extremely difficult to find and to verify. As Palestinians dispersed to different countries, it became increasingly more difficult even to define what Palestinian culture and theatre was and still is.

Despite the foregoing, two periods of development for Palestinian theatre can be discerned: the first was that which took place before the *nakbah*, when Palestine was still a geopolitical entity and when a majority of the inhabitants were Palestinians of Arab descent; the second is the period after 1948, which includes numerous contemporary initiatives to create a viable Palestinian theatre. Interestingly, both historic periods reflect a penchant towards a politicized national agenda.

The roots of indigenous Palestinian performance – like the roots of many Arab nations – are to be found in the songs and tales told by the region's many wandering storytellers, a tradition that remains popular in modern attempts to connect to audiences. Song and dance are part of communal activities and those with special skills in these arts have long been appreciated at weddings, birth celebrations, circumcisions and the many festivals celebrating such activities as successful harvests. The performative ritual is also to be found in Arab traditions surrounding death and burial. These latter events contain elegiac wailing, poetry, movement and even specific mourning costumes. One can add to this the rituals of religious festivals, both Islamic and Christian.

These cultural practices were not treated as theatre, partly because the concept of an independent theatrical art in the western sense did not exist in Palestine until the mid-nineteenth century, when the Arab and western worlds began to meet on such cultural grounds. Even here, the loss of Palestinian cultural archives has led researchers to have different opinions about the exact beginnings of European-style Palestinian theatre. One group of scholars has suggested that it began in 1913, the year when the Beirut-born, Egyptian-based actor George Abyad and his troupe visited major Palestinian cities, the first Arabic-language theatre company to do so. The troupe performed two plays, *Ghuneyat Al-Andalous* (*Andalusian Song*) and *Louis Al-Hadi-Ashar* (*Louis the Eleventh*).

Other scholars consider 1909 to be a more correct date as it marks the year that the literary club Al-Montada Al-Adabi was established in Al-Quds (Jerusalem) and performed the play *Salah al-Din al-Ayyoby* (*Saladin*). Still others feel that 1920 is the real beginning since it was in that year that the company Jamiyat Al Traki Wa Al Tamtheel Al Arabi (Arabic Society for Acting and Culture) was established in Al-Quds. This amateur group performed Arabic translations of Shakespeare's *Hamlet* and Molière's *L'Avare* (*The Miser*), among others. Some have even put the beginning as late as 1928, the year that Nasry al-Jouzy (1908–96) established his company, Jamaiyat Al-Funoon Wa Al-Tamtheel (Organization of Arts and Acting). He was the first Palestinian to perform original Arabic plays in Palestine. It was also as part of this troupe that the first Palestinian women appeared on the public stage.

Whatever the date, such a search for the birth of western-style theatre in Palestine is still only a partial recognition of the role that the performing arts have played in this land for thousands of years. At most, it is only a partial step toward understanding the historical and social conditions where something resembling a literary theatre was born, where writers such as Shakespeare and Molière began to be translated and a new way of thinking about performance began to be seen.

In fact, the westernization of Arabic education and culture had been going on long before such theatrical experiments. In the middle of the nineteenth century, European interest in the Middle East led to the establishment of many western-based missionary schools in Palestine – French schools in 1848, English and German schools in 1851, American schools in 1869, Russian schools in 1882 and Italian schools in 1891. These schools presented students with both western culture and new languages, all utilizing literary study as a key element of the pedagogy. Dramatic literature proved useful in such studies and another means through which a slow cultural conversion could take place. These schools attracted many wealthy families who wanted to give their children more opportunities in the 'modern' world.

Eventually some of those thus trained began to use these foreign forms to evolve an actual Arab art. Mohamed Aza Darouza (1887–1984), for example, worked in Nablus where he wrote from the mid-1920s a wide range of school plays including *Wufood Al-Norman Al-Ashra* (*The Ten Norman Emissaries*), *Akher Mulook Bani Serag* (*The Last Kings of Serag's Children*), *Saqr Kuraish* (*Kuraish's Eagle*) and *Al-Fallah Wa Al-Simsar* (*The Farmer and the Broker*). All these plays glorified the Arab past, questioned foreign cultural presence and bemoaned fraternal divisions in the country. Aza Darouza was also clearly defending the new idea of theatre as a viable art for the Arab world.

Literary circles, where plays were regularly read aloud and, in some cases, performed, began to become extremely popular. Most of the important literary circles would later combine political aims with cultural ones using these literary and performing arts to protest against and challenge Ottoman and British colonialism and/or to defend and promote Arab culture gen-

erally. Among these were Al-Shabibah Al-Masehiya (Christian Youth Circle) which was established in 1911; Al-Nahdah Al-Ektisadiya Al-Arabiyah (Arabic Economic Revival Circle) established by the journalist Naguib Nassar (1865–1948) in 1922; and Halakat Al-Adab (Literary Circle) which also began in 1922.

It was Halakat Al-Adab which had as one of its primary goals the development and encouragement of theatre arts in the country. One of its members, Jamil Al-Bahary (d. 1929), was a journalist who wrote (or adapted) sixteen plays; he also owned two newspapers and a book shop. One of Al-Bahary's plays was published in one of his newspapers, *al-Zahra* (*The Flower*). Written in verse, many of his works were tragedies with educational overtones. Among his most important works were *Katel Akheeh* (*His Brother's Killer*, 1919), *Sajeen Al-Qasr* (*The Palace Prisoner*, 1920), *Al-Liss Al-Zareef* (*The Humorous Thief*, 1922) *and Al-Watan Al-Mahboub* (*The Beloved Homeland*, 1923). Al-Bahary, who as early as 1916 had tried to establish an organization devoted exclusively to Arabic theatre, is arguably the most important pre-diaspora playwright in Palestine. He understood the ideological potential of theatre and believed that to exploit it, one had to be willing to work not only within the theatre's limits but also within limits acceptable to a society where traditional values and religious conservatism ruled. He perceived that conservative elements, for example, required him to write plays without female characters because he felt that it may be unacceptable to have women appear on stage, even if played by men.

The idea of literary circle theatre troupes had become even more popular by the mid-1920s. Theatre groups emerged within Nadi Al-Shabiba Al Orthodoksy (Youth Orthodox Club) in Jaffa, Al-Nadi Al-Adaby (Literary Club) in Nazareth, Al-Nadi Al-Orthodoksy (Orthodox Club) in Gaza and Al-Nadi Al-Thakafy Al-Islami (Islamic Cultural Club) in Jerusalem. Although the religious focus was clear in these organizations, it was their interest in new literary forms and their sense of national consciousness which set them apart from other such groups.

Al-Ferkah Al-Tamtheliyah Al-Arabiyah (Arab Acting Troupe), founded in 1929, tried to unite all the groups which were concerned with theatre. Among its leaders was Khalil Beidas (1875–1949), a teacher and journalist who had earlier founded *Majallat Al-Nafaees Al-Asreyah*, an arts magazine with a strong literary section.

The magazine often included translations by Beidas himself of modern European prose, particularly from the Russian, a language he himself spoke. Another frequent translator was Naguib Nassar.

Father Estefan Yousef was one of the significant dramatists to emerge from this literary ferment. Born in Nazareth in 1913, he directed religious schools in Jerusalem and then in Al-Lathekeyah (Latakia), Syria, in the 1940s. Among his plays (which now read quite melodramatically) were *Al-Sojanaa Al-Ahrar* (*The Free Prisoners*), *Siraa Bayna Al-Elm Wa Al-Deen* (*A Conflict Between Science and Religion*) and *Al Musiqah Khair Elaj* (*Music Is the Best Remedy*).

Perhaps the most prolific Palestinian writer of the latter period was Nasry al-Jouzy, the author of over a hundred plays between the 1920s and the 1970s. Among his best known are *Al-Haq Yalou* (*Truth Is Supreme*, 1927) and *Al Shumoo' Al Mohtarekah* (*The Burning Candles*, 1930). Several of his plays were directed by his brother, Jamil al-Jouzy, between 1922 and 1927 including *La Bod Lel Houb An Yantaser* (*Love Must Inevitably Win*) and *Ummi* (*My Mother*). Performed and read mostly in schools, his plays are clear and simple and always have a moral.

By the 1940s, dozens of theatrical troupes were in existence, especially in Jerusalem. But the increasingly strident political problems in the country were taking precedence over literary and theatrical creation, and the public was focusing its energies on the improvement of Palestinian society, the escalating confrontations between the Arabs, Jews and the British mandate government. Moreover, theatre in the European sense still had a limited audience, appealing as it did primarily to the educated, the cultured and the wealthy. The growing religious conservatism kept women not only out of most such groups but also in a separate part of the theatre when they did attend.

Even for those committed to theatre, the art was often seen more as a way to survey Arabic literature and rhetoric than anything else. Most texts were written in classical Arabic (see introductory essay on ARAB THEATRE AND LANGUAGE) using traditional verse forms. One can see this clearly in *Umru Al-Qayss Ibn Hajar* (1945) by Mohammed Hassan Alaa al-Din (b. 1917) and in *Watan Al-Shahid* (*Homeland of the Martyr*, 1947) by poet Borhan al-Din al-Ayboushy (b. 1911). An art only for dedicated amateurs – they wrote about it, translated it and tried to produce it – the theatre was basically seen at this point as just one more element in the evolution of Palestine's modern urban culture. Yet in the 1940s, Palestine was not really very urban and was not really very modern (only about 40 per cent of males and only 7 per cent of females received any sort of formal education, often only through elementary school). Even those who talked about theatre rarely if ever had seen a purpose-built theatre building since all performances were held in cinemas or on tiny, ill-equipped stages in the European schools.

Palestinian theatrical development after World War II was, in its turn, stopped in its tracks by the events of 1947 and 1948 as Palestinian Arabs either went to war or became refugees in their own land or just beyond its borders. Some artists in exile did write about the situation but it was rare when a dramatist's work was produced. This was partly because the drama of their reality far surpassed whatever they could put on stage, partly because the subject matter was not of interest in their new environments where they often found themselves destitute, culturally dazed and unfamiliar, and partly because their plays were often too polemic in nature for most companies and not very effective theatrically.

Some important works did emerge during the 1950s, however, such as *Eid Al-Jalaa* (*The Evacuation Feast*, 1956) by Nasry al-Jouzy and *Al Lahab* (*The Flame*) written by the poet Mahmoud Sief Al Din Al-Erany in the mid-1950s and published in 1977. Ibrahim Mata Ali used biblical references for some of his plays such as *Yakathat Al-Dameer* (*The Awakening of Conscience*) and *Al-Malak Al-Hadi* (*The Calm Angel*), both published in 1950. The poet Haroon Hashem Rashad wrote *Al Soual* (*The Question*), the only play among those written during the period to actually make it onto the stage, albeit not until 1975 when it was eventually performed by Al-Masrah Al-Qawmi (National Theatre) of Cairo.

Moeen Bisouson (1926–84) was one of the more successful Palestinian dramatists. A famous poet and professional journalist before becoming a playwright, he wrote political theatre featuring dramatized debates between Palestine and the various powers that contributed to its collapse, especially Israel. *Thawrat Al-Zunj* (*The Negroes' Revolt*), *Shamshoon Wa Dalelah* (*Samson and Delilah*, 1971) and *Al-Asafeer Tabni Ashashiha Bayna Al-Assabee* (*Birds Build Their Nests Between Fingers*, 1973) are among his most important plays. *The Negroes' Revolt* deals with the issue

Moeen Bisouson's *Thawrat Al-Zunj* (*The Negroes' Revolt*) directed and produced by Jawad al-Assadi.

of discrimination comparing Palestinians with the earlier African diaspora and even linking the Palestinian situation with that of the Native American, a people also displaced and disenfranchised by Europeans. The play was first performed in Cairo in 1970.

Shamshoon Wa Dalilah was performed at the Tawfiq al-Hakīm Theatre in Cairo in 1971. Dealing with the destiny of a Palestinian family who emigrated, it starts in suffering and ends with preparations for armed conflict. The modern Samson loses his hair to gunpowder, the innocent man fighting for justice and peace. *Al-Asafeer Tabni Ashashiha Bayna Al-Assabee* is an inspirational play urging the powerless to stand unshakable. The play was performed at the Arab Theatre Festival in Rabat in 1973. Two other plays of note by Bisouson are *Massat Jivara* (*The Tragedy of Guevera*) and *Mohakamat Ketab Kalelah wa Dimna* (*The Trial of the Book of Kalela and Dimna*). Not specifically about the Palestinian situation, in these works he writes about discrimination in general. Looking at his subject historically, he demonstrates his broad culture using very poetic language. Still later he wrote *Al Masrahiyah Dakhel Al Masrahiya* (*The Play Within a Play*) and *Sighat Qasr al Iham Al-Motaamed*.

Another important writer from this period was Ghassan Kanafany (1936–72). A novelist, short-story writer, literary critic and political commentator, he wrote three plays, *Al-Bab* (*The Door*, 1964), *Al Kubaa Wa Al-Nabi* (*The Prophet and the Hat*) and *Jisr Ela Al-Abadiyeh* (*A Bridge to Eternity*), a radio drama which was never broadcast. The first play was published during his lifetime but the other two were published only after he was assassinated by Israeli agents in Beirut in 1972. Both his plays and novels focus on home and exile, life and death comparing death with exile. To rebel against exile, he suggests, is to reaffirm life. Kanafany's plays differ from his novels in that they do not have Palestinian names and do not refer to Palestinian history, taking the more universal route. His play *Al-Bab*, for example, based on an old Arabian fable, is a dispute between humankind and its gods, between that which destroys personal will and the human fight for freedom. In his second play, *Al-Kubaa Wa Al-Nabi*, the existing world is rejected in favour of an imaginary one. His usual subjects appear – death and life, crime and innocence, doubt and certainty, injustice and revolution – but with a new philosophical tone clearly influenced by Sartre, Camus, Kafka and the Theatre of the Absurd. For Kanafany, freedom becomes an unobtainable dream, one not permitted in this world.

Ghassan Kanafany.

Another writer of note is Rashad Abo Shawor who wrote two plays – *Al-Helm Al-Falasteeny* (*The Palestinian Dream*) and *Al-Ghareeb Wa Al-Sultan* (*The Stranger and the Sultan*). The first was performed in 1975, the second was published in 1984. Like all these plays, they deal with oppositions: past and present, home and refugee camp, victory and defeat, friends and enemies, betrayal and patriotism, home and exile, death and birth, oppression and justice.

What is common to most of these works is that the conclusions of the plays are known almost from the beginning. It can easily be said that Palestinian theatrical writing in this period tended to be rather rhetorical, preaching as in a polemic or a morality play. This seems to be the case both in works of playwrights living within Palestine or in exile. Even the plays of Emile Habibi (1921–96), a well-known Palestinian author in Israel and a minority member of the Israeli Knesset between 1952 and 1972, fell victim to such predictability despite being written in colloquial Palestinian Arabic and

despite their usefulness in clarifying questions of Palestinian identity. His best play was *Luka'ibn Luka* (*Dwarf Son of a Contemptible Dwarf*, 1980).

The growth of Palestinian armed resistance to the occupation from the 1960s represented a historic about-face in Palestinian confidence and consciousness; a transformation from victim to actor, from defeat to struggle for future liberation. After long years in exile and the trials of refugee camps, Palestinians began to assert their identity and presence, exchanging the image of themselves as stateless and defeated fugitives for that of freedom fighters. Theatre was fertile ground for this idea and plays were used to investigate, solicit and preach. Independent amateur troupes run by Palestinians suddenly began to surface in most capitals in the Arab world. All these troupes played an essentially political role and the majority of productions were simple, rhetorical, and most often linked with national and political occasions and remembrances.

A Scene from *Al-Aeta Tout* (*The Tout Family*) by Al-Ghanhary Ashtafan Orkini directed by Jawad Al-Osary.

The Palestinian theatre in Syria was particularly active and representative of the early PLO period. In 1966 in Damascus, for example, on the initiative of the PLO, an Arab Association for Palestinian Theatre was formed – Jamaiyat al-Masrah al-Arabi al-Falasteny – whose aims were to raise awareness through theatre of the Palestinian question, to present issues of the Palestinian struggle on stage and to rebuild Palestinian culture and folklore. Performances growing from this work included theatre, dance and musical shows including poetry evenings. The association was ultimately supported by the Fatah faction of the PLO and often toured to other Arab countries. Composed of artists from Palestine as well as from Syria and Iraq, this Fatah Theatre was particularly active in 1968 and 1969, staging two plays, *Shaab Lan Yamout* (*A People That Will Not Die*) and *Al-Tareeq* (*The Way*), which depicted in fairly literal form the Palestinians as going from a lost people to revolutionaries, from exiles to a repatriated nation.

A successor company calling itself the Palestinian National Theatre Troupe was founded in 1970. One of its best known works was *Muhakamat Al-Rajol Allathi Lam Yuhareb* (*The Trial of the Man Who Did Not Fight*, 1971) written by the Syrian poet Mamdouh Adwan. Also staged was *Al-Koursy* (*The Chair*), directed by Khalil Tafesh and adapted from a text written by Moeen Bisouson, which depicted a presumed conspiracy to prevent Palestinians from fighting. Still another play was *Moasasat Al-Junoun Al-Wataniah* (*Institute of National Insanity*, 1977), written by the Palestinian-Israeli poet Samih Al-Qassem. A strong indictment of Israeli policy, it was directed by the Syrian Fawaz al-Sager. The artistic maturity of the Palestinian National Theatre Troupe was marked by its production of *Al-Ziyara* (*The Visit*), an adaptation by Mamdouh Adwan of the Egyptian novel *Yahdoth Fi Misr Al-Aan* (*Happening Now in Egypt*) by Youssef Al-Kaid. The troupe was supported from 1980 by the PLO Department of Information and Culture, and was long under the direction of the Iraqi actor-director Jawad Al-Osary who was able to find a balance between form and content, art and politics. Among Al-Osary's important productions were *Al-Aela Tout* (*The Tout Family*) by Al-Ghanhary Ashtafan Orkini and *Thawrat Al-Zunj* (*The Negroes' Revolt*) by Moeen Bisouson. Al-Osary also wrote and directed *Araas* and *Khuyout Min Al-Fidda* (*Silver Threads*), a prize-winner at the Carthage Theatre Festival in 1985.

Theatre also played an important role in politicizing the population following the 1967 war which brought all Palestinian land under Israeli occupation. This consciousness-raising mixed the cultural with the political, with the latter serving almost as a *raison d'être* for the former. Indeed, theatrical performances were seen as resistance against Israeli occupation. Within the Occupied Territories, this mixture helped to garner support and popularity for Palestinian theatrical troupes in the first half of the 1970s despite numerous attempts by Israeli authorities to stop or censor them. Beginning in the cities of Jerusalem and Ramallah, the movement spread to many smaller cities ebbing and flowing as the political situation changed.

Most theatre groups through this period were, as could be expected in such a situation, first and foremost political but there was one exception, the Balaleen (Balloons) Troupe, established in Jerusalem in 1971, one of Palestine's earliest professional companies. Balaleen's first performance was to be *Karkash*, a play by Samih Al-Qassem, but Israeli censors prevented it from opening. Under the direction of François Abu Salem, born and educated in Paris, the company had thirteen members and worked collectively. Relying most often upon improvisation, the troupe developed its material from daily reality and argued for change, attacked the Israeli occupation, and criticized Palestinian approaches as being too conservative. Determined to help bring about change, Balaleen searched for stylistic means by which it could activate the community. It regularly staged performances in cafés and shopping areas and developed its own music for its shows based on popular folk idioms. A number of its songs became well known in their own right. One particular Balaleen style called *hadiket al-balaleen*, a form of popular performance involving song, dance and text, began to be appreciated on its own as a specific theatrical genre. Indeed, one of the group's actor-singers, Mostafa Al-Kurd, became a star through the popularity of such music.

Among Balaleen's most important productions were *Qitt'et Hayah* (*A Slice of Life*), *El-Etmeh* (*The Darkness*, 1972) and *Nashret Ahwal Aljaaw* (*The Weather Forecast*, 1973). All were critical of aspects of Palestinian society: the role and treatment of women, the absence of effective leadership, the failure of the community to work collectively and the exploitation of workers. In the play *Thawb Al-Imbarator* (*The Emperor's Cloak*), the troupe criticized both military and autocratic rule. Other shows of note by the group included *Al-Kinz* (*The Treasure*), *Al-Aaraj Wa Shajarat Al-Joz* (*The Cripple and the Walnut Tree*) and *Taal Ahadethak Ya Saheby* (*Come Let Me Talk To You My Friend*), all produced in the early 1970s. Balaleen was one of the first to tour the countryside and eventually established a separate touring wing.

By linking popular urban and rural communities across the country, and finding significant support among intellectuals and students, Balaleen genuinely helped rejuvenate and reshape Palestine's national cultural identity. The company's political and artistic enthusiasm and its cooperative basis, however, also eventually led its members to take more and more divergent positions and ultimately to disagree over future artistic directions, politics and how far they could go in commercializing the work. The company split over these issues in 1974 and Abu Salem was expelled from the group.

That same year, Abu Salem founded a new troupe and called it Bila-Leen, a play on words referring to the original group but with a new meaning, 'no mercy'. Seeking answers that could also balance the issues and problems which ultimately killed Balaleen, the new group staged three productions before it too folded in 1975. The best known was *Al-Estethnaa wa Al-Qaeda*, an adaptation of Brecht's *The Exception and the Rule* reflecting the then current Palestinian situation. The company's two other shows were *Al-Ebra* (*The Moral*) and *Mosaraa Hurra* (*Free Style Wrestling*). The first dealt with freedom and dignity, the second with the eternal struggle between good and evil. Abu Salem tried to create another troupe in 1976 which he called Sandouk Al-Ajab (The Magic Lantern) with Mostafa Al-Kurd as its star. But that troupe was also short-lived, lasting only for four shows, the most successful of which was *Lamma Injanaina* (*When We Went Mad*).

In 1977, Abu Salem, some former members of Balaleen, and several actors from the Galilee – the Israeli side of Palestine – founded El-Hakawati (The Storyteller) Troupe. El-Hakawati was the longest lived of the companies, and played an important role in opening up and advancing Palestinian theatre. The group sought to create a new artistic language that could excite both the theatre professional as well as a general audience, and to find a balance between artistic expression as a value in and of itself while at the same time acknowledging and playing an important political role.

Rambunctiously visual and highly stylized, El-Hakawati's productions relied on fast action, vignettes and sketches which told stories or simply danced around them.

Among El-Hakawati's major productions were *Besm El-Ab Wa Al-Om Wa Al-Ibn* (*In the Name of the Father, the Mother and the Son*, 1978–9), *Mahjoob Mahjoob* (*Mahjoob Concealed*, 1980), *Alf Leila Wa Leila Fi Sook Al-Lahameen* (*A Thousand and One Nights in the Meat Market*, 1981–2, the title of which was changed by the censors from the original *A Thousand and One Nights of a Stone Thrower*), *Jalili Ya Ali* (*Ali the Galilean*, 1983–4), *Qisset Al-Ein Wa Al-Sin* (*The Story of the Eye and the Tooth*, 1985) and *Kufr Shamma* (*Shamma Village*, 1987). This last play is about a Palestinian who leaves his village to study abroad. Upon his return, now educated, he is unable to find his village which was completely destroyed in the occupation. It is the sad story of hundreds of destroyed Palestinian villages in the Galilee, but with the added alienation of the contemporary Palestinian situation.

Most of the scripts of El-Hakawati were group-written through a combination of improvisation and experimentation, and nearly all were directed by Abu Salem. Occasionally, El-Hakawati also utilized foreign texts in Arabic translations. One of its more successful and controversial shows was an adaptation of excerpts of Dario Fo's *Mistero Buffo*, called in Arabic *Hikayat Assalat Al-Ukhra* (*Stories of the Heretic's Prayer*). The play challenged and somewhat offended religious sensibilities by portraying the mysteries of Christ in a populist, almost ribald manner and in a very human way. The play opened in November 1985.

El-Hakawati's performances moved between cities on the West Bank and from there to villages and outlying areas, many of which had never seen theatre before. Like other theatre companies, many of their performances were prohibited by Israeli censors, particularly in villages and rural areas, on dubious security grounds. Unlike other companies, however, El-Hakawati in 1981 broke an unspoken taboo and began presenting shows in Tel Aviv for Jewish audiences as well. El-Hakawati was also one of the first Palestinian companies to undertake international touring of their plays. Providing synopses of their texts in various European languages, they succeeded in garnering a significant following in Europe and to some extent in the United States as well. By 1988, differences within the company grew, and several members left. El-Hakawati continued for a time, relying on joint productions with international companies, and during the *intifada*, the company spent much of its time out of the country. El-Hakawati finally folded in 1993.

Along with the Balaleen and El-Hakawati companies, many other theatre artists and companies made their first appearances in the 1970s and 1980s, their importance and length of existence differing significantly. Few of these troupes performed more than one work and many closed down even before their first performance. Dababees (Nails) was one of the few troupes to achieve moderate success. It was established at the end of 1972 in Ramallah and Al-Bireh by a group of educated building workers who also viewed theatre as an instrument to spread political and social awareness. Relying on collective artistic creation, the group produced several significant plays during its three years of existence, including *Al-Torshan* (*The Deaf*), *Al-Haq Ala Al-Haq* (*The Truth Is at Fault*), *Al-Intizar* (*Waiting*) and *Khawazeek* (*Shafts*), a play whose title was ultimately changed for security purposes to *Amarah Min Warak* (*A Building Made of Paper*). Dababees' work came to an abrupt halt with the arrest of most of its members.

Other troupes of note during this time in the West Bank include Al-Kashkool, established in Jerusalem in 1974. It performed only two works, *Kharoof Wa Nuss Kharoof* (*A Sheep and a Half*) and *Bela Enwan* (*Without an Address*). Al-Masrah Al-Falastini (Palestinian Theatre Troupe) began in Jerusalem in 1973 and stopped in mid-1987; it was built around Mohamad Al-Zaher, the group's playwright, director and administrator. Among its major productions were *Al-Rakissoon* (*The Dancers*), *Al-Tareek ela Al-Jaheem* (*The Way to Hell*), *Al-Jawharah* (*The Jewel*), *Al-Yad Al-Khamesah* (*The Fifth Hand*) and *Majama' al Kabadayat* (*The Tough Guys*), a comedy satirizing Israel's military. In his last work, *Man Al-'Aqer?* (*Who's Barren?*) Mohamad Al-Zaher took up the important societal issue of the liberation of women, associating it with the overarching problem of liberation from occupation. Sanabel (Wheat Stalks) Theatre Company, also from Jerusalem, made some impact during that time with active productions, the best received of which was *Natreen Faraj* (*Waiting for Release*, 1997), a 'Palestinianization' adaptation of *Waiting for Godot* and Christian mythology. The hero was anyone who could save the Palestinians from their dire situation. Al-Ruwat

Company later became active, and one of its productions, *Al-Zabbal* (*The Garbage Collector*), stood out.

Other companies of the time include Al-Nujoom (The Stars) in Tulkarem, Ferkat Al-Masrah Al-Sha'bi Al-Falastini (Palestinian Popular Theatre Troupe), Al-Farafeer (The Quails, a company which did seven productions between 1972 and 1984), Ferkat Al-Shumou' Al-Makdasiyah (Jerusalem Candles Troupe), Ferkat Al-Masrah Al-Ommali (Workers' Theatre Troupe) in Nablus, Ferkat Shabibat Deir Al Lateen (Latin Monastery Youth Troupe) in Beit Sahour, and Ferkat Al-Masrah Al-Jameii (University Theatre Troupe) in Bir Zeit. Few of those, however, survived very long or had any lasting impact on the theatre scene in Palestine.

Among the few theatre people who did operate over a relatively long period was George Ibrahim who from the early 1970s was active as a translator and adapter doing Arabic versions of such plays as Max Frisch's *The Firebugs*. In the early 1980s he started Masrah Al-Qasaba, a children's theatre in Jerusalem (the company played in schools there as well as in Nazareth and Galilee). By the mid-1980s the group started to explore more controversial issues and experimental forms. Ibrahim eventually got the group its own 100-seat theatre space where it not only produced shows but also held conferences, music events, film festivals and puppet shows. In 1994, Al-Qasaba co-produced with the Israeli Khan Theatre of Jerusalem a bilingual Arabic-Hebrew production of *Romeo and Juliet* which subsequently toured Europe. In 1997, Ibrahim adapted Athol Fugard's *Sizwe Banzi Is Dead* to reflect the problems of Palestinians living in the Occupied Territories who try to find work in Israel. Called *Ramzy Abul Majd*, the production was later seen at both the Carthage Festival and in Britian at the London International Festival of Theatre.

The spread of Arab/Palestinian theatre during this period may explain to some extent why the Israeli government decided to establish a cultural centre in Arab East Jerusalem, Beit Daood Lel Thakafah (House of David Cultural Centre). The centre offered courses in dance, singing and theatre, but was largely boycotted by most Palestinian theatre companies. At the same time, it prompted a group of educated Palestinians to form their own cultural centre called Al-Masrah Al-Hai (Living Theatre Centre) which performed a single play, *Al-Hallab* (*The Milkman*).

In 1983, El-Hakawati took a lease on an old burnt-out cinema in Jerusalem and, with donations and community help, succeeded in transforming it into the first Palestinian theatre centre in that city. With El-Hakawati as its resident company, it opened its doors in 1984. The centre had a theatre which seated 400 spectators and was well equipped with the latest in lighting, sound and computerized controls, another open space for rehearsals and smaller performances, and small offices. This was a double-edged accomplishment, however, as the broader community's dire need for space and the company's own expectations of using such a limited space as its own headquarters collided. This coincided with growing differences within the company and in 1988, as already noted, El-Hakawati split up and departed the centre.

The centre, however, was still in operation in the late 1990s as a community theatre, art and activities centre under the name of the Palestinian National Theatre, but with no resident company. The Palestinian National Theatre has been organizing arts exchange programmes, international festivals for puppet theatre, children's theatre, mime, and other such activities in addition to workshops and occasional training programmes. The theatre continues to host performances and occasionally produces plays, such as *Ansar* (1992), a play directed by Fateh Azzam and based on actor Nidal Al-Khatib's experience in the Israeli Ketziot Military Detention Centre in the Negev desert. An English version of *Ansar* later toured in the United States, Canada and the United Kingdom, and also played at the Amman (Jordan) Theatre Festival in 1996.

Virtually all the theatrical efforts and activities mentioned in this article took place under extremely difficult conditions. First and foremost was the Israeli occupation and its censorship apparatus, its overly broad security concerns and definitions, and its continuous obstruction of cultural work by Palestinians. Suddenly placed roadblocks often prevented performances from taking place (even if a permit had been granted in the first place). Israeli rules and regulations prevented the showing of the colours of the Palestinian flag in plays, and many scripts and productions (including Shakespeare) were censored. There were many instances in which actors and writers were imprisoned or administratively detained. These problems reached their highest pitch during the *intifada*, and did not end until 1993. It should be noted that the occupation imposed near total isolation of the Palestinian community from the broader international theatrical community, and in particular from the important Arab intellectual and artistic community. Thus, there was a dearth of new plays to produce and the community was left with only its own creativity. However, actors and directors, having heard about important Arab plays, at times created their own versions based on what they knew about them. Egyptian and Syrian plays have been particularly popular in this regard.

In addition to these many problems, Palestinian theatre groups have at times had difficulties with their own religious conservatives, particularly in the less urbanized communities.

Ansar (1992) directed by Fateh Azzam.

For example, pressure by conservatives temporarily stopped the theatrical movement in Nablus at one point in the mid-1970s, when Ferkat Al-Zaytoon company was attacked, not because of anything in its text or message but rather because women were on the stage.

Yet, despite all these difficulties, and at times perhaps because of these difficulties, Palestinian theatre survived. By the mid-1990s, a veritable cultural explosion began to take place in the country with an increase in both major and minor events. The year 1996, for example, saw twelve cultural festivals open across Palestine, many for the first time (some were revivals of earlier events after several decades). Among the larger festivals was the Palestine Festival, the year-long Jerusalem Festival, the Sabastia Festival and Ramallah Festival. The Palestinian National Theatre's annual children's theatre festival was postponed, however, due to repeated closures of the city of Jerusalem by Israeli authorities. Also in 1996, eight new theatre productions were seen and four performances from previous seasons were revived. The Ashtar Theatre School opened its doors in Ramallah as did a new Palestinian cultural centre, the Khalil Sakakini Cultural Centre.

This cultural thaw saw the return to Palestine of many prominent actors and artists who had previously been living in exile. Among them was the poet Mahmoud Darwish, editor of Al Karmel, a prestigious literary review which started up again in 1997. Darwish gave public readings of his poetry to capacity audiences at Bir Zeit and Al-Najah universities.

The mid-1990s saw some real exchange between Israeli-Palestinians and those living on the West Bank for the first time in many years. A number of Palestinians became known on the Hebrew stage, among them Makram Khoury, Salim Dhaou, Salwa Naqqara and Yousef Aby Wardeh. Most of these actors by the late 1990s, however, had chosen not to work any longer in Hebrew (despite winning prizes) and were performing only in Arabic plays in cities such as Haifa, Jaffa and Nazareth.

During this same period, Riad Masarweh, a resident of Nazareth who studied theatre in Europe, was active in adapting European scripts into Arabic and helping to get them staged (among these have been works by Brecht). Masarweh, for a time the artistic director of the municipal Cultural Centre of Nazareth, later began Ferkat Studio Al Masrah (Theatre Studio Troupe) which sponsors shows, classes and general lectures on theatre. Similarly, a National Arabic Theatre began operations in the early 1990s within the Haifa Municipal Theatre.

Finally, it should be noted that Masrah Al Ghorbal, a small theatre group in Shafa Amru, Galilee, founded in 1977, pioneered the establishment of Palestine's first Arabic Theatrical Union in 1983. This union has played a positive role in the coordination of efforts by all who care about the theatre.

Faysal Darraj with additional material by
Fateh Azzam
Translated by Christine Henein

Further Reading

Abd Raouf Mahammid, Muhammad. *Ma-sirt el-Haraka al-Masrahiya fi Adfa il Gharbiya 1967–87* [History of the theatrical movement in the West Bank 1967–87]. Im il Fahem, Israel: Markaz al-Thourath al-Arabiy-al-Taieba, 1989.

Abo il-Shabab, Wassef. 'Al kissa wal Riwaya, wal Masrahiya fi Falastien 1900–48' [The novel, fable and theatre in Palestine 1900–48]. In *Il Mousueha il Falastyniya* [Encyclopedia Palestina], vol. 3. Beirut, 1990: 127–63.

Abu-Ghazaleh, Adnan. *Arab Cultural Nationalism in Palestine during the British Mandate*. Beirut: Institute for Palestine Studies, 1973.

Anees, Mohamad. *Al Harakah Al Masrahiah Fee Al Manatek Al Mohtala* [The Palestinian theatrical movement in the occupied territories]. Jerusalem, 1979.

Ashrawi, Hanan Milhail. 'The Politics of Cultural Revival'. In *The Palestinians: New Directions*. Edited by Michael C. Hudson. Washington, DC: Georgetown University Centre for Contemporary Arab Studies, 1991. pp. 77–83.

Beidas, Khalil. *Masareh Al Athhan* [The theatre of the mind]. Beirut: Palestinian Union of Journalist Writers, 1978.

Bisouson, Moeen. *Al Aamal Al Masrahiya* [The theatrical works]. Beirut: Dra Al Awdah, 1979.

Bogart, Anne, *et al.* 'Caught in the Crossfire'. *American Theatre* 9 (December 1991): 26–35, 64–7.

Butitsiefa, Tamara Alexandrovna. *Alf Mil Am wa-Am ala Al Masrah Al-Arab* [A thousand and one nights of Arabic theatre]. Beirut: Dar il Farbi, 1981.

Doghman, Saad Al Din. *Al Osool Al Tarekhiyah Lenashaat Al Drama Fee Al Adab Al Araby* [Historical references for the beginning of drama in Arab literature]. Beirut: Arabic Beirut University, 1973.

Ersan, Ali Akla. *Al Thawaher Al Masraheyah Enda Al Arab* [The Arab theatrical phenomenon]. Damascus: Arabic Writers' Union, 1981.

Habibi, Emile. *The Secret Life of Said the Pessoptimist*. London: Zed Books, 1987.

Haydar, Yussef. 'Il harakah il masrahiye bil bilaad' [The Arabic theatre movement in the country]. In *Al-Falestinioun 1948–84*. Israel: Dar il-Mashreh, 1988. pp. 228–64.

Al-Jouzy, Nasry. *Falasteen Lan Nansaki* [Palestine, we won't forget you]. Damascus: Tarbeen, 1971.

Kanafany, Ghassan. *Al Athar Al Kamelah* [The complete works, part 3]. Beirut: Organization of Ghassan Kanafany, Dar Al Taleeah, 1978.

Khadra Jayyusi, Salma, ed. *Anthology of Modern Palestinian Literature*. New York: Columbia University Press, 1992.

Khory, Yousef Q. *Al Sahafa Al Arabiah Fee Falasteen 1876–1948* [The Arabic journal in Palestine 1876–1948]. Beirut: Moassassat Al Derasat Al Falasteniyah, 1976.

Laâbi, Abdellatif, ed. *Anthologie de la poésie Palestinienne contemporaine* [Anthology of contemporary palestinian poetry]. Paris: Messidor, 1990.

Lustick, Ian. *Arabs in the Jewish State: Israel's Control of National Minority*. Austin, TX University of Texas Press, 1980.

Malmborg, Ingvar von. 'Teater i den delade staden' [Theatre in the divided city]. *Teatertidningen* 17 no. 63 (1993): 42–6.

Al Masrah, Derasat Fe. *Wa Al Cenima Inda Al Arab* [Studies in Arab cinema]. Cairo: Al Hayaa Al Masreya Al Amah Lel Kotab, 1972.

Nigm, Mohamad Yousef. *Al Masraheyah Fe Al Adab Al Araby Al Hadeeth* [The play in contemporary Arabic literature]. Beirut: Dar Al Thakafa, 1980.

'Palestinian Theatre Under Occupation 1: The Palestinian Perspective'. *Theatre International* 5 (1982): 36–41.

'Palestinian Theatre Under Occupation 2: The Israeli Perspective'. *Theatre International* 5 (1982): 42–6.

S'adi, Ahmad. 'Between State Ideology and Minority National Identity: Palestinians in Israel and the Israeli Social Science Research'. *Review of Middle East Studies* 5 and in *Israel/Palestine: Fields for Identity*. London: Scorpion, 1992.

Said, Edward W. *Culture and Imperialism*. London: Chatto & Windus, 1993.

Sanbar, E.S. Hadidi, *et al.*, eds. *Palestine: l'enjeu culturel* [Palestine: the cultural game of chance]. Paris: Circé/Institut du Monde Arabe, 1997.

al-Sawahry, Khalil. *Zaman Al Ihtelal* [The time of occupation]. Damascus: Arabic Writers' Union, 1979.

al- Sharif, Maher, ed. *Le Patrimoine culturel palestinien* [Palestinian cultural heritage]. Paris: Sycamore, 1980.

Slyomovics, Susan. 'To Put One's Finger in the Bleeding Wound: Palestinian Theatre Under Israeli Censorship'. *The Drama Review* 35 (summer 1991).

Weir, Shelagh. *Palestinian Costume*. London: British Museum, 1989.

Yaghi, Abd al-Rahman. *Hayat Al Adab Al Falasteny Al Hadeeth: Min Awal Al Nahda Hata Al Nakba* [Modern Palestinian literature from the revolution until the disaster]. Beirut: Dar Al Afak al-Gadedah, 1981.

Ziad, Rawfeek. *An Al Adab, Al Adab Al Shaby Fee Falasteen* [The folk literature of Palestine: literature in Palestine]. Beirut: Dar Alawda, 1970.

PEOPLE'S DEMOCRATIC REPUBLIC OF YEMEN

(see **YEMEN**)

PERSIA

(see **IRAN**, Asia Volume)

QATAR

(Overview)

The peninsula of Qatar and its several offshore islands are located in the middle of the west coast of the Arabian Gulf. With an area of about 11,400 square kilometres (4,400 square miles), Qatar is surrounded by the Gulf on all sides except the south where it meets the borders of Saudi Arabia and the Emirate of Abu Dhabi. The population of Qatar is about 534,000 (1995 estimate) with some two-thirds of the population living in Doha, the capital. An ethnically mixed population, it is about 40 per cent Arab, 18 per cent Pakistani, 18 per cent Indian, 10 per cent Iranian and 14 per cent others. Arabic is the country's official language but English is commonly used. Islam is the dominant religion, with native Qataris members of the orthodox Sunni Wahhabi sect.

During the eighteenth century, most of the emirates in the area signed protective agreements with Britain. Qatar's agreement was ratified in 1868 during the reign of ash-Shaikh Mohammed Bin Thaani (the ruler from 1878 to 1913), a man considered to be the true founder of modern Qatar as a political entity. More than a century later, in 1971, Qatar became independent and an active member in world organizations such as the United Nations and the Pan-Arab Organization. A year later, ash-Shaikh Khaleefa Bin Hamad Al-thani became the Emir of Qatar. In 1949 oil was discovered within Qatar's borders and the country underwent a major economic and social change, becoming a wealthy nation which was able to bring in workers from abroad. Oil has remained the basis of the country's wealth ever since.

Music and dance along with storytelling have long traditions in this part of the world and Qatari experiences in these theatrical fields are similar to those in many other Islamic nations. As such, the introduction of a more literary theatre did not emerge until the 1960s. It was in the 1950s that more modern educational methods began to be adopted in the country and public schools began to be opened. It was at this period also that one could find the initial indications for the appearance of a modern theatre in the country.

Just prior to this period, amateur theatre activities began to be seen at social and community clubs around the country including Naadi at-Talee'a (Forerunner Club), Naadi al-Jazeera (Island Club) and Naadi Kibaar al-Muwaththafeen (Senior Staff Club). Naadi at-Talee'a, for example, was established in 1959 and not only staged theatre productions but also became involved in publishing magazines and organizing tours by visiting groups. The most important of the several stage plays presented by this group was *Al-Fattasha* (*The Searcher*), which satirically portrayed those who duped the naïve by claiming that they were able to heal through the evocation of spirits and the reciting of spells and incantations. Its later production of the play *Bayn al-Haadir Wa l-Maadi* (*Between the Past and the Present*) dealt with the various stages of Qatari history and the many changes that occurred in Qatar after the discovery of oil. Unfortunately, the pioneering activities of this club did not last long and the club closed its doors at the beginning of 1961. Dramaturgically, most of the group's presentations were called collective creations built by the actors and directors around particular themes.

Following that group's closing, the major

Al-Sadd Theatre Group's 1997 production of Saalim Maajid's *Stars on the Pavement*.

work in Qatari theatre moved to the Senior Staff Club which established theatre activities in 1961 under Hatmi Ahmad al-Hatmi, Mubaarak al-Hatmi and 'Atiyyat-allaah an-Nu'aymi. Composed only of men and creating plays with virtually all male roles, the club presented several plays of note including *Bidaaya Wa Nihaaya* (*Beginning and End*), '*Arab Falasteen* (*The Arabs of Palestine*) and *Naseehat Ab* (*A Father's Advice*). Other clubs such as the Jazeera Club even brought in theatre artists from the Gulf area to try to improve their productions. Ultimately, however, such work was less important in and of itself than it was as an indicator of a yearning for a more professional theatrical art in the country.

Another area where one could detect the beginnings of a modern theatre movement in the country during this same period was in schools and even scouting groups. Many foreign teachers were working in Qatar at this time and it was they who helped to initiate an active scholastic theatre in the late 1950s and early 1960s. In 1959, for example, Doha Secondary School presented the play *Bilaal Bin Rabaah*, which portrayed the life of one of the companions of the Prophet Muhammad and the various struggles to keep the faith. In 1963, the Religious Institute

presented the play '*Aalim Wa Taaghiya* (*A Scientist and a Dictator*) by Yousef al-Qirdaawi. The School of Industry presented a group of plays, among which were Molière's *Tabeeb Raghma Anfih* (*Le Médecin malgré lui/A Doctor in Spite of Himself*) in 1968 and an original work, *Matloub 'Ummaal* (*Labourers Needed*), in 1969.

Also in 1969, the Teachers College School presented two plays, *Saqr Kuraish* (*Kuraish's Eagle*), which dealt with the personality of 'Abdurahman ad-Daakhil and his role in founding the Islamic Arab Dynasty in Andalusia (southern Spain) and *Halaawat ath-Thowb Riq'atahu Minnu Wa Feeh* (*The Beauty of the Robe Is in Its Fabric*), written in the local vernacular and dealing with Arab customs and traditions.

By the late 1960s, the theatrical movement in Qatar entered a new phase as specialized theatrical companies began to appear. The first was al-Firqa ash-Sha'biyya lit-Tamtheel (Popular Company for Acting) established by Musa 'Abdurahman in 1968. During its two years of operation, it presented two major productions, *Bint an-Nawkhatha* (*The Sea Captain's Daughter*) and *ad-Daktoor Bou 'Allous* (*Doctor Bou 'Allous*), both of which grew out of improvisations, though written scripts did ultimately emerge. Both these scripts were important for they indicated that the theatre had begun to enter into the general public's consciousness. Both plays dealt with real problems and contemporary issues. During the 1980s, the group reestablished itself with the same name and presented *al-Feeraan* (*The Rats*) in 1985 and *Baay Baay Mishmish* (*Bye Bye Apricot*) in 1986.

A second group, Firqat al-Masrah al-Qatari (Qatari Theatre Company), was established in 1972 by Mohammed 'Abdalla al-Ansaari, who was also the director of the Teachers College Theatre at the time. A more or less private theatrical company, the Qatari Theatre presented several plays for younger audiences and later adult scripts among which were 'Abdalla Ahmad 'Abdalla's two plays *Sab' as-Sabamba'* (*The Beastly Beast*) and '*Aanis* (*The Old Maid*) in 1972, 'Aadil Saadiq's *Khaarij Min al-Jaheem* (*Coming Out of Hell*) in 1973 and Khaleefa as-Sayyid's *Min Toul al-Ghaybaat* (*After So Long*) in 1974. The company received state recognition from 1972 when it began to receive financial assistance from the Ministry of Information. The company continues operating into the late 1990s. Among its important productions have been *Marra w-Bas* (*Only Once*), which was

Qasim al-Ansari's 1994 production of Saaleh al-Manaa'i's *Sinan*, a production for young audiences

written by 'Ali Mirza Mahmoud and Kamaal Mehessi in 1974 and *Um iz-Zain*, which was written in the local dialect by 'Abdurahman al-Manaa'i in 1975. The latter play portrays an interim period of Qatari society when it moved from fishing and pearl diving to oil riches and institutions. This play was one of the first to deal with the clashing of values and the many accompanying social changes. A later play of note by this group was 'Aasim Toufeeq's and 'Abdalla Ahmad's *Souq al-Banaat* (*The Girls' Market*) in 1979.

Firqat Masrah al-Adwaa' (Lights Theatre Company) was established in 1966 by 'Abd ul-'Azeez Naasir. One of the longest continuing theatre groups in the country, its productions began to involve music and song. Among the company's many important productions have been the satire *al-Lawhaat ath-Thalaath* (*The Three Tableaux*) by Hasan Husain and *Hash-Shakl Ya Za'faraan* (*Is This the Way O Saffron*) written by 'Abdurahman al-Manaa'i. Other plays presented by this company have included *as-Saalfa Wa Ma Feeha* (*The Story and All About It*) by Mohammed 'Awwaad; *Mansour Qaahir al-'Amlaaqayn* (*Mansour the Conqueror*

of the Two Giants), a play for children written by Munsif al-Suwaisi; *Thalaatha 'Ala Waahid* (*Three on One*) by Hasan Husain, which satirically deals with the issue of polygamy; and Saalim Maajid's *Sawwaaq bil-Majistair* (*A Driver with a Masters Degree*), a critical portrait of changing Qatari society, especially its treatment of immigrant workers. In the last play, the dramatist portrays a Qatari worker suffering similar indignities while working in a fictional Asian country.

Firqat Masrah a-Sadd (Sadd Theatre Company) was established in 1973 at the Naadi a-Sadd ar-Riyaadi (Sadd Sports Club). This company has presented a wide range of original works, the most important of which have been *Bayt ul-Ashbaah* (*The House of Ghosts*) by Ghaanim as-Saleeti and Mustafa Ahmad, a play satirizing the practice of marrying young girls to old men – a situation usually prompted by greed on the part of the girl's father and which usually ended with the victimization of the girl; *Khuloud*, another play dealing with marriage problems, dowries and the role of women; and *'Illatna Feena* (*The Cause of Our Problem Is in Us*), co-authored by Marzouq Basheer and

Lights Theatre Company's 1980 production of Munsif al-Suwaisi's *Mansour the Conqueror of the Two Giants*.

Production of Hamad al-Rumaihi's *Bou Diryaah*, 1988.

Mustafa Ahmad, a play about individual sufferings built around the daily life of a broken family, an allegory, as some have argued, of the Arab world.

By the 1980s, the company had expanded its repertoire to include plays by dramatists from other Arab countries including the Egyptian Tawfiq al-Hakīm's *Majlis il-'Adl* (*The Court of Justice*) presented in 1981; the Syrian Sa'dallah Wanous's *'al-Feel Ya Malik uz-Zamaan* (*The Elephant O King of Eternity*) presented in 1982; and *Aneen as-Sawaari* (*Groans of Ship Masts*) produced in 1984 and adapted by 'Abdurahman al-Manaa'i from poems composed by 'Ali 'Abdalla Khaleefa. The company has also presented al-Manaa'i's *Ya Layla Ya Layla* (*O Night O Night*) in 1980, a drama about the dominance and tyranny of financial control and one of the country's classics; *Bou Diryaah*, written by Hamad al-Rumaihi which deals with the problematic relationship between a sea captain and those who work for him; and *Nujoum 'Ala r-Raseef* (*Stars on the Pavement*) written by Saalim Maajid about the struggle between a generation of conservative fathers and their sons who grew up to embrace new ways and novelties.

Such a relatively large amount of theatrical work and the production of so many new plays in a country with a low population density where theatrical art is still considered a novelty even in the 1990s and where older generations still have reservations about it eventually required more than box-office support to maintain its continuity. Indeed, it became imperative for the government to begin to sponsor at least some of these companies financially to ensure recognition of the art. School programmes were given the first boost in this direction in 1975 when a Theatrical Education Administration was established as a division of the Ministry of Pedagogy and Education with the goal of adding theatrical studies into various educational programmes. The Ministry of Pedagogy and Education thus became directly involved in the mid-1970s in funding training and for yearly scholastic theatrical competitions.

Most important, however, in the area of government sponsorship was the creation of the Arts and Culture Department of the Ministry of Information. Through its theatre division, it is the major national agency responsible for artistic, financial and human support. In most instances, recognized companies apply to the division when they wish to do a production. If approved, the company is given a sum of money – in the 1990s it was usually about 70,000 Qatari riyals – plus a smaller additional amount to cover part of the rent for the theatre. The theatre division also provides companies with technical and artistic support to cover additional needs in the form of materials, equipment and technicians. The theatre division sometimes covers costs to bring in actors from other countries (this has been especially important in attracting actresses from abroad since the theatre is still considered unsuitable for Qatari women).

Production of Hamad al-Rumaihi's *Ballad of Joy and Grief*, 1993.

Lobby of the Qatar National Theatre.

Auditorium of the Qatar National Theatre.

One of the most important achievements of the ministry was the building and furnishing of a National Theatre, an important space which was inaugurated in 1982. This theatre, supplied with the latest and most modern technical and artistic equipment, holds 500 spectators. It is also equipped with advanced facilities for simultaneous translation. Many of the groups rent this space.

The construction of the building was preceded by the creation in 1979 of a state company composed of the best actors from the many private groups operating across the country. Among the National Theatre company's important productions have been *al-Mughanni Wa l-Ameera* (*The Singer and the Princess*) by 'Abdurahman al-Manaa'i, and *Rihlat Juha Ila Jazeerat an-Nuzahaa'* (*Juha's Trip to the Nuzahaa' Island*), which was staged by the dramatist Munsif al-Suwaisi. Though the company still exists it produces only on rare occasions and its stage work has remained limited at best.

The theatre division has brought to Qatar a number of theatrical experts and specialists from abroad to set up programmes and organize training sessions. Among these have been Zaki Tulaimat, Sa'ad Ardash, Nabil al-Alfi, 'Ali ar-Raa'i and the dramatist Munsif al-Suwaisi.

Still another government agency supporting theatre has been the Supreme Council for Youth Welfare which established in 1983 a special theatrical division for performances given in youth centres. This division has set up many symposiums and training sessions in areas such as voice acting, design and directing. In 1983 as well, it set up its own company, the Classic Theatrical Arts company, which presented a range of Arabic productions including al-Manaa'i's *Hikaayat Haddaad* (*A Blacksmith's Tale*) and *Thaman al-Lu'lu'* (*The Cost of Pearls*); *al-Haqeeqa* (*The Truth*), which was created and staged under 'Uthmaan al-Hamaamsi; and Hasan Husain's *Haflat Tasaadum* (*A Clashing Performance*). The council has held playwriting competitions, and sponsors an annual theatrical festival for amateur clubs.

Most Qatari dramatists are concerned about retaining tradition within a rapidly changing contemporary world. The struggle for many Qatari playwrights therefore has been between past and future with their characters showing a deep-seated fear of change. In many scripts, families have therefore become central in showing discrepancies in thinking modes between the generations. Such splits between fathers and their sons have led to a serious disruption of the traditional family structure and

Qatar National Theatre Company's production of Ghanimi al-Sulaiti's *The Skirmish*.

relationships among various members of this once inviolate grouping. For more than a millennium, the social structure of societies throughout the Gulf area has been based on a strong adherence to customs, traditions and prevailing practice. The individual here has always strictly submitted to the rules of the family and the tribal grouping to which he or she belonged. As such, reality, in its social and cultural dimensions, reflects each individual's behavioural patterns. Once broken, society is threatened. Such a breakdown is obviously a fertile area for dramatic examination. Such issues have as a result formed the main dramatic plot for stage plays whether about marriage practices, polygamy or aberrant children. Audiences – mostly intellectuals – responded to such plays with enthusiasm and even with spontaneous reactions.

The very presence of such issues in Qatari theatre seems to represent a new desire for individualism and personal freedom, the waning of paternal authority and the cracking of a social structure. These themes are found clearly in such plays as 'Aanis (The Old Maid, 1972) by 'Abdalla Ahmad, Souq al-Banaat (The Girl's Market, 1980) by 'Aasim Tufeeq and 'Abdalla Ahmad, Khuloud and Naadi al-'Uzoubiyya (The Bachelors' Club) by Mohammed Mubaarak al-

'Ali, Ibtisaam Fi Qafas al-Ittihaam (Ibtisaam in the Dock) by Saaleh al-Manaa'i and az-Zawj al-'Aazib (The Bachelor Husband) by Mustafa Ahmad.

Many of the playwrights who deal with such issues remain attached to and support the old values and traditional standards. Consciously or unconsciously, therefore, most of these plays frequently end up in victory for the old values and prevailing traditions and in failure and retreat for the attempts to introduce changes and renewals. The girl is most often portrayed as unable to choose a suitable marriage partner, a situation which leads to marriage failure, a sense of defeat on the part of the girl, her confession of having been in the wrong and her final return to the mores acceptable by the family and society. One sees this in plays by Saaleh al-Manaa'i and in 'Aadil Saqr's Ibtisaam in the Dock, which ends with the retreat of the leading character from her previous stance of refusing a marriage forced upon her by her family, her confession of error and her return to her husband.

Since the 1980s, however, this automatic regression has begun to change and plays have started moving beyond the family, entering more vast horizons by dealing with national

Sufferings directed by Hamad al-Rumaihi.

Official Archives directed by Hamad al-Rumaihi, 1997.

Folklore Theatre Group's *A Noise in a Demi-Tasse*, March, 1997.

Masks directed in 1992 by Hassan Ibrahim.

and humanistic issues. Arab political concerns generally began to acquire a new and more immediate dimension on the Qatari stage. The play *O Night O Night* is considered among the most important in this new style. Shocking in many ways, it shows an absence of human conscience, greedy human beings full of self-interest and people focusing on their personal needs, desires and ambitions. Interestingly, al-Manaa'i wrote *O Night O Night* using the local dialect, but, when he later presented it at the Damascus Theatrical Festival, he rewrote it in classical Arabic. Tightly woven, artistically structured, serious in approach and conceptually rich, al-Manaa'i was able to examine heritage questions in all their economic, cultural and social dimensions. Considered a masterpiece in Qatar, the play focuses on the age-old struggles between good and evil, and freedom and justice.

One final area which should be noted here is that of puppet theatre. Qatar has long had shadow puppets but it was not until 1975 that a marionette theatre was established by Hassan Ibrahim, head of the Department of Theatrical Education Supervision, which was at that time a section of the Department of Cultural Affairs of the Ministry of Education. The company, which still gives occasional performances, received much assistance in its early years from the puppeteer Mohammed Kishk from Cairo.

Muhammed Abdul Rahim Kafoud
Translated by Maha and Tony Chehade

Further Reading

'Atwaan, Hasan. *Al-Hayaat al-Masrahiyya fi Qatar: Diraasa susyulujiyya Was Tawtheeq* [Theatrical life in Qatar: a sociological and documentary study]. Doha: H. 'Atwaan, 1987. 447 pp.

Kutayyib 'An al-Masrah al-'Aalami [A booklet on the world theatre]. Doha: Culture and Arts Administration, March 1981.

Majallat ad-Dawha [Doha Magazine].

Majallat al-'Ahd [Covenant Magazine].

Majallat al-Aqlaam al-'Iraaqiyya [Iraqi Writers Magazine].

Majallat al-Khaleej al-Jadeed [New Gulf Magazine].

Majallat at-Tarbiya [Education Magazine].

Mohammed Qaafoud, *al-Adab al-Qatari al-Hadeeth* [Modern Qatari Literature].

Othmaan al-Hamaamsi, *Taqreer al-Majlis al-A'ala l-Ri'aayat ash-Shabaab* [The Supreme Council for Youth Welfare report], 1983.

Taqreer 'An at-Tarbiya al-Masrahiyya Fi Dawlat Qatar [A report on theatrical education in Qatar], 1981.

RAS AL-KHAIMAH

(see **UNITED ARAB EMIRATES**)

SANA'A-YEMEN

(see **YEMEN**)

SAUDI ARABIA

Occupying most of the Arabian peninsula and covering an area of about 2,240,000 square kilometres (864,900 square miles), Saudi Arabia – the land of Mecca, the holy city of Islam – is bordered on the north by Jordan, Iraq and Kuwait, to the east by the Persian Gulf and Qatar, to the southeast by the United Arab Emirates and Oman, to the south by Yemen and to the west by the Red Sea and the Gulf of Aqaba. Saudi's population in 1995 was estimated to be 18.7 million. Arabic is the official language, although English is spoken in commerce and business. Islam is the only religion in the country as the practice of any other faith is forbidden within Saudi borders. The national capital is Riyadh.

Historically a land of contesting monarchies, modern Saudi Arabia – still among the most conservative of Arab states – dates to 1902 when Abd al-Aziz Ibn Saud launched a thirty year campaign to unite the Arabian peninsula. Since unification in 1932, the country has been a dominant force in Middle Eastern religion and business thanks in great measure to pilgrimage visits to Mecca by Muslims and to the peninsula's enormous oil wealth.

Culturally, Saudi Arabia has traditions in poetry and storytelling going back to pre-Islamic times. Particularly popular are music and dance performances, especially the men's sword dance know as the *Ardha*. In this dance, men carrying swords stand shoulder to shoulder and, from within the group, a poet steps forward to sing verses while drummers beat out the rhythm and the men go through extremely athletic and sometimes dangerous movements. In the Hijaz area, *al-sihba* folk music combines poetry and songs of Arab Andalusia from medieval Spain.

Another traditional song and movement combination is the *al-mizmar* which is performed in Mecca, Medina and Jeddah. Since the early 1980s, the Saudi Society for Culture and Art has been studying these traditional forms and recording them. In the 1990s, more than fifty folk dance and music groups existed in the kingdom.

Public performance traditions, however, are much less common, with theatre in the European sense not seen publicly until 1974. The first attempts to stage live theatre in the European sense go back only to 1960 when Sheikh Ahmad al-Sibaći tried to introduce western-style theatre for the first time in the kingdom. Living in Mecca, al-Sibaći, an historian and journalist, petitioned local administrative authorities to permit him a licence to build a stage and to produce plays. Gathering around him a distinguished group of young men with interests in writing, acting and directing, he began rehearsals for two original plays – *The Conquest of Mecca* by Muhammad Abdulla al-Malibari and *Musaylima the Liar* by Abdulla al-Abbasi. The first was directed by Muhammad al-Mushayyikh, later a vice-minister in the Ministry of Information, the second by an Egyptian director brought in for the production.

Though funds had been spent, though the productions were nearly ready to go and though press interest was high, the two productions had to be abandoned because of complaints by concerned citizens, in this case the Do Good and Avoid Evil Association which had made formal complaints about the theatre on religious grounds. Nevertheless, it is al-Sibaći who is credited with first introducing theatrical art to Saudi Arabia despite the fact that it was not until 1974 that Ibrahaim al-Hamdan staged the first public production in the capital – an adaptation of Molière's comedy *Le Médecin malgré lui* (*The Doctor In Spite of Himself*, called in Arabic *Doctor by Force*).

Even then the argument was made that Islam forbids theatre. Proponents of theatrical art, however, insisted that in the absence of specific statements in the Quran and in the traditions of the Prophet Muhammad, that no prohibition actually existed. Indeed, the Quran says nothing at all about theatre or even art. Even the old argument about not presenting 'images' made by certain Orientalists remained dubious at best since Islam forbids the worshipping only of idols or their images. So long as poets and artists draw their inspiration from the spiritual values of Islam, theatre, in and of itself seems clearly acceptable.

The fact is that painting, architecture and music have all flourished within Islamic environments for more than a millennium reflecting a wide variety of local cultural traditions while still observing the word of God, the central tenet of Islamic faith. Given such arguments, one can understand Islamic antipathy and general opposition to theatre in Saudi Arabia and other traditional Islamic countries only by comparing it to the responses of the early church in Europe, which also turned theatrical art out of its environs despite having helped it find its own earliest forms. As the Christian church distrusted theatre at that time so too has Islam been traditionally suspicious of this art of imitation.

In the late 1990s it is still a matter of opinion as to whether theatre should or should not be supported. Happily, the state has found no reason to withhold general and even financial support of theatrical art. It was this argument which was at the heart of the debate in 1960 about whether or not al-Sibaci's productions should be allowed to be seen, an argument that was as much social as it was doctrinal.

As well, similar debates took place prior to al-Hamdan's Molière production, and in the end, that show was allowed to be seen. By that time, attitudes had clearly relaxed somewhat. As well, al-Hamdan was a known quantity having already established a reputation as a responsible television director, while others saw a role for theatrical art in improving and shaping responsible citizens.

The earlier original play, *The Conquest of Mecca*, was itself certainly proper. A drama in three acts about the opening of Mecca by the Prophet, it looked at those who resisted him.

The author, al-Malibari, shaped his historical matter into dramatic form utilizing a series of flashbacks to create the balance between *jahilyya* (pre-Islamic ignorance) and Islam.

The author of the second play, al-Abbasi, had also tried his hand at historical matters, albeit in comic form, ridiculing in his play the apostasy of Musaylima and Sajah, a woman who, like Musaylima, was a counterfeit prophet. Perhaps the most controversial element was the fact that the author included a major female character in his play. Nevertheless, al-Abbasi skilfully handled character as well as plot. It must be said, however, that ultimately both of these early Saudi dramatists surrendered their plays to religious and ethical lessons rather than to the ultimate demands of the drama.

As for al-Hamdan's later Molière, it had been preceded by several plays written by him for television. Among these were *Second Chance* (1970–1), the story of a man who lived wrongly, *The House of Ghosts*, a horror story, and *Happy Dreams* (1971), a Ramadan series broadcast over thirty days relating the tale of a novice stage director who dreams a series of nightly adventures including one in which he was Ali Baba. A later series of his was *The Doer of Good* (1977) about a man who wishes to do good but winds up causing problems instead.

Al-Hamdan's major achievement as a playwright and director, though, rests with his stage work. Born in Riyadh, he was educated in Mecca and Cairo where he began seeing theatre. He later won a government award to study at Syracuse University in the United States. While at Syracuse, he attended courses in television production and directing. On his return he adapted the Molière play to a Saudi dialect and social setting. His version, it should also be noted, was actually based on two earlier Arabic translations of the play, one done by the Romantic poet Liyas Abu Shabak and the other by Ahmad al-Rifaci. The former was done more in a vernacular style (though maintaining the syntax of classical Arabic). In al-Hamdan's version, all the female characters were dropped including the sick patient who became here a male instead of a female to fit the social ethics that required men and women not to mingle in this very segregated society.

Shown only once on stage, the play was filmed for television and has been shown several times over the years. As well as attracting a new audience for theatre, this original Molière production also attracted many of those who worked on it to amateur careers in theatre with many becoming deeply involved in this new art.

The state ultimately supported their ambition and, in 1972, created a branch of the Saudi Society for Culture and Art. Based in Riyadh, the society now has six branches across the country in Jeddah, Abha, Al-Taif, Al-Quasim, Dammam and Al-Ahsa. Indeed, between 1974 and 1997, more than fifty plays had been written, directed and produced under the auspices of this organization. The organization's mandate includes general sponsorship of Saudi artists and the operation of a library, an information centre and the kingdom's first cultural centre, located in Riyadh.

The Saudi Society for Culture and Art was itself predated in its activities by the Society for Popular Arts, founded in 1970 by Abdulla Ċisa al-Barut, Abdul-Rahman al-Raquraqu, Hasan al-Cabdi, Hasan al-Manla and Ibrahim al-Duwaihi. This group offered space for reading, music and painting, the display of folk arts and a small museum. They also privately presented ten stage plays and four television plays during its four years of existence. When the Saudi Society for Culture and Art began, they joined forces and together produced a relatively large number of plays including al-Hamdan's 1976 drama, *Qitar Al-Hazz* (*Train of Luck*) about the inflation of land values in the wake of increased oil revenues beginning in 1973.

The Saudi Society for Culture and Art's theatre director was Abdul-Rahman al-Hamad. Active as both a playwright and director, he wrote his most significant play in 1979, *Medicine and Real Estate*, another cautionary tale about speculation and land values and one of many plays he wrote about social problems in the country. Other plays of note by al-Hamad were *Orphans* (1980) and *People Under Zero* (1987). Realistic with touches of irony, al-Hamad's work is nevertheless more dramatic than comic.

Another organization of note in the cultural field is the King Faisal Foundation which promotes both Arab and Islamic culture within Saudi and abroad. Based in Riyadh, it presents the annual King Faisal International Prize to individuals who have made a contribution to Arabic literature. The King Fahd Library in Riyadh is one of the major research facilities in the Middle East.

As an offshoot of this work came an interest in offering plays to young people. Abdul-Rahman al-Mraikhi was particularly active in this area staging the first play for young people in Saudi in Al-Ahsa in 1975, *Laylat Al-Nafila*

(*The Night of Nalfila*) which later toured the country. He ultimately wrote more than a dozen plays for young people, many of them produced and toured by the Ministry of Youth and Sports.

In the 1990s, the state was sponsoring various local festivals at which awards are presented for best play and best performances. Most popular at these festivals have been comedies, some with social commentary and some without. Serious dramas are rare. Among the issues raised by these modern Saudi plays are questions of social and ethical shortcomings including inflation, high dowries, cultural change and bribery. Many of these plays are originally written for television. Among the few significant plays originally written for the stage is Abdul-Rahman al-Shaċir's comedy *The End of the Walk* (1976), produced by the Saudi Society for Art and Culture.

Another important play of the 1980s was al-Hamad's *The Play and Its Production* (1982) in which plays are given the value of real estate and are suddenly taken seriously by the rest of society. In this comedy, a real estate firm becomes overnight a theatrical production company. Artistic value is measured in terms of the prices that can be charged for tickets and the ultimate box-office return. The debates between the artists involved and the real estate firm actually border on the absurd.

In addition to social comedies and theatre for young audiences, other styles that have been seen since the mid-1980s are monodramas, a form made popular by Abdul Aziz al-Squiċbi, who deals with individual alienation and social barriers, historical plays reflecting contemporary national problems such as *Al-Karamaniyya* by Ahmad Abd Al-Ruman and *Wa Muctasimah* by al-Dbaikhi, and folk-style plays which also have specific national viewpoints. A number of highly symbolic plays have been seen, including *The Locust* (1987) by Ali-Sad, where social change is treated as a swarm of locusts. The play attracted attention at the 1987 Carthage Festival in Tunisia.

In the 1990s audiences are growing for this still new art form and the state has become an even more active supporter. It can now be counted on to provide theatrical groups with spaces and modest funding. Additionally, the state has offered support for talented students to pursue advanced training in theatre while maintaining general support for dramatic activities in primary and secondary schools as well as at the university level. King Saud University, one of seven universities in the country, has built two modern stages and produces an average of six to eight new plays annually on its campus. The student directors at the university have an unusual amount of freedom in their choice of plays and more controversial work tends to be seen on the campuses than through the many semi-professional groups now in existence in the major cities.

Among the problems still faced by the country's theatre community, none is larger than the lack of a viable institute for theatrical training. Experts have to be brought in from abroad on an *ad-hoc* basis – mainly by schools and universities and the Saudi Society for Culture and Art. To this end, plans continue to be debated for the institution of a full degree programme in theatre studies at King Saud University while establishing a branch for theatre studies in the Department of Information.

Saudi theatre continues to mean in most instances a theatre for men only. Save the aforementioned unproduced play by al-Abbasi and two minor female roles in al-Hamdan's play *Al-Mababil* (both of which were played by men), women are still virtually non-existent in plays or in theatre groups. Syria, Egypt and Kuwait all began their theatres in this way but eventually allowed women to take a more active role both on-stage and off. Will it happen in Saudi Arabia? Some dramatists who have altered their plays to suit the social and cultural values of the country have come to see the creation of an entirely separate women's theatre as the best way to solve the problem.

Theatrical activities are certainly taking place at female schools and universities as well as in women's organizations but no one can predict the future here. In any event, little research has been done in this area. Perhaps it is worth noting that the Good Will Club – a women's group in Riyadh – has staged a play by al-Hamdan whose theme was male–female relationships within the Saudi family. In this play, *Monokilya* (1985), he relates the story of a Saudi husband and wife who spend a summer holiday in Greece where the husband is caught making passes at a Greek woman. Women played all the roles in this production, which was done privately under the sponsorship and protection of the women's group itself.

Nazeer El-Azma

Further Reading

Abd Allah, Malhah. *Athar al-badawah 'ala al-masrah fi al-Saudiya* [The impact of Bedouin lifestyle on Saudi theatre]. Cairo: Matba'at Nasr al-Islam, 1994. 185 pp.

El-Azma, Nazeer. *The Saudi Theatre: A Critical Study*. Riyadh: Literary Club, 1992.

Eberhard, Frank. *Buhnewagen für das KFCC in Riyadh* [Revolving platform for the KFCC in Riyadh]. *Bühnentechnische Rundschau* 84 no. 4 (1990): 44–5.

Al-Khatib, Nasir. 'Madkhal Ila Dirasat Al-Masrah' [An introduction to the study of theatre in Saudi Arabia]. Diploma thesis, Higher Institute of Theatrical Arts, Cairo, 1984. 148 pp.

Al-Malibari, Muhammad Abdu'llah. *The First Theatre in Saudi Arabia* [in Arabic]. Mecca: Majallat Quraysh, 1960.

Al-Mirqrin, Abdu'l-Rahman. 'Bidayat Al-Masrah Al-Saudi' [The beginnings of the Saudi theatre]. BA dissertation, Higher Institute of Theatrical Arts, Cairo, 1979. 94 pp.

Al-Molla, Jasim. *Annual Report on Student Theatrical Activity at King Saud University*. Riyadh: King Saud University. Reports began 1983.

SHARJAH

(see **UNITED ARAB EMIRATES**)

SOCIALIST PEOPLE'S LIBYAN ARAB JAMAHIRIYA

(see **LIBYA**)

SOMALIA

Officially the Somali Democratic Republic, Somalia is one of the few places in the world where one can obtain myrrh, an indigenous aromatic gum resin highly valued in ancient times as an ingredient of perfume and incense. Located on the Horn of Africa, directly south of the Arabian peninsula and bordered by Ethiopia and Kenya to the west, Djibouti to the northwest and the Indian Ocean to the east, Somalia covers an area of 637,660 square kilometres (246,200 square miles). In 1995, the population was estimated at 8.9 million, with another 4 million or so Somalis living outside the country. The national capital is Mogadishu.

About 70 per cent of Somalis still live as nomads, travelling with their herds not only through Somalia but also through parts of Kenya and Ethiopia. Somalis also constitute a majority of the population in Djibouti. The official language of the country is Somali, which, despite attempts to introduce Arabic script, continues to be written in the Roman alphabet. Arabic and English are also widely used.

Several historians have suggested that Somalis first came to this land by sea from the Arabian peninsula while others argue that Somalis originated in Africa. Whatever the truth, traditional Somali belief suggests that all Somalis are descended from two brothers – Somali and Sab. This hereditary connection has led to strong alliances as well as bloody feuds with the majority of Somalis being the more nomadic of the two groups. Following the arrival of fleeing Muslim immigrants to Abyssinia (now Ethiopia) in the seventh century trying to escape Kurashite oppression, Islam started to spread in Somalia. The country is now almost totally Muslim with most following Sunni beliefs.

Mogadishu has been a major trading centre for nearly 1,500 years. So widespread was its fame that in 1427 it was visited by an envoy from Peking; an envoy from Mogadishu visited Peking the next year and two years later a Chinese trading fleet came to Mogadishu. The country has been a centre for invasions over the millennia with northern Somalia, by 1885, having become a British protectorate known as British Somaliland. In 1894, Italy gained control over Somali regions along the Indian Ocean, calling them Italian Somaliland, while Emperor Menelik of Ethiopia claimed the Somali area of Ogaden. Thus divided for the first half of the twentieth century, pressure for independence led the country to become a United Nations trusteeship in 1950. In June 1960 British Somaliland became formally independent and a month later was joined by Italian Somaliland to create what was called the Somali Republic. Ethnic rivalries erupted, however, and by 1964 Somalia was waging war on its biggest neighbour, Ethiopia, over land claims in the Ogaden region. The ensuing defeat led the country to shift its diplomatic ties from the Soviet Union to the United States. Somalia joined the Arab League in 1974.

In 1987, continuing political insurrections led to a full-scale civil war with rebel forces overthrowing the government in 1991. Since that time, wars between clan factions, interim presidents and a fervent political climate have meant that no party has ever really been able to gain full control of the country. As of 1998, no interim government had been recognized internationally and no functioning government was in place.

Culturally, language has long been one of the problem areas in Somalia. Indeed, the country's lack of a written language until 1974 meant that its history and cultural beliefs had to be kept through an oral literature easily accessible to people. So complicated has this been that the country's higher education curriculum is written in Italian and English while lower levels use a colloquial Somali containing much Arabic terminology.

From the late nineteenth century and up until independence, the two colonial Somalilands – the Italian one in the south with Mogadishu as its capital and the British one in the north with Hargeisa as its capital – had relatively little contact with one another and travel was not permitted between the two colonies. As a result, traditional performative events were kept as local as possible while a European-style mostly musical theatre came to Somalia through the countries of their foreign administrators.

The first modern theatre performance in the Italian-controlled part of the country has been dated quite precisely by Mohammed Sheikh Younis Yalho in his MA thesis at Baghdad's Institute of Arab Studies (1985: 85). According to him, it was in 1938 that the head of the Italian Catholic Church in Somalia hosted a visiting Italian opera troupe which included a Greek singer named Binella and performed several operas and opera excerpts for the Italian expatriate community in Mogadishu. Somalis did not attend any of the performances, though, since the Italian authorities did not permit the intermingling of Somalis and Europeans. Yet these performances still had an impact on young Somalis, who would watch through openings in the wall of the theatre, some of them night after night.

It was during World War II that the actor-singer-director Maalo Nour created one of the first modern-style theatre groups in the southern part of the country. Calling it Kooxda Badda (Naval Company), it was comprised of young musicians, singers, dancers and would-be actors. It offered musical shows at various points in the year, the major event being performances during Ramadan. Without a lot of money, costuming reflected what was available, varying between the folkloric and the military. For the Ramadan performances, the British Army looked after security and order. At the end of the Ramadan month, a parade was held and the governor of the region would distribute prizes to the best performances.

Eventually the members of Kooxda Badda began including political songs and sketches which brought it to the attention of the independence movement. The Somali Youth Unity Party, for example, more or less adopted the group. Indeed, the company received most of its funding from the party until 1952 when, with the assistance of Mohammed Sheikh Gaibu, an Italian lawyer, Radio Mogadishu began operating and took over funding for the group. Calling itself the Radio Mogadishu Artists' Company, the new company performed both on radio and in independent productions. In those days it was an all-male group since tradition did not allow women to appear on a public stage. All female roles were therefore played by young men.

In 1958 the company started to perform plays outside of Mogadishu and this new kind of musical theatre containing at its centre political messages began to spread to other cities and into the countryside. In that same year, four women joined the company – Khadija Abdalla Dalbess, Fatima Kassim Halool, Aisha Abdu and Halima Khalif Magol.

In the northern region, a local form of musical theatre called *balwoow* began to be seen as early as 1943. Created by the singer-producer Eid-Eid (real name Eid Sanmu) in the city of Zaila on the Somali–Djibouti border, Eid Sanmu's company performed to the accompaniment of the Arabian drum, mostly in a series of solo numbers, some with commentary on current issues.

In 1946 the Hargeisa Company began in the north. By 1954, under the direction of Abdalla Farsha, it was touring to other cities including Mogadishu with a popular musical evening called *The Disagreement*, a show which touched on the country's political problems and espoused national unity.

Other companies soon emerged in the south, also doing various forms of musical theatre. Among these was the Najmat Mogadishu Company (Somali Star Company), Esood Banadir, and a group called Don't Repeat My Name. None of the groups had a proper theatre and most played outdoors. The year 1954 also saw the first performances of non-musical, text-based plays and by 1956 a cinema was made available to these Mogadishu theatre groups.

After independence, the new Somali government decided to commit resources to the growing number of musical theatre companies around the country. Rather than direct funding, though, the government chose to cover the costs of cinema theatre rentals for up to three performances. Most popular of the cinema spaces was the Hamar Theatre and later the Africa Theatre.

The reputation of some of these groups began to grow both nationally and internationally. In 1966 a group calling itself the Somali National Theatre Company, for example, visited the

People's Republic of China and group members were invited to meet the Prime Minister, who offered to build a proper theatre for the group in Mogadishu. Thus was the Somali National Theatre built in the centre of the city. Also provided was technical and musical equipment. The new theatre had a significant and positive impact on the development of the Somali theatre, attracting new audiences and inspiring new groups such as Horsib (one of the most important Somali groups over the next two decades), the Somali Crescent and the Lions of the Cities, the smallest of the companies.

Audiences looked at this new art with mixed feelings. Young people generally found it to be lively and exciting; older audiences were not so convinced. Particularly troubling for them was the presence of women in the companies and serious religious concerns were raised on these grounds. Such concerns continued to cause problems for Somali artists right into the 1990s.

Through the 1960s, however, all these groups were relatively free to perform and there was little interference from religious or government groups. Seen as a commercial trade practised by professional artists, the theatre was flourishing at this point. Unfortunately, when the new military regime took over in 1969, problems emerged. One of the state's first acts was to virtually nationalize all theatre groups, making them all part of the state apparatus. Later the regime amalgamated the Radio Mogadishu Company and Horsib into one group called Wabri, which was made the official artistic leader of the country.

Through the 1970s, following the government's lead, groups came into being only under the auspices of unions, government ministries and businesses. Among the new groups to emerge during the 1970s were Iftin (The Light), connected to the police force; Heegan (Ready), part of the Ministry of Education and Training; Conkod (Thunder), part of the workers' union; Hasus (Reminiscence), part of the General Trade Union; Halgan (Struggle), part of the political Vanguard Forces; Danan (Ringing Out), part of the Revolutionary Union for the Somali Youth; and the Art Company, part of the Movement of Somali Cooperatives.

All these groups officially worked for and belonged to the state with administrators chosen by the state and earning salaries that were kept secret from other members. Salaries of company members were also guaranteed by the state. But independent groups simply stopped operating and state laws banned the establishment of new theatre companies.

By 1991, war had paralysed the theatre in virtually all parts of the country. While many artists left at this time, some individuals wrote and staged plays clandestinely and in many cases taped the plays on cassette and distributed the tapes widely. It is in this form that many plays of the period have survived. Among the most interesting of these is *Lancrorlusal* (*Landcruiser*), a short play about the shutdown of electricity in Mogadishu which was accompanied by the appearance of a group of senior government officials driving through the city in Landcruiser vehicles. The play was produced by the Wabri company, supported, ironically, by the Ministry of Defence. Another play of note performed in this period was the allegory *Shabeelnaagood* (*Leopard Among the Women*), which spoke to audiences poetically and allegorically so as not to run into trouble with censors.

Structure of the National Theatre Community

Until theatre activities in the country were paralysed by war in 1991, all companies were state owned and funded on a loan basis. If money was made on a production, the loan had to be paid back. The state also took 1 per cent of any profits. In return for funding, all companies were expected to support government policies.

Between 1988 and 1990, the period during which the government of Siad Barre was at its weakest, commercial productions were also allowed to exist. Performed on a total risk basis by the artists, some shows actually allowed artists to earn a living from their work. Officially, though, such approaches were not permitted.

The Wabri company, funded by the Ministry of Defence, was the biggest theatre company in the country. Rehearsals for most productions lasted one to two weeks. Productions were traditionally advertised in two ways – through large street signs and by hiring cars to roam neighbourhoods with megaphones.

The Union of the Somali Artists was active in establishing international contacts and tried to set basic living standards. It is the only arts union in the country. Theatre tickets are extremely cheap – less than the price of a cup of tea.

Artistic Profile

Companies

Beyond the eighteen or so state theatre companies in Somalia there is one company not subject to state control – the Banadir Lions. Established during the Italian colonization in Mogadishu, its work is essentially folkloric. From the 1980s, it professionalized quite significantly and set standards in the field of dance theatre. Most other groups performed a music and dance-based repertoire before war closed their activities.

Dramaturgy

There are many Somali writer-directors. Among the most important of those who began writing in the 1940s and 1950s are Qassim Malou, Abdi Sanmu, Al-Keifu and Maalo Nour. Those working in the 1960s and 1970s include Hassan Sheikh Moumin (b. 1930), author of *Shabeelnaagood* (*Leopard Among the Women*, 1966); Ali Safli (1933–81); Osman Adem (b. 1939), who wrote under the pen-name Askari (soldier); Mohammed Ibrahim Hadrawi (b. 1947); and Mohammed al-Sanjab. Most of these writers were affiliated with particular theatre groups during their careers.

Moumin was born in the city of Borma in the province of Autle in the northwest. An outstanding poet, he wrote particularly strong plays against colonialism among which was *Shabeelnaagood*, which criticized the behaviour of the Somali politicians after independence. Among other notable plays by Moumin are *Laba Isasi Siri* (*Two Cheaters*) and *Gobanimo* (*Freedom*). His plays are all written in Somali. In 1977, following the independence of the Djibouti Republic, he was sent by the Somali government to Djibouti to help organize the new theatre companies emerging there. He returned to Somalia in 1979 to head the National Theatre in the city of Hargeisa and later became manager of the Wabri company.

Safli was born in the city of Audoiny on the Somali–Ethiopian border in the province of Tagdheer. Educated in the city of Barbar on the Aden Gulf, his first artistic works appeared in 1956 in the form of patriotic songs, some of which were broadcast on Hargeisa Radio. In 1963, he wrote his first important play *Indhsarcad* (*Insurrection*). Set in northern Kenya after that country's independence from Britain and focusing on this region's desire to become part of Somalia, the play was a blend of poetry and realism. The play was also highly critical of the way Somalia handled this sensitive issue. Among his other plays are *Cat and Mouse*, *Travel*, *The Country Man in the City* and *A Soldier on Route 1*. Other plays of his deal with such issues as marriage and love relationships. All his plays were written in Somali.

The writer Osman Adem (Askari) moved to Mogadishu after independence. Among his major plays are *Maanta Iy Cadhi* (*Sitting Today*), *Araga Sog Daadkuba Uu Kula Tegiyee* (*Wait and You Will Be Taken By the Floods*), *Balan Iyo Geeri* (*The Pledge and Death*) and *Wadhav Iyo Shimbiro Wat Iska Hayaam* (*The Birds and the Catapult*, 1976). The last is his best known play, a social drama in fifteen scenes set in Mogadishu and in Rome.

Directors, Directing and Production Styles

Among the most prominent directors in the country are Mohammed Ibrahim Hadrawi, a playwright, poet and politician, and Saeed Salih Ahmed (b. 1946). Both received training abroad and established their reputations in the 1970s and 1980s.

Hadrawi was born in Hargeisa and joined the Wabri company in 1972, becoming well known for staging a number of provocative political plays such as *Without Pains*, a nationalistic play which questioned the then current political leadership. In response, he was exiled to a village in central Somali where he was forced to stay from 1976 to 1979. After his release, he wrote and staged another controversial play that attracted wide attention across the country, *Bidoon Um*

(*Without Mother*, 1980). Once again, he was imprisoned, not being released this time until 1984.

Ahmed was born in Mogadishu and studied directing in Italy. Among his major productions have been three plays by Adem (Askari) – *Wadhav Iyo Shimbiro Wat Iska Hayaam*, *Balan Iyo Geeri* and *Maanta Iy Cadhi*.

Music Theatre
Dance Theatre

The northern Somalian theatre has relatively little music or dance in comparison to the southern theatre in and around Mogadishu which tends to involve much music, drum accompaniment and dance. There is no play that does not start with music and music is played between scenes. More specifically, when there is music in the northern theatre, it is usually done as a solo with little movement. The musical sections of the southern plays, on the other hand, involve much group movement.

In the northern theatre the director, the playwright and the composer are often one and the same person. It is not unusual to find that this person is a leading actor as well. This is not always so true for the southern theatre. The number of instruments used and the size of the cast is generally twice as large in the south, averaging between thirty and forty persons.

Dance itself has long been part of Somali tradition and plays a major part in community events such as weddings, harvests and religious celebrations. With the emergence of the modern theatre, though, particularly in the south, dance has taken on a separate life and professional dancers can now make popular and profitable careers. Many dancers are famous across the country.

Theatre for Young Audiences
Puppet Theatre

In 1979 the Academy of Science, Art and Literature held a conference to look into the establishment of a theatre for children in Somalia. Attending were representatives of both UNESCO and UNICEF. Though no concrete action came from the meeting, it was a serious attempt to establish a children's theatre in the country.

Until that time, the only other attempt at creating theatrical performances for children was done on Mogadishu Radio, a show aimed at teaching children about Somali traditions and customs. When television began in the country, the radio programme was transferred to television and became a kind of children's theatre.

Theatre has never been part of the educational curriculum. There are no puppet theatres in the country.

Design
Theatre Space and Architecture

Design is not among the priorities of Somali theatre. That said, design elements can be seen to a greater degree in southern Somali theatre than in the north. Costuming is of key importance especially in folk shows and performances involving particular periods or social groupings. Traditionally, men wear shorts with a kind of loose skirt. Shoes are made of animal hides. Women's dresses are tied at the left shoulder.

Among the few designers working in the

theatre are Ali Suleiman, Khalif Mussa and Mohammed Kinyaro. The first has a university degree in design, and the others are graduates of art institutes.

In terms of theatre spaces, in Mogadishu the major theatre was constructed by the Chinese government in 1969 and was the first theatre to be built in Somalia. With 2,500 seats, it is a standard proscenium, also used regularly by the government for social events. It is the largest theatre in Somalia.

The Hargeisa State Theatre is located in the heart of that northern city and was constructed by the government in 1974. Also a basic proscenium, it too accommodates 2,500 and

has been used for public meetings and even weddings.

In all capital cities of the sixteen provinces there are smaller theatres owned by the state. Because of high rental costs, a number of groups have made arrangements with cinema owners to stage shows in these movie halls. In Mogadishu there are twenty-one cinema houses and in Hargeisa there are six. In addition to these spaces there are small stages in most of the eighty-two community centres across the country. It is in these spaces that most touring shows are played. They are also used for community meetings and can hold as many as 5,000 people.

Training

There are no specialized theatre training institutions in the country. As a result many performers have gone abroad for training to such countries as the United States, Italy, the former Soviet Union, North Korea, China and Sudan for either short courses lasting a month or two or for longer training extending over several years. The state has traditionally paid for such

training through competitive scholarships.

The government has regularly invited specialists from abroad to come to major cities and set up training courses. Such courses are mainly directed toward experienced performers. Those who obtain some form of certification are hired by the big state companies such as Wabri and Horsib.

Criticism, Scholarship and Publishing

There are no specialized agencies conducting theatre research in the country and criticism is woefully lacking. One of the few arts programmes – *Sanka Iya Sanaaninta'* (*Art and Artists*) – is broadcast weekly on Mogadishu Radio. Mostly interviews, it features playwrights and well-known singers and actors. The state-owned newspaper *October* from time to time includes theatre news and occasional essays.

Abdullah Said Hersi
Translated by Yacob Idris

(See also DJIBOUTI)

Further Reading

Ahmed, Abdulghder Saeed. 'The Somali Theatre'. Unpublished article, n.d.

Balho, Mohammed Shiekh Yousef. 'Modern Somali Literature'. MA thesis, Institute of Arab Studies and Research, Baghdad, 1985.
Luterkort, Ingrid. 'Finding a Theatre for Somalia'. *Theatre International* 9 (1983): 17–23.
Moumin, Hassan Sheikh. *Leopard Among the Women: Shabeelnaagood – A Somali Play*. Translated by B.W. Andrzejewski. London: Oxford University Press, 1974. 230 pp.
Sheik-Abdi, Abdi. *Tales of Punt: Somali Folktales*. Macomb, IL: Dr Leisure, 1993. 135 pp.
Younis, Mohammed Abdulmuniem. *The Somalia Nation and People*. Cairo: Dar Al-Nahdha al-Masriyah [Egyptian Nahdha Centre], 1962.
Al-Zaher Hamdi. *The Story of Somalia*. Dar al-Shaab Bil-Qahirah [The People's Centre in Cairo], 1977.

SOMALI DEMOCRATIC REPUBLIC

(see **SOMALIA**)

SOUTH YEMEN

(see **YEMEN**)

SUDAN

The largest country on the African continent, Sudan spans 2,505,800 square kilometres (967,500 square miles) and shares borders with Egypt to the north, Ethiopia and the Red Sea to the east, Kenya, Uganda and Zaïre to the south and the Central African Republic, Chad and Libya to the west. The population of the country, estimated in 1995 to be 30.1 million, is 52 per cent African and 39 per cent Arab with the former mostly in the southern half of the country and the latter mostly in the north. Minorities include large communities of Beja peoples, Jamala and Nubians. Some one hundred languages are spoken in Sudan, with Arabic being the country's official language and English widely understood. Among the many African languages spoken are Nubian and Ta Bedawie along with diverse dialects of various Nilotic, Nilo-Hamatic and Sudanic languages. Three-quarters of Sudanese Muslims follow the Sunni faith and live in an area where Islamic culture is very strong. Some 17 per cent of the people – mostly in the south – follow tribal or indigenous beliefs, with about 5 per cent of the population listed as Christian, mostly Roman Catholic. The Sudanese capital is Khartoum.

Connected for a long part of its modern history to the Ottoman Empire, Sudan from 1898 until 1956 was controlled by Britain through Egypt and was known through this period as the Anglo-Egyptian Sudan. Granted independence in 1956 in the midst of a civil war and economic decay, Sudan was for nearly two decades torn between its prosperous Muslim north and its less wealthy African and Christian south. Isolated from each other under British rule, the substantial cultural differences between the two territories escalated until full civil war took place. In 1958, General Ibrahim Abboud overthrew the new government in a military

coup, dismissed the Parliament, proclaimed himself Prime Minister and declared martial law. Fighting continued, however, for another eleven years until Colonel Joafar el-Nemery, who came to power in a bloodless coup in 1969, brought an end to it in 1972 by granting limited autonomy to the south. An uneasy peace lasted until 1983 when he introduced Islamic rule and religious fundamentalists gained new powers. Two years later (1985), el-Nemery was himself overthrown. A State of Emergency was called in 1987 and the army took full control of the country once again in 1989.

The country was ruled through the early 1990s by a fifteen-member Revolutionary Council but through this period controls deteriorated, the south continued to push for full independence and the southern part of the country remained a war zone. As a result, many – especially in the south – were faced with economic ruin and starvation.

Though differently rooted than the country's politics and religion, Sudan's theatre also has two distinct strands – one essentially Arab-Islamic and following trends in modern Arab theatre; and another rooted in indigenous African traditions and built around communal events, that is, events without the European distinction between artist and audience. Both traditions are rich in music, dance and ceremony and records indicate that from at least the early nineteenth century travellers had been commenting on the many colourful events to be seen here.

It was in the early part of the twentieth century that European-style theatre began to be seen with some regularity when Shakespearian drama began to be taught and produced by students at Gordon Memorial College, an institution founded in 1902 and which eventually developed into the University of Khartoum. The influence of Arabic dramatic writing in the European style began to be felt shortly thereafter with many Arabic teachers arriving in the country – mostly from Egypt, Syria and Lebanon – teaching and producing plays by dramatists from their own countries. In both cases, the Sudanese were fascinated 'recipients'.

The first Sudanese to be attracted to these new styles tended to be both politicized and intellectually daring. Among these were Siddiq Fareed (1889–1941), who came in touch with English drama at Gordon College. He later became associated with the country's growing Lebanese and Egyptian communities through whom he learned about Arabic plays. Daringly anti-colonial, he concentrated on plays that tried to raise national consciousness. In 1938, he was elected a member of the committee of sixty that led the Graduates' Congress, an event which was the embryo of national political parties, calling for self-determination in Sudan. Others involved in similar dramatic activities were Ismael al-Azhari, later the first Prime Minister of Sudan; Khidir Hamad, later a member of the five-member Sovereignty Council; Muhammad Ahmed Mahgoub, also a later Prime Minister; and Nasir al-Hag Ali, later the first Sudanese vice-chancellor of the University of Khartoum.

Another pioneer, Hussein Mallasi (1894–1946), in collaboration with Egyptian expatriates, formed a theatre company that was active from 1910 to 1924 in Port Sudan. He too had links with the national movement. His company had to stop functioning after the 1924 uprising, however, because of a colonial backlash that hit all cultural and educational institutions. Even Ali Abdul Latif, leader of the uprising, acknowledged that he regularly took part in backstage preparations for many plays and was a frequent visitor to performances at the Egyptian Club.

By 1933 Sudanese were themselves writing plays. It was that year that Khalid Abdul Rahman Abdul Rous (1908–85) wrote, co-directed and acted in *Tajouj*, his version of a well-known Sudanese legend and the first original Sudanese play of note. Until then, plays were either adaptations into classical Arabic of English or French plays, or were written by Egyptian or Lebanese nationals. *Tajouj* was a clarion call for the new movement and encouraged many others to write for theatre. Among them Ibrahim al-Abbadi (1890–1981), Sayyid Abdul Aziz and Al Khalifa Yousif Al Hassan. Later plays by these writers all focused on Sudanese themes, were written in colloquial

Sudanese Arabic, directly or indirectly called for unity of the Sudanese people, and celebrated Sudanese history and values (implicitly rejecting cultural emasculation). Their productions were also usually fundraising efforts for the Ahlia Schools, the alternative educational system set up by the national movement. Many of the plays used the populist Duo-Bait poetic tradition. The two leading writers in this style were Rous and al-Abbadi, both of whom experienced several encounters with colonial censorship.

With Sudan's burgeoning theatrical movement reaching its maturity in the late 1930s on the bedrock of the national movement, it became patronized by the most respectable elements in society. Even Sayyid Abdul Rahman Al Mahadi, one of the religious leaders of the time, in an apparent effort to influence the national movement, hosted a theatrical performance in his own house, a rare event for someone of his stature.

But the emergence of a national drama – despite such exceptional moments – was not easy. Following the first performance of *Tajouj* in 1933, for example, the playwright found himself in trouble with authorities at the religious institute in which he studied because

Khalid Abdul Rahman Abdul Rous.

Tahia Zarough, one of the most prominent actresses of the 1970s and 1980s.

fundamentalist teachers disapproved of his including women characters in the play which required male actors to dress as women. To them, it was tantamount to public transvestism, which is strictly proscribed by Islam. Yet the play was recognized by a wider public and the style deeply planted.

Ironically, with the evolution of recognized political parties in the Sudan in the 1940s, theatre activities waned since colonial rule could now be openly challenged. It was at this point that many people turned from theatre to the formation of political structures and more specifically toward the formation of programmes for independence. Evidence of this change can be seen in the brief history of the Sudanese Company for Acting and Music, a group formed in 1948 in Omdurman. The group was given a plot of land on which they could build a theatre as well as the right to raise money for the project. But as politics came to replace theatre, those involved simply forgot about the theatre entirely. Indeed, the plot of land is still barren and the company's name is now simply a dim memory.

After independence in 1956, the country's poets, actors and activists took on other roles and quickly became Sudan's parliamentarians, ministers and political leaders. The civil war raging at this time simply pushed the idea of theatre even further to the background. In 1958, Talaat Fareed, the Minister of Information and the younger brother of theatre pioneer Saddiq Fareed, tried to bring into being a national theatre in Khartoum, a building more than anything else. Based on earlier unfinished plans by the British colonial administration, the theatre was inaugurated in 1959 and became a centre for visiting companies from overseas and for local artists. There was, however, no resident company included in the planning and no sustained theatrical activity. Jugglers, jokers and revue performers instead made their reputations here, among them Uthman Humaida and Ismael Khorshed. In 1967, the National was reorganized to present short seasons of its own work.

In 1964 the military *junta* was overthrown but civil war in the south raged on. Despite this, parliamentary democracy was restored and the arts began to breathe again. Theatre benefited from two very far-reaching measures: the setting up in 1966, with the help of two Soviet experts, of Firqat Al-Funun Al-Shabiyya (National Folk Dance Troupe) and the establishment in 1969 of the Institute of Music and Drama to teach both theoretical and practical theatre. For the former, dozens of dancers were selected from their tribal areas and brought to Khartoum where their dances were refined for the stage. The company included a rather large administration, a rehearsal space and a number of technicians. The troupe proved to be a resounding success, both at home and abroad. It also solved a problem that seemed intractable, demonstrating that multiculturalism could be a source of strength rather than strife. In a country where more than a hundred languages were spoken and where a civil war had continued unabated for thirteen years, it was heartening for many to see a troupe transcending language barriers and proving on the stage that recognition of different cultures was not only feasible but also enjoyable.

In 1969, however, a second *coup d'état* took place and parliamentary democracy and freedom of expression were again lost. Once more, the theatre's vulnerability was exposed. Nevertheless the Institute of Music and Drama, though shaken, survived as did the National Folk Dance Troupe. By 1972, the country's one-party regime even established a Department of Culture which,

Asia Abdel Majid (Um Eihab).

the rebels in southern Sudan to end seventeen years of fratricidal war in 1972, several companies were formed, the most significant of which was Skylark in 1978. Writers, actors and directors such as Line Rel Deng and Joseph Obok also began to make an impact. Gradually a situation similar to that in the 1930s was created. Theatre companies mushroomed and the art was again seen as a means of both celebration and dissent, a way to think individually, a way to discuss matters without asking permission and a way to criticize the totalitarian way of life with a reasonable chance of getting away with it. Thus the 1970s saw the emergence of an unprecedented number of well-organized theatrical companies, which made maximum use of the National Cultural Festival, an event organized regularly by the government.

The 1980s' shift towards religious intolerance saw the institution of the Sharia (Islamic common law) imposed. Again, cultural life suffered. Books were burned in the streets in Omdurman, public whippings became common, limbs were amputated as punishments and even crucifixions were seen. Theatre, which brought both sexes into close proximity – something not approved of by religious authorities – came to a gradual halt. No law was passed against it but an atmosphere was created in which it simply could not function. When civil war again began in the south, theatrical life was once more all but smothered. By 1985, the new regime was overthrown and Sudan regained parliamentary democracy and freedom of expression. Once more, the door was open for further developments in theatrical activities. Since this time, a cautious theatrical community has begun to re-emerge.

however, with the National Council for Arts and Letters (established 1971), sought to control all cultural activities including theatre. The two bodies formed a bureaucratic octopus that devoured most of the funds made available for the arts. After paying for salaries, buildings, cars and staff, little was left for the artists.

When the regime signed an agreement with

Structure of the National Theatre Community

Though there is a National Theatre building in Sudan there is no real national theatre company. The space itself is, for the most part, rented out on a low-cost basis to other groups. Through the years attempts were made to establish a real company but most fell apart for lack of sufficient funding.

The only fully professional company in the country is the National Folk Dance Troupe whose salaries are paid by the state. All other troupes exist on a semi-professional or an

amateur basis and their seasons are presented without any financial guarantees. About twelve such groups exist, all of them in the capital of Khartoum. There are several groups that occasionally put on performances in the provinces, mainly in Port Sudan, Medani, Al-Obeid, Kassala, Kosti and Al-Fashir.

To use the National's facilities, companies simply approach the National's administration with a play and a required production period. If approved, the group usually performs for about two weeks; if it finds an audience, it transfers to the 2,000-seat Friendship Hall where it performs on a purely commercial basis paying a high rent for this well-equipped and centrally situated theatre.

Probably the worst enemy of theatre companies in Sudan is the tax system, with companies required to pay at least four kinds of taxes to various government bodies. This makes it extremely difficult for them to break even in the end and discourages outsiders from investing in their work.

Artistic Profile

Companies

The al-Fadil Saeed Company was influenced by the Egyptian actor Amin al-Hinaidi who was teaching in Khartoum in the early 1950s. Immediately after independence, Saeed, an actor, began to present sketches utilizing two characters, Bint Guddaim, a crafty old woman who comments on changing values and changing times, and Al Ajab (the surprised one), a simple person who inevitably and inadvertently collides with authority or bureaucracy. These two char-

Director, actor-manager and playwright al-Fadil Saeed.

acters made Saeed famous and later they were presented on radio and television. In 1967 he moved on to presenting full-length plays, mostly revolving around the character of Al Ajab. The plays are usually put together by improvisation, with the final text arrived at only when the play is ready for dress rehearsal. Even then, the text is often changed from one performance to another.

Saeed is a playwright-actor-manager-director and his productions clearly put him at the centre. Such a personal focus has led to the formation of at least three breakaway groups formed by young members. The strength of Saeed's company can also be found in its mobility. It tours to the most remote regions of the country and has a faithful following almost everywhere. The company is also very strong when it comes to social criticism of the establishment.

The National Folk Dance Troupe was founded in 1966 in the breathing space between two coups and as a result of the high hopes that followed the 1964 revolution. Two years after its foundation, a Soviet choreographer named Ramazin was invited to give the group some specific dance training. The company owes a great deal to his efforts and dedication. All sixty dancers are considered as full-time employees who get a regular salary. They rehearse at the troupe's centre in Omdurman; this has a small rehearsal stage and a capacity of 300.

The dancers usually perform pieces from a repertoire of fifteen tribal dances selected from across the country. The troupe has toured throughout the Arab world, Africa, Europe and China and has participated in many festivals. The troupe went through a lean period in the early 1980s when the regime in power tried to dissolve the Ministry of Culture and Information and attached the National Folk Dance Troupe to, incredibly, the Ministry of Defence. During this period, many dancers left. The troupe is now back in the fold of the Ministry of Culture and Information.

Nimat Hammad, the first woman to establish a theatre company in Sudan.

Other active companies in the country include Firqat Adwa Al-Masrah (Theatre Lights Company), Firqat Al-Masrah Al-Hur (Free Theatre Company), Firqat Toar Al-Jar (Pulling Ox Company), Firqat Al-Masrah Al-Sudani (Sudanese Theatre Company), Firqat Omar Al-Khidir (Omar Al-Khidir Company, previously Firqat Al-Ard or Land Company), Firqat Khalid Abdul Rous (Khalid Abdul Rous Company), Firqat Nimat Hammad (Nimat Hammad Company – the only company – founded in 1979 – headed by a woman), and Firqat Aaza (Aaza Company).

Two more or less avant-garde companies are Firqat Al-Asdiqa (Friends' Company) founded in 1979 and specializing in musical satire, and Firqat Al-Sadeem (Cloud Company) founded in 1982. The latter championed street theatre and even went to audiences in densely populated quarters of the capital. There are no companies in the provinces.

Dramaturgy

Khalid Abdul Rahman Abdul Rous and Ibrahim

al-Abbadi are the undisputed founders of Sudanese playwriting. Before them texts were performed in English or in classical Arabic mainly for the benefit of students and the expatriate community. Among the Arabic plays performed were scripts by the Egyptian poet Ahmad Shawqi and by the Lebanese playwright Najb al-Haddad.

Rous and al-Abbadi changed all this and wrote about Sudanese themes in the vernacular. Their characters were from the countryside and the values of these characters were tribal (honour, community, nobility and revenge) The mixture of singing and chanting in their poetic plays, coupled with performances by famous singers between the acts of the plays, gave their works real popularity and power connecting their productions to communal ceremonies and ancient rituals. The fact that both men were also politically engaged linked their work for audiences to daily events. Despite the politics, however, they will be remembered not as political artists but rather as artists of the first order, writers whose statements were as valid in the 1990s as they were in the 1930s.

Tajouj (1933) by Rous was based on both fact and legend. According to this legend, a poet gets married to a very beautiful woman whom he loves deeply. On their wedding night, he asks her to parade in front of him totally naked, approaching him, moving away and then returning to him again. She is shocked and annoyed by his request, considering it deeply humiliating. She accepts, however, but with a single proviso – that he agrees to a request from her. He promises that he will accept anything she might ask. She then parades in front of him. When he is satisfied, she makes her request to him: an immediate divorce. He must, of course, agree and, alone thereafter, he dies in misery. She, in turn, will die at the hands of a tribal chief when a major conflict is triggered by her beauty. Rous's play is highly symbolic.

Al-Mak Nimir (1937) by al-Abbadi is also based on this legend but with a more realistic emphasis. Two lovers find themselves in trouble because the chief of a neighbouring tribe has heard about the beauty of the girl and is determined to marry her. The couple escape. They are overtaken and in a duel the young man kills the chief and has to take refuge with a third tribe. War is about to break out between the two tribes but reconciliation and peace are finally arranged.

Although Rous and al-Abbadi dominate early Sudanese playwriting, there are other dramatists of note. Among them is Abdallah Attayeb (b. 1921), an authority on Arabic poetry, who in 1955 wrote and staged a trilogy whose plot was taken from the court of Haroun Al-Rasheed in Baghdad. The plays were written in classical Arabic poetry, and were arguably the first Sudanese musicals in anything approaching the modern usage of the term. Attayeb broke away from the strait-jacket of classical Arabic poetic forms and established himself as one of those few who pioneered poetic 'renewal' in the Arabic-speaking world. Another is Hassan Abdul Majeed (d. 1980), a graduate of Gordon Memorial College. His best work was *Al-Rafdh* (*Rejection*, 1972), which discussed questions of the young rebelling against old values and determined to reject them.

During the early 1970s, playwrights such as Uthman Nisairi, Salma Babiker, Ali Abdul Ghayyoum, Shawqi Izzuldin, Najiyya Al-Wasila, Azma Al-Wakiel, Abdul Basit Sabdarat and others tried to create yet another theatrical revival. They were strongly resisted by Muslim fundamentalist students, however, who opposed performances involving both men and women. A clash ensued in which one student was killed.

During the same period, Hamadna Allah Abdul Qadir (b. 1928) was Sudan's most popular playwright. His three major successes were *Al Mundhara* (*The Mirror*, 1970), *Khutubat Suhair* (*The Engagement of Suhair*, 1971) and *Fi Intizar Omar* (*Waiting for Omar*, 1972). In his private life, Qadir was a senior civil servant who visited England from time to time and was particularly impressed with the works of George Bernard Shaw. Later a director of the Department of Culture, and dean of the Institute of Music and Drama, his plays use a highly refined colloquial prose on themes related to urban life. Qadir wrote about a world of classes and an increasingly nuclear family. In his drama *Khutubat Suhair*, for example, a family prepares itself for a visit on the occasion of an engagement. But the host family must conceal its secret: the father is an alcoholic. When sober he is great and loving but when drunk he is a monster. Unfortunately, he borrows money and gets drunk, returning in time to spoil the occasion. Through these characters he explores the validity of Sudanese marriage traditions and values. The father is, in this sense, not the only villain of the piece.

Yusuf Khalik (b. 1946), Yusuf Aidabi (b. 1944), Abdullahi Ali Ibrahim (b. 1943) and Khalid al-Mubarak (b. 1937) all have daringly experimented with and utilized street theatre, traditional games, Sufi rituals and tribal ceremonies. All have also written about the theatre. Khalik, a poet who was forced to leave Sudan at one point for political reasons, advocated the use of new forms to express a new content. A student of theatre in the former East Berlin, he first drew attention to his work with adaptations of plays by García Lorca and his own rewriting of the Tajouj legend. Aidabi, who wrote a doctoral dissertation on 'Mythology in Contemporary Arabic Theatre', was at one time dean of the Institute of Music and Drama. His play *Hisan Al-Bayaha* (1974) was a dramatization of an eighteenth-century manuscript about early Sudanese poets and wise men. Ali Ibrahim was awarded a PhD in folklore from the University of Indiana in the United States. One of the most accomplished prose writers in the country, he uses colloquial language in his plays (many of which have been done on the streets) and mixes elements of narration with dramatic presentation. For his part, al-Mubarak – with a PhD in drama from the University of Bristol (England) and for four years the dean of the Institute of Music and Drama, writes most of his plays in classical Arabic. Many are based on Sufi and African tribal rituals.

Three other writers whose work was first seen in the late 1970s are Hashim Siddiq (b. 1944), who studied at the East 15 Acting School in London; Badr-al-Doin Hashim (b. 1937), who studied in England and Romania; and Omar al-Hamidi (b. 1937), a novelist, painter and designer. Siddiq, an actor, poet and well-known dissident, was arrested several times for his political activities. A teacher of theatre at the Institute of Music and Drama, his fame rests primarily in the area of musical theatre. His best known piece is *Napata Habibati* (*Napata My Beloved*) which caused an uproar and demonstrations in 1973. Indeed, the president of the country reportedly disguised himself to see the performance. Highly entertaining, the play used ancient rituals to make contemporary statements. A revival in the late 1980s, after the restoration of democracy, was also well received.

Al-Doin Hashim wrote several realistic plays (similar to those of Hamadna Allah Abdul Qadir) that established his reputation. His best play is *Safar Al-Jafa* (1976), about migration of young men from the countryside to urban centres. Omar al-Hamidi's main achievement – in a society obsessed with sexual taboos – is the ability to discuss sex in an open way. *Napata*

Playwright Hashim Siddiq.

Habibati, a scathing criticism of totalitarian rule, was performed again in 1983.

Among writers who have emerged since the mid-1980s are Al-Tayib al-Mahdi, who won a German television drama competition; Izzaldin Hilali, a poet, actor and increasingly successful playwright; Osman Ali al-Faki, whose play *Al-Hafila* was well received at the Damascus Festival in 1986; Muhammad Sharif Ali, another actor-director turned playwright; Khattab Hassan Ahmed; Abdul Muttalib al-Fahal; and Jamal Hassan Saeed.

Directors, Directing and Production Styles

The leading director, in both consistency and high standards, is Makki Sinada (b. 1944). A teacher, he also paints, writes for radio and acts. A student of stage design in Cairo, he regularly designs the plays he directs. Among his major productions have been plays by Qadir, Siddiq's *Napata Habibati*, al-Mubarak's *Haza La Yakoon Wa Tilk A Nazra*, which was stopped from representing Sudan at the Damascus Festival five days before the actors' departure

because it questioned the regime, and Hashim's *Safar Al-Jafa*, which anticipated the country's drought of the 1980s.

Al-Faki Abdul Rahman (b. 1933) became the director of the reorganized National Theatre in 1967 and stayed in this position for several years. He insisted on a definite budget, a regular season and opened the door to new ideas. He sponsored revivals of plays from the golden 1930s. He personally directed *Al-Mak Nimir* for the opening of the first season in 1968 and encouraged women to act, presenting Asia Abdul Magid with her first role. Al-Faki, the godfather of modern theatre in the Sudan, studied in Egypt (1953) and England (1961–3).

Uthman Gamar Al-Anbiya (b. 1942) was trained in drama at the Croydon College of Art in England. Controversy surrounded one of his early productions, which included a dramatized religious marriage ceremony and its attendant festivities (a Shaiqiyyash tribe ceremony) in 1979. Another strong production was his theatrical adaptation of a poem by M.A. Magzoub about traditional celebrations on the occasion of the annual anniversary of the birth of the Prophet Muhammad. Long resident in Saudi

Makki Sinada.

Arabia, Uthman directed in Riyadh University a play by the Syrian playwright Sa'dallah Wanous, *Mughamarat Ras Al-Mamlouk Gabir*, which relied on Sudanese *hakawati* forms.

Music Theatre
Dance Theatre

Aside from the work of the National Folk Dance Troupe which brings together traditional musicians and dancers from all over the country for regular seasons in Khartoum, music and dance forms can be seen across Sudan on social and communal occasions. The *zar*, for example, is a highly dramatic ceremony. The participants – mainly women – dance with a focus on impersonation. It is said that the dancers go into a trance and are 'transformed' into other characters. Others assist the new character into appropriate costumes and the dancer then speaks and behaves in line with the new personality. In the end, the costumes are removed and the dancers return to their original selves. *Zar* survives despite its non-Islamic roots. In 1987 the leader of the most famous *zar* group in Khartoum was involved in a legal battle with religious neighbours, who sought his eviction. *Zar* is not specifically a Sudanese ritual. It is known – with slight variations – in Egypt, Ethiopia (where it probably originated) and the Gulf states.

The chanting of verses from the Quran is a performance done by a *madih* who travels from village to village; through his performances he spreads news and information, becoming the centre of a circle of listeners who also chant and join in appreciatively. The *madih* himself moves around the circle playing a tambourine.

The investiture of the Reth (king) of the Shilluk (a nilotic tribe) is a breathtaking theatrical spectacle in which the whole tribe takes part.

The event is full of music, dance, mock battles, sacrifices and competitions. It has been filmed by the BBC and by German television.

Another spectacle is the rain-maker's ritual. In it, the *kujur* – a combination of rain-maker and medicine-man – goes through a series of very theatrical rituals dancing in full regalia. *Kujurs* are very popular and influential in non-Muslim areas of Sudan. One *kujur* dance has even been incorporated into the National Folk Dance Troupe's repertoire.

Baramka is a communal ceremony involving the drinking of tea. People sit in a circle with teapots and cups in the centre. The tea is prepared and poured in specifically prescribed ways with the participants singing and offering forms of praise.

In its original setting, Nubian wrestling in the mountains of central Sudan was and still is more of a theatrical spectacle than a sports event. The dress, the careful stage management, the social gathering, the set of rules preceding and following the actual event, all underline the almost choreographed theatricality.

The *mugai* – the court jester of Darfur tradition – formally vanished with the end of the Fur Sultanate in 1916. But the memory and spirit of this dancer-singer who conveyed to the sultan the woes and sorrows of the state survives. There are many *mugais* who still entertain even without a sultanate in Darfur Province.

Theatre for Young Audiences
Puppet Theatre

Puppetry is not a well-known art in Sudan. Nevertheless one company does exist and performs on an occasional basis. Firqat Al-Arais (Puppet Company) was founded in 1976 with Romanian help and training. Romanian experts trained the company both in Bucharest and Sudan. The company shares the same building as the National Folk Dance Troupe and the State Acrobatic Company. There are no groups in the country specifically doing theatre for young audiences.

Design
Theatre Space and Architecture

A breakthrough in the evolution of Sudanese stage design came with the organization of regular theatre seasons at the National Theatre in 1967. A decision was taken by the artistic and administrative staff that design should be part of the total theatre experience and that the design team should come from the ranks of recent graduates of Khartoum College of Fine Arts.

Salih Al-Amin (b. 1947) was one of these graduates; he joined the National Theatre in 1969. The National later sponsored him to study in France, where he stayed for five years (1973–7). His stage designs for *Safar Al-Jafa*, *Darih Wad Al-Nour* and *Al-Asad Wal Jawhara* were memorable. Salih introduced design techniques to the National's stage and allowed easy groupings. Later, his work moved away from realism towards a symbolist quality. He

also confirmed a new tradition of bringing in designers at the beginning of each new project.

Other names in this rare specialization are Farouk Ajabani, who studied in the former East Germany after graduation from Khartoum College of Fine Arts, and Salah Al-Ubaid, also a graduate of the College of Fine Arts and later head of stage design at the National Theatre.

As for theatre spaces, small groups use a variety of locations but the most prestigious is the National Theatre in Khartoum. Another space widely used is the 2,000-seat Friendship Hall in Khartoum, also a proscenium stage. In the provinces, open-air theatres exist in the cities of Kassala, Port Sudan, Medani, Al-Damazin, Dongola, Al-Obaid, Al-Nuhood, Nyala, Al-Fashir and Juba. The latter is a multipurpose conference hall built with Kuwaiti aid.

Training
Criticism, Scholarship and Publishing

Teaching of drama as literature began in 1902 with the founding of the Gordon Memorial College in Khartoum. Shakespeare was taught and produced. Indeed, part of the physics department building was designed to serve as a backstage area for an open-air theatre and the site is still intact. The teaching of theatrical subjects as part of the curriculum, however, was introduced only in the early 1970s by Adrian Welch as part of courses offered at the department of English. The programme survived for only four years after Welch's return to England. No similar programmes now exist.

In literary areas, though, drama is regularly taught. In the Arabic department at the University of Khartoum, Muhammad Al-Wathiq Yusuf taught a theoretical course in Arabic drama for many years while both the French and Russian departments teach dramatic theory. Extra-curricular activities in the French department include theatrical productions. The department of extra-mural studies has occasionally offered practical theatre courses.

The Institute of Music and Drama (IMD) was

founded in 1969 through the efforts and commitment of one man – Abdul Majid Abu Hasabu (d. 1985). His efforts came as a response to calls for the establishment of such an institute by several pressure groups which felt that a school could significantly add to the growth of Sudanese culture. The initial syllabus and a detailed timetable for four years of study was prepared by the Egyptian expert Nabil Al-Alfi. The founding dean, Al-Mahi Ismael, acquired rented premises and made contracts with part-time teachers from other institutions as well as from members of the expatriate community in Khartoum. In 1976 the IMD was moved under the sponsorship of the National Council for Higher Education. This improved the chances of sending teaching assistants abroad for further study.

The IMD remains the single most decisive factor in the development of theatre in Sudan. All holders of key positions in radio, television and at the National Theatre are now graduates of the IMD as are a vast majority of actors and directors in the country. Many of its graduates are also quite successful in finding work in the cultural field, particularly in the Gulf states.

The language of instruction at the IMD is Arabic. Its main courses are acting and directing, stage design and criticism. Ancillary courses include history of art, film appreciation and literature. In order to graduate, acting and directing students must stage a short play under supervision. Students of criticism present a dissertation. Stage design students present a major design project.

Graduation performances and projects have become an annual attraction for Khartoum residents. Under the umbrella of 'academic freedom', students and supervisors can even present performances that are socially critical. The IMD has an average of twenty students graduating annually.

An IMD journal, *Al Musiqa Wal Masrah* (*Music and Drama*) edited by Khalid al-Mubarak Mustafa published three issues in the 1980s but ceased for financial reasons.

There are no regular theatre reviewers in Sudan though graduates of the IMD and others review plays from time to time. Discussions are

Actor Mohammad Naeem Saad.

occasionally held after performances. Hashim Saddiq has presented a television programme entitled *Drama* and a similar programme exists on radio.

Numerous diploma dissertations are written at the IMD covering all aspects of Sudanese drama from television and radio performances to dissertations on left-wing theatre groups. As for theatre publishing, since 1958 only twelve plays have been printed in Sudan (plus seven printed abroad). Needless to say, there are no publishing houses that specialize in this field.

Khalid Al-Mubarak Mustafa

Further Reading

Al-Fadil, Amal. 'Alttarika Al Masrahiyya Fi Al Soudan' [Theatre practice in Sudan]. MA thesis, Omdurman University, Omdurman, 1978.

Ali Ibrahim, Abdullahi. *An Introduction to His Plays 'Al Jarh Wal Ghanoug*. Khartoum, 1986.

Ali Al-Waki, Uthman, and Saad Yusuf. *Al Haraka Al Masrahiyya Fi Assoudan*. Khartoum, 1979.

Filewod, Alan. 'Underdeveloped Alliance'. *Canadian Theatre Review* 53 (winter 1987): 39–42.

Hussain, M. Rida. *Al Drama Lil Huwat*. Khartoum, 1979.

Al-Mubarak Mustafa, Khalid. *Arabic Drama: A Critical Introduction*. Khartoum: Khartoum University Press, 1986.

——. *Harf Wa Nuqt'a*. Khartoum, 1980. 158 pp.

Al-Nisairi, Uthman Jaafar. *Al Masrah Fi Al Soudan 1905–1915*. [Theatre in Sudan 1905–1915]. Khartoum, 1969. 15 pp.

Rabha, M. Mahmoud. 'Masrah Al Arais fi Assoudan' [Arab theatre in Sudan]. Dissertation, Institute of Music and Drama, Khartoum, 1978.

Sinada, Makki. 'Al Masrah Al Soudan. Zawahiruhu Wa Qadayah'. Unpublished paper, 1979.

Al-Tayed, Ahmed. *Tarikh Al Fann Al Masrahi*. Edited by Uthman Hassan. Khartoum, 1984. 41 pp.

'Uthman, al-Fatih Mubarak. *Masrah Firqat al-Asdiqaa': Bayna l-Qawl al-Yawmi Wa l-Qawl al-Masrahi, ad-Dahiq wa Ma'zaq al-Marji'iyya: Masrahiyyat Bayaan Ragm Namudhhan* [The Asdiqaa' theatrical company: between what is said daily and what is said on the stage, laughter and the authority's predicament: the stage play proclamation of an exemplary number]. Khartoum: Nadi al-Masrah al-Sudani, 1989. 23 pp.

SYRIA

One of the longest continually inhabited parts of the world, the Middle Eastern land that is now called Syria – and more specifically its capital, Damascus – can trace its history back to approximately 5000 BC. Now bordered by Turkey to the north, Iraq to the east, Jordan and Israel to the south and Lebanon and the Mediterranean Sea to the west, the country has a land area of 185,180 square kilometres (71,500 square miles). The country's population in 1995 was 15.4 million with an annual growth rate of 3.6 per cent, one of the highest in the world. Arabic is the official language, and both English and French are widely understood. Of the 90 per cent of the population who are Muslims, three-quarters follow Sunni beliefs.

As a land bridge between Europe and Asia, Syria was a common historical stopping ground. Remnants of Phoenician, Assyrian, Hellenistic, Roman, Byzantine, Arab, Babylonian and Ottoman empires are scattered across the country in impressive ruins too numerous to mention by name. Indeed, some of them are ancient theatres.

In AD 636 Syria was conquered by the Arab peoples from across the Arabian peninsula and joined the growing Arabic-Islamic Empire. By the end of the eleventh century, however, the Christian Crusades reached the region and incorporated regions of Syria into their territorial spoils. The Crusaders were overthrown a century later and the country was ruled until 1516 by the Mameluks. After 1516 it became part of the Ottoman Empire where (linked with Lebanon, Palestine and Jordan) it remained until World War I. It was then that an alliance was established between Britain the Arabs and to help the area free itself of Ottoman control. Once free, however, Syria became a French mandate of the League of Nations (1922)

resulting in further control and deeper hostile feelings.

Nationalistic sentiments ultimately led to riots and strikes until independence was achieved in 1946. Syria then became a republic and a charter member of the United Nations. Political instability followed the creation of the new republic, though, and after several coups throughout the 1950s and 1960s, the Ba'th party came to power in 1963. In 1970, the then Defence Minister Hafiz al-Asad took political control, remaining in power through the late 1990s.

Even before the appearance of Roman colonists, Syria had its own performative events. The roots of Syrian performance can be found, as in Egypt and many other Arab countries, in storytelling and, to some extent, in shadow theatre. As well, one must recognize the extensive use of song and dance in folk celebrations and related traditions. All, however, connect back to the storyteller, known as *al-hakawati*; and the shadow theatre (with its many stories) known as *khayal al-zhil*. The storyteller was always given a place of honour when people congregated in cafés or houses. There *al-hakawati* would relate and enact popular sagas to his very enthusiastic listeners. The tale would often be interrupted by casual comments from the audience, which would side first with one character and then with another. The most important tales in the storyteller's repertoire were legends of historical characters and situations such as adh-Dhaahir Baybars, 'Antara Bin Shaddaad, az-Zeer Saalem, Hamza al-Bahlawaan (Hamza the Acrobat) and Bani Hilaal (The Hilaal Clan).

The shadow theatre, *khayal al-zhil*, seems to have emerged later and was flourishing during the Ottoman period where it connected to

Ottoman-style *karagöz*. In Damascus it was called *khaymat al-karakoz* (the clown's tent) because the *karakozaati* (clown) or *fannaan khayal al-zhil* (shadow theatre artist) would always begin by erecting a tent in or near a café. Shadows were thrown from the back onto a white screen by lanterns. The figures themselves were made of perforated and coloured leather (a material which would resist wear and tear and the passage of time) with hinged body parts connected by strings that were held by the *saahib khayal al-zhil* (master puppeteer) who would move them as needed. Accompanying the puppet's movements was a story in dialogue delivered by the *karakozaati*, who would change the tones and inflections of his voice to fit the different characters.

Though subjected to many alterations and improvisations, the texts of the *karagöz* stories were considered the property of the puppeteer himself and could be bequeathed by him, most often to his eldest male child whom he would train to take over the company. In the nineteenth-century directory *Qaamous as-Sinaa'aat ash-Shaamiyya (Damascan Industries Directory)*, al-Qaasimi considered the *khayal al-zhil* as a major industry which 'greatly flourishes in the winter time'. The money collected from the audience in the café would normally be divided into two portions, one half for the café owner, the other for the *karakozaati*.

Shadow theatre was widespread during the latter half of the nineteenth century, its subject matter rife with immoralities and scandalous sexual references. In fact, when the enlightened Ottoman governor, Midhat Pasha, the ruler in Damascus, was touring the city in 1878 to check on its spiritual and social affairs, he was shocked at the large number of cafés where such *karagöz* tales and sagas were performed. Midhat Pasha castigated the Damascan notables for the city's low level of morality and blamed them for attending performances with such shameful scenes and obscene utterances.

Another document to be cited as testimony to the importance of this art form and the role it played in social life was the politician Fakhri al-Baroudi's memoirs. Writing in the early twentieth century, he said,

> in our time, the intellectual recreation which all people go to see during Ramadan and children attended during the evenings the rest of the year [is the *karagöz*]. Other shadow theatre styles change their characters as the seasons, whereas the *karagöz* characters, who

appear every season, are permanent. These characters include Karagoz himself, the main character; al-Mudallal (The Pampered) who is the youngest; Quraytim al-Khayyal (Quraytim the Horseman), an Egyptian-speaking Arab; Abu Argeela Qashqo Bakri Mustafa; and Um Karagoz (Karagoz's Mother); and Karrash the donkey. . . . One of the most famous to practise this trade was Khalid Bin Habeeb whose father Habeeb was one of the most learned people in music and song.

The Habeeb family was probably the one that produced the most important of the *khayal al-zhil* artists in Syria and continued passing the techniques and secrets of this art form from generation to generation until those in the family practising shadow theatre ended in the 1950s. The family still possesses the marionettes, puppets, white screens and other paraphernalia, as well as the texts of the plays in copybooks. The latter use a special shorthand involving the insertion of symbols between the letters to render the document unreadable by anyone else.

The scripts presented in the shadow theatre were quite varied in subject matter, and so flexible in structure that improvisation and interaction with the concerns of audiences were a regular feature. Over the centuries, shadow theatre shows were repeatedly banned and the subject of police harassment (almost always under the pretext of obscenity, which usually meant simply overstepping the prevailing social norms). Another regular charge was disturbing the peace, which meant opposing the political status quo. During the time of French mandate, particularly, *khaymat al-karagoz* practitioners were exposed to regular and official harassment due to their stinging attacks on French colonialism and occupation, exactly what had occurred during the days of Ottoman rule.

During the latter half of the twentieth century, great efforts have been made to collect and publish what is still available of the many shadow theatre scripts. The *Majallat al-Hayaat al-Masrahiyya (Theatre Life Magazine)* – a Ministry of Culture quarterly founded in 1977 which specializes in theatre – has regularly published articles about shadow theatre groups, particularly those in Aleppo and in coastal areas.

A more literary theatre in Syria began to emerge toward the end of the eighteenth century, first done by those who came from abroad and later picked up by local amateurs.

Such early work became more varied in form during the nineteenth century. During this same period political and social relations with the west grew more complicated ranging from expanded commercial activities to interference in the affairs of the Ottoman government, from insisting on protection for religious minorities to an increase in the number of evangelizing missions. The opening of European-style schools were high on the agenda as western influence increased during the first decades of the nineteenth century. Most of those attending such schools believed that they could acquire from the west enlightenment and progress along with independence from the Ottoman government. Perhaps naïvely, they also hoped to acquire those things without bringing upon themselves the ordeal of still another colonial master. Clearly, the power of Enlightenment philosophy and the apparent scientific and material progress of the west obscured any sense of political danger. At the same time the indigenous population saw a dissolution of religious and military feudalism, elements that had been used to dominate Arab provinces during the Ottoman Empire. As all this occurred, a bourgeoisie began to gradually emerge. Along with it came a wide range of new ideas about the nature of the state, the nature of society and particularly about the nature of culture.

The growth of such elemental changes set a positive environment for the birth of a literary theatre. The first major theatrical initiative was taken by Marun al-Naqqash (1817–55), a cultured businessman who studied languages and various art forms and who travelled widely both for business and his own general education. On one of his visits to Italy, he attended several plays, an art form that impressed him for its ability to reach a wide popular public as well as to foment social change. Al-Naqqash, a native of Sidon (in present-day Lebanon), returned home and organized the first public presentation of an Arabic stage play in Beirut. Well aware of the cultural importance of his work as well as its pioneering nature, he sought not just to copy western theatre but to plant and cultivate it in a variety of ways.

In a statement written for that first production, he delineated his objectives very carefully declaring that he was presenting his audience with 'foreign gold cast in an Arab mould'. From that point of view, it is possible to understand his first two plays – al-Bakhil (The Miser), which is not an adaptation of Molière's L'Avare, and an adaptation of several popular tales in the stage play Abu'l-Hasan al-Mughaffal (Abu'l-Hasan the Fool). His productions included dance and song and improvised comedy. In such a mix, al-Naqqash was offering his own unique solution to the problem of cultivating a new art form in a traditional Arabic environment. Those theatrical pioneers who followed him had to find their own solutions to that same problem. A century and a half later it can be said that many of al-Naqqash's ideas are still relevant in terms of freshness and the depth of their perspectives.

The dreams of al-Naqqash to establish a professional theatre in Syria were in truth never equalled by the reality of his on-stage productions and late in his life he became pessimistic and perhaps even bitter. Indeed he called the creation of such a theatre in Syria at that time 'something farfetched'. Nevertheless, after his death others stepped in to carry the dream to the next level. One of those was ash-Sheikh Ahmad Abu Khalil al-Qabbaani (c.1833–1902) who worked in Damascus, a city which had earlier seen a number of visiting foreign companies from Egypt. As well, western plays had been studied in schools.

The initial efforts of al-Qabbaani were built around the idea of establishing a more or less permanent company in the capital. A student of languages and religious studies, al-Qabbaani pursued in his early years a career in commerce but at the same time he also worked on developing his musical and singing talents. He became particularly well known for his singing of al-muwash-shahaat (a vocalized verse form of Terza Rima) and the music for raqs as-samaah (samaah dance) to the point that his business affairs began to take second place in his life. There is little information about how al-Qabbaani's interest in theatre was developed. It may well have come about as a result of his awareness of al-Naqqash's work or from attending performances presented by visiting theatrical companies or even by some school theatre he was in. What is sure is that his musical talents led him to embellish his own stage productions with vocal music. In this sense, he can be considered as well as one of the important pioneers in music theatre in the Arab world.

Some theatre historians have suggested that 1865 was the real beginning of al-Qabbaani's theatrical work. During that year, he gathered around him a number of his friends and joined them in rehearsing a stage play titled Naakir al-Jameel (The Ingrate). Performed in his grandfather's house for an audience composed of friends and relatives, the positive reaction to the performance encouraged him to continue his work. Some time later he presented a second production entitled *Waddaah* (*The Conspicuous One*) in a café. The audience was again impressed with his performance and the fact that this new art was being presented by one of their own. For both productions, al-Qabbaani wrote the script, directed, acted, composed tunes and trained singers in addition to performing most of the organizational and administrative tasks.

Al-Qabbaani continued his work during the administration of Midhat Pasha, the enlightened Ottoman *waali* (provincial ruler), who brought about many significant cultural reforms in Damascus. In this instance, Midhat Pasha encouraged al-Qabbaani to establish a permanent theatre, offering not only financial assistance, but also moral support. Al-Qabbaani had apparently been waiting for such an opportunity and quickly sold off his business and established his theatre in the section of Damascus called Khaan al-Jumruk (Customs Quarters). The new theatre cost him all the money he had. In that theatre, he presented a number of his most important performances including *Abu' l-Hasan al-Mughaffal* (*Abu' l-Hasan the Fool*). These were huge successes, and al-Qabbaani's theatre became a phenomenon and one that greatly influenced Damascus social life as attested to by large audiences and the intense resentment of conservative *mashaayikh* (religious leaders) who quickly lined up to attack the new art.

Indeed, almost from the moment that Midhat Pasha stepped down as ruler of Damascus in 1879, the *mashaayikh*, led by Sa'eed al-Ghabraa', petitioned the Ottoman sultan decrying the theatre and requesting its banning. Ash-Shaikh Sa'eed al-Ghabraa took the petition with him to Istanbul and, as he stood facing the sultan, shouted, 'Help us O Prince of the Faithful! Immorality and debauchery are rampant in Damascus, dignity and good reputation have been violated, virtue is dead, honour has been buried alive and men and women are mixing socially.' The sultan soon issued a decree closing al-Qabbaani's theatre, but the reactionaries were still not satisfied. They had it burned to the ground, inciting their followers to such acts and rendering al-Qabbaani's existence in Damascus virtually impossible. He soon left for the city of Homs, where, for a while, he worked with his company and some of the enlightened people from there such as Dawoud Qustanteen al-Khouri before moving finally to

Egypt, where he resumed his theatrical work without such pressures. Thus did religious and cultural reactionaries, with a violence approaching terrorism, kill a major attempt at establishing a literary theatre in Syria.

Interestingly, a reading of al-Qabbaani's eight plays reveals nothing that could or should have provoked such strong reactions. In fact, the emergence of such a theatre was part of a Syrian enlightenment movement, a renaissance which empowered the new middle class. This was at the root of the anti-theatre reaction. The fact that al-Qabbaani also introduced dancing and singing into his presentations and took most of his subject matter from popular tales – especially from *The Thousand and One Nights* – just made it all the more popular. He also left room in his productions for improvisation and interaction with audiences. Thus, the theatrical presentation became a social event in which the audience learned to become active and socially critical. In that fertile milieu, the theatre's power began to manifest itself as a force for change, thus increasing the irritation of the religious right.

The argument was made that because acting provides a representation of what should remain an elevated mental picture, the mere presence of represented kings and princes on a stage can diminish their stature and dignity. An actor's slip of the tongue may render a king laughable or a prince ridiculous. Such elements, which are part of the nature of theatrical performances and not necessarily even within scripts, were among the things that most worried conservative thinkers and led them to argue that theatre was a fierce enemy that needed to be confronted.

Al-Qabbaani's amateur performances continued from 1865 until about 1878 on a regular basis and then on an occasional basis until 1881, the year his theatre was burned down.

In total, he authored or adapted fifteen scripts of which eight are extant. These include *Haroun ar-Rasheed Ma' al-Ameer Ghaanim Bin Ayyoub Wa Qout al-Quloub* (*Haroun ar-Rasheed with Prince Ghaanim Bin Ayyoub and Qout al-Quloub*); *Haroun ar-Rasheed Ma' Uns al-Jalees* (*Haroun ar-Rasheed with Uns al-Jalees*) and *al-Ameer Mahmoud Najl Shaah al-'Ajam* (*Prince Mahmoud the Son of the Persian Shah*), inspired by and derived from *The Thousand and One Nights*; *'Antar Bin Shaddaad*, inspired by a popular biography; *Metridaat Aw Lubaab al-Gharaam* (*Metridat or The Heart of Passion*) by Racine; *Hiyal an-Nisaa' ash-Shaheera* (*The Famous Ploys of Women*) based on a work by Blusia; *Junfiyaf Ameerat al-'Afaaf* (*Genevieve*

the Princess of Chastity); and Naakir al-Jameel
(The Ingrate).

In the early decades of the twentieth century,
despite continuing religious pressure, amateur
groups continued to emerge, groups which were
encouraged significantly by French authorities
during their colonial stay in the country between
the 1920s and 1940s. These decades were also a
time when authors and artists generally began to
realize the importance of developing a national
culture, particularly one that would reflect the
Arab character of the country, articulate its
problems and express its ambitions. Although
the fruits of that endeavour did not appear until
the 1950s, such development became a national
obsession.

After World War II, there was an obvious
increase in the number of plays dealing with
loyalty, courage and allegiance to national
ideals. Many were presented by an-Naadi al-
Fanni (Artistic Club) in Damascus, one of the
many amateur clubs that by this time could be
called semi-professional. That is, though all the
actors were officially amateurs holding other
jobs, they presented their productions on a
regular basis (every week or every two weeks and
for special occasions or celebrations) generating
income by selling tickets to employees of government institutions, merchants and the social elite.

Another well-known club was Ma'had al-
Aadaab Wa al-Funoun (Arts and Literature
Institute), established in 1948. By the mid-
1950s, most of the members of this club had left
to join another club, an-Naadi ash-Sharqi
(Eastern Club) which had itself been established
in 1954. The newer club played an important
role in energizing the theatrical movement. By
the 1960s, it was even offering classes to its
members, many of whom subsequently opted
for professional careers. Among those who later
established such professional careers were
Nouhaad Qala'i (b. 1928), Mahmoud Jabr (b.
1935), Khaldoun al-Maleh (b. 1938) and
Mohammed Shaheen (b. 1931). Plays of import
done by the Eastern Club included al-Ustath
Klinof (Mr Klinof) – written by Bramson,
adapted and directed by Shaheen and Thaman
al-Hurriyya (The Price of Liberty) – written by
Robles, adapted by Zuhair Baraq (b. 1933) and
directed by Shaheen.

In general, the club was staging mostly foreign
plays from the international repertoire but
almost all were adapted to the local reality deep-
ening their impact. Indeed, the importance of
the Eastern Club was partly because it was able
to 'Syrianize' its plays. As well, the club used a

local accent in its productions rather than the
Egyptian dialect used by all actors to that time in
imitation of Najib al-Rihani (1892–1949), an
Egyptian actor of Syrian origins, who created
the theatrical character known as Kishkish Bek.
This character was so well known and loved
that many Syrian actors used to compete in
imitating him.

Credit for 'Syrianizing' the theatre must more
specifically go to the man who was among the
first to become a professional actor in Syria,
'Abd ul-Lateef Fat-hi (1916–85). Fat-hi realized
early in his career that the Syrian theatre must
acquire its own characteristics and special features and not simply imitate the theatre of other
countries if it wanted to draw in Syrian audiences. This interest made him a natural choice to
become the first manager of al-Masrah ash-
Sha'bi (The People's Theatre), the first government-sponsored theatre, which operated from
1964 to 1970 when it was merged with al-
Masrah al-Qawmi (National Theatre).

The spread of clubs and theatrical companies
was not limited to Damascus. The city of
Aleppo, the second largest city in Syria, also
boasted a number of groups, the most famous
of which was Firqat al-Masrah ash-Sha'bi
(also called the People's Theatre company).
Established in 1956, the group boasted two
actors who went on to major careers: Ahmad
'Adaas (b. 1924) and Bashār al-Qādi (b. 1934).
These two actors later moved to the capital as
their careers evolved. They were soon followed
by two actresses, the sisters Thanaa' Dibsi (b.
1941) and Tharaa' Dibsi (b. 1944), among the
first women to become professional actresses in
the country.

During the 1950s, the dream of most theatre
people was to establish a national theatre. In
1958, with the creation of the United Arab
Republic initiated by Syria and led by Egypt, a
Ministry of Culture was at long last begun and
along with it came the beginning of a real pro-
fessionalization and the hoped-for national
theatre. This was the beginning of a golden age
for Syrian theatre. Audiences increased for
theatre generally and serious new plays began to
be seen which mirrored the country's numerous
social and political changes.

At the same time, theatre artists began to
enjoy steady incomes while working in an
atmosphere that was more secure than ever,
more settled and more humane. Their work was
even part of a coherent cultural plan, far different from their previous individuated tribulations
and chaotic lives and their work for private

companies which were always at the mercy of the owners of theatre buildings, financial backers and producers. The theatre itself suddenly became more than a social event and professional careers were no longer looked upon as something dubious. Theatre was at long last seen as being part of both the culture and the national economy.

In 1959, a series of meetings between the directors of the major cultural clubs and theatrical companies, and officials of the Arts Directorate (whose specific function within the Ministry of Culture was to take care of all artistic endeavours whether theatrical or musical) resulted in the creation of a new company which would be attached to the Ministry of Culture. It was that company which was the core of the National Theatre. Based in Damascus, the actors in this company would, for the first time, be employees of the government.

One must mention here that when the National Theatre was established by the government in 1960, it was one of two theatre groups to receive state funding. The other was al-Masrah al-'Askari (Military Theatre) funded by the Army Political Guidance Administration. Among those who joined this theatre were several established amateur and professional actors such as Ahmed Ayyoub (b. 1912), Sa'd ud-Deen Baqdounis (b. 1924), Mahmoud Jabr and Mona Waasif. Unfortunately, this theatre did not have a clear concept of such things as script selection or audience preferences. In 1961, the company presented three performances (all directed by Mohammed Shaheen) – al-Aydi an-Naa'ima (The Soft Hands) by Tawfiq al-Hakīm, al-Lusous (The Robbers) by Schiller and al-'Itr al-Akhdar (The Green Perfume) by an unknown playwright. In 1962, al-Masrah al-'Askari presented Ufoul al-Qamar (The Moon is Down) by Steinbeck and Makhlab al-Qutta (The Cat's Claw) by Golden Smith, and, under the direction of Shaheen, the company performed Tabeebun Raghma Anfihi (Le Médecin Malgré lui or The Doctor in Spite of Himself) by Molière. The Military Theatre, like the National, ultimately depended on the production of foreign scripts, most presented without any change of text or locale.

From the 1960s, the Ministry of Culture began to show new interest in encouraging local playwriting. As a result of that interest, a playwriting contest was organized by al-Majlis al-A'la lil-Aadaab (The Arts Council) with a number of interesting scripts emerging from this initiative.

By the beginning of the 1970s, the theatre-on-tour division of al-Masrah al-'Askari began to show signs of rejuvenation. This division, which normally offered presentations of variety shows and short plays in military and assembly centres, began to present performances in the form of evening parties where interaction with the audience was direct and quite often interlaced with improvised dialogues with the spectators. Along with this development, directors with an academic background began to join the theatre as a way to fulfil their compulsory military service. Among them were Hasan 'Uwayni (b. 1942) who in 1974 directed Laylat al-Qatl (The Night of Murder) by Michael Roman; Manuel Jiji (b. 1946) who directed al-Musta'sim al-Jadeed (The New Musta'sim) by Safwaan 'Akki and Jaasim al-Khaalid by Nadeem Mu'alla Mohammed, both in 1978; Fouad ar-Raashid (b. 1943) who directed Insu Hirositraat (Forget Hirositraat, 1978) by Gregory Goren; Tawfik al-Mu'adhthin (b. 1944) who staged Domer 'Aashiqan (Domer in Love, 1979) by Mohyi ud-Deen al-Baraad'i; and Sa'eed Jokhdaar who directed Deek al-Jinn (1980). In 1982, the Military Theatre's last production opened – al-Marhoum (The Deceased), written by Branislav Noshlitch and directed by Manuel Jiji.

Following the lead of the national government, the Municipality of Aleppo also gave support to the creation of a theatre in 1968. First called Masrah ash-Sha'b (People's Theatre), in 1980 it changed its name to the National Theatre of Aleppo. Chosen to run the new theatre by the Ministry of Culture was Husain Idilbi (b. 1939) who had done his theatrical studies in Austria. The company opened on Christmas night 1968 with Habata al-Malaak Fi Baabil (The Angel Descended in Babel) by Friedrich Dürrenmatt.

A further storm of debate over the theatre's social role emerged with the creation of al-Masrah at-Tajreebi (Experimental Theatre), a group established in 1976 by playwright Sa'dallah Wanous and director Fawwāz as-Sāhir. This company sought to create a more direct theatre language and presentational style utilizing feedback and ongoing social research. Al-Masrah at-Tajreebi strove to do away with the proscenium arch, changing as well the internal architecture of the theatre. The goal was to find an Arabic working style that would be recognizable to audiences as well as distinct from European forms. For its first production in 1977, the company presented Wanous's Arabic adaptation of Gogol's Yawmiyyat Majnoun

(*Diary of a Madman*). The first productions, however, revealed no significant changes in style. By 1979, however, for the group's production of *Rihlat Handhala* (*The Journey of Handhala*) the seats were brought closer to the stage and by 1980, the stage was completely removed for Osvaldo Dragun's *Thalaath Hikaayaat* (*Three Stories*).

The company began to emphasize 'spectacle' allowing significant room for improvisation. The subject of all its plays was consistently that of the little man and the economic and social conditions which caused his suffering and daily miseries. After three productions, however, the company ceased operations for lack of funds. The new theatrical language that was being sought required financial support to retrain actors and to restructure the theatre building; it also needed a much greater commitment within the society towards real freedom of speech.

The torch of experiment was soon passed onto a new private company, Firqat al-Mukhtabar al-Masrahi (Theatre Workshop Company) which included two key members of the former company – actor Zinaati Qudsiyya (b. 1947) and director Waleed al-Quwatli (b. 1939). In 1978, the new group staged *Qissat Hadeeqat al-Hayawaan* (*Zoo Story*), a production of the play by Edward Albee done in the 'poor theatre' style using a virtually empty stage and an emphasis on the actor's physical and vocal skills. That presentation met with an unexpected success, due in great measure to the subject matter of the piece: isolation and consumerism.

Through the 1970s, an increase in the number of plays by Syrian writers could be clearly seen even at the National Theatre, which staged plays by Sidqi Isma'eel (1924–84) and Wanous. The former was known both in the field of literature and literary criticism and his play *Ayyaam Salamoun* (*Solomon's Days*) was presented by the National Theatre in 1972 while Wanous's play *Sahra Ma' Abi Khaleel al-Qabbaani* (*An Evening With Abi Khaleel al-Qabbaani*) was presented at the National Theatre in 1974. Other Syrian writers whose work was presented at the National Theatre at this time included Farhan Bulbul, whose play *al-Mumathiloun Yataraashaqoun al-Hijaara* (*Actors Throwing Stones at Each Other*) was presented in 1975; Riyaad 'Ismat, whose play *Lu'bat al-Hub Wa th-Thawra* (*The Game of Love and Revolution*) was presented in 1976; and Mamdouh 'Idwaan, whose play *Hamlet Yastayqidh Muta'kh-khiran* (*Hamlet Wakes Up Late*) was presented in

1978. During this period, Syrian plays tended by and large to be political, something which attracted audiences particularly because of the ongoing Arab–Israeli struggle and the effect of that struggle on the internal conditions in the country.

At the same time, a new generation of directors entered the theatre armed with academic degrees and the experiences and plays they had seen in the countries where they had studied (most had graduated from theatre schools in the former Soviet Union and Bulgaria). The professional path facing these newly graduated directors was not easy. Most had to combat both bureaucratic and career obstacles, a state of affairs that prevented most from getting any start at all. Some of those whose careers were already established argued that it was still too early for this group of young directors to join the National Theatre and so that influential door was closed to them. Most, therefore, went in other ways: some simply gave up while the others knocked on every door they could find and accepted every job that was offered whether in youth companies, university companies or amateur workers' groups.

Probably the most distinguished director from this generation was Fawwāz as-Sāhir (1948–88) who had studied theatrical direction at the GITIS Institute in Moscow with one of Stanislavski's former students. First working at al-Masrah al-Jaami'i (University Theatre) then at Masrah ash-Sha'b (People's Theatre) in Aleppo, as-Sāhir staged important productions, such as *Haleeb ad-Duyouf* (*Milk for Guests*), a play by the Moroccan playwright Ahmad at-Tayyib al-Balah. He subsequently moved to the capital where he staged at al-Masrah al-Jaami'i in 1975 a trio of scripts by the Argentine Osvaldo Dragun and two Syrian writers, Mamdouh 'Idwaan and Riyaad under the collective title *Nakoun Aw La Nakoun* (*To Be or Not To Be*). The successful and always controversial works of as-Sāhir attracted wide attention at the University Theatre. In 1976, he did *Rasoul Min Qarya* (*An Emissary from a Village*), by the Egyptian writer Mahmud Diyab, a provocative play about war and peace. As-Sāhir's theatrical work passed through a variety of phases, most specifically from a theatricalized event with the director in total control to later productions that depended heavily on the actor and script. Among his successful productions in this latter phase was William Saroyan's *Sukkaan al-Kahf* (*Cave Dwellers*) in 1988.

Another influential director was Naa-ila al-

Atrash (b. 1949), who had studied in Bulgaria. She found, as most of her colleagues did, that the University Theatre was the place to offer her an opportunity to express and prove her skills. In 1974, she staged *Fi Intihaar Godot* (*Waiting for Godot*) in an adaptation by Mamdouh 'Idwaan. She also presented 'Idwaan's *Lail al-'Abeed* (*Night of the Slaves*) in 1977 and Alfred Faraj's *az-Zeer Saalem* in 1984. Other important directors from this generation were Hasan 'Uwaiti (b. 1942), who had also studied in Bulgaria, Mahmoud Khudour (b. 1946) and Manuel Jiji (b. 1946). 'Uwaiti's major productions at this time included Mahmud Diyab's *Idhbatou as-Saa'aat* (*Correct the Watches*), in the National Theatre in 1973, 'Idwaan's *az-Ziyaara* (*The Visit*) in 1980 and Waleed Ikhlaasi's *Qatl al-'Asaafeer* (*Bird Killing*) in 1984. Khudour's most important shows were *Hamlet Yastayqith Muta-akhiran* (*Hamlet Wakes Up Late*, 1977) by Mamdouh 'Idwaan and the Dale Wasserman musical *Man of La Mancha* (*Rajul al-Mancha*, 1979) adapted by 'Idwaan. Jiji worked mostly with the Military Theatre and his important productions included *Unshoudat Angola* (*The Lusitanian Bogey*, 1981) by Peter Weiss and *al-Um* (*The Mother*, 1982) by Brecht.

Along with an increase in serious scripts and major productions in the 1980s there was also an enormous growth in the number of commercial theatre productions. Indeed, commercial companies grew not only in the capital, but also in the provinces. These theatres dealt with political subjects but added in sexual titillation, broad comedy and even dance. Though popular, the general level of work was not particularly high.

Two such commercial theatrical companies, out of the many which began, stand out, however. Both are predominantly family-owned enterprises and both continue operating in the 1990s. The first, Firqat Dabaabees (Needles Company), was begun in 1973 by the Qanou' family. The company's resident playwright, Ahmad Qanou' (1937–96), has said that his group was influenced by the Thorns Theatre, and that the name of the company Dabaabees (Needles) is quite close in meaning to the word Shawk (Thorns). Some of their most successful shows have been *Sawaareekh* (*Missiles*, 1975), *al-'Izz lir-Rizz* (*Power to the High Ranking*, 1979), *al-Manaafeekh* (*The Pumps*, 1977) and *Qisma Wa Naseeb* (*Fate and Luck*, 1985).

A second private group of note established in 1997 is Firqat Mahmoud Jabr (Mahmoud Jabr Company) the name being that of its leading actor, who also writes and directs. Among the major productions of this group have been *an-Nahb* (*The Looting*, 1977), *Hammaam Maqtou'a Maytu* (*A Bath Without Running Water*, 1979) and *al-Mu'allim* (*The Teacher*, 1979).

Generally done in the local dialect, commercial productions can and do run for several years. One such example was the hit play by Ahmed Qblaawi's *Laylat Uns* (*An Evening's Entertainment*, 1984), which was first presented under the direction of Hishaam Shirbatji.

By the end of the 1980s and into the 1990s, the number of performances of plays has declined and few new companies have emerged. The National Theatre now rarely stages more than two or three shows a season. A stagnation in Syrian theatre is evident. As a result, the National Theatre's actors have begun to move towards television serials. Nevertheless, the Syrian entertainment industry – specifically television and cinema – has increased in production of both local television serials and movies. The loss of playwright Sa'dallah Wanous to cancer in 1997 added to the general diminution of an already weakened theatre community.

Structure of the National Theatre Community

There are dozens of theatres in Syria ranging from the government-supported National Theatre in Damascus to municipally supported theatres such as the National Theatre of Aleppo. There are professional theatres with long and distinguished histories and smaller experimental groups which come and go in relatively short periods of time. Commercial groups also exist, mostly in Damascus which is still the centre of Syrian culture and has the largest number of official theatrical companies (those subsidized by the government), as well as most of the private and commercial companies.

The official theatrical companies include Firqat al-Masrah al-Qawmi (National Theatre), Firqat al-Masrah al-Jawwaal (Theatre-on-Tour

SYRIA

Company) and Firqat al-Masrah al-'Askari (Military Theatre Company).

Among the private companies, it is difficult to ascertain an exact number because most of them come and go far too quickly. These companies are often named for their owners, the families involved or the leading actors. The most established of these groups are Firqat Mahmoud Jabr (Mahmoud Jabr's Company), Firqat Tishreen (October Company) and Firqat Dabaabees (Needles Company).

Located in northern Syria, the city of Aleppo, which is the largest and most important city after Damascus, has one official company, Firqat al-Masrah al-Qawmi (National Theatre

of Aleppo) in addition to several privately owned theatrical companies. In the coastal city of Latakia, there is a National Theatre Company subsidiary. In the city of Homs, there are two companies, one connected to the Cultural Centre there and the other called Firqat al-Masrah al-'Ummaali (Workers' Theatre).

The Damascus Festival is the most important theatre festival in the country and among the most important in the Arab world. A biennial event, it now alternates years of operation with Tunisia's Carthage Festival. The annual Mahrajaan Basra lil-Funoun ash-Sha'biyya (Basra Folklore Arts Festival) is held every year in September.

Artistic Profile

Companies
Dramaturgy
Directors, Directing and Production Styles

Rafeeq as-Sabban (b. 1931) was the National Theatre's first director-manager when the company was created in 1960. His background was impressive: he had studied law in France and nurtured a personal interest in the cinema and theatre. On his return to Syria, rather than practising law, he concentrated all his efforts on artistic activities especially the theatre. Under as-Sabbaan, the leadership of the new theatre took as one of its first responsibilities to train audiences to enable them to better appreciate new theatrical styles and ideas. To that end, the National Theatre's repertoire, during its first season, included a number of works that had never before been seen in Syria including works by Aristophanes, Molière, Albert Camus and two Egyptian playwrights, Tawfiq al-Hakīm and Mahmud Taymur. The company's first two performances, presented in February 1960, were Braksajoura (an adaptation of an Aristophanes play by al-Hakīm and directed by Rafeeq as-Sabbaan) and al-Muzayyafoun (The Phony), written by Mahmud Taymur and directed by Nouhaad Qala'i. Trying to act as a bridge between the international theatre and a local audience whose theatrical knowledge was still in its developmental stages, they were careful to offer a well-balanced assortment of what they considered to be international theatre.

In 1961, as-Sabban established Nudwat al-

Fikr Wal-Fann (Intellectual and Artistic Circle). Composed mostly of younger company members, it began arguing for a greater emphasis on western classics to make audiences more appreciative of the history of the theatre. It was ultimately funded to present plays such as Sophocles' Antigone, Shakespeare's The Merchant of Venice, Julius Caesar and Twelfth Night, and performances of Molière's an-Nisaa' al-Mutahadhliqaat (Les Précieuses ridicules). By the mid-1960s, the focus of the group became a bit more contemporary and plays by Shaw began to be seen such as Rajul ul-Aqdaar (Man of Destiny).

The Nudwat al-Fikr Wa'l-Fann separated from the parent company in 1963, re-establishing itself as Firqat al-Funoun ad-Draamiyya lit-Talivizion (Theatre Arts for Television Company) and staging a number of previously successful plays while adding into the mix new plays such as as-Sultaan al-Haa'ir (The Bewildered Sultan) by Tawfik al-Hakīm, Banaadiq al-Um Karaar (Señora Carrara's Rifles) by Brecht, Macbeth by Shakespeare, al-Khajoul Fi al-Qasr (The Bashful in the Palace) by Tirso de Molina and al-Jilf (The Boor) by Chekhov.

After the departure of Sabban, the Ministry of Culture hired the Jordanian director, Hani' Snobir, who had studied theatrical direction in the United States, to run the National Theatre. Among Snobir's major productions were Abtaal Jadduna (Our Grandfather's Heroes) by the Egyptian playwright Ya'qoub ash-Sharouni,

Shitra by Rabindranath Tagore, *al-Mufattish* (*The Government Inspector*) by Gogol, *al-Ashbaah* (*Ghosts*) by Ibsen and *Rajul al-Aqdaar* (*Man of Destiny*) by Shaw. It should be noted that during this period the National Theatre continued to present a mix of plays from various countries and periods.

Around this same time, the first group of Syrian actors and directors who had gone to Egypt to study at the Higher Institute of Dramatic Arts in Cairo returned to Damascus. All joined the National Theatre on their return. Among these were 'Ali 'Uqla 'Irsaan (b. 1940), As'ad Fudda (b. 1938) and Khudr ash-Sha'-'aar (b. 1939). They brought with them scripts they had rehearsed and performed as part of their studies, including plays by such internationally known authors as Ben Jonson and Tennessee Williams (*Volpone* and *The Glass Menagerie* among others.) These younger actors and directors, following along the path that had been trodden before them, emulated their predecessors in their belief that their main function was to build a bridge between western theatre and Syrian audiences. None really paid attention to local realities or to the limitations of such viewpoints and none showed any real interest in the production of Syrian plays.

It is worth noting that those who were directing the National Theatre had no particular dramaturgical experience. This is certainly clear from the types of plays produced (consecutively) at one point in the mid-1960s: *al-'Aadiloun* (*Les Justes/The Just*) by Albert Camus, *Hiwaayat al-Hayawanaat az-Zujaajiyya* (*The Glass Menagerie*) by Tennessee Williams, *Mirwahat al-Laydi Windarmeer* (*Lady Windermere's Fan*) by Oscar Wilde and *Madrasat al-Fadaa'ih* (*The School for Scandal*) by Sheridan.

Despite the fact that Syria in the 1960s witnessed a thunderstorm of political, social and economic changes, that the decade was one in which a new social class, with peasant and blue-collar origins, rose to positions of authority, and that for the first time ever the Syrian government was taking an interest in culture, the National Theatre seemed totally unconcerned with what was occurring. It is not an exaggeration to say that the National Theatre at this point in its development isolated itself from contemporary Syrian life. As a result, most of the important growth and experimentation in the Syrian theatre in the decade of the 1960s emanated not from the National but from the many privately owned companies operating in Damascus.

One such group was Firqat al-Masrah (Theatre Company) which was established in 1969 by playwright Sa'dallah Wanous (1941–97). Wanous was a graduate of Cairo University where he studied literature and later worked in journalism. After completing theatrical studies in France, he began writing plays. The company also included directors 'Alaa' ud-Deen Kawkash (b. 1942), Haani ar-Roumaani, Yousef Hanna and Usaama ar-Roumaani.

Three plays by Wanous highlighted the first seasons of the new company – *Haflat Samar Min Ajl 5 Huzairaan* (*An Evening's Entertainment for 5 June*, written in 1968), *al-Feel Ya Malik uz-Zamaan* (*The Elephant O King of All Times*, 1970) and *Mughaamarat Ra's al-Mamlouk Jaabir* (*The Adventure of Jaabir the Slave*, 1970). The first was probably the most important of the three for that play dealt with the subject of the 1967 Six Day War against Israel, a defeat for the Arab cause. His suggestion was that it was a defeat only for those who ruled the country and not a defeat for the people. The play caused an intense controversy – both for its content and its form, a controversy never seen before or since in any Arab country.

Wanous's *The Adventure of Jaabir the Slave* was also unique in its attempt to create a new form of Arab theatre (as opposed to imitating European forms) modelling itself on popular Arab storytelling. Transforming a café into a theatre, the story being told to those around the narrator in this case was a political allegory, one which marked the real beginning of political theatre in Syria. The company had a clear and distinct viewpoint both about society and theatre and the means by which an effective and original theatre could be achieved. Along with writing such plays, Wanous also published a number of theatrical manifestos (later collected and published in *al-Ma'rifa* (*Review*, issue 104, 1970) and later as a book under the title *Bayanaat li-Masrah 'Arabi Jadeed* (*Manifestos for a New Arab Theatre*). The manifestos called for politicizing the theatre, inciting the audience to action, initiating direct dialogue, enlightening them about fundamental issues and urging them to take a stand on such issues. His company, however, eventually ceased operation because of a lack of ongoing funding and continuing problems caused by censorship.

By 1969, a new company emerged determined to focus its work on social issues – Masrah ash-Shawk (Theatre of Thorns). Determined to 'provoke' its audiences and to prick its conscience, the group's first performance was given at the

Soviet Cultural Centre in Damascus. Run by 'Umar Hijju and Duraid Lahhaam, the latter a well-known film and television actor, Masrah ash-Shawk performances were typically composed of several pieces, with almost no connection between them, dealing in a critical manner with such issues as bureaucracy, suppression, cheating, misrepresentation and political abuse. Their performances rarely utilized scenery, props or theatrical effects; in fact, the stage was almost empty except for placards which would provide information or commentary. Such an unusual approach to the work caused an uproar and heated discussions during the first Damascus Theatre Arts Festival, held in May 1969, a festival which attracted groups from not only Syria but also Lebanon, Jordan, Kuwait and Egypt (the festival now alternates biennially with Tunisia's Carthage Festival). Also in attendance were groups from the Democratic Republic of Germany, the Soviet Union and Bulgaria.

Masrah ash-Shawk was simply a protest against a social reality rife with crises and problems. Any resemblance between the Masrah ash-Shawk's work and that of other groups mentioned is probably purely coincidental. Hijju, for example, was neither an academic nor an artist, and had never studied the theatre. Rather he was someone with genuine social concerns. Others who joined him – writers and artists such as Zakariyya Taamir, 'Alaa' ud-Deen Kawkash and Sa'dallah Wanous – were the ones with a theatrical background but they too saw the value of social provocation. Unfortunately, the work quickly lost its sharpness and became little more than provocation without an effective theatricality.

The National Theatre of Aleppo from its creation in 1968 presented two or three productions each year. In 1969, it presented its first Syrian play, *al-Ayyaam allati Nansaaha (The Days That We Forget)* by Waleed Ikhlaasi (b. 1935) and directed by Husain Idilbi and *'Ali Janah at-Tabrizi Wa Taabi'ahu Quffa (Ali Janah at-Tabrizi and His Servant Quffa)* by Egyptian dramatist Alfred Faraj and directed by Bashār al-Qādi. Later productions ranged from Chekhov, *Kayf Tas'ad Doun An Taqa' (How to Ascend without Falling)* to other plays by Ikhlaasi and *Haleeb ad-Duyouf (Milk for Guests)* by the Moroccan playwright at-Tayyib al-'Ilj and directed by Fawwāz as-Sāhir.

It is noteworthy that those in responsible positions in the theatre realized the importance of presenting plays in Arabic and in the local dialect at a time which could be described as representing the rise of the Syrian script. Unfortunately, the scripts of the many international plays seemed, generally speaking, randomly chosen. The playwright Ikhlaasi played an important and positive role in the life of the People's Theatre. The presence of Arabic scripts in general and Syrian ones in particular could be attributed to the efforts exerted by Waleed Ikhlaasi. In 1976, however, the activities of the theatre ceased when the Municipality of Aleppo abandoned its financial support. In 1980, though, it was reopened under the name Masrah Halab al-Qawmi (Aleppo National Theatre) after it had won sponsorship from the Ministry of Culture.

Another group to begin operations at this time was Firqat al-Masrah al-Jawwaal (Theatre-on-Tour Company), which was established in 1970 also under the sponsorship of the Ministry of Culture. Determined to effect a change in the relationship between theatre and audience, the theatre took its productions to factories and farming communities. To this end, director 'Alaa' Kawkash, actor 'Umar Hijju and their small company toured the villages of southern Syria living in the various communities. After listening to the stories and problems of the people in these communities, they returned to Damascus where they created stylized documentary plays about their experiences. One such was scripted for the group by playwright Sa'dallah Wanous. From its official inauguration in 1971, the Theatre-on-Tour Company set up its productions to encourage interaction with the audiences. Many such shows led to enthusiastic debates among the communities watching them. Unfortunately, by the late 1970s the group ceased touring rural areas and instead began offering one or two productions in the major towns each year. Indeed, its repertoire, which began to include productions of Molière, soon became indistinguishable from that of the National Theatre.

Another company of note from this period was Firqat al-Maqha (Café Company), a group established and led by the playwright Ahmed Qablaawi (1937–84) and the actor Talhat Hamdi (b. 1940). Firqat al-Maqha attempted to find its niche between the National Theatre and the various commercial groups that had also sprung up at this time. The company utilized a café format and for a time it had a real following, but by 1976 it had ceased operations. Among its important collective creations during its short life were its 1972 play, *al-'Umr Ilkum Maat (May You Live Long, He Is Dead)*, *Awwal*

Fawaakihat ash-Shaam Ya Fantum (*The First Fruits of Damascus O Phantom*), a play that dealt with the October War and the downing of Israeli warplanes, and the 1976 play *Turra Willa Naqshi* (*Heads or Tails*).

Another private theatrical company, well known during the 1970s and radically different from such experimental groups, was Firqat Tishreen (October Company), established in 1974 by actors Duraid Lahhaam, Nouhaad Qala'i and dramatist Mohammed al-Maghout. The influence of the Theatre of Thorns on the work of Firqat Tishreen was quite clear, especially in its use of political satire and song and dance. Some of its many successful productions include *Day'at Tishreen* (*The Tishreen Village*, 1975), *Ghirba* (*Homesickness*, 1977), *Kaasak Ya Watan* (*Cheers, Homeland*, 1979) and *Shaqaa'q an-Nu'maan* (*Anemones*, 1987). Though the company does not receive any financial subsidies from the government, it has continued operating into the 1990s. The major reason for its success is due to the popularity of Duraid Lahhaam on the one hand, and, on the other, this company's ability to find the middle ground between the serious and less serious aspects of commercial theatre.

Not discussed so far has been the country's large number of amateur theatres. These groups occupy a special place. On the one hand, they have played an important role in supplying professional theatres with new faces and, on the other hand, they have provided work opportunities for professional directors. Highly regarded by most theatre people and often well funded, many can be considered as semi-professional.

The most important of the amateur theatres is al-Masrah al-Jaami'i (University Theatre), which began its activities in 1971. The Foreign Languages Departments were almost all involved in its beginnings with some productions part of the prescribed curriculum and others dealing with matters of special interest to university people. The al-Masrah al-Jaami'i reached its current high status during the mid-1970s. Indeed, the group's production of *An Nakoun Aw La Nakoun* (*To Be or Not To Be*) attracted more attention than those of professional groups when it was presented during the sixth Damascus Theatre Arts Festival.

The al-Masrah al-Jaami'i has regularly provided the first working opportunities for professional directors such as Khalil Tafesh (b. 1947) who, in 1974, directed *Jisr Arta* (*The Arta Bridge*) by George Theotoka; Toufeeq al-Mu'ath-dhin (b. 1944) who, in 1980, directed *Muqaabala Suhufiyya Fi Buenos Aires* (*A Press Interview in Buenos Aires*) by Henry Borovik; Fouad ar-Raashid (b. 1943) who, in 1982, directed *an-Naseeha* (*The Advice*) from a text by Mark Twain; and Ilya Qajmeeni who, in 1981, directed *Malhamat Gilgaamish* (*The Epic of Gilgamesh*). Besides the University Theatre, there is al-Masrah al-'Ummaali (Working-Class Theatre), an organization with branches in different cities that was established in 1975. The group ceased operations in 1983. Involving a mix of amateurs and professionals across the country, it sponsored an annual festival in which the many affiliated groups from the provinces participated. Al-Masrah al-'Ummaali was itself a subsidiary of the General Federation of Labor Unions, which administered this theatre and provided it with financial assistance. The winning play during each festival would be presented for a week or two in the theatre of the General Federation of Labor Unions in Damascus as well as in various community centres.

One of the most distinguished companies affiliated with this organization was Firqat al-Masrah al-'Ummaali Fi Homs (Workers' Theatre Company of Homs) which was itself established in 1973. In 1975, its name was changed to Firqat al-Masrah al-'Ummaali (Workers' Theatre Company). Heading this group, which has continued its operations despite the demise of most of the other working-class groups in the country, is the playwright and director Farhan Bulbul. Between 1973 and 1985, this company presented nineteen productions of which five were specifically for children. Some of its most successful shows have been *al-Mumath-thiloun Yataraashaqoun al-Hijaara* (*The Actors Are Throwing Stones at Each Other*, 1975) written and directed by Farhaan Bulbul, *Jawhar al-Qadiyya* (*The Crux of the Matter*, 1976) written by Naadhim Hikmat and directed by Farhaan Bulbul, *al-'Ush-shaaq La Yafshaloun* (*Lovers Don't Fail*, 1977) written and directed by Farhaan Bulbul, *al-Qura Tas'ad Ila al-Qamar* (*The Villages Ascend to the Moon*, 1979) an adaptation of Brecht's *Caucasian Chalk Circle*, *Ya Haadir Ya Zamaan* (*O Time That Is Present*, 1980) written and directed by Farhaan Bulbul and *al-Malik Huwa al-Malik* (*The King Is the King*, 1985) written by Sa'dallah Wanous and directed by Bulbul.

Music Theatre
Dance Theatre

Dance and music are of enormous importance in Syrian cultural tradition and there have been many experiments by directors aimed at using these forms in the more literary theatre. None, however, has led to particularly original or unusual work.

There is only a single company in the country specializing in folk dance – Firqat Umayya (Umayya Company) – established in 1960 as a subsidiary of the Ministry of Culture from which it receives financial support. The company is composed of forty artists including twelve dancers, six vocal chorus members, sixteen musicians and six directors.

Distinguished for its folk and heritage shows, the company has played in several Arab countries and even further abroad. Some of its most important works include pieces choreographed by 'Umar al-'Aqqaad – al-Moulawiyya (Whirling Dervish, 1961) and as-Samaah (1962), Kamal Karkutli's al-'Urs (The Wedding, 1966), Sa'eed Zu'aytir's al-Hurriyya (Liberty, 1968) and Husaam Tahseen's as-Sahraa' (The Desert, 1970).

In 1968, a modern dance group Firqat Zenoubia (Zenoubia Company) was established but it has worked only on an occasional basis.

Theatre for Young Audiences
Puppet Theatre

The ancient shadow theatre of karagöz has a long history in Syria as earlier discussed (see opening historical section). European-style puppet theatre featuring marionettes and glove-puppets dates only from about 1960 when the Ministry of Culture established the Masrah al-'Araa'is (Puppet Theatre) which tours mostly to schools in Damascus. This group includes sixteen men and women artists in addition to technicians and administrators. The group has its own workshop to make puppets.

The company's repertoire is based on Arabic adaptations of well-known children's stories ranging from The Three Bears (1960) and Laila and the Wolf (1961) to Hikaayat Nasr ud-Deen (The Nasr ud-Deen Story, 1972) and al-Kalb al-Abyad (The White Dog, 1986). Only in the 1990s were dramatists beginning to look seriously at this field and that of theatre for young audiences. Among the writers who have tried their hands

with original works are Dalaal Haatim (b. 1938) and Hasan Yousef (b. 1948), a novelist and journalist. Salwa al-Jaabri (b. 1941) returned to Syria after studying abroad and has long been the company's administrator and main director.

The concept of a specific theatre for young audiences did not appear in Syria until even later – 1983. Previously, children's shows were unorganized and presented intermittently with supervision provided alternatively by organizations such as the Ministry of Education or the Organization of Pioneers. The group is composed of graduates of al-Ma'had al-'Aali lil-Funoun al-Masrahiyya (Higher Institute for Theatre Arts). For many years the group was run by director 'Adnaan Jawda (b. 1943). Among the group's most popular performances were Aladdin and the Magic Lantern, Cinderella, and al-Qit Abu Jazma (The Cat Abu Jazma), an adaptation of a Brothers Grimm fairytale.

Design
Theatre Space and Architecture

Design is not a major feature in Syrian professional theatre although in the late 1980s and 1990s it began to be taken more seriously as an independent element. As well, it must be said that there are virtually no indoor purpose-built theatre spaces in the country.

The National Theatre in Damascus, for example, a 450-seat proscenium space, was originally the al-Qabbaani cinema and before that a storage space. The Military Theatre too has about the same capacity and was also a cinema. Masrah Ittihaad Naqabaat al-'Ummaal (Federation of Labor Unions Theatre) in Damascus is slightly smaller at 350 seats while the Masrah Halab al-Qawmi (National Theatre of Aleppo) is one of the largest indoor spaces with a capacity of 720. Masrah Daar ath-Thaqaafa Fi Homs (House of Culture Theatre in Homs) is one of the few spaces that was actually designed as a theatre. It too is a proscenium space and has a capacity of 600. Masrah al-Markaz ath-Thaqaafi al-'Arabi (Arab Cultural Centre Theatre) in Latakia has a capacity of 350 seats as does Masrah al-Markaz ath-Thaqaafi (Cultural Centre Theatre) in Tartous.

There are several Roman amphitheatres dating back to the second century BC. One such is Masrah Basra (Basra Theatre), situated 120 kilometres south of Damascus. Among the world's best preserved and largest amphitheatres, it has a capacity of 15,000 and was equipped with 'sound and light' in the mid-1970s. Unlike other Roman theatres built into hillsides, the theatre at Bosra is a free-standing structure. A fortress built around the theatre accounts for its excellent state of repair. This theatre is also the home of the Mahrajaan Basra lil-Funoun ash-Sha'biyya (Basra Folklore Arts Festival) which is held annually in September. Ballet, theatre and folklore companies perform on this stage every summer and an annual international dance and music festival takes place in the Roman theatre in October.

Another Roman theatre is Masrah Jablé (Jablé Theatre) on the Syrian coast. Architecturally, it is similar to the Ba'ra Theatre and has the same number of seats. This theatre has been renovated and equipped with a 'sound and light' system and is popular for folk arts and amateur festivals.

Training
Criticism, Scholarship and Publishing

Prior to 1978, the date when al-Ma'had al-'Aali lil-Funoun al-Masrahiyya (Higher Institute for Theatre Arts) was established, no formal training centre for actors existed in Syria. In fact, the number of actors who had studied in any formal way was quite small with most of those studying in Egypt. The institute has two divisions: Dramatic Literature/Critical Studies and the Acting Division, the latter being the first established.

The Acting Division is highly selective, accepting only fifteen to twenty students each year from the more than seven hundred who apply. The institute's entrance exam includes questions on theatrical knowledge and an audition is required. Until 1991 the institute was run by Ghassan al-Maleh.

On the publishing side, in the 1960s, the Ministry of Culture began to publish a series of world drama in Arabic as well as a number of books on various aspects of theatre art. It also published *al-Ma'rifa* [Review] which devoted one entire issue (no. 34, 1964) to the theatre. Other issues of this magazine devoted to the theatre include nos. 104 and 105, both in 1970. In 1977, *Majallat al-Hayaat al-Masrahiyya* (*Theatre Life Magazine*) began publication. Established by playwright Sa'dallah Wanous and funded by the Ministry of Culture, this quarterly looks at theatrical trends not only in Syria but across the Arab world and internationally. In his introduction the first issue of this magazine, Wanous wrote:

This magazine aspires to create a societal milieu for Arab theatrical thought and world theatrical thought and for whatever is between both in the form of interaction and exchange. It aspires also to crystallize Arab and world theatrical experience presenting the best studies about them. The magazine's goal is to transform its pages into a theatrical stage that expresses all that can be said about the theatrical movement, to uncover weaknesses and obstacles, to expose and deal with problems through open discussions and to arrive at solutions. Its ambition is to adopt every new idea in the theatre that can be useful.

Another useful theatre publication is *al-Mawqif al-Adabi*, a monthly published by the Union of Arab Writers. It features special sections in which theatrical activities in Syria are reported on and debated. From time to time, the Higher Institute for Theatre Arts publishes books about the theatre. Among its publications are the first translations into Arabic of Stanislavski's writing.

During the 1970s, theatre reviews in newspapers began to be written by people with specific training in the field. From this point on, the best reviewing looked not only at the scripts but also at the entire theatrical experience. Prior to the 1970s, little of any value was said by reviewers in Syria. Among the best of the post-1970s reviewers are Riyaad 'Ismat (b. 1948) who studied English literature at the University of Damascus and theatre in Britain and later wrote a book on reviewing theatrical productions under the title *Buq'at Daw'* (*A Spot of Light*), Nabeel Haffaar (b. 1945) who studied German literature as well as theatre, and Nadeem Mu'alla Mohammed (b. 1949) who studied theatre theory and wrote a book on reviewing *al-Judraan al-Arba'a* (*The Four Walls*, 1980).

> *Sa'dallah Wanous (deceased) and*
> *Nadim Mohammed*
> *Translated by Maha and Tony Chehade*

Further Reading

Aadel, Abu Shanab. *Masrah 'Arabi Qadeem, karagūz* [An old Arab theatre, karagöz]. Damascus: Ministry of Culture, n.d.

Aliksan, Jaan. *al-Wilaada ath-Thaaniya lil-Masrah Fi Souriyya* [The second birth of the theatre in Syria]. Damascus: Union of Arab Writers, 1983.

'Arourki, Badr ud-Deen. 'at-Tajriba al-Masrahiyya Fi Souriyya' [The theatrical experience in Syria]. *Majallat al-Mawqif al-Adabi* 1 (1972).

——. 'adh-Thaahira al-Masrahiyya al-'Arabiyya Ba'd al-Khaamis Min Huzayran' [The Arab theatrical phenomenon after 5 June]. *al-Ma'rifa* [Review] 104 (1970).

Arsan, Ali Okla. 'Teatr Sirii zivet i boretsia' [Syrian theatre lives and struggles]. *Teatr* 46 (March 1993): 128–33.

al-Baaroud i, Fakhri. *Mudhakkaraat al-Baaroudi* [al-Baaroudi's memoirs]. Beirut and Damascus: al-Hayaat, 1951.

al-Bahra, Nasr ud-Deen. *Ahaadeeth Wa Tajaarib Masrahiyya* [Theatrical discussions and experiences]. Damascus: Union of Arab Writers, 1977.

Chalala, Elie. 'Sa'dallah Wanous Calls for Restoration of Theatre, the "Ideal Forum" for Human Dialogue'. *Al Jadid* 2 (June 1996).

Dhureil, 'Adnaan Bin. *al-Masrah as-Souri Mundhu Abi Khaleel al-Qabbaani Ila l-Yawm* [The Syrian theatre from Abi Khaleel Al-qabbaani to today]. Damascus: Damascus Distribution Office, 1971.

al-Farra, Ahmed Nouhaad. 'al-Masrah Fi Halab' [The theatre in Aleppo]. *Majallat al-'Umraan* 20–2 (1967).

'Fi Qadaaya al-Masrah al-'Arabi al-Hadeeth' [Concerning the affairs of the modern Arabic theatre]. *Majallat at-Tareeq* 2 (April–May 1986).

Hassan, Fatme Sharafeddine. 'Wanous' Perspective of Theatre: A Balance Between National Tradition and Universalism'. *Al Jadid* 2 (June 1996).

al-Jindi, Adham. *A'laam al-Adab Wa al-Fann* [Noted personalities in art and literature]. Damascus, n.d.

Kilaani, Ibraheem. 'at-Ta'leef al-Masrahi 'Indana' [Our way of writing for the theatre]. *Majallat al-Ma'rifa* [Review] 34 (1964).

Mabradzi, Z. 'Stanovlenie sovremennoj sirijskoj dramaturgii, 1847–1973' [The creation of modern Syrian dramaturgy, 1847–1973]. Dissertation, ANSSSR, Institut Vostokovedenija, Moscow, 1989. 200 pp.

Majallat al-Hayaat al-Masrahiyya [Theatrical Life Magazine] 4, 5, 6, 7, 8 and 9 (1977–9).

Majallat al-Ma'rifa [Knowledge Magazine] 34 [special issue about the theatre] (1964).

Mohammed, Nadeem Mu'alla. *al-Adab al-Masrahi Fi Souriyya* [Theatrical literature in Syria]. Damascus: Mu'assasat al-Wihda (Unity Institution), 1986.

Moosa, Matti. 'Naqqash and the Rise of the Native Arab Theatre in Syria'. *Journal of Arabic Literature* 3 (1972): 106–17.

Najm, Mohammed Yousef. *al-Masrahiyya Fi al-*

Adab al-'Arabi [The stage play in Arabic literature]. Damascus: Daar ath-Thaqaafa Press, n.d.

al-Qaasimi, Mohammed Sa'eed, Jamaal ud-Deen al-Qaasimi and Khaleel al-'Athm. *Qaamous as-Sina'aat ash-Shamiyya* [Directory of Syrian industries]. Damascus: Daar Tlas Publishing, 1988.

Qattaaya, Salmaan. *al-Masrah al-'Arabi Min Ayn Wa Ila Ayn* [The Arabic theatre from where to where]. Damascus: Union of Arab Writers, 1972.

Shanab, 'Aadel Abu. *Bawakeer at-Ta'leef al-Masrahi Fi Souriyya* [First fruits of theatrical writing in Syria]. Damascus: Union of Arab Writers, 1978.

Subhi, Muhyiddeen. 'Nusous Masrahiyya Min as-Sittinaat' [Theatrical scripts from the 1960s]. *Majallat al-Mawqif al-Adabi* 1 (1972).

'Theatre in Syria'. *Lotus: Afro-Asian Writings* 19 (1974): 74–93.

Ullrich, Peter. 'Zwischen Damaskus und Palmyra: Streiflichter vom syrischen' [Between Damascus and Palmyra: sidelights of Syrian theatre]. *Theater der Zeit* 38 (1983): 40–3.

Wanous, Sa'dallah. *Bayanaat li-Masrah 'Arabi Jadeed* [Declarations for a new Arabic theatre]. Beirut: Daar al-Fikr al-Jadeed Publishing, 1988.

TRUCIAL OMAN

(see **UNITED ARAB EMIRATES**)

TRUCIAL STATES

(see **UNITED ARAB EMIRATES**)

TUNISIA

Situated in north Africa between Algeria and Libya, Tunisia is part of the Arab area known as the Grand Maghreb. Occupying a strategic position along the western basin of the Mediterranean, it has a land area of 162,160 square kilometres (63,170 square miles) and a population of some 9 million of which about 1 per cent speak Berber. For the others, Arabic is the mother tongue though French is almost universally used in business, industry, the mass media and for teaching. English usage is growing and in the 1990s was being taught widely. Some 98 per cent of Tunisians are Muslims following the Malachite sect. The national capital is Tunis.

An Arab country, Tunisia has deep roots in Africa and is the inheritor of many great civilizations, the most prestigious being the Carthaginian. It has also been part of the Roman and Byzantine empires and is now part of the French community of nations, having been a colony of France for some seventy-five years between 1881 and 1956.

Following World War II and the Allied victory – a victory gained with Tunisian participation – France refused Tunisia's requests for political independence, a decision which led to armed resistance. Under Habib Bourguiba, leader of the Neo-Destour Party, Tunisia achieved that independence in 1956. A year later, the monarchy was abolished and Bourguiba was elected the new republic's first president, remaining in this position for thirty years. Old, sick and no longer really in control, he was replaced by Zine Al-Abidine Ben Ali in 1987. It was the new president who led the nation through a tumultuous period of legal changes resulting in new democratic processes and a much more effective economy. The same year as the country's independence, Tunisian women were liberated from the weight of ancient traditions thanks to the passage of a series of family and personal laws.

Culturally, Tunisia's identity, though rooted in Arab and Muslim traditions, has also consistently remained open to European ideas. Before the end of the eighteenth century, for example, following the liberal lead of Hamouda Pacha and Ahmed Bey the First a number of significant reforms took place including the abolition of slavery, the establishment of a series of polytechnical schools and, a bit later, the enactment of the first national constitution in an Arab-Muslim country. Another great reformer, Khereddine Pacha, introduced modern styles of teaching and encouraged relatively liberal practices and ideas which were ultimately reflected in both the country's open approach to publishing and its free press.

By 1962, unprecedented support began to be given to culture generally and theatre in particular. The state was actually the leader in creating a national arts infrastructure and it prevailed in the construction of a number of theatres, cultural and youth centres as well as libraries. Several international theatre festivals, film festivals, fine arts exhibitions and popular music events were in inaugurated. In response to the urging of established artists, a Higher Institute of Dramatic Art, a Higher Institute of Music and an Institute for Art and Architecture, Technology and City Planning were created.

Before the introduction of European-style theatre at the end of the eighteenth century, both popular and traditional Tunisian culture was rooted in poetry, music, dance and storytelling.

In the areas surrounding Tunis and in provincial towns as well as in the country, one could always find *meddahs* and *fadouls* (storytellers) recounting and enacting their many tales about the great periods of Tunisian and Arab history, and relating heritage tales such as *Al-Jaziyya al-Hilalyya*, *Saif al-Yazal*, *Foutouh ach-Cham* and *Al-Antaryya*. Also seen, especially on religious occasions, were the adventures of the characters from the *karagöz* shadow theatre, a style which clearly reflected the influence of Ottoman/Turkish culture on popular Tunisian culture between the seventeenth and twentieth centuries. As well, one could see Sicilian-style puppet theatres which showed, among other things, enactments of epic sea battles between the frightening Christian pirates and the Ottoman Muslims.

Through published articles, educated and cultured people in Tunisian society at the beginning of the twentieth century became aware of major theatrical events taking place in Syria and in Egypt. European theatre groups regularly passed through Tunis. Performing for the most part at the Municipal Theatre (begun by colonial authorities in 1902 but not opened until 1909) and the Rossini Theatre (opened in 1903) in Tunis, such groups – mostly French and Italian – served as early models for later European-style theatrical initiatives.

The modern Tunisian theatre was born amid these cultural and political conditions, that is, between colonial oppression at the beginning of the twentieth century and the crystallization of the country's Islamic Arab character in the last decades of the century. In 1908, a Tunisian theatre company was begun by a group of employees and artisans in Tunis. Calling themselves an-Najma (Star Troupe), they launched their first season with the Arab play, *al-Qaa'id al-Maghribi* (*The Maghrebi Leader*).

During the four decades from 1910 until independence in 1956, major Egyptian theatrical figures such as Salama Hijazi (in 1914), George Abyad (in 1921 and 1932), Yusuf Wahbi (in 1927 and 1950) and Zaki Tulaymat (in 1954) appeared in Tunis and attracted much attention to this more literary style of theatre. Offering short seasons of dramas, comedies and musicals, many of these visiting artists also led workshops in directing and acting.

By 1910, European-style theatre began to spread even beyond the capital. Over the next forty years, more than a hundred companies were established, some remaining active for a decade or two, others barely lasting the lifespan of a rose. Two of the most important of these early groups were ach-Chahama (Gallantry) and al-Adab (Letters) established in 1910 and 1911 respectively. Set up as legal entities with the approval of both national and colonial authorities, these groups took their members from the amateur group, al-Jawq at-Tunisi al-Masri (Tunisian-Egyptian Company), which was made up, as its name suggests, of Tunisian and Egyptian amateurs. Each of these groups presented a range of dramas and comedies over the next decade interrupted only by World War I. Most were presented in classical Arabic with others presented in Tunisian dialect to audiences eager to acquaint themselves with the art.

Both of the new companies sought to find a balance between world classics (Shakespeare and Molière, for example) and Arabic-language plays. Both companies allowed women on their stages, a challenge not only because society was suspicious of such activities but also because up to that time women were generally uneducated and few could read. Nevertheless, some did make significant careers as actresses. In general the work done by these theatres was uncontroversial and espoused such values as freedom, brotherhood and tolerance. A benevolent and humanistic movement, its leading actors included Ibrahim al-Akoudi (1890–1942), Mohammed Bourquiba (1881–1930), al-Habib al-Mani' (1881–1952), Ahmed Bouleyman (1884–1976) and Ach-Chérif Ben Yekhelf (1897–1968).

Colonial officials had decided to encourage theatre in the hope of 'Frenchifying' Tunisian citizens. But these same authorities soon became wary of criticism by certain artists and groups, especially the members of al-Adab, and began monitoring their activities. During World War I, in fact, social criticism of colonialism ran high. During the ensuing decades, criticism by writers and theatre people was continuous and it became an effective weapon which was used over and over again even in later years against anything perceived to be national oppression.

Mahmud Messadi, who wrote 'As-Sudd in 1940, is credited as having been one of the first people to attempt to create a 'Tunisian theatre'.

Early in the post-World War I era, the two companies merged into a new group called at-Tamthil al-'Arabi (Arab Acting Troupe). Artistic control of the new company was given to the Egyptian actor George Abyad who in 1921 had just completed a theatrical tour in Tunisia. Abyad's 1921 tour had attracted particularly great attention. He had produced a number of

Shakespeare's *Othello* directed by Tawfik al-Jebali, 1998.
Photo: Abou Rabïi

very popular new Egyptian plays during his visit including *Luwees al-Haadi 'Asher* (*Louis the Eleventh*), *ash-Sharaf al-Yabaani* (*Japanese Honour*) and *Fat-h Bayt al-Maqdis* (*The Conquest of Jerusalem*). As artistic director of the new group, Abyad approached his task with enthusiasm. He began by offering acting classes for his new group whose première was to be in the season of 1922–3. This new generation of Tunisian theatre people was well prepared and offered several seasons of particularly high quality; those so trained eventually became the leaders of the Tunisian theatre over the ensuing three decades. Among these figures were such well-known theatre people as al-Béchir Methenni (1901–72), Mohamed al-Habib (1903–80), Tahar Belhaj (1900–59), Allala Sfaïhi (1892–1970) and Chédli Ben Friji (1903–45). Abyad's success in developing this next generation, in fact, far surpassed his successes on the stage during his stay at this time.

Between the 1920s and the early 1950s a dozen or so groups of note emerged in and around Tunis. Among the most important of these were al-Masrah al-Kamili (Kamili Theatre, 1924–8), Firqat as-Saâda (Happiness Company) supported by the Liberal Constitutional Tunisian Party (founded 1920) of this same period, al-Masrah al-Fukaahi (Comedy Theatre) which employed social criticism to challenge existing problems, Firqat al-Mustaqbal at-Tamthili (Future Acting Company, 1927–36), Firqat al-Ittihad al-Masrahi (Theatre Union Company, 1936–49), Firqat al-Kawbab at-Tamthili (Acting Star Company, 1942–51), Firqat Ittihad Kawakib at-Tamthil (Union of Acting Stars Company, 1947–9) and Firqat al-Masrah (Theatre Company), which was among the first groups to sponsor national competitions for new plays.

A number of groups were led by women, an idea which emerged at this time under the general banner of al-Qyada an-Nissaya (Women's Leadership), an organization which fought in its work for female equality. Among the groups which took up the challenge and appointed female directors were Firqt Fadhila Khitmi (Fadhila Khitmi Theatre, founded 1929), Firqat Wassila Sabri (Wassila Sabri Company, 1937–40), Firqat al-'Ichra Tayiba (Good Fellowship Company, founded in 1940) and Firqat Noujoum al-Fan (Artistic Stars

Jalila Baccar in *Familia* (1993) directed by Fadhel Jaibi.
Photo: Mahmoud Chalbi

Company, founded by Chafia Rochdi in 1949). In many of these groups women played all the roles including traditional male ones.

During this period Tunisian plays began to be seen more and more as well as some of the plays that Abyad had presented, both his own and scripts by other Arabic dramatists. Plays written in classical Arabic taught Tunisians the history of Africa, the Maghreb, the Arabian peninsula and Andalusia. Those written in Tunisian Arabic offered social criticism and moral lessons. All attacked colonial hegemony and helped to develop a national spirit and character. This latter role was especially important in the 1952–4 struggle against French colonialism.

The year 1953 saw the situation change significantly. The municipality of Tunis established the country's first municipally funded professional theatre troupe that year and shortly thereafter a union was established for theatre artists and theatre companies. The new municipal company, Firqat Médina Tunis lil-Masrah (Tunis City Theatre), was run by Hammady al-Jaziri (1926–87), an actor, director and playwright. A new sense of professionalism saw long-term administrative planning taking place in this and other theatre troupes, the diversification of repertoire and the beginning of genuine

ongoing financial support by various levels of government. The company's best known director was Aly Ben Ayed (1930–72) who studied theatre at the Markaz ad-Diraasaat al-'Ulya ad-Dramiyya (Centre for Advanced Studies in Drama) in Cairo and then in Paris at the Théâtre National Populaire, where he worked with Jean Vilar.

When Tunisia achieved full independence in 1956, the first ruling political party – Neo-Destour Party, later renamed the Parti Socialiste Destourien – showed particular interest in supporting national cultural initiatives. In 1962 the government established the first Ministry of Culture with theatre its most important foundation and, as one government statement put it, as a symbol of 'the national character that must be safeguarded.'

Among the first directors of the new municipal company were Mohammed 'Abd al-'Aziz al-'Agrebi (1902–68), Hassen Zmerli (1906–83) and Aly Ben Ayed, who was an actor well versed in French, English, Egyptian and Tunisian theatrical cultures. It was due to Ben Ayed's efforts that the company began modernizing its work both on-stage and off. Among these changes was the discarding of on-stage exaggeration in favour of a more Stanislavski-based realism in both acting and design. He was instrumental in commissioning new translations of works by Shakespeare and Casona, Molière and Goldoni and through adaptation making them more suitable for Tunisian society; he also introduced plays by such writers as Albert Camus, García Lorca, Tawfiq al-Hakīm and *Murad III* by the Tunisian al-Habib Boulares. Ben Ayed insisted that the company tour as widely as possible both in and out of the country and he took them as far away as Algeria, Morocco, Egypt, Lebanon, Iran, Austria and France, where the group took part in the Theatre of Nations Festival in Paris.

In 1964, the Neo-Destour Party provided encouragement and funding for a national theatre festival which later expanded to a second and then to a major international festival by the 1980s. This Mahrajaan Ayyam Qartaaj al-Masrahyya (Carthage Theatre Journeys Festival) is now the major international festival in the Arab world. Two other Tunisian festivals are the Mahrajaan al-Hammamet ad-Duwali (International Hammamet Festival) and Mahrajaan Masrah al-Maghrib al-'Arabi (Arab Maghreb Theatre Festival). Primarily Arab-language troupes participated in the early festivals although on occasion other language companies have been seen. The festivals have allowed Arab groups to compare their work and to challenge one another artistically.

By 1966, another troupe was established by Abd al-Mouttalib Zaâzâ' – Firqat al-Masrah at-Tajribi (Experimental Theatre Company). That company introduced to Tunisia the plays of Brecht, a dramatist who would come to dominate the Tunisian theatre in the 1970s and 1980s with his ideologies, doctrines, techniques and plays. The first Brecht to be seen was *al-'Istithnaa' Wa l-Qaa'ida* (*The Exception and the Rule*). Though the Experimental Theatre Company itself did not remain active for very long its activities were a real precursor for research into political theatre techniques.

The group was a prelude to the work of the Firqat Médina le Kaf (City of Kaf Company), established and managed by the distinguished man of theatre al-Moncef Suwaisi in 1967. Kaf, situated in a rural area in northwest Tunisia near the Algerian border, had never before had a theatre troupe of any kind. Part of a national theatrical decentralization policy for the propagation of the professional theatrical art in the country, the establishment of Kaf Company was not an isolated act for it was preceded and then followed by the establishment of other regional companies including the Firqat Médina Sfax

(City of Sfax Company) in 1964, Firqat Médina Bizerte (City of Bizerte Company) in 1968 in the far north, Firqat Médina Gasfa (City of Gafsa Company) in 1972 (situated on the Chott al-Jarid Road, Gafsa, in the southwestern region), Firqat Médina al-Kairouan (City of Kairouan Company) in 1973, Firqat Médina Sousse (City of Sousse Company) in 1974 and Firqat Médina al-Mahdia (City of al-Mahdia Company) in 1976.

The experiences of the Kaf Company were unique in its pioneering of performances outside the capital. The company itself had been selected by Souissi from young actors from Kaf. Once cast, they were trained in acting, voice and movement and then put on stage to face audiences, not only in Kaf, but also in the capital and other locales. Eventually the company played successfully at several of the major festivals, doing politically committed plays by playwrights from Tunisia such as Samir Ayadi, Mustafa Fersi and Tijani Zalilaa, from Egypt such as Alfred Faraj, and from Lebanon. All of these writers dealt with issues of import to Arab societies. The company itself followed the populist methods of the French director Roger Planchon with whom Soussi studied as well as the ideas of Brecht. Some of these plays were even critical of the Bourguiba regime whose economic ideology (cooperation and socialism) ended in failure in 1969.

Over the next eight years, the regime tried to forbid opposing opinions, a strategy which led to public riots in 1978. Once again theatre people used their art to attack the regime; the government responded with harsh censorship policies. Many theatre people left the country at this time fearing for their lives, only to find that Tunisian police officials would still be following them even into France and the Gulf. Such actions contributed significantly to the loss of credibility ultimately sustained by the Bourguiba regime.

Throughout this turmoil, the City of Tunis Company and those groups still working outside the capital continued offering seasons but with varying degrees of success. Even new theatres began to operate during this difficult time – al Masrah al 'Umumi (General Theatre), a state-run facility, and two private companies, al-Masrah al-Hour (Free Theatre) and al-Masrah al-Jadid (New Theatre). All of these were established on a more-or-less private basis opening still another level of theatrical endeavours in the country. Other private groups quickly followed the lead of these three, particularly the lead of the New Theatre. Among the groups emerging

The Phou Theatre's 1989 production of *Saken Fi hay Essaïda* directed by Raja Ben Ammar-Moncef Sayem.
Photo: Mahmoud Chalbi

at this time were Masrah Phou (Phou Theatre, in 1979), Masrah ad-Daïdahana (Ad-Daïdahana Theatre, 1980), al-Masrah al-'Oudhour (Organic Theatre, 1981), Masrah al-Ardh (Earth Theatre, 1984), Masrah Sanimar (Sanimar Theatre, 1984), and al-Masrah al-Muthallath (Triangular Theatre, 1985).

Most of those involved with these groups had some experience with European theatre but, in general, much less experience with Arabic theatre. As a result, new European styles were adopted over more local ones, particularly in playwriting. Collectively created plays became popular and plays by individual writers became less produced. Nevertheless, plays continued to take on social issues and were staged in a variety of styles including what came to be called environmental theatre, a style favoured by al-Masrah Fil-Bayt (Theatre in the House). The Ad-Daïdahana Theatre, for its part, still focused on individually written scripts but its productions tended to adapt each playwright's work significantly. The director became all powerful in such groups.

Each group seemed to carve out its own area: the Earth Theatre, for example, was unique in its concern with rural matters both in its choice of scripts and its approach to production. For most of these private groups, classical Arabic began to disappear in their plays being replaced by Tunisian colloquial Arabic in an attempt to reach audiences more easily.

Several events occurred in 1982 which would significantly change the theatrical map of the country: the creation of the Tunisian National Theatre company, the creation of the Carthage Theatre Journeys Festival and the establishment by al-Moncef Souissi of the country's first serious theatre magazine, *Fadha'aat Masrahiyya* (*Theatrical Areas*). These events played an effective role in introducing Tunisians to Arab, African and Mediterranean theatres while at the same time acquainting other countries with the new Tunisian theatre. In 1988, Mohamed Idris (b. 1944) – an actor, director and playwright – became manager of the National. A student of Arabic literature and theatre in France, Idris had earlier participated in the establishment of the Gafsa Theatre Company.

Though the government provided financial and material support to all these groups, its Lajnat at-Tawjih al-Masrahi (Theatrical

Tawfik al-Jebali's 1992 production of *Femtella* at El Teatro
Photo: Mahmoud Chalbi

Orientation Committee) was still functioning as a censorship of sorts for playwrights, directors and, in financial terms, the companies as a whole. Such harassment was more severe for those in the public sector than for their counterparts in the private sector. During this same period, a new brand of religious fundamentalism had begun to appear and in 1987, when the Bourguiba regime finally came to an end, it began to have an impact on national theatre life.

In the 1980s and 1990s, a number of new institutions emerged serving cultural activities. Among them were the National Dance Centre of Borj El Baccouche and the International Cultural Centre in Hammamet and its transformation into a Cultural House of the Mediterranean specializing mainly in theatre performances. The National Ensemble of Popular Arts, based in Tunis, was presenting choreographed versions of folk styles, including sword dances and various exorcistic rites. Numerous brotherhoods, attached to the shrines of local saints, also gave dance performances in courtyards, with the dances sometimes going on all night.

Through this same period, many of the smaller groups managed to obtain their own spaces such as Madar Theatre, Hamra Theatre and El Teatro (two theatre spaces – one of 253 seats and the other, also used for rehearsals, of 120 seats). An active theatre centre, El Teatro is primarily a creation and meeting space for artists established in 1987 under the direction of Tawfik al-Jebali (b. 1944). Subsidized by the Tunisian government when there is political agreement with El Teatro's policies, its most successful shows have been *Klem Ellil* (*Night Talks*, 1989) by Tawfik al-Jebali, *Babour Australia* (1990) by Mohammed Fellag, and *Jadal* (1997) by the Lebanese dramatist Marcel Khalifa. El Teatro shows have been seen in Egypt, Syria, Lebanon, Brazil, Argentina, Italy, Spain, France and Germany. 'Our goal', says Jebali, 'is to dismantle the image many western theatre professionals have of Arab theatre as just sand, folklore and dance.'

As for the professional life of theatre people in Tunisia, all tend to take on a variety of responsibilities. Actors are often playwrights and directors, too. A number of theatrical figures, however, have stood out during this period specifically as dramatists and need to be mentioned in this brief account. Among them are Mohammed al-Jaïbi (1878–1938),

El Teatro's 1989 production of *Klem Ellil* (*Night Talks*).
Photo: Mahmoud Chalbi

Mohamed al-Habib (1903–80), Ahmed Khéreddine (1905–67), Khalifa as-Stambouli (1919–48), Izziddine al-Madani (b. 1938) and the aforementioned Tawfik al-Jebali.

Mohammed al-Jaïbi is generally agreed to be the first Tunisian playwright of note. His play *as-Sultaan Bayn Judraan Yaldiz* (*The Sultan Amid the Walls of Yaldiz*, 1909) was presented for the first time by the Ibraheem Hijazi Company on the stage of the Rossini Theatre in Tunis. A politician and long-time member of the Tunisian Liberal Constitutional Party, al-Jaïbi was also a journalist who established the *as-Sawaab* newspaper in 1904 and *Khéreddine* magazine in 1906.

Mohamed al-Habib was a theatrical apprentice under George Abyad. Trained as a lawyer, he wrote several plays, a number of which were historical, in the early 1930s including *al-Wathiq bi-Llaah al-Hafsi, Tariq Bin Zyad, Amir Sujilmasa* (*The Prince of Sujilmasa*), *Salambo, ar-Rachid Wa al-Barmika* (*ar-Rachid and the Barmikas*), *Abu Ja'ar al-Mansour* and *Abu 'Abdallah as-San'aani*. The administrator of Firqat al-Mustaqbal at-Tamthili in 1926 and Firqat al-Kawbab at-Tamthili in 1938, he also wrote theatre reviews as a journalist and wrote one successful novel, *Basala Turkiyya* (*Turkish*

Tawfik al-Jebali.

Courage). His lectures on Arabic music, acting and directing attracted wide audiences and contributed much to the development of later generations of Tunisian dramatists. He was generally considered to be the most prominent Tunisian dramatist from the 1930s to the end of the 1950s.

Ahmed Khéreddine was a playwright and a poet (writing in both classical and colloquial Arabic). Among his plays in classical Arabic were *al-Kahena*, *Bardr ad-Douja*, *Shibl ul-Faatimiyyeen* (*The Cub of the Fatimids*), *al-Mou'iz Bin Badis*, *al-Joundi al-Majhoul* (*The Unknown Soldier*), *al-Jaza'* (*The Retribution*) and *Omar Ben Abdelaziz*. He also wrote a large number of sociological plays in the local Tunisian dialect, a collection of stories and a collection of poetry.

Khaleefa as-Stambouli (1919–48) was an actor, director and a playwright. His best plays were *Ziyaadat Allaah al-Aghlabi*, *al-Mu'iz li-Din Illaah as-Sanhaji*, *Qal'a Tahtariq Aw Suqout Maliqa* (*The Fort Burns or The Fall of Maliqa*), *al-Intiqam ar-Rahib* (*The Terrible Revenge*), *Ana l-Jani* (*I Am the Perpetrator*), *I'raf Esh Kun Tukhalit* (*Know With Whom You Associate*), *al-Hub al-Ithri* (*Platonic Love*), *Masra' at-Tughat* (*The Death of the Oppressors*), *Ah Fulousi* (*Oh My Money*) and *'Aqibat al-Khamr* (*The Consequence of Drinking Wine*). Most of these plays were produced many times during his life and continue to be produced even in the 1980s and 1990s. Well constructed and effectively plotted, they featured easily understood language and complex characters.

Izziddine al-Madani is one of the best known playwrights of the Tunisian theatre. His most important plays include *Thawrat Sahib al-Himar* (*The Revolt of Sahib al-Himar*) directed by Aly Ben Ayed in 1970; *Diwan Thawrat az-Zanz* (*The Record of the Negro Revolution*) directed by al-Moncef Souissi in 1972; *Rihlat al-Hallaj* (*The Journey of the Hallaj*) directed by Souissi in 1973, by al-Béchir ad-Drissi in 1982 and by Chérif Khaznadar in 1985 in Tunis, Paris and Marseilles; *Ta'azi Fatimiyya* (*Fatimid Condolences*) directed by Abdallah Rouached in 1975; *al-Ghufran* (*The Pardon*) presented in 1976 in Casablanca; *Mawlay as-Sultan al-Hassan al-Hafsi* (*My Lord the Sultan al-Hassan al-Hafsi*) directed by Souissi. In addition, he wrote *at-Tarbee' Wa at-Tadweer* (*Squaring and Circling*) which he directed himself in 1978 and which was staged by Ra'ouf al-Basti in 1984 and by Sameer al-'Asfouri in Cairo in 1985.

Perhaps the country's most widely known theatre person has been al-Moncef Souissi (b. 1944), who began his career as an actor and later became a director. A manager of the City of Kaf Company and later the City of Tunis Company, he helped to establish and later manage the Tunisian National Theatre; for many years he directed the Carthage Theatre Festival. The son of the actor and playwright Izziddine Souissi, al-Moncef studied theatre in Tunisia, then continued his advanced theatrical studies in France with the director Roger Planchon. He was almost the best example of the success of the administrative decentralization of theatre in the country and has promoted Arabic playwriting widely. In 1979, he began to teach theatre in the Gulf. He has acted in, directed and produced more than fifty stage plays to date.

There has been a strong movement since the 1980s toward a study and appreciation of what has been called the Arab heritage in theatre with a number of directors and scholars focusing their attention on earlier Arabic plays and plays from other Arabic countries. Among these directors and writers are Izziddine al-Madani, Hamadi Mizzi (working at the Sinbad Theatre) and Fadhel Jaziri (working mostly at Firqat al-Masrah al-Jadid) and known for such heritage-based productions as *an-Nouba* (*The Shift*), *al-Hadhra* (*The Presence*) and *an Nujoum* (*The Stars*).

Few Tunisian theatre groups have specifically focused on theatre for young audiences. In 1994, however, a conference on the subject was held in Tunis and it was agreed that festivals should in future include such work in their programming.

As for training, there is one major institution in Tunisia – the Higher Institute for Theatre Arts in Tunis. This centre began in the mid-1970s giving *ad-hoc* courses. By 1972 it had evolved a more permanent status now training actors and directors for both public and private theatres, film and television as well as theatre critics. A number of scholars have emerged in the 1980s and 1990s, among them Mohammed Moumin in the field of aesthetics, Faouzia Mizzi and Badra B'chir in theatre sociology, Mohamed Abaza, Mohammed al-Madyouni and Mahmoud al-Majri in criticism and Omar Ben Salim, Moncef Charfeddine and Mohammed Idris Massaoud in documentation. Many of these people are now looking closely at Arab heritage theatre and are studying Tunisian theatre and theatre activities in other Arab countries.

Izziddine al-Madani
Translated by Maha and Tony Chehade

El Teatro's 1993 production of *Weilon* based on Diderot's *The Actor's Paradox*.
Photo: Mahmoud Chalbi

Further Reading

Abbassi, Ezzeddine. *L'Écriture théâtrale en Tunisie post-coloniale 1964–1982: mutations et problèmes* [Post-colonial playwriting in Tunisia 1964–1982: mutations and problems]. PhD dissertation, Université de Paris X, 1985.

Aziza, Mohamed. *Les Formes traditionnelles du spectacle* [Traditional forms of spectacle]. Tunis: Société Tunisienne de Diffusion, 1975.

Bahr, Mohamed. *Le Chant et la musique dans le théâtre arabe en Tunisie* [Song and music in Arab theatre of Tunisia]. Paris: Université de Paris III, 1984. 104 pp.

B'chir, Badra. 'Apertu sur la recherche théâtral en Tunisie' [Summary of theatrical research in Tunisia]. *Revue Tunisienne des Sciences Sociales* 48–49 (1997): 11–22.

——. 'La Combinatoire dramatique du théâtre en Tunisie' [The dramatic combination of theatre in Tunisia]. *Revue Tunisienne des Sciences Sociales* 44 (1976): 37–72.

——. 'Contre le social, famille et théâtre' [Against the social, the familial and the theatre]. In *Des relations interpersonnelles dans la famille Maghrébine* [Interpersonal relations in the Maghreb family]. Tunis: Cahiers du CERES [Centre d'Étude, et de Recherche, Économique et Social], 1988.

——. 'Éléments du fait théâtral en Tunisie' [Elements of theatrical activity in Tunisia]. Tunis: Cahiers du CERES [Centre d'Étude, et de Recherche, Économique et Social], 1993. 218 pp.

——. 'Évolution des formes de créativité et dynamique sociale: l'apport de la comédienne tunisienne au théâtre en Tunisie' [The evolution of creative styles and social dynamics: the contribution of the actor in Tunisian theatre]. In *Théâtre et changement social* [Theatre and social change]. Tunis, 1995.

——. 'L'Inadéqation formation théâtre-emploi' [The inadequacies of training and theatre employment]. *Revue Tunisienne des Sciences Sociales* 52 (1978): 11–42.

Ben Halima, Hamadi. *Nisf Qarn Min al-Masrah al-'Arabi bil-Bilaad at-Tounisiyya (1907–1957)* [A half-century of the Arab theatre in Tunisia (1907–1957)]. Tunis: Tunis University Publications, 1974.

Ben Salim, Omar. 'ar-Rasid al-Masrahi bi-Wizarat ath-Thaqaafa' [Theatrical assets in the ministry of culture]. *Literary Series*, 8th issue, Tunis University Social and Economic Studies and Research Centre. Tunis: City of Tunis Press, 1993.

Ben at-Tajani, Hamda. *Hayati al-Masrahiyya* [My theatrical life]. Tunis: City of Tunis Press, 1981.

Charfeedine, Moncef al-Moncef. *Taareekh al-Masrah at-Tounisi Munthu Nash'atihi Ila Nihaayat al-Harb al-'Aalamiyya al-'Oula* [The history of the Tunisian theatre from its inception to the end of World War I]. Tunis, 1972.

——. 'Le théâtre'. *Institute Belle-Lettres Arabes Revue* 30 no. 20 (1967): 411–18.

Un demi-siècle de théâtre Arabe en Tunisie (1907–1957) [A half-century of Arabic theatre in Tunisia (1907–1957)] Tunis, 1974.

Ghazi, Mohammed Farid, "al-Masrah al-'Arabi Fi Tunis, Tarikhuhu Wa Ittijaahatuhu Min Nash'atihi Ila Sanat 1918' [The Arab theatre in Tunisia: its history and orientation from its inception to 1918]. *al-Fikr Magazine* (July 1961): 36–52.

'Hammamet Festival'. *World Theatre* 15 (May–July 1966): 300–1.

El Houssi, Majid. *Pour une histoire du théâtre tunisien* [A history of Tunisian theatre]. Padova: Francisci Editore, 1982.

Idris, Mohammed Massaoud. *Dirasaat Fi Tarikh al-Masrah at-Tounisi 1881–1956* [Studies on the history of Tunisian theatre 1881–1956]. Higher Institute of Theatre Arts, Tunis: Daar Sahar Publishing, 1993.

Jaziri, Hammadi. 'Le situation de théâtre en Tunisie' [The current theatre in Tunisia]. *African Arts/Arts d'Afrique* 1 no. 3 (1968): 40–1, 92–3.

Karrou, Ab l-Qasim Mohammed. 'Abd ar-Razzaq Karabaka'. In *Distinguished Personalities of the Arab Maghreb Series*. Tunis: City of Tunis Press, 1965.

'Littérature et arts du spectacle à Tunis: 1966–1967' [Literature and the performing arts in Tunis]. *Institut des Belles-Lettres Arabes Revue* 120 (1968).

Machut-Mendecka, Ewa. 'Niespokojny teatr tunezyjski' [Restless theatre in Tunisia]. *Dialog* 29 no. 4 (April 1984): 127–34.

Madani, Izziddine. 'al-Masrah at-Tounisi' [The Tunisian theatre]. In *Encyclopédie du Théâtre*. Edited by Michel Corvin. Paris: Bordas Press, 1991.

——. and Mohammed as-Saqanji. *Ruwwaad at-Ta'leef al-Masrahi Fi Tunis* [Pioneering playwrights in Tunisia]. Tunis: Tunisian Distribution, 1986.

al-Madyouni, Mohammed. 'Ishkalaat Ta'seel al-Masrah al-'Arabi' [The problem of establishing the origin of the Arabic theatre]. *Carthage Theatre Studies and Research Series*. Tunis: Bayt al-Hikma Publications, 1993.

——. *Masrah Izziddine al-Madani Wa at-Turaath* [Izziddine al-Madani theatre and heritage]. Tunis: Daar Rasm Tunis, 1983.

Al-Majri, Mahmoud, Izziddine al-Madani, Rida Bin Hameed, Mohammed Momen, Faouzia al-Mizzi, and Izziddine al-'Abbasi. 'Dirasaat Fi al-Masrah at-Tounisi' [Studies on the Tunisian theatre]. *Cultural Life Magazine*, Tunis, n.d.

Maquoi, Azza. *Karagoz i el culte a la negativitat* [Karagöz and the cult of the negation]. Translated by Montserrat Benet. Barcelona: Institute del Teatre, 1984. 192 pp.

Mediouni, Mohamed. 'About the Obstacles and Perspectives of Tunisian Theatre Institutions'. *Theatre Studies Magazine of the ISAD*, 1995.

——. 'Theatre Phenomenon in Tunisia in the Twentieth Century: A Reading of the Tunisian Theatre Process'. In *Aspects of Tunisian Civilization in the Twentieth Century*. Tunis: La Faculté des Lettres Manouba, 1996.

——. 'The Way Towards Theatre in Maghreb'. *Tunisian University Yearbook* 38 (1995): 109–68.

al-Mizzi, Hamadi. *at-Tansheet al-Masrahi al-Madrasi Fi Tounis* [Stimulation of school theatres in Tunisia].Tunis: Daar ar-Riyaah al-Arba' Press, 1985.

Mohammed, Yahya. *Fi ad-Darb al-Masrahi* [On the theatrical path]. Tunis: City of Tunis Press, 1988.

Rebolledo, Maria Victoria Gonzalez. *Una Panoramica del Teatro Tunecino Contemporaneo (1900–1975)* [Survey of contemporary Tunisian theatre (1900–1975)]. Granada: Grupo de Investigacion Estudios Arabes Contemporaneos, 1991.

as-Samlaali, al-Haadi, *Thikrayaat Fannaan* [Memories of an artist]. Tunis: City of Tunis Press, 1982.

Saqanji, Mohammed. *Firqat Médina Tounis lil-Masrah: Safha Mushriqa Min Hayaat al-Masrah al-'Arabi Fi Bilaadina* [The city of Tunis theatrical company: a shining page out of the life story of the Arabic theatre in our country]. Tunis: Kahiya, 1988.

Severin, Micheline B. 'Théâtromania' [Theatre mania]. *L'Avant Scène Théâtre* 974 (1995): 49–51.

Thiry, Jacques. 'Pour une approche du théâtre tunisien contemporain' [An approach to contemporary Tunisian theatre]. In *Théâtre de Toujours, d'Aristote à Kalisky* [Eternal theatre: from Aristotle to Kalisky]. Edited by Gilbert Debusscher and Alain van Crugten. Brussels: Éditions de l'Université de Bruxelles, 1983.

Tomiche, Nada. 'Le théâtre' [The theatre]. In *La Littérature arabe contemporaine* [Contemporary Arab Literature]. Paris: Maisonneuve & Larose, 1993.

TURKEY

(Europe Volume)

UAE

(see **UNITED ARAB EMIRATES**)

UMM AL-QAWAIN

(see **UNITED ARAB EMIRATES**)

UNITED ARAB EMIRATES

(Overview)

A federation founded in 1971 and consisting of seven emirates – Abu Dhabi, Dubai, Sharjah, Ras al-Khaimah, Umm al-Qawain, Ajman and Fujairah – the United Arab Emirates (UAE) is located on the Arabian Gulf and shares borders with Qatar and Saudi Arabia to the west, Saudi Arabia and Oman to the south, Oman and the Gulf of Oman to the east, and the Gulf Sea to the north and northwest. The total land area of the UAE is approximately 83,600 square kilometres (32,280 square miles) with a 1995 population estimated at 2.9 million. The UAE capital is Abu Dhabi.

Indigenous Emirians are Arabic, descended from Arabic tribal confederations that dominated the peninsula for over 2,500 years. However, only some 20 per cent of the country's population are currently from the UAE, with less than half the total population actually of Arabic descent. The majority is now composed of immigrants to the region – east and southeast Asians as well as a small population of Europeans, in addition to the Arab communities who came to the Emirates as a result of the post-World War II oil boom in the region. Despite these numbers the population has remained overwhelmingly Muslim (96 per cent). The UAE's official language is Arabic with English and Urdu widely spoken in major cities. During the last quarter of the twentieth century, the UAE has made education, health and social services available free to all its citizens with the petroleum-rich areas of Abu Dhabi and Dubai exercising a generally accepted political dominance.

Theatre in the Emirates is still in a neophyte phase in comparison to similar movements in other Arab countries. Indeed, theatre in the European sense did not emerge until after World War II. The 1950s – when such forms were first introduced – can best be described as a period of imitation during which actors from the region would do little more than copy the poses and styles of well-known Arab and Hollywood actors. Eventually some of the better actors began offering their own characterizations; during this period improvisation dominated and scripts were little more than excuses for actors to amuse audiences. The best of the actors, however, began to join together to form groups and to work on a more-or-less amateur basis. Most groups were short-lived and quickly unravelled at the first group problem. Such groups emerged in many social and community clubs, often with the same core of actors appearing under different sponsorships. Even for the most experienced actors, theatre could not be counted on as any kind of a professional career.

Indigenous forms of performance – generally rooted in dance and music – remained at the heart of most performative events, both religious and communal. But the introduction of European-style stage performances affected the public perception of such performances and rendered them somehow 'unworthy'. One cannot speak of theatre in the Emirates, however, without at least mentioning such folk events and noting the many songs and masque-like shows related to the sea: rituals of the departure and return of pearl-diving ships with impressive farewell and welcoming scenes, the ritualized unfurling of sails and the distribution of singing

roles to accompany work, and scenes performed by townspeople relating to the sea and its many hardships. In the desert, such folk arts continue including competitive poetry recitals, falconry, horse breeding and camel racing, all done with swirls of colour and an impressive sense of the theatrical. Throughout the country there remain a wide variety of seasonal celebrations, all rooted in performative traditions ranging from recitations of the Quran and storytelling to family events such as weddings and circumcisions.

Some dances are seen at almost all such occasions including *al-Ayalah* or the Bedouin *ar-Razeef*, both war dances performed in many Arab countries under different names. In the Emirates, dances with religious connotations include *al-Maalid*, *al-Mirdad* and *al-Zaat*, a dance aimed at communicating with the spiritual world. More secular dances with strong theatrical elements include *al-Midaan* (The Battlefield), *al-A'araas* (The Brides) and *as-Sibaqaat* (The Races).

One row of participants performing the *al-Ayalah* folk dance at a wedding.

It was the appearance of cinema in the Emirates during the 1950s which first generated interest in live scripted performances. At the same time inter-Arab cultural exchanges began to grow, ranging from scouting and school trips to visits from touring Arab theatrical groups (mostly Egyptian). Also affecting this development were many teaching missions from other Arab countries, especially from Palestine, Egypt, Jordan, Iraq and Syria before and after the Emirates were united. Teachers from these missions usually organized plays as a teaching device. In 1958, for example, as part of a programme during the Sharjah School's annual celebration, a temporary stage was erected on which comedy skits were performed by students about desert nomads trying to get along in the city as well as jokes and social critiques about such activities as smoking and drinking. Many Emirates actors began their careers in such shows. Similar sketches were later performed in social clubs, precursors to fully scripted shows. Perhaps the most distinguishing characteristic of this genre was its flood of repetitive words and gestures, elements later seen in more sophisticated productions. But without trained artists, proper facilities and financial sponsorship, it was difficult for such work to coalesce into a truly professional movement.

By the early 1960s, however, important new initiatives were beginning to be seen. One such was a new respect for the author and a reduction in the use of improvised material by the actors. Another was the emergence of autonomous directors. These new elements could be seen clearly in such important productions as *Tawwil Umrak We-Shba'e Tamashah* (*Long Life and Full Scenery*) and *Wukalaat Sayhoun* (*Sayhoun's Agents*) by Jumm'a Gharib, himself both an author and director. Later came Wathiq as-Samarra'i, author and director of the play *Min Ajl Waladi* (*For My Son*) staged in 1963 at the Nadi-as-Sha'b (People's Club) in Sharjah with the participation of Mohammed Shafar, Mohammed al-Nakhi and Hasan Saif, the most distinguished members of the ar-Rawla Café's theatre group. In this production, many of the elements of modern theatrical work began to be seen – adequate rehearsal (three months), direction and even design with the roles of author and director clearly differentiated. The play was presented, however, only once. Because of its significance, though, audiences came from as far away as Dubai, Ajman and Ras al-Khaimah. After the success of this production, the group produced another play by the same author, *al-*

Adaalat (*Justice*). Later in 1963, the Nadi-Sh-Sha'b (Youth Club), an acting group from Dubai staged another play by as-Samarra'i, *Samiheeni* (*Forgive Me*), a play later performed in Qatar by Qatari actors. By early 1964 other clubs – such as Nadi-el-Khaleej (Gulf Club) in Dubai and Nadi-el-Uruba (Arab Club) in Sharjah – began presenting plays, including one about the Palestinian question.

Early on in its history, the acting group of an-Nadi-el-Ahli (National Club) in Abu Dhabi was presenting mostly revues and short pieces. Led by noted actors Yousef Hamadeh, Thani Bin Fitr and Saif al-Kubaisi, directors Mohammed al-Jenahi and Mohammed Ssawwan, and female impersonators Mohammed Yaseen and Yousef Sa'ad, in 1969 the group presented *Qahwat Ehaenaish* (*Ehaenaish's Café*), a work that went far beyond the limits of its earlier sketches. Its success encouraged the group to move, during the same year, to present the play *Tabib Fi-l-Qarn al-Ishreen* (*Doctor in the Twentieth Century*) written and staged by Wathiq es-Samarra'i.

A similarly structured play, *Qadi-el-Furaij* (*The Suburban Judge*), was later presented by the acting group of Nadi-el-Khaleej (Gulf Club), established by Mohammed Safar. Such innovative stage activities spread to other acting groups including Nadi-Sh-Shu'la (Flame Club) in Ajman, Nadi-Sh-Shurtah (Police Club) in Abu Dhabi, Nadi-n-Nasr (Victory Club) in Dubai and An-Nadi-el-Umani (Omani Club) in Ras el-Khaimah. Among the latter group's important early productions were *Ghala'e el-Muhoor* (*Costly Dowries*) written by Hamad Sultan and directed by Sa'eed Bumwaian for the Omani Club; *al-Fa'r* (*The Rat*) written by Awwad Nasrallah and directed by Murad Kamel for the Police Club; *Yawmiyyat Arqoob* (*Arqoob's Diaries*) written by Yousef Hamada with group direction for the Police Club; and *Arian ou Layeth a la Mafsakh* (*The Newlyweds of Layeth a la Mafsakh*) written and directed by Hanna Sa'adeh for the Police Club.

In 1971, coinciding with the declaration of union among the Emirates, came the establishment of various Union ministries, some dealing with various aspects of theatre. The Ministry of Information and Culture, for example, established a Theatre Division, the Ministry of Education established a Scholastic Theatre Division and the Ministry of Youth and Sports organized the Dubai National Youth Theatre Company. This latter company took as its members the best of the various actors working in the many clubs at the time. Out of this company, two further groups evolved. The first came under the umbrella of the Sharjah Folk Arts Society which ultimately became the Sharjah National Theatre Troupe. The second grew from the Oman Club Theatre Group which later gave rise to the Ahli (National) Theatre Group (later the Saqr ar-Rushood Theatre Troupe) in Ras el-Khaimah.

By 1975, these groups had all established themselves on an almost permanent basis, had presented plays that went beyond the many early amateur efforts and clearly recognized the roles of playwright and director and the importance of adherence to the script. Among major productions during this period were *Irhamouni Ya Naas* (*Oh People! Give Me Your Mercy*) by Mohammed Hamdan and directed by Husain Abu-l-Makarim, *Nokhathaht-l-Ghaws* (*The Pearl Captain*) by Abdullah Umran and directed by Abdullah al-Mutawwa, *Ayna eth-Thiqa* (*Where Is the Confidence*) by Mohammed Bakheet and collectively staged, *Istahil Illi Ili* (*I Deserve What Is Mine*) and *al-Layl Wa-l-Bahr* (*The Night and the Sea*) written and directed by Mahfouz al-Maghazi and *Ghaltat Abu Ahamad* (*Abu Ahamad's Mistake*) written and directed by Fouad Ubaid (the UAE government's choice for the 1975 Youth Festival in Libya).

That same year the Ministry of Information and Culture invited the Egyptian actor and director Zaki Tulaymat to carry out a study aimed at raising the performance level still further. The first part of Tulaymat's final report proposed practical ideas for the improvement of the movement. The second part was a listing of specific items needed to accomplish this growth. The report also included an addendum which proposed budgets. Overall the report identified and dealt with four important areas – artists, scripts, audiences and theatre in schools.

The Ministry of Information and Culture eventually earmarked a special budget for the development of theatrical activities while continuing to support a range of companies across the Emirates. As well, a number of theatres – either independent or as part of cultural centres – were constructed with capacities ranging between 500 and 1,000 seats. Among the theatres built at this time were the National Theatre, the Cultural Foundation and Al-Ain, Ajman, Bada'e Zaayid and Al-Fujairah Cultural Centres.

In the mid-1970s, after he directed *Shames En-Nahar* (*Day' Sun*) by Tawfiq al-Hakīm for Masrah Esh-Sharjah El-Wattani (Sharjah

National Theatre), Saqr ar-Rushood was named head of the ministry's Theatre Division. Almost immediately he established Firqat Masrah al-Imarat al-Qaouni (UAE National Theatre Troupe), a new company attached to the Theatre Division. In order to make new scripts more available, he put into effect the idea of a 'script bank' for which he organized a national playwriting competition. He also appointed experts such as Ibraheem Jalal and Abd-ur-Rahman as-Saleh (b. 1943), Khlifah al-Ouraifi, Abdul-Kareem Awadh and later advisers such as Fadel Az-Zu'bi, Farouk Ohan, Ar-Raieh Abdul-Qader, Yahya el-Hahajj and Fathi Diyab, from outside the Emirates.

Between 1978 and 1980 groups from other Arab countries were invited to perform in the UAE. Among these were the Kuwaiti Arab Gulf Theatre Troupe, which staged *Teb Um Usfour* (*Teb Bird's Mother*) and *Shal'e as-Sa'ada* (*The Happiness Chalet*), two plays by Mubarak Suwaid; the Kuwaiti Arts Theatre Troupe with its production of *Azubi as-Saalmiyyah* (*The Salmiyyah Bachelor*) by Husain Abd-ur-Rida and directed by Ahmad Abd-ul-Halim, and the Syrian Comedy Theatre Troupe, which presented *Jawz et-Tintayn* (*The Husband of Two*) and *Aah Min Hurmati* (*Oh! From My Wife*), two comedies by Sa'ad-ud-Deen Baqdounis and directed by Nizar Fouad and *Al-Mudhhek al-Mubaki* adapted and directed by Ibraheem Jalal for the Sharjah National Troupe.

Through the 1980s and into the 1990s theatre groups in the Emirates have presented a variety of plays in both classical and colloquial Arabic dealing with a wide range of subjects including such controversial social issues as dowries and the westernization of traditional lifestyles. Among the most important have been *El-Maal Maal Abouna* (*The Wealth Is Our Father's*), an adaptation from Ali Salem's *Bi'r al-Qameh* (*The Wheat Well*) written and directed by Khalifah al-Ouraefi for the Saqr ar-Rushood Theatre Troupe; *Dayayah ou Tuyuruha* (*A Chicken and its Birds*), an adaptation of Tawfiq al-Hakīm's *Majlis al-Adl* (*The Justice Council*) directed by Abdullah al-Manaa'i for the Sharjah National Theatre Troupe; *Qaadi Modail 80* (*The 1980s' Model Judge*) directed by ar-Reeh Abd-ul-Qaadir for the Dubai Society Theatre Group; *Ya Ghaafil Laka al-Laah* (*O Forgetful One, I Leave You to God*) by Dha'in Jumm'a and directed by Fathi Diyab for the National Youth Theatre Group; *Kalimat Haqq* (*A Word of Truth*) directed by Kareem Makhzanji for the theatre group of Um al-Qayuween Society; *Al-Fereeg*

(*The Suburb*) by Al-Latteef al-Mafeez and directed by Al-Lattef el-Qarqae for Sharjah National Theatre; and *Ma Taf'al Tijahi* (*What You Do For Me*) by Ismail Abdullah and directed by 'Ali Mas'ud for the Khorfakkan Society Theatre Group.

In 1983, the Ministry of Information and Culture extended invitations to several Arab theatrical groups to present some of their performances in the UAE. Among them were *Tismah Tidhak* (*Please Laugh*) directed by Mansour al-Mansour of the Kuwaiti National Theatre Company; *Kan Ya Ma Kan* (*Once Upon a Time*) by Yousef as-Sayyid and directed by Sa'ad az-Jazzaaf of the Bahraini Jazeera (Island) Club Theatre Troupe; and two monodramas – *Yawmiyyat Majnoun* (*A Madman's Diary*) adapted, acted and directed by Sa'edi Younis and *Nufous Ariyah* (*Naked Souls*) by Abd ur-Rahman Abou Zahra and performed for As-Slam Egyptian Group. Both plays were seen in Dubai, Sharjah and Fujairah.

The Theatre Division conducted a survey at this time of theatre spaces to pinpoint the specific needs of each and to upgrade them where possible. Also founded was the Layla Theatre for Children (in 1984) run by the female director Souad Jawad. Jawad directed a children's play entitled *Baet el-Haywanat* (*Animal House*) by Faiq el-Hakeem and *Layla wa Bhe'b* (*Layla and the Wolf*) which she wrote in 1984.

The country's first theatre magazine, *Majallat 'ar-Rawla al-Masrahiyya* (*ar-Rawla Theatrical Magazine*), emerged in the 1960s. First published as a monthly pamphlet by the Sharjah National Theatre Troupe in 1979 in the form of two typewritten issues edited by Mohammed Abdullah with an editorial staff from the members of the troupe, the third issue was published in the form of a full magazine in 1963 by al-Matba'ai al-Iqtisadiyya (Economic Press) in Dubai and edited by the Cultural Committee of the Sharjah National Theatre Troupe. The new publication contained a report on the first Theatrical Training Session, a series of meetings sponsored by the Ministry of Information and Culture between March and August 1982. By 1985, the *ar-Rawla* magazine was publishing

Al-Mudhhek al-Mubaki (1980) adapted and directed by Ibraheem Jalal for the Sharjah National Troupe.

Souad Jawad's 1983 production of *Baet el-Haywanat* (*Animal House*) by Faiq el-Hakeem at the Layla Theatre for Children.

four issues per year and was being edited by Ash-Sheikh Ahmad Bin Mohammed al-Qaasimi. Each issue included interviews, studies, panel discussions and reviews of local, pan-Arab and international theatrical activities such as festivals in Damascus, Baghdad, Rabat and Carthage, and even reports from as far away as Barcelona. Also in each issue were texts of new scripts. Another magazine beginning at this time was *Turaath Wa Funoon* (*Heritage and Arts*). Published by the Dubai Society for Popular Arts since 1980, the magazine has always included reports on theatre events.

In the mid-1980s, several major new plays and productions appeared – *Ghalat Fi Ghalat* (*Error Upon Error*) by Sulaiman aj-Jaasim and directed by Abdullah al-Manaa'i for the Fujairah National Youth Theatre Acting Troupe and later chosen as the UAE entry for the Carthage Theatre Festival where it was directed by Abdullah al-Ustaath; and *Juth-Tha Ala ar-Raseef* (*A Corpse on the Sidewalk*) written by the Syrian Sa'dallah Wanous and directed by Abdullah al-Manaa'i for the Fujairah National Youth Theatre Troupe. It was later staged at the Arab Theatre-on-Tour Festival in Morocco as was *Ma'esaat Abi-el-Fadl* (*The Tragedy of Abi-*

el-Fadl) adapted by Khalifah al-Uraifi and directed by Majdi Kamel. All of these plays were originally performed during the first Sharjah Days National Festival in 1984. The festival included panel discussions and group debates.

The most important and more or less professional company in the country in the 1990s has been the National Theatre Troupe, whose members mostly work through the ministry and, when they are not performing with the National Troupe, work with other acting groups in the Emirates. It has performed one or two plays each season since its inception. Among the most successful have been *Al-Awal Tahawal* (*The Former Has Changed*) and *Ili Malah Awal Malah Tali* (*He Who Has No Past Has No Future*), both by Abdul Aziz Assura'ie, and *Al-Fakh* (*The Trap*) by Mahfouz Abdul Rahman. All three were directed by Saqar ar-Rushood. The troupe has mounted *Dawaier al Kharse* (*Department of the Water Jar*) by Abdul Rahman el-Saleh, directed by Moncef Suwaisi and *Al-Wareeth Wal Lu' Lu'e* (*The Heir and the Pearl*) adapted and directed by Farouk Ohan, among others. All performances toured the seven Emirates and most participated in Arab theatre festivals.

Ghalat Fi Ghalat (*Error Upon Error*) by Sulaiman aj-Jaasim, directed in 1984 by Abdullah al-Ustaath at the National Theatre.

Other important troupes are Firqat Masrah Khalid (Khalid Theatre Troupe) established in 1972 as part of the Sharjah Folk Society; Firqat Masrah Khorfakkan Ash-Sha'bi (Khorfakkan Popular Theatre Troupe) established in 1979 as part of the Khorfakkan Folk Society; and Firqat al-Masrah at-Tajreebi (Experimental Theatre Troupe) established in Dubai in 1981.

All theatrical troupes must be licensed by the Ministry of Social Affairs with the Ministry of Culture providing such licensed troupes with annual financial support. The Theatre Division also has direct artistic responsibility for all public productions and advises on directors and actors.

The Ministry of Education sponsors two annual theatrical festivals, the School Activities Festival and the Military Schools Cultural Festival. International Theatre Day is used for a festival held every 27 March (first celebrated in the UAE in 1980). A new production is the centre of the World Theatre Day celebration, which includes speeches and panel discussions about the current status of theatre in the country.

The UAE has participated in several Arab theatrical festivals with entries nominated by the Ministry of Information and Culture. Among these have been the Damascus Theatre Arts Festival, the Arab Theatre-on-Tour Festival in Morocco, the Carthage Festival and Youth Festivals in Libya, Damascus and Kuwait, the Gulf Theatre Touring Festival and the Cairo International Experimental Theatre Festival.

In truth, however, it must be said that, even in the late 1990s, theatre is still very much a minority art form in the Emirates. In total, there are probably less than 150 people involved in spoken theatre on the professional or semi-professional level and productions are rare and special events during the year. Even more rare are the few indigenous plays with most productions being adaptations of western plays by dramatists such as Molière and O'Neill or production of writers from other Arab countries such as Sa'dallah Wanous, Tawfiq al-Hakīm and Yousif al-Aa'ni. There are only two Emirates playwrights worthy of the name – Abdul Rahman as Saleh (b. 1950) and Ahmad Rashid Thani (b. 1963). Saleh has written many plays including *As-Saied al-Mudeer* (*Mr Director*) and *Hikayaht Lam Tarwiha Shahrazad* (*A Tale Hasn't Been Told*

Al-Wareeth Wal Lu' Lu'e (*The Heir and the Pearl*) adapted and directed by Farouk Ohan.

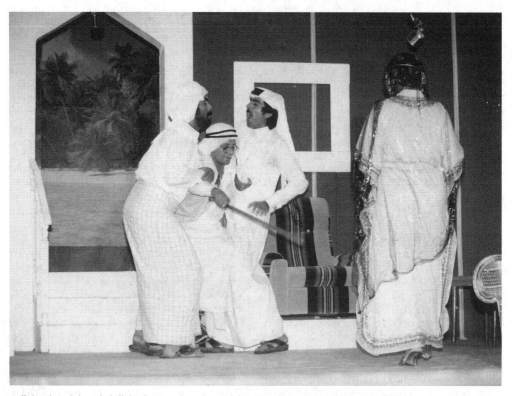

Mullah Ghreeb by Abdullah al-Ustaath, adapted from Molière's *Tartuffe* for Khalid Theatre Group, 1981.

By Shahrazad). Thani has written *El-ardhe-B-Tetkalam Urdu* (*The Land Speaks Urdu*), *Qafass Madagashqar* (*Madagascar Cage*) and *Elab-U-Ghuol Eseter* (*Play and Say God Bless Me*).

*Farouk Ohan, Mohammed Ben Ahmad
Assuwadi, Abdul Wahhab Ar-Radhwan and
Abdul Hameed Ahmad
Translated by Maha and Tony Chehade*

Further Reading

Abd ul-Qadir, Abd ul-Ilah. *al-Masrah Fi-l-Imaraat: Ru'ya Naqdiyya* [The theatre in the Emirates: a critical examination]. Abu Dhabi: Far' Bin Dasmal Press, 1985. 160 pp.

——. *Tarikh al-Harakah al-Masrahiyah Fi Dawlat al-Imarat, 1960–1986*. Al-Shariqah: Ittihad Kuttab wa-Udaba' al-Imarat, 1989. 298 pp.

Duwaib, Rif'at Mohammed. *Kitaab Aghaani al-A'raas Min Dawlat al-Imaraat al-Arabiyyah al-Muttahida* [Wedding songs from the United Arab Emirates]. Abu Dhabi: Ministry of Information and Culture, Kathim Press, 1982. 200 pp.

George, Jose. 'The Arrest and Trial of Malay Indians in the United Arab Emirates'. *TDR* 38 no. 2 (1994): 138–49.

Jumm'a, Dha'in. *Karraas An al-Masrah al-Madrasi* [School theatre in the UAE]. Abu Dhabi: National Press, 1985. 16 pp.

Majallat Kulliyat al-Adaab Li Jami'at al-Imaraat [Literature in the Emirates]. Dubai: 'al-Bayaan' Commercial Press for Emirates University. Since 1985.

Muhadaraat Al-Mawsam Ath-Thaqaafi Li Wizarat Al-I'laam Wa Th-Thaqaafa Munthu'l Aam 1971 Hatta Al-Aan [Cultural lectures sponsored by the Ministry of Information and Culture since 1971]. Abu Dhabi: Ministry of Culture. Annual series.

an-Nuwais, Abdullah. *Kitaab al-I'laam Wa-t-Tanmiya* [Cultural information and development in the UAE]. Abu Dhabi: Union Institute for Journalism, Publishing and Distribution, 1981.

Ohan, Farouk. 'Al-Ihtifaal al-Masrahi Fi Taqaleed Ar-Raqs Ash-Sha'bi: Raqsat al-Alayalah Fi al-Imaraat al-Arabiyyah al-Muttahida' [Theatrical festivities in the traditions of popular dances: the 'ayala' dance in the United Arab Emirates]. *Majallat al-Ma'thouraat as-Sha'biyya* [Popular Legacies Magazine] (January 1988): 41–61.

Taboor, Abdullah. *Al-Arabiyyah al-Muttahidah Bi-Imarat Ra's al-Khaimah* [The theatrical movement in Ras al-Khaimah]. Ras al-Khaimah: Nakheel Press, 1985.

Thani, Ahmad Rashid. *al-Masrah fi al-Imarat: al-hadir wa-al-mustaqbal* [al-Shariqah]: Da'irat al-Thaqafah wa-al-I'lam, Hukumat al-Shariqah, Dawlat al-Imarat al-'Arabiyah al-Muttahidah, 1994. 213 pp.

UNITED ARAB REPUBLIC

(see **EGYPT** and **SYRIA**)

YEMEN

(Overview)

The modern Yemen Republic was formally established in 1990 through unification of the Yemen Arab Republic (Yemen-Sana'a or North Yemen) and the People's Democratic Republic of Yemen (Yemen-Aden or South Yemen). On unification, the city of Sana'a in the north was designated as the political capital of Yemen, with Aden, the former capital of South Yemen, designated as the commercial capital.

One of the world's oldest suppliers of frank-incense, myrrh, spices and other luxury items, and now beginning to develop its oil and natural gas reserves, Yemen, on the southwest corner of the Arabian peninsula, is bordered by the Red Sea to the west and the Arabian Sea to the south. Yemen has a land area of 527,970 square kilometres (211,190 square miles). The Bab el-Mandeb, a strait along Yemen's southwestern coast, links the Indian Ocean with the Red Sea

and has been an important trading route for over three thousand years.

The population of the country – estimated in 1995 to be about 14.7 million – is predominantly Arab in respect to both language and culture. However, significant distinctions exist between Yemenis in the north and those in the south in areas of religion, tribal affiliation and occupation. Although almost all are Muslim, the northern mountains are home to the Zaidi, a Shiite sect, while low-lying areas are dominated by Sunni Muslims, who are quite distinct culturally and economically from the Zaidi. The two groups have often been at odds on social and political issues. Those resident on the coastal plain tend to be of Arab-African descent while the rest of the country is predominantly Arab.

Yemen is also home to small Christian, Hindu

and Jewish enclaves. The country has one of the world's lowest literacy rates with only 38 per cent of the population able to read and write. Still relatively undeveloped and closed to most of the world for long periods in its history, in the 1990s Yemen began to open up to commercial trade with other nations.

One of the earliest centres of the Arab world, ancient Yemen was well known by other early civilizations including the Egyptians, Greeks and northern Arabs. The scholar 'Abd ul-Hameed Younis has suggested that ancient Yemeni civilization never completely disappeared but rather metamorphosed through the ages into nomadic Bedouin communities carrying their civilization with them as they moved through the Arabian peninsula. Yemenis also actively participated in the spread of Islam in the seventh century.

From the sixteenth century until the end of World War I when it gained its independence, North Yemen was part of the Ottoman Empire while Aden (South Yemen) was under British control from 1839 and did not gain its independence until 1967. After independence, in the 1970s two civil wars broke out in Yemen and it was only in 1989 that progress was made toward a political association related to the development of oil reserves and natural gas supplies.

During the Gulf War (1990–1) Yemen supported Iraq, resulting in the expulsion of most Yemeni workers from Saudi Arabia, and in 1992 border clashes between Yemen and Saudi Arabia further escalated tension. The Yemeni economy was also overburdened at this time by an influx of refugees from the civil war in Somalia. Again in 1994, tensions between the north and south erupted into civil war in Yemen. By the end of that year, an uneasy peace had again settled over the nation.

In Yemen, as in most other Middle Eastern countries, poetry holds a special cultural place. Each Yemeni village has a resident poet who expresses official community sentiments on special occasions. Each village has its own method of expressing community greetings by singing poems it has prepared. Although such poetry developed through lines of tradition over the centuries, modern poetic styles are taking the older forms and moulding them into new modes of expression. Such poetry nevertheless maintains the two dominant streams. The first has as its purpose to foster a spiritual connection with God, the second expresses a more epic and heroic romantic poetry. It is only since the 1980s

A traditional dance.
Photo: Françoise-Eric de Repentigny, CIDA

that Yemeni poetry has been translated into more innovative forms.

Historians have suggested that the first appearance of theatre in most societies can be found in conjunction with religious rites and prayer gatherings. One can assume that in Yemen too an ancient theatre was born from religion. Indeed, the country has witnessed a huge number of religions from the worship of stone artefacts, trees, rain and animals, to the worship of the Sun, Moon, Venus and other heavenly bodies and, later, the worshipping of God according to the teachings of Moses, Jesus and finally Muhammad.

According to the scholar Mohammed Tawfiq in his book *Jawf al-Yaman* (*Inside Yemen*) and what others have written about religious life and the role of such rites of worship in the country, it would not be difficult to imagine that Yemen too would have created a theatre from such a rich religious background. Many questions about ancient Yemeni civilization and the possible existence of a Yemeni theatre, however, still lie buried in the sands here and such questions will not be resolved until the traces of those early civilizations are unearthed by archaeologists and their story is told by historians.

A musician playing a *d'oud*, an instrument that resembles a mandolin.
Photo: Françoise-Eric de Repentigny, CIDA

Lest anyone believe that this speculation is not rooted in fact, it should be noted here that a theatre was unearthed near the site of the destroyed Ma'rib Dam. As for a literary history, Ben Ezra, an eighteenth-century Jewish scholar, has suggested that the Book of Job – one of the most dramatic in the Old Testament – had Yemeni Arab origins and that it may have been written in Yemen around the twentieth century BC and then translated into Hebrew. Though the original Arabic text is lost, historians point to the many names in the book, names that connect it culturally and linguistically to pre-Islamic Yemen.

The major book in the theatre field is Sa'eed 'Aulaqi's *Sab'oun 'Aaman Min al-Masrah Fi l-Yaman* (*Seventy Years of Yemeni Theatre*, 1980). In it, he points out that modern theatrical activities started in Yemen in 1904 when an Indian theatrical company visited Aden bringing along with it a number of musicians, singers and actors as well as a large number of tame animals, peacocks, pigeons and other multi-coloured singing birds. This event, performed to entertain Indian workers in Aden, though not Yemeni, probably had an indirect effect on later theatrical developments, in that it led some edu-cated Yemenis to start thinking about the possi-bility of starting similar activities on their own.

The first Yemeni group to engage in western-style acting was established by students of the Government School in 1910. This school group presented the play *Julius Caesar* on a small stage that was erected in a tennis court behind the Ministry of Education building in the Crater Quarter. That performance, the first Arabic the-atrical presentation in Aden, was the initial step in the process of establishing a more modern Yemeni theatre. In the beginning, stage perfor-mances relied on translated foreign plays that were of Indian or English origins. At a later point, stage plays were written in Arabic using Arab historical subjects.

These initial scholastic efforts were later aug-mented by the theatrical activities of various companies such as the 1929 performance of the play *Salaah ud-Deen al-Ayyoubi*, and the spreading of theatrical activities outside the con-fines of Aden to Lahaj, where plays, derived from historical, religious and romantic stories were occasionally presented.

Sa'eed 'Aulaqi also indicates that the Yemeni theatre at the time completely relied on roman-tic and historical plays because the Yemenis, politically cut off from the rest of the Arab world, found in such plays a kind of bridge linking them with their past. In such plays, Yemenis also reflected their longings for freedom and independence.

Most of these early efforts at writing literary plays were done in verse or, at the very least, in prose with a strong rhythmic cadence, literary forms with soul-stirring language. Such school theatre productions of historical plays reached their peak in the late 1950s when political ideas began to be seen even in schools. Audiences, though small at this time, would usually include government employees. In Aden, occasional films were also seen which attracted people from both north and south (movies in North Yemen were not seen until 1963).

The first printed theatrical work to be widely read in Yemen was *Pygmalion*, a play written in verse by the poet and playwright Mohammed 'Ali Luqmaan. First printed in 1948, it was also the first fully scripted play to appear on a non-scholastic Yemeni stage. In an introduction, 'Ali Luqmaan wrote, 'Pygmalion is a Greek legend that captivated Bernard Shaw [and] also [Egyptian dramatist] Tawfiq al-Hakīm. . . . Each of those two writers chose different con-ceptual and artistic modes while creating their own version.'

But *Pygmalion* was not the only play of note from this period. Others included *Musaafir Layl* (*Night Traveller*) by Salaah 'Abd as-Sabour, *Fi Ard al-Jannatayn* (*In the Land of the Two Edens*, 1963) by poet Mohammed ash-Sharafi, *Saif Bin Thee Yazin* (1964) by poet Mohammed Abdu Ghaanim, *Samraa' al-'Arab* (*The Arab Brunette*, 1966) by 'Ali Luqmaan and *Hareeq Fi San'aa'* (*A Fire in Sana*, 1974) by ash-Sharafi.

Ash-Sharafi's *Fi Ard al-Jannatayn* (*In the Land of the Two Edens*) is a four-act verse play dealing with the tragic reign in Yemen of Imam Ahmad in the 1940s and 1950s. In the second act, the Imam is seen isolated in his castle and surrounded by his concubines, one of which, Muhsina, was entrusted with the task of running the affairs of the country. The last act includes scenes about the final days of the Imam's rule. A poetic work, the play combined comedy and tragedy.

Hareeq Fi San'aa' (*A Fire in Sana'a*), ash-Sharafi's second work, is a three-act play, which dealt with the true story of a fire that started in a movie house during a famine. Religious leaders argued that it had been caused by the shameful films being shown but the people understood that famines had also come before. Indeed, the play symbolized the greater conflagration that was consuming the whole country at that time under the Imam's regime.

Ghaanim's *Saif Bin Thee Yazin* was a stage adaptation of a long poem published by him earlier – *'Ala sh-Shaati' al-Mas-hour* (*On the Magic Beach*). Looking at the events historically referred to as the story of the Christians of Najraan, the play is a military epic of belief and invasion.

Eighteen years after writing his first play, 'Ali Luqmaan wrote his second drama *Samraa' al-'Arab* (*The Arab Brunette*) but the play, not as strong as his earlier play, was never staged. Derived from Arab history, it alludes to various national symbols and was written during the armed revolt against the British occupation of Aden. Although set in the third century AD – during the hegemony of the Roman Empire over Tadmur in present-day Syria – it was clear that Tadmur stood for Aden, the Roman Empire represented the British Empire and Khayraan, the vassal Arab ruler, was a symbol representing the contemporary professional politicians or even those sultans who offered their services to foreign colonists.

The Yemeni independence revolution succeeded in destroying the walls of cultural isolation which the country had suffered from for centuries, especially the North. In the next few years, such early occasional attempts at creating a literary theatre were replaced by, first, an amateur theatre of considerable energy and later by an even more serious quasi-professional theatre connected to styles being seen in other Arab countries. Both the amateur companies and the government-sponsored ones began to be seen by the late 1960s.

In 1971, Firqat al-Masrah al-Watani (National Theatrical Company) was established in Aden. Two years later, a similar company, with the same name, was established in Sana'a. This second company not only was active in presenting a number of Yemeni, Arab and international plays on stage in Yemen, but also performed several plays on radio and television. Perhaps the two most important plays presented by the National Theatrical Company in Sana'a in its early days were *al-Fa'r Fi Qafas al-Ittihaam* (*The Mouse in the Dock*) by 'Abd al-Kaafi Mohammed Sa'eed and *al-Jarra* (*The Earthen Jar*). The former, a symbolic play, dealt with the destructive role played by a mouse in causing the destruction of the Ma'rib Dam in ancient Yemen; the latter was first written by the Italian playwright Luigi Pirandello and directed by Husain al-Asmar. Pirandello's original was about the tyranny of the feudal lords in Italy against peasants and craftsmen. In the Yemeni version, the director heavily adapted the plot and characters to fit a more local milieu.

'Ali Ahmad Bakathir (1910–69) is the most prolific Yemeni playwright. Born in Indonesia of Arab parents and brought up in Yemen, he moved to Egypt in 1934 and remained there for the rest of his life. Bakathir began his literary life as a poet and was deeply influenced by the plays of the Egyptian poet and playwright Ahmad Shawqi. Bakathir wrote three plays in verse but then decided that prose was a more natural theatrical language. Bakathir had actually written his first play in verse before he left Yemen having read some of Shawqi's work there. Entitled *Humam* and published in 1934, the connections between the two writers were clear. His next two plays were equally influenced by his reading of Shakespeare, whose masterpieces were written in verse but a verse significantly different from Arabic poetry with its strict rules of metres and rhymes. Bakathir's second and third plays were ultimately written in blank verse – a translation of *Romeo and Juliet* and a drama entitled *Ikhnaton and Nefertiti*.

Bakathir ultimately wrote more than twenty plays, most of the later ones in prose and most generally better suited for reading than staging. In choosing to write plays in prose on historical subjects, Bakathir was also later influenced by the Egyptian playwright Tawfiq al-Hakīm. Among his major historical plays are *al-Fir'awn al-Maw'ud* (*The Promised Pharaoh*, 1945), *Ma'sat Udib* (*The Tragedy of Oedipus*, 1949), *Sirr Shahrazad* (*The Secret of Shahrazad*, 1953), *Uziris* (*Osiris*, 1959), *Al-Za'im al-Awhad* (*The Supreme Leader*) and *Abu Dalama*. Among his major non-historical plays – both comedies and social dramas – are *Gulfadan Hanum* (*Madame Gulfadan*), written in the local vernacular; *Habl ul-Ghasil* (*The Clothesline*), also written in the local vernacular; *Shayluk al-Jadid* (*The New Shylock*, 1945), about the Palestinian problem; *Sha'b Allah al-Mukhtar* (*God's Chosen People*, 1945); *Ilah Isra'il* (*God of Israel*); *Musmar Juha* (*Juha's Pin*), about the British occupation of Egypt; *Dr Haazim*, a modern domestic drama; *Imbiraturiyya fi' l-Mazad* (*An Empire for Auction*, c.1953), a political satire that takes up where *God's Chosen People* leaves off; *al-Dunya Fawda* (*This Chaotic World*, c.1957); and *Qitat wa Firan* (*Cats and Mice*, c.1959).

Other notable Yemeni playwrights include the aforementioned scholar Saeed Aulaqi (b. 1940), a writer and dramatist from the former South Yemen who has written plays about the two revolutions of North and South Yemen. He has also published several plays including *Nidaa' al-Ard* (*The Land's Call*), *Fawq al-Jabal* (*On the Mountaintop*), *al-Qawi Wa l-Aqwa* (*The Strong and the Stronger*), *at-Tirka* (*The Inheritance*), *Mashrou' Zawaaj* (*The Marriage Project*) and *al-Mahzala al-Idaariyya* (*The Administrative Farce*).

Abd al-Majeed al-Qadi (b. 1934) is a short-story writer and dramatist originally from the district of Taiz. Working for the Ministry of Culture in Aden, he published two plays, *Bint al-Daudah* (*Al-Daudah's Daughter*) and *al-Fata Mansour al-Mansour* (*Young Man Mansour*). His writings reflect a deep involvement with and commitment to social progress and change within the country.

Mohammed ash-Sharafi (b. 1940), born in the district of Hajja, also published more than twenty volumes of poetry and plays. A government diplomat, among his most noted plays are *In the Land of the Two Edens*, *Al-Intithaar Lan Yatoul* (*Waiting Will Not Be Too Long*), *Al-Ghaa'ib Ya'oud* (*The Absent One Returns*), *At-Tareeq Ila Ma'rib* (*The Road to Ma'rib*), *Mawta bi-La Akfaan* (*The Dead Without Shrouds*) and *Min Mawaasim al-Hijra Wa l-Junoun* (*Seasons of Migration and Madness*). He has been unusually active in issues connected to women's rights, a major theme in his writing.

Other playwrights of note include Ahmad Dahmash, author of *al-Wa'i* (*Awareness*); Ahmad Mohammed ash-Shaami, author of *Muhaakama Fi Jannat ash-Shu'araa'* (*A Trial in Poets' Paradise*); Hasan al-Lawzi, author of *as-Suraakh Fi Mahkamat?* (*Shouting in the Court of?*); 'Abd ul-Kaafi Mohammed Sa'eed, author of *Unshoudat as-Sab'ayn* (*The Song of the Two Lions*), *as-Safar Fi th-Thalaam* (*Travelling in the Dark*), *Mughtarib Ila l-Abad* (*Immigrant Forever*) and *'Abdaan* (*Two Slaves*); 'Abdalla al-Hayfi, author of *al-Jazaa'* (*The Retribution*), *al-Khubz Wa l-'Ilm* (*Bread and Science*), *ad-Dameer Fi Ijaaza* (*A Conscience on Leave*), *Madrasat al-Mughaffaleen* (*The School of Fools*) and *Shay' La Bud Minhu* (*Something That Must Be*); and 'Ali Luqmaan, author of *al-'Adl al-Mafqoud* (*The Lost Justice*), *ath-Thill al-Manshoud* (*The Sought-after Shadow*), *Adonees Aw Ard as-Salaam* (*Adonis or the Land of Peace*) and *Qays Wa Layla* (*Qays and Layla*).

Also al-Qarshi 'Abd ur-Raheem Salaam, author of *Salaat at-Turaab* (*The Soil Prayer*) and *Ma' ish-Shams Yaji'oun* (*They Came with the Sun*); Mohammed al-Hayfi, author of *li-kul Shay' Nihaaya* (*Everything Has an End*); Mohammed az-Zarqa, author of *Laylat al-'Eed* (*The Eve of the Holiday*) and *Kullun Lahu 'Aalamahu al-Khaas* (*Each Has His Own Special World*); Mohammed ash-Shihaari, author of *al-Jeneraal Wa l-Barlamaan* (*The General and the Parliament*), *az-Zawaaj ad-Daa'i'* (*The Lost Marriage*) and *Tinba' Min Bayn al-'Aseed* (*Springs from the Gruel*); and Mohammed Muthna, author of *al-Qaadimoun Ma' il-Fajr* (*Those Arriving at Dawn*).

There is one arts association in the country – the Federation of Yemeni Men of Letters and Authors.

Abdul Aziz Makaleh
Translated by Maha and Tony Chehade

Further Reading

'Aulaqi, Sa'eed *Sab'oun 'Aaman Min al-Masrah Fi l-Yaman* [Seventy years of Yemeni theatre]. 1980.

Al-Haddad, Abdul-Rahman. *Cultural Policy in the Yemen Arab Republic*. Paris: UNESCO, 1982. 74 pp.

Luqmaan, Hamzah 'Ali. *Qisas min tarikh al-Yaman*. Sana'a: Dar al-Kalimah, 1985. 93 pp.

Rahumah, Muhammad Mahmud. *Dirasat fi al-shi'r wa al-masrah al-Yamani*. Sana'a: Dar al-Kalimah, 1985. 184 pp.

Zuwiyya, Jalal, compiler. 'Yemen' In *The Near East (South-west Asia and North Africa): A Bibliographic Study*. Metuchen, NJ: Scarecrow Press, 1973: 306–409.

YEMEN ARAB REPUBLIC

(see **YEMEN**)

FURTHER READING

The following selected bibliography was prepared by *WECT* staff in association with the Theater Research Data Center at Brooklyn College, publishers of the *International Bibliography of Theatre*. Essential books that deal with particular countries included in this volume can generally be found at the end of the respective national articles. The books included here tend to be of a more general nature.

Reference Works/Dictionaries/ Encyclopedias/Bibliographies

Naga, Abdul. *Recherche sur les termes de théâtre et leur traduction en arabe moderne.* [Research into theatrical terms and their translations into modern Arabic]. Algiers, 1973.

Omotoso, Kole. 'Arabic Drama in North Africa'. In *Theatre in Africa.* Edited by Oyin Ogunba and Abiola Irele. Ibadan: Ibadan University Press, 1978.

'Selected Bibliography of Arabic Drama'. *Theatre Three* 6 (fall 1989): 65–8.

Souissi, Moncef. 'L'État législatif du théâtre arabe' [Legal status of Arab theatre]. *Congrés Internacional de Teatre a Catalunya 1985.* Actes, vol. 3, sections 4, 5, 6. Edited by Jordi Coca and Laura Conesa. Barcelona: Institut del Teatre, 1987.

Tomiche, Nada and Cherif Khaznadar. *Le Théâtre arabe* [Arab theatre]. Paris: UNESCO, 1969. 229 pp.

Theatre History

Aziza, Mohamed. *Regards sur le théâtre arabe contemporain* [A look at contemporary Arab theatre]. Tunis: Maison tunisienne de l'édition, 1970.

Badawi, M.M. 'Modern Arabic Drama Outside Egypt'. *Theatre Three* 6 (fall 1989): 53–64.

Buonaventura, Wendy. *The Serpent and the Sphinx.* Como: Lyra, 1986. 221 pp.

Bushrui, S.B. 'Casablanca: The Arab Theatre'. *World Theatre* 15 (September 1966): 419–22.

'Glance at the Origins of the Arab Theatre'. *World Theatre* 14 (November 1965): 607–9.

Kadiri, Ali. 'Arab Theatre Seminar, Casablanca, 17–20 November 1966'. *Afro-Asian Theatre Bulletin* 2 no. 2 (1967): 25–7.

Landau, Jack M. 'The Arab Theatre'. *Middle East Affairs* 4 (March 1953): 77–86.
'The Precursors of the Arab Theatre'. *World Theatre* 16 no. 2 (1967): 188–93.

Al-Ra'i, Ali. 'Arabic Drama Since the Thirties'. *Modern Arabic Literature* (1992): 402–3.
——. *Al Masrah fil watan al arabi* [Theatre in the Arab world]. Kuwait, 1987.

Criticism and Aesthetics

al-Ahmed, Ahmed Sulaimaan. *Diraasaat Fi al-Masrah al-'Arabi al-Mu'aasir* [Studies on the contemporary Arab theatre]. Damascus: al-Ajyaal [Generations] Publishing House, 1972.
Allen, Roger. 'Drama and Audience: The Case of Arabic Theatre'. *Theatre Three* 6 (fall 1989): 7–20.
Al-'Aqqad, A.M. 'The Theatre: Why It Has Not Developed Among the Arabs'. *Al-Kitab* 8 (December 1949): 649–52.
Bushrui, S.B. 'Shakespeare and Arabic Drama and Poetry'. *Ibadan* 20 (October 1964): 5–16.
Khouri, Chaki. *Le Théâtre arab de l'absurde* [Absurdist Arab theatre]. Paris: A.G. Nizet, 1978. 190 pp.

Manzalaoui, Mahmoud. *Arabic Writing Today*, 2 vols. Cairo: American Research Centre in Egypt, 1968–77.
Mubarak, Khalid. *Arabic Drama: A Critical Introduction*. Khartoum, Sudan: Khartoum University Press, 1986. 95 pp.
Al-Ra'i, Ali. *al-Masrah Fi al-Watan al-'Arabi* [The theatre in the Arab world]. Kuwait: 'Aalam al-Ma'rifa [World of Knowledge] no. 25, 1980.
Various. *Al masrah al arabi bainal nakli wal ta'sis* [Arab theatre: between limitation and creation]. Kuwait, 1988.
Wanous, Sa'dallah. *Bayanat li masrah arabi jadid* [Manifesto for a new Arab theatre]. Beirut: Dâr al-Farâbî, 1988.

Theatre Arts

Boyd, Douglas A. *Broadcasting in the Arab World.* Ames: Iowa State University Press, 1993.
Cocteau, Jean. *Maalesh: A Theatrical Tour in the Middle East.* Translated by Mary C. Hoeck. Westport, CT: Greenwood Press, 1978.
Karachouli, Regina and Wolfgang Hauswald. 'Vielfalt der Mittel und Genres' [Diversity of means and genres]. *Theater der Zeit* 44 no. 4 (1989): 61–4.
Landau, Jack M. *Studies in the Arab Theatre and Cinema.* Philadelphia: University of Pennsylvania Press, 1958.
Lindaw, Ya'qoub. *Diraasaat Fi l-Masrah Wa s-Sinema 'Ind al-'Arab* [Studies about the Arab

theatre and cinema]. Translated by Ahmed al-Maghaazi. Cairo: Egyptian Public Book Organization, 1972.
Najm, Mohammed Yousef. *al-Masrahiyya Fi l-Adab al-'Arabi al-Hadeeth* [The theatrical play in modern Arabic literature]. Beirut: Beirut Publishing House, 1956.
Oukla Irsan, Ali. *Al zawaher al masrahia indal'arab* [Arabic forms of performance]. Damascus, 1981.
Slauth, Georg and Sami Zubaida, eds. *Mass Culture, Popular Culture and Social Life in the Middle East.* Boulder, CO: Westview Press, 1987.

Anthologies

Jayyusi, Salma Khadra and Roger Allen, eds. *Modern Arabic Drama: An Anthology.* Indiana: University of Indiana Series in Arab and Islamic Studies, 1995. 480 pp.

Puppet and Mask Theatre

'Adel Abu-Shanab. *Karaküz*. Damascus: Ministry for the Preservation and Promulgation of Antiquities, n.d.

Landau, Jack M. 'Arab Shadow Play'. *Atlantic*

Monthly 98 (October 1956): 142–3.

——. *Shadow Plays in the Near East*. Jerusalem: Palestine Institute of Folklore and Ethnology, 1948.

Music and Dance Theatre

Farrah, Ibrahim and Adam Lahm. 'Sizing Up Realities in Ethnic Dance'. *Arabesque* 8 (July–August 1982): 4–5, 20.

Izzard, Molly. 'The Music of the Arabian Gulf'. *Dilmun: A Journal of Archaeology and History in Bahrain* 9 (1980): 4–9.

Traditional Theatre

Bayatly, Kassim. 'La tragedia religiosa araba' [Arabic religious tragedy]. *Quaderni di Teatro* 8 no. 32 (May 1986): 111–15.

Faik, Ala Yahya. *Theatrical Elements in Religious Storytelling of Medieval Islamic Culture*. Ann Arbor: University of Michigan, 1986. 154 pp.

Reynolds, Dwight Fletcher. *Heroic Poets, Poetic Heros: The Ethnography of Performance in Arabic Oral Tradition*. Ithaca, NY: Cornell University Press, 1995. 243 pp

INTERNATIONAL REFERENCE

SELECTED BIBLIOGRAPHY

The following is a list of significant theatre books that have been published since the early 1960s. For a complete listing of world theatre publications, see Volume 6 of this encyclopedia, *World Theatre Bibliography/Cumulative Index*. This section was prepared with the collaboration of the Belgian scholar René Hainaux and the Centre de Recherches et de Formation Théâtrales en Wallonie with the assistance of collaborators from Europe, North and South America, Africa, the Arab World and Asia and the Pacific.

Reference Works/Dictionaries/Encyclopedias/Bibliographies

Attisani, Antonio. *Enciclopedia del teatro del' 900.* [Theatre encyclopedia of the twentieth century]. Milan: Feltrinelli, 1980. 598 pp.

Bailey, Claudia Jean. *A Guide to Reference and Bibliography for Theatre Research.* 2nd ed. Columbus, OH: Ohio State University Libraries, 1983.

Banham, Martin, ed. *The Cambridge Guide to World Theatre.* Cambridge: Cambridge University Press, 1988. 1,104 pp.

Brauneck, Manfred, and Gérard Schneilin, eds. *Theaterlexikon: Begriffe und Epoche. Bühnen und Ensembles* [Theatre lexicon: terms and periods. Stages and ensembles]. Hamburg: Rowohlt, 1986. 1,120 pp.

Bryan, George G., ed. *Stage Lives: A Bibliography and Index to Theatrical Bibliographies in English.* Westport, CT Greenwood Press, 1985. 368 pp.

Cao, Yu, and Wang, Zuo Ling, eds. *China's Great Encyclopedia of World Theatre and Drama.* Beijing/Shanghai: China's Great Encyclopedia Press, 1989. 583 pp.

Carpenter, Charles A., *Modern Drama Scholarship and Criticism 1966–1980: An International Bibliography.* Downsview, ON: University of Toronto Press, 1985. 650 pp.

Cohen, Selma Jeanne, ed. *International Encyclopedia of Dance.* Oxford: Oxford University Press, 1995.

Coreman, Linda, Charles A. Carpenter and Rebecca Cameron, compilers, 'Modern Drama Studies: An Annual Bibliography'. *Modern Drama* 36 (June 1993): 179–348.

Corvin, Michel. *Dictionnaire encyclopédique du théâtre* [Encyclopedic dictionary of theatre]. Paris: Borduas, 1991.

Couty, Daniel, and Alan Rey, eds. *Le Théâtre* [Theatre]. Paris: Borduas, 1980.

Cruciani, Fabrizio and Nicola Savarese, eds. *Teatro* [Theatre]. Milan: Garzanti, 1991. 353 pp.

Dahlhaus, Carl. *Pipers Enzyklopädia des Musiktheaters* [Piper's encyclopedia of music theatre]. 5 vols. Munich: Piper, 1986–.

D'Amico, Silvio, ed. *Enciclopedia dello spettacolo*

[Encyclopedia of the performing arts]. 11 vols. Rome: Le Maschere, 1954–66.

Eaker, Shirley, ed. *The Back Stage Handbook for Performing Artists*. 3rd revised ed. New York: Back Stage Books, 1995. 304 pp.

Elias, Marie and Hanan Kassab-Hassan, eds. *Dictionary of Theatre: Terms and Concepts of Drama and the Performing Arts* [Arabic-French-English]. Beirut: Librairie de Liban, 1997.

Esslin, Martin, ed. *The Encyclopedia of World Theater*. New York: Scribner, 1977.

Fielding, Eric, gen. ed. *Theatre Words: An International Vocabulary in Nine Languages*. Prague: Publication and Information Exchange Commission of OISTAT, 1993.

Fliotsos, Anne L. 'Listservs for Laymen: Accessing Theatre Information' *Theatre Topics* 5 (March 1995): 81–7.

Gassner, John, and Edward Quinn, eds. *The Readers' Encyclopedia of World Drama*. New York: Thomas Y. Crowell, 1969. 1,030 pp.

Giteau, Cécile. *Dictionnaire des arts du spectacle: Théâtre-Cinéma-Cirque-Danse-Radio-Marionettes-Télévision-Documentologie* [Dictionary of the performing arts: Theatre-Film-Circus-Dance-Radio-Puppetry-Television-Documentation]. [French, English and German]. Paris: Dunod, 1970. 430 pp.

Gregor, Josef, and Margret Dietrich. *Der Schauspielführer: Der Inhalt der wichtigsten Theaterstücke aus aller Welt*. [The play guide: synopses of the most important plays from the whole world]. 15 vols. Stuttgart: Anton Hiersemann, 1953–93.

Hainaux, René, ed. *Stage Design Throughout the World*. 4 vols. London: Harrap and New York: Theatre Arts Books, 1956–75.

Hartnoll, Phyllis, and Peter Found, eds. *The Concise Oxford Companion to the Theatre*. 2nd ed. New York: Oxford University Press, 1992. 586 pp.

——. *The Oxford Companion to the Theatre*. 4th ed. London: Oxford University Press, 1983. 934 pp.

Hawkins-Day, Mark, ed. *International Dictionary of Theatre*. Vol. 2: *Playwrights*. Detroit/London/Washington: Gale Research International/St James Press, 1994. 1,218 pp.

Hochman, Stanley, ed. *McGraw-Hill Encyclopedia of World Drama*. 2nd ed. 5 vols. New York: McGraw-Hill, 1984.

Hoffmann, Christel, ed. *Kinder- und Jugendtheater der Welt* [Children's and youth theatre of the world]. 2nd ed. Berlin: Henschelverlag, 1984. 276 pp.

Kienzle, Siegfried. *Schauspielführer der Gegenwart. Interpretation zum Schauspiel ab 1945* [A guide to contemporary plays: an interpretation of plays since 1945]. Stuttgart: Alfred Kröner Verlag, 1978. 659 pp.

Koegler, Horst, ed. *The Concise Oxford Dictionary of Ballet*. Oxford: Oxford University Press, 1987. 458 pp.

Kullman, Colby H. and William C. Young. *Theatre Companies of the World*. 2 vols. New York/London: Greenwood Press, 1986.

Leleu-Rouvray, Geneviève, and Gladys Langevin, eds. *International Bibliography on Puppetry: English Books 1945–1990*. Paris: Institut International de la Marionnette/Associations Marionnette et Thérapie, 1993. 281 pp.

McCoy, Ken. 'A Brief Bibliography of Internet Theatre Resources Beyond Email: Excerpts from Ken McCoy's Guide to Internet Resources in Theatre and Performance Studies'. *Theatre Topics* 5 (March 1995): 89–94.

Matlaw, Myron. *Modern World Drama: An Encyclopedia*. London: Secker & Warburg, 1972. 960 pp.

Mikotowicz, Thomas J., ed. *Theatrical Designers: An International Biographical Dictionary*. Westport, CT: Greenwood Press, 1992. 365 pp.

Mokulski, S.S., and P.A. Markov, eds. *Teatralnaia Entsiklopedia* [Theatre encyclopedia]. 6 vols. Moscow: Sovietskaia Entsiklopedia, 1961–7.

Molinari, Cesare. *Storia universale del teatro* [Universal history of the theatre]. Milan: Mondador, 1983. 358 pp.

Morey, Carl. 'Under the "O" for Opera'. *Opera Canada* 34 (spring 1993).

Ortolani, Benito, ed. *International Bibliography of Theatre*. 7 vols. New York: Theatre Research Data Center, 1985–93.

Parker, Roger, ed. *The Oxford Illustrated History of Opera*. Oxford/New York: Oxford University Press, 1994. 541 pp.

Pavis, Patrice. *Dictionnaire du théâtre: termes et concepts de l'analyse théâtrale*. [Dictionary of the theatre: terms and concepts of theatrical analysis]. 2nd ed. Paris: Éditions Sociales, 1987. 477 pp.

Philpott, A.R. *Dictionary of Puppetry*. London: MacDonald, 1969. 291 pp.

Queant, G., ed. *Encyclopédia du théâtre contemporain* [Encyclopedia of contemporary theatre]. Paris: Olivier Perrin, 1959. 211 pp.

Rischbieter, Henning. *Theater-Lexikon*. [Theatre lexicon] Neuausgabe, Zurich-Schwäbisch Hall: Orell Füssli, 1983. 484 pp.

Sadie, Stanley, ed. *The New Grove Dictionary of Opera*. 4 vols. London: Macmillan, 1992.

Salgado, Gamini and Peter Thomson. *The Everyman Companion to the Theatre*. London: J.M. Dent, 1985. 458 pp.

Schindler, Otto G. *Theaterliteratur: Ein Bibliographischer Behelf für das Studium der*

Theaterwissenschaft [Theatre literature: a bibliographic guide for theatre studies]. 3 vols. Vienna: Institut für Theaterwissenschaft, 1973.

Shemanski, Frances. *A Guide to World Fairs and Festivals.* Westport, CT/London: Greenwood Press, 1985. 309 pp.

Shigetoshi, Kawatake, ed. *Engeki Hyakka Daijiten* [Encyclopedia of world theatre]. 6 vols. Tokyo: Heibonsha, 1960–2.

Swortzell, Lowell, ed. *International Guide to Children's Theatre and Educational Theatre: A Historical and Geographical Source Book.* Westport, CT: Greenwood Press, 1990. 360 pp.

Trapido, Joel, Edward A. Langhans and James R. Brandon, eds. *An International Dictionary of Theatre Language.* Westport, CT/London: Greenwood Press, 1985. 1,032 pp.

Veinstein, André, and Alfred Golding, eds. *Performing Arts Libraries and Museums of the World/Bibliothèques et musées des arts du spectacle dans le monde.* 4th ed. Paris: Centre National de la Recherche Scientifique, 1992. 773 pp.

Wilcox, R. Turner. *The Dictionary of Costume.* New York: Scribner, 1969. 406 pp.

Theatre History

Ahrends, Günther and Hans Jürgen Diller, eds. *Chapters from the History of Stage Cruelty.* Tübingen: Gunter Navr Verlag, 1994. 171 pp.

Anderson, Jack. *Ballet and Modern Dance: A Concise History.* 2nd ed. Princeton, NJ: Princeton Book Company, 1992. 287 pp.

Arnott, Peter. *The Theatre in its Time.* Boston, MA: Little, Brown, 1981. 566 pp.

Aslan, Odette. *L'Art du théâtre* [The art of theatre]. Verviers: Marabout, 1963. 672 pp.

Awad, Louis. *Al masrah al âlami* [World theatre]. Egypt, 1964.

Beneventi, Paolo. *Introduzione alla storia del teatro-ragazzi* [An introduction to the history of children's theatre]. Florence: La casa Usher, 1994. 213 pp.

Brockett, Oscar G. *History of the Theatre.* 6th ed. Boston, MA: Allyn & Bacon, 1990. 680 pp.

Calendoli, Giovanni. *Storia universale della danza* [General history of dance]. Milan: Mondadori, 1985. 288 pp.

Dumur, Guy, ed. *Histoire des spectacles* [History of the performing arts]. Encyclopédie de la Pléiade Collection. Paris: Gallimard, 1965. 2,010 pp.

Heszke, Bela. *Szinhaz: Szinhaz torteneti breviarium* [Theatre: Breviary of theatre history]. Budapest: Simonffy, 1995. 95 pp.

International Theatre Institute. *World of Theatre 1988–1990.* Moscow: Culture Publishing, 1991. 172 pp.

——. *World of Theatre 1990–1992.* Bangladesh: ITI, 1993. 275 pp.

Jurkowski, Henryk. *Dzieje teatru lalek: od wielkiej reformy do współczesności* [History of the puppet theatre: from theatre's reform to today]. Warsaw, 1984.

——. *Écrivains et marionnettes: quatre siècles de littérature dramatique* [Writers and puppets: four centuries of dramatic literature]. Charleville-Mézières: Institut National de la Marionnette, 1991.

Kostelanetz, Richard. *On Innovative Performances: Three Decades of Recollections on Alternative Theatre.* London: McFarland, 1994. 276 pp.

Kuritz, Paul. *The Making of Theatre History.* Englewood Cliffs, NJ: Prentice-Hall, 1988. 468 pp.

Kybalova, Ludmila, Olga Herbenova and Milena Lamarova. *The Pictorial Encyclopedia of Fashion.* New York: Crown, 1968. 604 pp.

Londré, Felicia Hardison. *The History of World Theatre: From the Restoration to the Present.* 2 vols. New York: Continuum, 1991. 644 pp.

Meyer, Dennis, ed. *Perspective on the Tomato Action: Theatrical Innovation in the Sixties and Seventies.* Amsterdam: Theatre Instituut Nederland, 1994. 220 pp.

Molinari, Cesare. *Teatro* [Theatre]. Milan: Mondadori, 1972.

——. *Theatre Through the Ages.* New York: McGraw-Hill, 1975. 324 pp.

Moore, Michael F. *Drag! Male and Female Impersonators on Stage, Screen and Television.* Jefferson, NC/London: McFarland, 1994. 301 pp.

Mordden, Ethan. *The Fireside Companion to the Theatre.* New York: Simon & Schuster, 1988. 313 pp.

Nagler, A.M. *A Sourcebook in Theatrical History.* New York: Dover, 1952. 611 pp.

Nicoll, Allardyce. *The Development of the Theatre: A Study of Theatrical Art from the Beginnings to the Present Day.* 5th ed. London: George G. Harrap, 1966. 318 pp.

Niculescu, Margareta. *Teatrul de păpuşi în lume* [Puppet theatre in the world]. Berlin: Henschelverlag and Bucharest: Meridiane, 1966. 230 pp.

Nutku, Özdemir. *Dünya Tiyatrosu Tarihi* [A history of world theatre]. 2 vols. Ankara: Ankara Universitesi dil ve Tarih Coğrafya Fakültesi Yayınları, 1973.

Ottai, Antonella, ed. *Teatro Oriente/Occidente* [Oriental/occidental theatre]. Biblioteca Teatrale 47. Rome: Bulzoni, 1986. 565 pp.

Pandolfi, Vito. *Storia universale del teatro drammatico* [World history of dramatic art]. 2 vols. Turin: Unione Typografico-Editrice, 1964. 1,626 pp.

Pronko, Leonard C. *Theater East and West: Perspectives Toward a Total Theater*. Berkeley: University of California Press, 1967. 280 pp.

Roose-Evans, James. *Experimental Theatre: From Stanislavksi to Peter Brook*. 2nd ed. London: Routledge, 1989. 224 pp.

Sallé, Bernard. *Histoire du théâtre* [History of the theatre]. Paris: Librairie Théâtral, 1990. 320 pp.

Wickham, Glynne. *A History of the Theatre*. New York/ Cambridge: Cambridge University Press, 1985. 254 pp.

Zamora Guerrero, Juan. *Historia del teatro contemporáneo* [History of contemporary theatre]. 4 vols. Barcelona: Juan Flors, 1961–2.

Criticism and Aesthetics

Allegri, Luigi. *Lat drammaturgia da Diderot a Beckett* [Dramaturgy from Diderot to Beckett]. Rome: Laterza, 1993. 206 pp.

Appia, Adolphe. *Oeuvres complètes* [Complete works]. 3 vols. Edited by Marie L. Bablet-Hahn. Lausanne: L'Age d'Homme, 1983–8.

Artaud, Antonin. *Oeuvres complètes*. [Complete works]. 25 vols. Paris: Gallimard, 1961–90.

Aston, Elaine. *An Introduction to Feminism and Theatre*. London: Routledge, 1995. 166 pp.

Barba, Eugenio. *Beyond the Floating Islands*. New York: PAJ Publications, 1986. 282 pp.

——. *The Floating Islands*. Holstebro, Denmark: Thomsens Bogtrykkeri, 1979. 224 pp.

——. *The Paper Canoe: A Guide to Theatre Anthropology*. Translated by Richard Fowler. London/New York: Routledge, 1995. 187 pp.

——, and Nicola Savarese. *The Secret Art of the Performer: A Dictionary of Theatre Anthropology*. Edited and compiled by Richard Gough. London: Routledge, 1991. 272 pp.

Bawtree, Michael. *The New Singing Theatre*. Bristol: Bristol Classical Press; New York: Oxford University Press, 1991. 232 pp.

Beckerman, Bernard. *Dynamics of Drama*. New York: Drama Book Specialists, 1979. 272 pp.

Bentley, Eric. *The Dramatic Event*. Boston, MA: Beaucou Press, 1956. 278 pp.

——. *The Life of the Drama*. New York: Atheneum, 1964. 371 pp.

——. *The Playwright as Thinker*. New York: Reynal & Hitchcock, 1946. 382 pp.

Bharucha, Rustom. *Theatre and the World: Performance and the Politics of Culture*. London/New York: Routledge, 1993. 254 pp.

Bikkulova, I. *Analiz dramaticeskogo proizvedenija* [Analysis of a dramatic work]. Moscow: Ministerstvo obrazovanija, 1994. 45 pp.

Birringer, Johannes. *Theatre, History and Post-Modernism*. Bloomington: Indiana University Press, 1991. 240 pp.

Boal, Augusto. *Theatre of the Oppressed*. New York: Theatre Communications Group, 1985. 197 pp.

Bondarcuk, S.F. *Vospitanie pravdoj* [Education with the truth]. Moscow: Prosvesenije, 1993. 143 pp.

Brecht, Bertolt. *Kleines Organon für das Theater* [A little organon for the theatre]. Frankfurt: Suhrkamp Verlag, 1958.

——. *Schriften zum Theater* [Writings on the theatre]. 7 vols. Edited by Werner Hecht. Berlin: Aufbau Verlag, 1963–4.

Brook, Peter. *The Empty Space*. London: MacGibbon & Kee, 1969. 141 pp.

——. *The Open Door: Thoughts on Acting and Theatre*. New York: Pantheon, 1993. 147 pp.

Brustein, Robert. *The Theatre of Revolt*. Boston, MA: Little, Brown, 1964. 435 pp.

Carlson, Marvin. *Theories of the Theatre: A Historical and Critical Survey from the Greeks to the Present*. Ithaca, NY/London: Cornell University Press, 1993. 553 pp.

Clark, Barrett H. *European Theories of the Drama*. New York: Crown, 1965. 628 pp.

Constantinidis, Stratos, E. *Theatre Under Deconstruction? A Question of Approach*. New York: Garland, 1993. 336 pp.

Craig, Edward Gordon. *On the Art of Theatre*. London: Heinemann, 1911, 1968. 295 pp.

——. *Towards a New Theatre*. London: J.M. Dent, 1913.

Davidson, Clifford, Johnson Rand and John A. Stroupe, eds. *Drama and the Classical Heritage: Comparative and Critical Essays*. New York: AMS Press, 1993. 299 pp.

Davis, R.G. 'Deep Culture: Thoughts on Third-World Theatre'. *New York Theatre Quarterly* 6 no. 24 (November 1990): 335–42.

Deldime, Roger. *Foi de théâtre* [Faith in theatre]. Morlan Welz: Lansman, 1993. 127 pp.

Diamond, Elin. *Unmaking Mimesis: Essays on Feminism and Theatre*. London/New York: Routledge, 1997. 226 pp.

Dolfi, Anna and Carla Locatelli, eds. *Retorica e interpretazione* [Rhetoric and interpretation]. Rome: Bulzoni, 1994. 337 pp.

Dort, Bernard. *Théâtre en jeu* [Drama in performance]. Paris: Seuil, 1979. 334 pp.

——. *Théâtre réel* [Real theatre]. Paris: Seuil, 1971. 300 pp.

Epskamp, Kees P. *Theatre in Search for Social Change: The Relative Significance of Different Theatrical Approaches*. The Hague: Centre for the Study of Education in Developing Countries, 1989.

Esslin, Martin. *The Field of Drama*. London: Methuen, 1987. 190 pp.

——. *The Theatre of the Absurd*. Garden City, NY: Doubleday, 1961. 364 pp.

Frye, Northrop. *Anatomy of Criticism*. Princeton, NJ: Princeton University Press, 1957. 383 pp.

Goodman, Lizbeth. *Contemporary Feminist Theatres*. London: Routledge, 1992. 272 pp.

Graver, David. *The Aesthetics of Disturbance: Anti-Art in Avant-Garde*. Ann Arbor: University of Michigan Press, 1995. 253 pp.

Grotowski, Jerzy. *Towards a Poor Theatre*. New York: Simon & Schuster, 1968. 262 pp.

Innes, Christopher. *Avant-Garde Theatre, 1892–1992*. London/New York: Routledge, 1993. 262 pp.

Ionesco, Eugène. *Notes et contrenotes* [Notes and counternotes]. Paris: Gallimard, 1962. 248 pp.

Jurkowski, Henryk. *Szkice z teorii teatru lalek* [Essays on the theory of puppetry]. Łodz: Polunima, 1993. 183 pp.

Kalb, Jonathan. *Free Admissions: Collected Theatre Writings*. New York: Limelight, 1993. 218 pp.

Kaye, Nick. *Postmodernism and Performance*. London: Macmillan, 1994. 180 pp.

Kidd, Ross. *The Performing Arts, Non-Formal Education and Social Change in the Third World: A Bibliography and Review Essay*. The Hague: Centre for the Study of Education in Developing Countries, 1981.

Kondo, Dorinne K. *About Face: Performing 'Race' in Fashion and Theatre*. New York: Routledge, 1997. 277 pp.

Kosteljanec, B.O. *Drama i dejstvie* [Drama and action]. St Petersburg: GATI, 1994. 112 pp.

Kott, Jan. *Shakespeare Our Contemporary*. Garden City, NY: Doubleday, 1964. 241 pp.

Mackintosh, Iain. *Architecture, Actor and Audience*. London/New York: Routledge, 1993. 184 pp.

Malkin, Jeanette. *Verbal Violence in Contemporary Drama*. Cambridge: Cambridge University Press, 1992. 256 pp.

Melrose, Susan. *A Semiotics of the Dramatic Text*. London: Macmillan, 1994. 338 pp.

Meschke, Michael. *In Search of Aesthetics for the Puppet Theatre*. Translated from the Swedish by Susanna Stevens. New Delhi: Indira Gandhi National Centre for the Arts and Sterling Publishers, 1992. 176 pp.

Metzidakis, Stamos. *Difference Unbound: The Rise of Pluralism in Literature and Criticism*. Amsterdam/Atlanta: Rodopi, 1995. 268 pp.

Middleton, D.K. 'The Theatre of Affect'. PhD dissertation, University of Hull, 1993.

Mitchell, Arnold. *The Professional Performing Arts: Attendance Patterns, Preferences and Motives*. 2 vols. Madison, WI: Association of College, University and Community Arts Administrators, 1984.

Musati, Luigi Maria. *Le parole del teatro* [The words of theatre]. Ancona: Transeuropa, 1995. 251 pp.

Oddey, Alison. *Devising Theatre: A Practical and Theoretical Approach*. London/New York: Routledge, 1994. 254 pp.

Pavis, Patrice. *Theatre at the Crossroads of Culture*. London: Routledge, 1991. 256 pp.

Poniz, Denis. *Komedija in mesane draske zvrsti* [Comedy and mixed dramatic forms]. Ljubljana: ZPS, 1995. 206 pp.

Problemy teatral nosti [Problems of theatricality]. St Petersburg: Ministerstvo kul'tury Rossii, SPLITMik im. N.K. Cerkasova. Kafedra zarubeznogo teatra, 1993. 152 pp.

River, Julie, and Germaine Dellis. *L'Enfant et le théâtre* [The child and the theatre]. Brussels: Labor, 1992. 155 pp.

Schechner, Richard. *Between Theatre and Anthropology*. Philadelphia: University of Pennsylvania Press, 1985. 342 pp.

——. *By Means of Performance: Intercultural Studies of Theatre and Ritual*. Cambridge: Cambridge University Press, 1990. 320 pp.

——. *Environmental Theatre*. New York: Hawthorne, 1973. 339 pp.

——. *Performance Theory*. London: Routledge, 1988. 320 pp.

Schechter, Joel. *Satiric Impersonations from Aristophanes to the Guerilla Girls*.

Carbondale/Edwardsville, IL: Southern Illinois United Press, 1994. 188 pp.

Schra, Emile. *Peter Brook en het eiland van ver-beelding: intercultureel theaterwerk 1970–1995* [Peter Brook and the island of imagination: intercultural work in the theatre, 1970–1995]. Amsterdam: Passe Partout/International Theatre and Film Books, 1995. 196 pp.

Schutzman, Mady, and Jan Cohen-Cruz, eds. *Playing Boal: Theatre, Therapy, Activism.* London/New York: Routledge, 1994. 246 pp.

Scolnicov, Hanna, and Peter Holland, eds. *The Play out of Context: Transferring Plays from Culture to Culture.* Cambridge: Cambridge University Press, 1989. 240 pp.

Seltzer, Daniel. *The Modern Theatre: Readings and Documents.* Boston, MA: Little, Brown, 1967. 495 pp.

Solovjev, V.B. *ABC of an Actor, Director and Teacher of Amateur Theatre.* Syktyukar: Komi Rippkrno, 1994. 156 pp.

Soule, L.A. 'Character, Actor and Anti-Character'. PhD dissertation, University of Exeter, 1994.

Stanislavski, Konstantin. *The Collected Works of Konstantin Stanislavsky.* Sharon Marie Carnicke, gen. ed. 10 vols. London: Routledge, 1993–.

——. *Sobraniye Sochinenii* [Collected works]. 7 vols. Moscow: Iskusstvo, 1954–60.

Strehler, Giorgio. *Per un teatro umano: pensieri scritti parlati e attuali* [For a humanized theatre: contemporary written thoughts and discussions]. Milan: Feltrinelli, 1974. 363 pp.

Styan, J.L. *Modern Drama in Theory and Practice.* 3 vols. Cambridge: Cambridge University Press, 1981–3.

Toro, Fernando de. *Theatre Semiotics: Text and Staging in Modern Theatre.* Translated by John Lewis. Edited by Carole Hubbard. Frankfurt/Madrid: Die Deutsche Bibliothek, 1995. 201 pp.

Trillis, Steven. *Towards an Aesthetics of the Puppet: Puppetry as a Theatrical Art.* New York: Greenwood Press, 1992. 181 pp.

Turner, Victor. *Antropologia della performance* [The anthropology of performance]. Bologna: Il Mulino, 1993. 295 pp.

——. *From Ritual to Theatre: The Human Seriousness of Play.* New York: PAJ Publications, 1982. 127 pp.

Ubersfeld, Anne. *L'École du spectateur* [The school for theatregoers]. Paris: Éditions Sociales, 1981. 352 pp.

——. *Lire le théâtre.* [Reading performance]. Paris: Éditions Sociales, 1977. 280 pp.

Wandor, Michelene. *Carry On, Understudies: Theatre and Sexual Politics.* London: Routledge, 1986. 224 pp.

Theatre Arts

Alberts, David. *Rehearsal Management for Directors.* Portsmouth, NH: Heinemann, 1995. 160 pp.

Bablet, Denis. *La Mise en scène contemporaine* [Contemporary directing]. Brussels: Renaissance du Livre, 1968.

——. *Les Révolutions scéniques du XXième siècle* [The scenic revolutions of the twentieth century]. Paris: Société Internationale d'Art XXième siècle, 1975. 388 pp.

Barba, Eugenio and Nicola Savarese. *The Secret Art of the Performer: A Dictionary of Theatre Anthropology.* Translated by Richard Fowler. New York: Routledge, 1991. 272 pp.

Barton, Lucy. *Historic Costume for the Stage.* London: A. & C. Black, 1961. 609 pp.

Bellman, Williard F. *Scenography and Stage Technology.* New York: Thomas Crowell, 1977. 639 pp.

Benedetti, Robert L. *The Actor at Work.* Englewood Cliffs, NJ: Prentice-Hall, 1981. 286 pp.

Berney, K.A., ed. *Contemporary Women*

Dramatists. London/Detroit/Washington, DC: St James Press, 1994. 335 pp.

Blunt, Jerry. *The Composite Art of Acting.* New York: Macmillan, 1966. 450 pp.

Boldrini, Maurizio. *La voce recitante: un percorso contro-verso* [The acting voice: a controversial course]. Rome: Bulzoni, 1994. 95 pp.

Bowskill, Derek. *Acting: An Introduction.* Englewood Cliffs, NJ: Prentice-Hall, 1977. 278 pp.

Braun, Edward. *The Director and the Stage: From Naturalism to Grotowski.* London: Methuen, 1982. 218 pp.

Burris-Meyer, Harold, and Edward C. Cole. *Scenery for the Theatre: The Organization, Processes, Materials and Techniques Used to Set the Stage.* Revised ed. Boston, MA: Little, Brown, 1971. 518 pp.

Ching, Francis D.K. *Architecture, Form, Space and Order.* New York: Van Nostrand Reinhold, 1979. 394 pp.

Cole, Toby, and Helen K. Chinoy. *Actors on Acting: The Theories, Techniques and Practices of the Great Actors of all Times as Told in Their Own Words*. Revised ed. New York: Crown, 1970. 715 pp.

Condee, William F. *Theatrical Space: A Guide for Directors and Designers*. Lanham, MD/London: Scarecrow, 1995. 206 pp.

Currell, David. *The Complete Book of Puppet Theatre*. Totowa, NJ: Barnes & Noble, 1985. 312 pp.

Del Ministro, Maurizio. *Il testo com sopravvivenza* [Text as survival]. Rome: Bulzoni, 1994. 205 pp.

Dennis, Anne. *The Articulate Body: The Physical Training of the Actor*. New York: Drama Book Publishers, 1995. 208 pp.

Duerr, Edwin, ed. *The Length and Depth of Acting*. New York: Holt, Rinehart & Winston, 1962. 590 pp.

Duess, Bart. *Waarheid of doen? Handleiding voor intercultureel-theater met jongeren voorzien van regels, voorbeelden en fotos* [Truth or dare? Guidelines for intercultural theatre for youth, with rules, examples and photos]. Amsterdam: Stichting Artisjok/Nultwingtig, 1996. 70 pp.

Dunaeva, E.A. *Avtor ty* [You the author]. Moscow: Firma NT-cent'r, 1994. 200 pp.

Fingerhut, Arden. *Theatre: Choice in Action*. New York: HarperCollins, 1995. 379 pp.

Gaulme, Jacques. *Architectures scénographiques et décors de théâtre*. [Scenographic architecture and theatre design]. Paris: E. Magnard, 1985. 144 pp.

Gillibert, Jean. *L'Acteur en création* [The actor in creation]. Toulouse: Presses Universitaires du Mirail, 1993. 206 pp.

Gorelik, Mordecai. *New Theatres for Old*. New York: Dutton, 1962. 553 pp.

Grady, Sharon. 'Between Production and Reception: Constructing Experience and Meaning in Theatre Work for Young Audiences'. PhD dissertation, University of Wisconsin, Madison, 1995. 441 pp.

Grebanier, Bernard. *Playwriting*. New York: Thomas Y. Crowell, 1961. 386 pp.

Hagen, Uta. *Respect for Acting*. New York: Macmillan, 1973. 227 pp.

Hodge, Francis. *Play Directing: Analysis, Communication and Style*. Englewood Cliff, NJ: Prentice-Hall, 1994. 426 pp.

Institut del Teatre de Barcelona. *El teatre d'ombres arreu del mon: les grans tradicions* [Shadow puppets of the world: The great traditions]. Barcelona: Institut del Teatre, 1984. 192 pp.

Izenour, George C. *Theater Design*. New York: McGraw-Hill, 1977. 631 pp.

Jones, David Richard. *Great Directors at Work: Stanislavsky, Brecht, Kazan, Brook*. Berkeley: University of California Press, 1986. 290 pp.

Kahn, David and Donna Breed. *Scriptwork: A Director's Approach to New Play Development*. Carbondale/Edwardsville, IL: Southern Illinois University Press, 1995. 183 pp.

Luere, Jeane, ed. *Playwright Versus Director: Authorial Intentions and Performance Interpretations*. Westport, CT Greenwood Press, 1994. 179 pp.

Machlin, Evangeline. *Speech for the Stage*. New York/London: Routledge/Theatre Arts Books, 1992. 254 pp.

Mali gledaliski vedez [Little theatre know-all]. Ljubljana: Fairy Tale Theatre, 1993. 111 pp.

Malkin, Michael R. *Traditional and Folk Puppets of the World*. New York: A.S. Barnes, 1977. 194 pp.

Mello, Bruno. *Trattato di scenotecnica* [A treatise on scene design]. Novara: G.G. Gorlich, Instituto Geografico de Agostini, 1979.

Mielziner, Jo. *Designing for the Theatre: A Memoir and a Portfolio*. New York: Atheneum, 1965. 242 pp.

Milnes, Rodney, ed. *Opera Index*. London: Opera, n.d.

Niccoli, A. *Lo spazio scenico: storia dell'arte teatrale* [Scenic space: a history of theatre art]. Rome: Bulzoni, 1971.

Parker, Wilford Oren, and Harvey K. Smith. *Scene Design and Stage Lighting*. Revised ed. New York: Holt, Rinehart & Winston, 1979. 597 pp.

Payne, Darwin *Scenographics*. Carbondale/Edwardsville, IL: Southern Illinois University Press, 1994. 237 pp.

——. *Scenographic Imagination*. Carbondale/Edwardsville, IL.: Southern Illinois University Press, 1993. 328 pp.

Pecktal, Lynn. *Designing and Drawing for the Theatre* New York: McGraw-Hill, 1995. 601 pp.

Pilbrow, Richard. *Stage Lighting*. New York: Drama Book Specialists, 1979. 176 pp.

Pywell, Geoff. *Staging Real Things: The Performance of Ordinary Events*. London/Toronto: Associated University Presses, 1994. 177 pp.

Quigley, Austin E. *The Modern Stage and Other Worlds*. New York/ London: Methuen, 1985. 320 pp.

Rayner, Alice. *To Act, To Do, To Perform: Drama and the Phenomenology of Action*. Ann Arbor: University of Michigan Press, 1994. 165 pp.

Saint-Denis, Michel. *Theatre: The Rediscovery of Style*. London: Heinemann, 1960. 110 pp.

——. *Training for the Theatre*. New York: Theatre Arts Books, 1982. 242 pp.

Sanford, Mariellen R. ed. *Happenings and Other Acts*. London/New York: Routledge, 1995, 397 pp.

Schreck, Everett M. *Principles and Styles of Acting*. Reading, MA: Addison-Wesley, 1970. 354 pp.

Segal, Harold B. *Pinocchio's Progeny: Puppets, Marionettes, Automatons and Robots in Modernist and Avant-Garde Drama*. Baltimore, MD: Johns Hopkins University Press, 1995. 373 pp.

Shershaw, Scott Cutler. *Puppets and Popular Culture*. Ithaca, NY: Cornell University Press, 1995. 252 pp.

Sherzer, Dina and Joel Sherzer, eds. *Humour and Comedy in Puppetry: Celebration in Popular Culture*. Bowling Green, OH: Bowling Green State University Popular Press, 1987. 151 pp.

Sorell, Walter. *Storia della danza: arte, cultura, societa*. [History of dance: art, culture, society]. Bologna: Il Mulino, 1994. 491 pp.

Spolin, Viola. *Improvisation for the Theatre: A Handbook of Teaching and Directing Techniques*. Evanston, IL: Northwestern University Press, 1963. 397 pp.

Stern, Lawrence. *Stage Management*. Boston, MA: Allyn & Bacon, 1995. 353 pp.

Sweet, Harvey and Deborah M. Dryden. *Complete Book of Drawing for the Theatre*. Boston, MA: Allyn & Bacon, 1995. 323 pp.

——. *Handbook of Scenery, Properties and Lighting*. 2 vols. Boston, MA: Allyn & Bacon, 1995. 269 and 227 pp.

Szabo, G. Laszlo. *Levetett maszkok* [Without masks]. Bratislava: Madach-Posonium, 1994. 180 pp.

Tidworth, Simon. *Theatres: An Architectural and Cultural History*. New York: Praeger, 1973. 224 pp.

Trefalt, Uros. *Osnove lutkovne rezije* [Basics of direction in puppet theatre]. Ljubljana: ZKOS, 1993. 191 pp.

Vasle, Juan. *Pevci so tudi ljudje: pogovori z opernimi in koncertnimi pevci* [Singers are people too: interviews with opera and concert singers]. Koper: Ognjisce, 1993. 199 pp.

Walne, Graham, ed. *Effects for the Theatre*. London/New York: A. & C. Black/Drama Book Publishers, 1995. 150 pp.

Warthen, William B. *The Idea of the Actor*. Princeton, NJ: Princeton University Press, 1984. 269 pp.

Watson, Lee. *Lighting Design Handbook*. New York: McGraw-Hill, 1990. 458 pp.

Whitmore, Jon. *Directing Postmodern Theatre: Shaping Signification in Performance*. Ann Arbor: University of Michigan Press, 1994. 242 pp.

Willingham, Ralph. *Science Fiction and the Theatre*. Westport, CT: Greenwood Press, 1994. 213 pp.

Withers-Wilson, Nan. *Vocal Direction for the Theatre: From Script Analysis to Opening Night*. New York: Drama Book Publishers, 1993. 115 pp.

Wylie, Kathryn. *Satyric and Heroic Mimes: Attitude as the Way of the Mime in Ritual and Beyond*. Jefferson, NC/London: McFarland, 1994. 254 pp.

Zaporah, Ruth. *Action Theatre: The Improvisation of Presence*. Berkeley, CA: North Atlantic, 1995. 275 pp.

Zarrilli, Phillip B. *Acting (Re)Considered: Theories and Practices*. London/New York: Routledge, 1995. 378 pp.

Zizn sceny I kontraktnyj mor: sbornik [Stage life and the world of contracts: collection]. Moscow: GITIS, 1994. 198 pp.

WRITERS
AND NATIONAL
EDITORIAL COMMITTEES

ALGERIA

Writer: Abdallah El Rukaibi (Professor, Algiers University; former Cultural Counsellor, Algerian Embassy, Damascus, Syria)
Reader: Debbie Folaron (PhD Candidate, Comparative Drama and Literature, Binghamton University, New York)

BAHRAIN

Writer: Mohamed A. al-Khozai (Director of Culture and National Heritage, Bahrain)
Reader: Hussein Al Riffaei (Actor; Director; Executive Director Al Sawari Theatre Troupe, Bahrain)

COMOROS ISLANDS

Writer: Staff

DJIBOUTI

Writer: Staff
Reader: Rianne Tamis (Professor, Arabic Literature, University of Nijmegen, the Netherlands)

EGYPT

Writers: Samir Awad (Researcher, National Centre for Theatre Research, Egypt), Ahmed Abdel Hameed (Journalist; Theatre Critic),

Abdul Aziz Hammouda (Playwright; Professor, Faculty of Arts, Cairo University, Egypt), Shawky Kamis (Poet; Playwright; Critic; Dramaturge, Department of Theatre, Ministry of Culture), Sami Khashaba (Journalist; Theatre Critic), Ahmed Zaki (President, International Theatre Institute, Egypt)
Readers: Dina A. Amin (Director; PhD Candidate, University of Pennsylvania), Arthur Goldschmidt (Professor, Department of History, Penn State University)

IRAQ

Writers: Ahmad Fiyyaad al-Mufraji (Director of Research, National Film and Theatre Organization), Sami Abd al-Hameed (Actor; Voice Teacher; Theatre Academy Professor), 'Abd ul-Ilaah Kamaal ud-Deen, 'Ali Muzaahim 'Abbaas, Yaaseen an-Nusayr and Yousif al-A'ni (Playwright; President, International Theatre Institute, Iraq)
Reader: Mohammed Darweesh (PhD; Managing Editor, *Gilgamesh: A Journal of Modern Iraqi Arts*)

JORDAN

Writers: Zein Ghanma (Theatre Instructor; Director, Amman, Jordan), Nader Omran (Director, Amman International Theatre Festival, Amman, Jordan)

KUWAIT

Writer: Staff with Fuad al-Shatti (President, Kuwaiti Center of the International Theatre Institute)
Reader: Stephen H. Franke

LEBANON

Writer: Nabil Abou Mrad (Theatre Department, University of Lebanon, Beirut)
Readers: Shawn Cramer (Independent Scholar, Middle Eastern History), Stephen P. Sheehi (Assistant Professor, Arabic Literature, University of Utah)

LIBYA

Writer: Staff

MAURITANIA

Writer: Mohamed El Hassan Weld Mohamad El Mostafa (Critic; Playwright)
Reader: Aly Boubou Gandega (Director, Troupe Yillenkaré, Nouakchott, Mauritania)

MOROCCO

Writer: Abdelkrim Berrechid (Director; Playwright)
Readers: Abdullah Benahnia (Professor, English and Curriculum Development, English Department, Institute of Public Administration, Riyadh, Saudi Arabia), Fatima Chebchoub (Playwright; Director; Actress; Professor of Theatre, Meknes University, Morocco), Debbie Folaron (PhD Candidate, Comparative Drama and Literature, Binghamton University, New York), Stephanie Saad (Independent Scholar, Development Studies, Brown University, Providence, Rhode Island)

OMAN

Writer: Abd-Elkarim Bin Ali Bin Jawad

PALESTINE

Writers: Faysal Darraj (Writer; Theatre Critic),
Fateh Azzam (Former Director, Palestinian National Theatre; Programme Officer for Rights and Culture, Ford Foundation)
Readers: Muhammad Hirzalla (MA, Paris), Jennifer Lee Ladkani (PhD Candidate, Ethnomusicology, Florida State University)

QATAR

Writer: Muhammed Abdul Rahim Kafoud (Minister of Education and Higher Education; Former Dean, Faculty of Humanities and Social Sciences, University of Qatar)

SAUDI ARABIA

Writer: Nazeer El-Azma (Professor, Arabic Department, King Saud University, Riyadh, Saudi Arabia)
Reader: Abdellah Benahnia (Professor, English and Curriculum Development, English Department, Institute of Public Administration, Riyadh, Saudi Arabia)

SOMALIA

Writer: Abdullah Said Hersi (Professor, National University of Somalia)

SUDAN

Writer: Khalid Al-Mubarak Mustafa (Associate Professor of Drama, Khartoum University; Director, Khartoum University Press; Playwright; Drama Critic)
Reader: Hrant Alianak (Playwright; Director)

SYRIA

Writers: Nadim Mohammed, Sa'dallah Wanous (deceased)
Readers: Miriam Cooke (Chair, Asian and African Languages and Literature, Duke University, Durham, North Carolina), Shawn Cramer (Independent Scholar, Middle Eastern History), Stephen Tamari (Professor, Sidwell Friends School, Washington, DC) Heiko Wimmen (Journalist, Beirut, Lebanon and Berlin, Germany)

TUNISIA

Writer: Izziddine al-Madani (Playwright;
Adviser to Minister of Culture, Tunisia)
Readers: Zeyneb Farhat (Director, El Teatro,
Tunis), Debbie Folaron (PhD Candidate,
Comparative Drama and Literature,
Binghamton University, New York), Mohamed
Mediouni (Professor, Modern Literature and
Theatre, University of Tunis I)

UNITED ARAB EMIRATES

Writers: Abdul Hameed Ahmad (Writer;
Critic), Mohammed Ben Ahmad Assuwadi
(Secretary-General, UAE Cultural Foundation),
Farouk Ohan (Theatre Department Manager,
Ministry of Information and Culture, Abu
Dhabi, UAE), Abdul Wahhab Ar-Radhwan
(Director, UAE Radio)
Reader: Cherif Wehbe

YEMEN

Writers: Najwa Adra (Adjunct Assistant
Professor, Hofstra University, Hempstead, New
York), Abdel Aziz Makaleh (Essayist; Poet;
President, Sana'a University, Sana'a, Yemen)

INDEX